This Is True Grace

The Shaping of Social Behavioural Instructions by Theology in 1 Peter

Joyce Wai-Lan Sun

MONOGRAPHS

© 2016 by Joyce Wai-Lan Sun

Published 2016 by Langham Monographs
An imprint of Langham Creative Projects

Langham Partnership
PO Box 296, Carlisle, Cumbria CA3 9WZ, UK
www.langham.org

ISBNs:
978-1-78368-184-6 Print
978-1-78368-186-0 Mobi
978-1-78368-185-3 ePub
978-1-78368-187-7 PDF

Joyce Wai-Lan Sun has asserted her right under the Copyright, Designs and Patents Act, 1988 to be identified as the Author of this work.

All rights reserved. No part of this publication may be reproduced, stored in a retrieval system or transmitted, in any form or by any means, electronic, mechanical, photocopying, recording or otherwise, without the prior written permission of the publisher or the Copyright Licensing Agency.

British Library Cataloguing in Publication Data
A catalogue record for this book is available from the British Library

ISBN: 978-1-78368-184-6

Cover & Book Design: projectluz.com

Langham Partnership actively supports theological dialogue and an author's right to publish but does not necessarily endorse the views and opinions set forth, and works referenced within this publication or guarantee its technical and grammatical correctness. Langham Partnership does not accept any responsibility or liability to persons or property as a consequence of the reading, use or interpretation of its published content.

Contents

Abbreviations ix

Chapter 1 1
Introduction
   1.1 Review of Scholarship 1
      1.1.1 Form-Critical Approach 1
      1.1.2 Social-Scientific Approach 2
   1.2 Approach of This Study 5
   1.3 Plan of This Study 9
   1.4 Working Hypothesis 11

Chapter 2 17
Theological Vision of 1 Peter
   2.1 The Christ-Messiah in 1 Peter 20
      2.1.1 The Suffering Christ-Messiah 21
      2.1.2 The Exalted Christ-Messiah 30
      Section Summary 34
   2.2 The Christian Elect Exiles of Diaspora in 1 Peter 34
      2.2.1 The Christian Elect 39
      2.2.2 The Christian Exiles 47
      2.2.3 The Christian Elect Exiles of Diaspora 52
      Section Summary 54
   2.3 Christ-Christians Unity in 1 Peter 55
      2.3.1 The Christ-Christian Spiritual House 57
      2.3.2 The Christian Elect Diaspora Determined by Christ 59
      Section Summary 63
   2.4 Chapter Conclusion 63

Chapter 3 65
Social Behavioural Instructions in 1 Peter
   3.1 The Governing Principle (2:11–12) 75
   3.2 Christian Engagement in Civil Life (2:13–17) 80
      Section Summary 85
   3.3 Christian Engagement in Household Life (2:18–3:7) 86
      3.3.1 Exhortations to Slaves (2:18–25) 87
      3.3.2 Exhortations to Wives (3:1–6) 92
      3.3.3 Exhortations to Husbands (3:7) 96

    Section Summary..97
    3.4 Christian Engagement in Daily Social Life (3:9–4:6) 98
        3.4.1 Do Not Return Evil for Evil (3:9–12) 98
        3.4.2 Suffer for the Sake of Righteousness (3:13–22) 100
        3.4.3 Do Not Accomplish the Will of the Gentiles (4:1–6)......106
        Section Summary..113
    3.5 Christian Engagement in Suffering for the Name of Christ
    (4:12–4:19) 114
        Section Summary..118
    3.6 Chapter Conclusion..118

Chapter 4 121
The Jewish Elect Exiles of Diaspora
    4.1 Social Engagement of the Jewish Elect Exiles of Diaspora 126
        4.1.1 Jewish Diaspora Engagement in Civil Life 127
        4.1.2 Jewish Engagement in Household Life...........................140
        4.1.3 Jewish Engagement in Daily Social Life 144
        Section Summary: Jewish Resonances in 1 Peter 155
    4.2 Diaspora Consciousness of the Jewish Exilic People of God 158
        4.2.1 Diaspora's Longing for Return 160
        4.2.2 Diaspora's Belonging to the Native Country 166
        Section Summary: Jewish Resonances in 1 Peter 173
    4.3 Chapter Conclusion..174

Chapter 5 177
Comparison Text I: Revelation
    5.1 Social Behavioural Instructions in Revelation............................181
        5.1.1 Purpose of the Revelation Social Behavioural
        Instructions 182
        5.1.2 Social Behavioural Instructions of Revelation.................193
        Section Summary: Features of Petrine Social Behavioural
        Instructions 198
    5.2 Shaping of Social Behavioural Instructions by Theology in
    Revelation 201
        5.2.1 Messiah-Christ in Revelation 202
        Subsection Summary 210
        5.2.2 Christian Messianic Army in Revelation 210
        Section Summary: Features of the Shaping of Social
        Behavioural Instructions by Theology in 1 Peter....................218
    5.3 Chapter Conclusion..219

Chapter 6 221
   Comparison Text II: The Epistle to Diognetus
      6.1 Christian Social Engagement Portrayed in the *Epistle to Diognetus* 224
         6.1.1 Christian Engagement in Civil Life............................230
         6.1.2 Christian Engagement in Household Life 231
         6.1.3 Christian Engagement in Daily Social Life.....................234
         Section Summary: Petrine Resonances in the *Epistle to Diognetus*..236
      6.2 Shaping of Social Behavioural Instructions by Theology in the *Epistle to Diognetus* 237
         6.2.1 All-loving God/Christ in the *Epistle to Diognetus*.............238
         6.2.2 Christian Resident-Aliens in the *Epistle to Diognetus*........244
         Section Summary: Features of the Shaping of Social Behavioural Instructions by Theology in 1 Peter...................251
      6.3 Chapter Conclusion...252

Chapter 7 255
   Conclusion

Bibliography... 261
   Primary Sources 261
   Dictionaries, Lexicons and Grammars...................................263
   Secondary Literature 264

Abbreviations

Bib. Hist.	Diodorus, *Bibliotheca Historica*
BECNT	Baker Exegetical Commentary on the New Testament
ed.	edition
GLAJJ	Stern, Menahem. *Greek and Latin Authors on Jews and Judaism*. 3 vols. Jerusalem: Israel Academy of Sciences and Humanities, 1974–1984
Hdt.	Epicurus, Προς Ηροδοτον
JIWE	Noy David. *Jewish Inscriptions of Western Europe*. 2 vols. Cambridge: Cambridge University Press, 1995
LNTS	Library of New Testament Studies

Except listed above, abbreviations generally follow those in Patrick H. Alexander, *The SBL Handbook of Style: For Ancient Near Eastern, Biblical, and Early Christian Studies* (Peabody, MA: Hendrickson, 1999) and Barbara Aland, *Greek-English New Testament: Greek Text Novum Testamentum Graece, in the Tradition of Eberhard Nestle and Erwin Nestle* (9th rev. ed.; Stuttgart: Deutsche Bibelgesellschaft, 2001). Titles not mentioned in these works or above are spelled out in full.

CHAPTER 1

Introduction

This study investigates the coherence between the social behavioural instructions and the theological teachings in 1 Peter. The question I intend to address is: How and in what respects are the Petrine social instructions shaped by the author's theological vision?

1.1 Review of Scholarship

Although it appears nothing phenomenal in expecting the ethics of a NT writing to flow from its theological visions, the notion that the Petrine social ethics are de facto derived from the author's theological/religious conviction as his "ultimate concern"[1] is more often assumed, or indeed time and again neglected, than seriously considered in Petrine scholarship.

1.1.1 Form-Critical Approach

Since the time of R. Perdelwitz, Petrine scholarship in the early decades of the twentieth century had been dominated by the belief that 1 Peter was a composite work. Besides Perdelwitz, who views 1 Peter as composed of a baptismal homily (1:3–4:11) and a shorter letter (1:1–2 and 4:12–5:14),[2] Preisker also regarded the letter as comprising the different parts of a baptismal liturgy with 1:3–12 as a prayer-psalm (*Gebetspsalm*), the actual baptism between 1:21 and 1:22, 4:12–19 as an eschatological apocalyptic

---

1. I borrow this term from Michael LaFargue, "Sociohistorical Research and the Contextualization of Biblical Theology," in *The Social World of Formative Christianity and Judaism: Essays in Tribute to Howard Clark Kee*, ed. Jacob Neusner et al. (Philadelphia, PA: Fortress Press, 1988), 4.

2. R. Perdelwitz, *Die Mysterienreligion und das Problem des 1 Petrusbriefes: ein literarsicher und religionspeschichtlicher Versuch* (Giessen: Topelmann, 1911), 16–26.

discourse (*eschatologischen Offenbarungsrede*), and so on.³ Preisker's proposal was then modified by Cross who argued that 1 Peter represents parts of an Easter baptismal rite.⁴ In similar fashion, Boismard also located four earlier baptismal hymns preserved in the letter.⁵

Even when 1 Peter was accepted as having been written as a single document, form-critical considerations remained scholars' focus and deterred serious attention to the relationship between the letter's overall theological vision and social ethics. For instance, although accepting 1 Peter as genuinely epistolary, Moule proposed that the author actually sent "two forms of epistles," one (comprising 1:1–4:11 and 5:12–14) for those not yet under actual duress and one (comprising 1:1–2:10 and 4:12–5:14) for those who were facing real persecutions.⁶ Likewise, Selwyn argued for the presence of two primitive baptismal catechisms and a source with persecution in view behind the letter.⁷ Beare also found a "separate composition" of a baptismal sermon in 1:3–4:11.⁸ In the face of this general treatment of 1 Peter as a segregate entity, there is no surprise that G. L. Green complained in 1979; "There has been relatively little written which seeks to give a synthetic and comprehensive evaluation of the theology of the epistle, let alone of the ethics."⁹

1.1.2 Social-Scientific Approach

Although the literary unity of 1 Peter is commonly recognized nowadays, scholars continue to underrate the role of theology/religious conviction as

---

3. H. Windisch, *Die katholischen Briefe*, 3rd rev. and augmented ed. with appendix by H. Preisker, HNT 15 (Tübingen: Mohr [Siebeck], 1951 [1st published, 1911]), 156–161.

4. F. L. Cross, *I. Peter: A Paschal Liturgy* (London: A. R. Mowbray, 1954), 36–41.

5. M.-É. Boismard, *Quatre hymnes baptismales dans la première épître de Pierre*, LD 30 (Paris: Cerf, 1961).

6. C. F. D. Moule, "The Nature and Purpose of 1 Peter," *NTS* 3 (1956/1957): 7.

7. Edward Gordon Selwyn, *The First Epistle of St. Peter: The Greek Text with Introduction*, 2nd (repr.) ed. (London: Macmillan, 1952 [1st published, 1946]), 365–466.

8. Francis Wright Beare, *The First Epistle of Peter: The Greek Text with Introduction and Notes*, 3rd rev. and enlarged ed. (Oxford: Blackwell, 1970 [1st published 1958]), 25–27.

9. G. L. Green, *Theology and Ethics in 1 Peter*, PhD diss (University of Aberdeen, 1979). It is noticeable, however, that Green also failed to look for a better integrated theological perspective or a coherent theme of social ethics in 1 Peter especially with reference to its extensive use of OT language and images. His account of the relationship between the Petrine theology and ethics remains fragmentary.

the author's *ultimate concern* when he formulates the Petrine social strategies for Christians. With the application of a "social-scientific approach" to Petrine studies pioneered by John Elliott,[10] scholars' interest shifted to the social dimension of the text including its social context and intended impact on the Christian community.[11] Hence, 1 Peter is often read as a "vehicle"[12] to further certain concrete interests of the Christian community in the context of the contemporary socio-economic conditions of the wider world.[13] For example, Elliott argues that the purpose of the Petrine strategy is to promote Christians' internal cohesion and external distinction,[14] while Balch sees the primary purpose of the Petrine household code as to reduce tension between the church and the wider society.[15] In similar vein, both Talbert[16] and Carter[17] regard "Christians' survival in a hostile environment" to be the aim of the Petrine exhortations.

What follows from this functionalist approach is that the Petrine theology is often viewed as likewise "functional" in serving the real purpose of the letter. Therefore, Bechtler, designating his position as similar to "moderate functionalism," describes his interest in interpreting the Petrine christological references as lying in their *function* to facilitate Christians embracing their liminal place in the hostile society.[18] Likewise, Carter also regards the Petrine theology as "legitimating" Christians' submission and

---

10. John H. Elliott, *A Home for the Homeless: A Social-Scientific Criticism of 1 Peter, Its Situation and Strategy* (Eugene, OR: Wipf & Stock, 2005). This is the paperback edition of *A Home for the Homeless: A Sociological Exegesis of 1 Peter, Its Situation and Strategy* (Philadelphia, PA: Fortress, 1981) with a new preface, introduction and subtitle.

11. Cf. John H. Elliott, "Social-Scientific Criticism of a Biblical Text: 1 Peter as an Example," in *Social-Scientific Approaches to New Testament Interpretation* ed. David G. Horrell (Edinburgh: T&T Clark, 1999), 340.

12. Ibid.

13. Cf. LaFargue, "Sociohistorical Research," 3–16.

14. Elliott, *Home*, 231.

15. David Balch, *Let Wives Be Submissive: The Domestic Code in 1 Peter*, SBLMS 26 (Atlanta, GA: Scholars Press, 1981), 81.

16. Charles H. Talbert, "Once Again: The Plan of First Peter," in *Perspectives on First Peter*, ed. Charles H. Talbert (Macon, GA: Mercer University Press, 1986), 146–148.

17. Warren Carter, "Going All the Way? Honoring the Emperor and Sacrificing Wives and Slaves in 1 Peter," in *A Feminist Companion to the Catholic Epistles and Hebrews*, eds. Amy-Jill Levine and Maria Mayo Robins (London: T&T Clark, 2004), 32–33.

18. Steven Richard Bechtler, *Following in His Steps: Suffering, Community, and Christology in 1 Peter*, SBLDS 162 (Atlanta, GA: Scholars Press, 1998), 23–40.

even cultic participation in civic and domestic spheres.[19] As LaFargue observes, "The functional model eliminates methodologically a priori the possibility of finding anything transcendent in theological writing and makes serious 'theological' study . . . impossible."[20]

In addition, scholars' efforts to understand the Petrine social behavioural instructions with reference to the various resources, theories and models appropriated from social-scientific studies such as the "conversionist sects,"[21] the "Japanese immigrants" and "Detroit Mexican immigrants" to America,[22] the "African tribal societies"[23] and the "peasant societies in Malaysia,"[24] further divert their attention from viewing the Petrine overall theological vision as the *ultimate* frame of reference with which the letter's social behavioural instructions are formulated, and, thus, should be understood.

However, this availability of a diverse range of social-scientific resources has also resulted in a wide variety of (and sometimes inherently incompatible) understandings of the Petrine instructions, as is evidenced by the Balch-Elliott debate which was once described as an "obvious and prominent 'storm centre' in the interpretation of 1 Peter."[25] The conflicting conclusions reached by Elliott and Balch, as to whether 1 Peter calls for Christians' internal cohesion and, thus, identity maintenance (Elliott)[26] or their assimilation to the secular society (Balch),[27] together with the diverse social-scientific-exegetical proposals in response to this debate, such as

---

19. Carter, "Going," 26–29.
20. LaFargue, "Sociohistorical Research," 12.
21. Elliott, *Home*, 73–78.
22. David L. Balch, "Hellenization/Acculturation in 1 Peter," in *Perspectives on First Peter*, ed. Charles H. Talbert (Macon, GA: Mercer University Press, 1986), 89.
23. Bechtler, *Following*, 118–125.
24. E.g. Carter, "Going," 31–32; David G. Horrell, "Between Conformity and Resistance: Beyond the Balch–Elliott Debate towards a Postcolonial Reading of First Peter," in *Reading First Peter with New Eyes: Methodological Reassessments of the Letter of First Peter*, eds. Robert L. Webb and Betsy Bauman-Martin (London: T&T Clark, 2007), 117.
25. Horrell, "Between Conformity," 112.
26. Elliott, *Home*; Elliott, "1 Peter, Its Situation and Strategy: A Discussion with David Balch," in *Perspectives on First Peter*, ed. Charles H. Talbert (Macon, GA: Mercer University Press, 1986), 61–78.
27. Balch, *Let Wives*; Balch, "Hellenization/Acculturation," 79–101.

"unqualified conformity,"[28] "*both* social cohesion *and* social adaptability,"[29] "*neither* fully integrated to *nor* entirely removed from society,"[30] "polite resistance reflecting a nuanced negotiation between conformity and resistance,"[31] and "a combination of a modified acculturation, a rather low form of structural assimilation, a modified marital assimilation, very low identificational assimilation, and very low, close to non-existent attitude-, behavioral relational- and civic assimilation,"[32] actually demonstrate the need for a recovery of the letter's overall theological context as the *ultimate* frame of reference to govern proper understanding of the Petrine instructions.[33]

1.2 Approach of This Study

In the following study, I wish to add one more dimension to the current discussion on the Petrine social engagement by placing the letter's social behavioural instructions within the letter's own theological context and understanding them with reference to the author's own theological/religious convictions as his *primary and ultimate concern*. I will take what LaFargue calls an "empathic entrance"[34] and engage the text from "an insider" perspective of the author as a member of the Christian believing community.

The reason for my approach is that the task of studying an individual example of Christian *internal correspondence* such as 1 Peter is *by its nature* different from the task of seeking to understand Christianity *as a religious movement* in its socio-historical context. First Peter is a letter from one Christian to others. Participants to the correspondence shared the same religious conviction and allegiance to one unique God, and, thus, also shared their own priorities, worldviews and value judgments which even their contemporaries could not fully understand. While understanding

---

28. Carter, "Going," 23–33.
29. Talbert, "Once Again," 146–148.
30. Bechtler, *Following*, 155.
31. Horrell, "Between Conformity," 110–143.
32. Torrey Seland, *Strangers in the Light: Philonic Perspectives on Christian Identity in 1 Peter*, Biblical Interpretation Series 76 (Leiden: Brill, 2005), 172–189.
33. Individual assessments of these proposals will be provided in chapter 3.
34. LaFargue, "Sociohistorical Research," 4.

Christianity as a social phenomenon can be achieved by "observation with detachment" as an "outsider,"[35] and indeed requires "objectivity" to be "scientifically valid,"[36] one can hardly grasp what the Petrine text may have meant for the parties without regard to their unique primary concern and perception of their own existence. As Wilken comments, "We would expect the self-understanding of the Christians to differ from the view of outside observers – the Christians 'read' themselves quite differently than their contemporaries 'read' them . . ."[37]

Although from an outsider viewpoint, social tension may turn Christians sectarian and distance them from the influence of the larger world,[38] Christians themselves may view their own existence as resident-aliens with self-dignity (e.g. 1 Pet 2:9–10) and regard their continuous engagement with the pagan world as the proper mode of service to God (2:5, 9). Likewise, although the Petrine exhortations on submission by slaves and wives may be viewed, from an (modern) outsider point of view, as "colluding" with the existing system in exploiting the weak,[39] "foregoing power through submission" may just be what the Petrine author himself understood as what Jesus Christ exemplified on the cross, and what Christian slaves and wives should follow for a higher purpose of gaining room to maintain their ultimate allegiance to God in their difficult situations.[40]

In order to seek this "empathic understanding" of the Petrine theology and social ethics, I will attempt to allow the voice of the Petrine author to be heard by explicating his "way of seeing things" and paying attention to "the (apparently) more obvious meanings of the text."[41] Instead of looking

---

35. Cf. Gerd Theissen, *Social Reality and the Early Christians: Theology, Ethics and the World of the New Testament*, trans. Margaret Kohl (Edinburgh: T&T Clark, 1993), 24.

36. Cf. Derek Tidball, *An Introduction to the Sociology of the New Testament* (Exeter: Paternoster, 1983), 16; Susan R. Garrett, "Sociology of Early Christianity," *ABD* 6 (1992): 91.

37. Robert L. Wilken, "Toward a Social Interpretation of Early Christian Apologetics," *CH* 39 (1970): 439.

38. Cf. Elliott, *Home*, 112–118, 148–150.

39. E.g. Jennifer G. Bird, *Abuse, Power and Fearful Obedience: Reconsidering 1 Peter's Commands to Wives*, LNTS 442 (London: T&T Clark, 2011), 89–101.

40. These issues will be further dealt with in my exegesis of the relevant Petrine text.

41. Cf. Stephen C. Barton, "Historical Criticism and Social-Scientific Perspectives in New Testament Study," in *Hearing the New Testament: Strategies for Interpretation*, ed. Joel B. Green (Grand Rapids, MI: Eerdmans, 1995), 75–76. See also Garrett, "Sociology,"

for the *hidden agenda* or the *ulterior motive* of the text, I will attempt to understand the author's primary (theological) concern *as apparent from the text* and inquire how this concern is seen giving rise to his formulation of the corresponding mode of Christian social engagement.

In fact, since the Balch-Elliott debate, both Dryden and Thurén have published their works concerning the relationship between the Petrine theology and ethics.[42] Both of them are rhetorical studies and, thus, different from my present focus. Dryden seeks to classify 1 Peter as a paraenetic epistle and is still concerned only with how theology serves to accomplish the paraenetic ends of the letter.[43] In Thurén's work, his purpose is to explain "how the paraenesis is motivated in 1 Peter"[44] by constructing an ideological structure behind the text. He chooses to rely on modern rhetorical theories[45] and notably is not interested in revealing what the author had in mind.[46]

One literary feature of 1 Peter, to which both Dryden and Thurén have failed to pay sufficient attention, is the extensive use of OT language and images by the author. Indeed, 1 Peter has already been observed as having "the highest concentration, relative to its size, of OT references in the entire NT."[47] Therefore, I will particularly consider how such concentration of OT language constitutes the integral fabric in the construction of the author's theological vision of the current reality and Christians' existence on earth.

95, for an observation of Elliott's contrasting between "implicit" sociological concerns and "explicit" theological phrasing of 1 Peter.

42. J. de Waal Dryden, *Theology and Ethics in 1 Peter: Paraenetic Strategies for Christian Character Formation*, WUNT 2/209 (Tübingen: Mohr Siebeck, 2006); Lauri Thurén, *Argument and Theology in 1 Peter: The Origins of Christian Paraenesis*, JSNTSup 114 (Sheffield: Sheffield Acacemic Press, 1995).

43. Dryden, *Theology*, 1–13.

44. Thurén, *Argument*, 13.

45. Ibid., 30–57.

46. Ibid., 187, 220.

47. Andrew Mūtūa Mbuvi, *Temple, Exile, and Identity in 1 Peter*, LNTS 345 (London: T&T Clark, 2007), 6. See also William L. Schutter, *Hermeneutic and Composition in 1 Peter*, WUNT 30/2 (Tübingen: J. C. B. Mohr, 1989), 43; David G. Horrell, *1 Peter*, NTG (London: T&T Clark, 2008), 31; Reinhard Feldmeier, *The First Letter of Peter: A Commentary on the Greek Text*, tran. Peter H. Davids (Waco, TX: Baylor University Press, 2008), 26–27.

In fact, recent decades have witnessed a surge of scholarly interest in locating the dominant theological symbol (the controlling metaphor) in 1 Peter. The metaphors proposed include "covenant,"[48] "diaspora,"[49] "Israel,"[50] "idea of exile"[51] and so on. It is immediately noticeable that these metaphors underscore the Petrine identification of the Christian community with Israel and, some of them, especially with the exilic Jewish Diaspora.[52] However, these studies tend to *assume* that 1 Peter is solely concerned with resisting assimilation without *actually* investigating the social engagement of Israel especially in the Diaspora (διασπορᾶς, 1 Pet 1:1), and without taking sufficient consideration of the tension of both "resistance" and "accommodation" within the Petrine social ethics as betrayed by the Balch-Elliott debate.

It is here that I consider it necessary to go behind the text and investigate its socio-political context in order to facilitate an empathic understanding of the text.[53] I will conduct a historical investigation into the actual social engagement of the Jewish Diaspora in order to clarify the author's vision when he designated Christians as "elect exiles of Diaspora" (ἐκλεκτοῖς παρεπιδήμοις διασπορᾶς, 1:1) with the aid of primary literary and epigraphic evidence. In addition, I will pay attention to the text's socio-political and cultural milieu in the course of my exegetical analysis by resorting to primary and secondary sources in order to throw light on the circumstances which aroused the author's (theological) concern, and on the implications of his social behavioural instructions to the original readers. My approach to engage the text is therefore both literary and historical.

Besides literary and historical analysis, I will also highlight the features of the Petrine theology and social ethics by comparing the letter with two other early Christian writings – Revelation, which belongs to a similar

---

48. John W. Pryor, "First Peter and the New Covenant," *RTR* 45 (1986): 1–4, 44–51.

49. Troy W. Martin, *Metaphor and Composition in 1 Peter*, SBLDS 131 (Atlanta, GA: Scholars Press, 1992), 144–267.

50. Paul J. Achtemeier, *1 Peter: A Commentary on First Peter*, Hermeneia (Minneapolis, MN: Fortress Press, 1996), 69–73.

51. Mbuvi, *Temple*, 22–33.

52. These proposals of the Petrine controlling metaphors will be individually assessed in chapter 2.

53. Cf. LaFargue, "Sociohistorical Research," 5.

geographical and temporal context to 1 Peter, and the *Epistle to Diognetus*, which falls into the trajectory of 1 Peter in the understanding of Christians' earthly existence as "resident-aliens" (ὡς πάροικοι, *Diogn.* 5.5; cf. τῆς παροικίας ὑμῶν, 1 Pet 1:17; ὡς παροίκους καὶ παρεπιδήμους, 1 Pet 2:11) in the second century. A comparison with Revelation will serve to place 1 Peter within the larger religious landscape of Asia Minor to which the original readers of both 1 Peter and Revelation belonged. A comparison with *Diognetus*, on the other hand, will help to verify the findings of my analysis of the Petrine text.

Therefore, I am not proposing to dispense with socio-historical investigations in the attempt to understand a biblical text nor do I intend to question the value of scholars' effort to read 1 Peter against the socio-economic and political conditions behind the text. What I wish to achieve in this study is to add another perspective to the current discussion on the Petrine social strategy by placing the author's own theological/religious conviction as the *starting point* of investigation and utilizing socio-historical data as "an essential aid for imaginatively entering into"[54] the author's way of perceiving the current reality when formulating his mode of social engagement for Christians.

Hence, although my approach is basically literary and historical, I will continue using the terms originally employed in social-scientific studies, such as identity, accommodation, social strategy and so on, for the ease of discussing the issues which have long been the interest of scholars engaging in social-scientific research of 1 Peter.

1.3 Plan of This Study

As already hinted in the foregoing, the following discussion will comprise (1) an exegetical study of 1 Peter, (2) a historical study of the Jewish exilic people in the Diaspora and, (3) a comparison of 1 Peter with Revelation and the *Epistle to Diognetus*.

In my exegetical study in chapters 2 and 3, I will explore the overall Petrine theological vision and social behavioural instructions paying special attention to the author's extensive use of OT language and images.

---

54. I borrow this phrase from LaFargue, "Sociohistorical Research," 8.

Chapter 2 demonstrates that against the author's eschatological vision portrayed in terms of the Jewish expectations, Jesus Christ is underscored as the expected Messiah but paradoxically submitted to human suffering essentially as a resident-alien on the cross. Christians are then positioned as "elect exiles of Diaspora" amidst pagan alienation inheriting the self-definition and eschatological redemption hope of the Jewish Diaspora. It is precisely in the light of this theological self-understanding that Christians' sense of identity is perceived as based on their privileged status before God rather than derived from being different from the wider culture.

Based on the analysis in chapter 2, chapter 3 will engage the Balch-Elliott debate by arguing that the Petrine Christian social strategy reflects the form of "differentiated resistance" which is perceived as the congruent behavioural expression of Christians' identity as "elect exiles of Diaspora" and as a token of their finding solidarity with the Messiah-Christ by following in his steps. "Ultimate allegiance to God" will be seen as the overriding boundary of Christians' accommodation to the pagan culture to ensure their remaining in the grace of God (1 Pet 5:12).

In the historical study of the Jewish Diaspora social engagement in chapter 4, I will argue that the Petrine author's appropriation of Jewish self-definition to Christians includes their social strategy so that the Jewish social engagement becomes the frame of reference to which the Petrine social behavioural instructions can be understood. "Differentiated resistance" will be demonstrated to be also the form of Jewish strategy especially in Asia Minor and Rome, with "ultimate allegiance to God" once again the primary concern of the Jewish Diaspora.

Chapters 5 and 6 will then compare the relationship between Petrine theology and social ethics with that in Revelation and the *Epistle to Diognetus*. These chapters seek to argue that for the early Christians like the Petrine author, theological/religious conviction was their primary consideration when formulating their Christian social strategies. Chapter 5 will contrast the Petrine strategy of "differentiated resistance" with the "total resistance" in Revelation. This difference in their forms of social engagement will be shown as due to the authors' different theological perceptions of the relationship between Christ and the world as reflected by the cross and, thus, their understanding of Christians' existence on earth. On the other hand, chapter 6 will verify the findings in the previous chapters by demonstrating that "differentiated resistance" is also perceived in *Diognetus* as the congruent identity expression of Christians as "resident-aliens" with "ultimate allegiance to God" their primary concern. Christians' distinctive identity will again be shown as not depending on maintaining difference from the wider culture but as derived from their new status brought about by the sacrifice of Jesus Christ.

The final chapter 7 will summarize my findings in this study. A reflection on Christians' formulation of their social engagement amidst a socially-estranged environment and on the continuous cooperation between the theological approach and socio-historical approach to investigate Christian social behaviour will also be offered.

1.4 Working Hypothesis

Since much scholarly effort has already been spent to ascertain the background of 1 Peter with traits of consensus emerging, I only wish briefly to present my view on the historical situation of the text as the working hypothesis of my study.

It is clear that 1 Peter is a letter written to the churches in Asia Minor (1 Pet 1:1). The references to their former life as one in ignorance (πρότερον ἐν τῇ ἀγνοίᾳ ὑμῶν, 1:14), their futile way of life inherited from their ancestors (τῆς ματαίας ὑμῶν ἀναστροφῆς πατροπαραδότου, 1:18), their having been no people (ποτε οὐ λαός, 2:10) and having taken part in idolatry before their conversion (ἀθεμίτοις εἰδωλολατρίαις, 4:3), also make it quite certain that the original readers were mostly Gentile Christians, although the presence of Jewish Christians cannot be ruled out.[55]

The questions on authorship and, thus, the date of the letter are more difficult to answer. The clearest clue is 1 Peter 1:1 in which the author addresses himself as "Peter" who, according to early Christian traditions (e.g. Eusebius, *Hist. eccl.* 2.25.5–8), was martyred during Nero's persecution of Christians. Hence, 1 Peter could have been written before 64

---

55. Achtemeier, *1 Peter*, 51; Horrell, *1 Peter*, 47–48; Joel B. Green, *1 Peter*, The Two Horizons New Testament Commentary (Grand Rapids, MI: Eerdmans, 2007), 5–6.

CE.⁵⁶ However, I agree with many scholars that 1 Peter is pseudonymous.⁵⁷ Among the reasons so far offered by scholars, I find it particularly convincing that despite the author's self-address as Peter, the letter itself actually does not witness a close relationship or even a personal acquaintance of the author with the earthly Jesus. Even in places where the earthly life of Jesus is relevant and where one might expect an eyewitness to provide a personal account (e.g. 1:18–21; 2:22–25; 3:18–22), the author only draws from existing christological traditions and OT references rather than giving his own testimony. Where a saying of Jesus could have been cited to support his exhortations (e.g. 4:8, 14), the author again notably chooses to rely on OT references.⁵⁸

In addition, it is commonly accepted that "Babylon" in 1 Peter 5:13 refers to Rome as the archenemy of the holy people of God.⁵⁹ This perception was especially accentuated after 70 CE to link Rome with the world power responsible for the destruction of Jerusalem. It is therefore understandable why Rome as a code name for Babylon is testified in Jewish literature after 70 CE (*4 Ezra* 3.1–2, 28–31; *2 Bar.* 10.2–3; 11.1–2; 67.7; *Sib. Or.* 5.143, 159). The Petrine reference of Rome as Babylon is strong evidence of its date after 70 CE.

This observation of pseudonymity is also consistent with 1 Peter 1:1 in which the Christian addressees are said to be situated over the whole of Asia Minor. Even if Christianity started to grow in Asia Minor with Paul's first missionary journey (Acts 13:13–14:25) in the 50s CE, it is doubtful

---

56. Contra J. Ramsey Michaels, *1 Peter*, WBC 49 (Waco, TX: Word Books, 1988), lvii–lxi.

57. E.g. Leonhard Goppelt, *A Commentary on 1 Peter*, trans. John E. Alsup, ed. Ferdinand Hahn (Grand Rapids, MI: Eerdmans, 1993), 48–53; Beare, *First Epistle*, 43–50; Bechtler, *Following*, 42–47; Horrell, *1 Peter*, 20–23.

58. M. Eugene Boring, "Narrative Dynamics in First Peter: The Function of Narrative World," in *Reading First Peter with New Eyes: Methodological Reassessments of the Letter of First Peter*, eds. Robert L. Webb and Betsy Bauman-Martin (London: T&T Clark, 2007), 29, 35. Contra Robert H. Gundry, "'Verba Christi' in 1 Peter: Their Implications concerning the Authorship of 1 Peter and the Authenticity of the Gospel Tradition," *NTS* 13 (1967): 336–350; Robert H. Gundry, "Further Verba on Verba Christi in First Peter," *Bib* 55 (1974): 211–236, whose attempt to locate a long string of allusive quotations of Jesus' sayings is considered by most scholars as not convincing.

59. E.g. Goppelt, *Commentary*, 374–375; C. E. B. Cranfield, *The First Epistle of Peter* (London: SCM Press, 1950), 123; Achtemeier, *1 Peter*, 353–354.

that the Jesus movement could have spread throughout the whole area during the lifetime of Peter, not to say to have the network of communication built between the church in Rome and those in the various provinces of Asia Minor.[60]

As for the exact date of the letter, although many scholars recognize that 1 Peter is alluded to in Polycarp's *Letter to the Philippians* (e.g. *Pol. Phil* 1.3; 2.1, 2; 8.1)[61] which sets the letter's *terminus ad quem* around 110–130 CE,[62] little information is provided in the text to throw light on its *terminus a quo*. However, several considerations seem to render a proposal possible.

If Babylon as the code name of Rome began to generate after 70 CE, a period of time is needed before it could be so well known from Rome to each province of Asia Minor as to become a cipher between the author (Babylon, 5:13) and the addressees. On the other hand, since 1 Peter is alluded to in Polycarp's letter, it is probable that 1 Peter was already well circulated around 110–130 CE, so that it was also mentioned in Christians' correspondence. These considerations actually fit in the report of Pliny written about 111–112 CE that there were Christians in Asia Minor who had renounced their faith as far as twenty-five years before (*Ep.* 10.96), probably under pressure of persecution.[63] Therefore, a reasonable case can be made by viewing these factors together to date 1 Peter to sometime around the 90s CE possibly in the reign of Domitian.

Although a number of Petrine scholars identify Domitian's reign as a period of imperial persecutions of Christians which affects their judgment on the dating of 1 Peter,[64] many scholars nowadays, especially those engaging in studies on Revelation, recognize that there is no concrete evidence of widespread state-initiated persecution of Christians at the time of Domitian.[65] Thus, to date 1 Peter to the 90s CE is consistent with the

---

60. See also Beare, *First Epistle*, 30; Feldmeier, *First Letter*, 33.

61. See Achtemeier, *1 Peter*, 44–45 for a judicious evaluation of the evidence of dependence. Eusebius, *Hist. eccl.* 4.14.9 also noted Polycarp's use of 1 Peter.

62. See Michael W. Holmes, "*Polycarp*, Epistle to the Philippians," in *The Writings of the Apostolic Fathers*, ed. Paul Foster (London: T&T Clark, 2007), 124.

63. Also Achtemeier, *1 Peter*, 48. Contra Beare, *First Epistle*, 32.

64. E.g. Balch, *Wives*, 137; Bechtler, *Following*, 49–50; Green, *1 Peter*, 8–9.

65. E.g. Leonard L. Thompson, *The Book of Revelation: Apocalypse and Empire* (New York: Oxford University Press, 1990), 15–17, 95–115; Adela Yarbro Collins, *Crisis and*

situation of the readers, who were more likely to be facing alienation and hostility primarily from pagan neighbours as a result of their change of lifestyle after conversion to become Christians (3:15; 4:4, 14–16). Such hostility was expressed mainly in the form of verbal accusations (2:12, 15; 3:9, 16; 4:4) while those Christians in vulnerable situations, such as slaves, may also be open to physical abuse (cf. κολαφιζόμενοι, 2:20). In cases of extreme hostility and as testified by Pliny's letters (*Ep.* 10.96–97), private hatred and accusations could, in some cases, end up Christians being brought before the Roman authorities (cf. 3:15)[66] and even having to face death for being Christian.[67]

The persecutions which Christians had to face were, therefore, primarily the result of their new religious orientation. The test (πειρασμός, 1:6; 4:12) which they had to go through was the temptation to renounce their faith and relapse to their traditional piety (cf. 1:14–18), as Pliny testified to be the case twenty-five years earlier (*Ep.* 10.96). It is against this tendency towards apostasy that the Petrine author expressly underlines his purpose of writing the letter as procuring the readers to stand firm in the true grace of God (ταύτην εἶναι ἀληθῆ χάριν τοῦ θεοῦ εἰς ἣν στῆτε, 5:12), that is, the eschatological salvation (1:10, 13; 3:7)[68] to be revealed in the last time (1:5) and the goal (τέλος, 1:9) of Christians' earthly life of faith (πίστεως, 1:9; cf. πίστις, 1:5, 7, 21; 5:9). Therefore, the primary concern of the Petrine author is Christians' holding fast to their ultimate allegiance to God so as to remain in God's salvation. This "ultimate allegiance to God" is by no means merely a matter of "inner commitments"[69] but has to be trans-

---

Catharsis: The Power of the Apocalypse (Philadelphia, PA: Westminster Press, 1984), 69–73; David A. deSilva, "The Social Setting of the Revelation to John: Conflicts Within, Fears Without," *WTJ* 54 (1992): 274; Grant R. Osborne, *Revelation*, BECNT (Grand Rapids, MI: Baker, 2002), 7–9.

66. Although I agree with many scholars that ἀπολογίαν in 3:15 refers to Christians' defense of their faith primarily in informal inquiries happened in the daily social life, private accusations can also result in formal court proceedings. See note 128 on page 101 below. This observation is consistent with the fact that ἀπολογία is also used to refer to the defence in a legal action, for example in Acts 25:16; Phil 1:7, 16 and 2 Tim 4:16.

67. Bruce W. Winter, *Seek the Welfare of the City: Christians as Benefactors and Citizens* (Grand Rapids, MI: Eerdmans, 1994), 18; Horrell, *1 Peter*, 57–58.

68. Michaels, *1 Peter*, 41.

69. Contra Carter, "Going," 28–29.

lated into concrete visible behaviour, as I am going to demonstrate in the following study.

CHAPTER 2

Theological Vision of 1 Peter

As I argued in the previous chapter, the purpose of 1 Peter is to encourage Christians to stand firm in the grace/salvation of God in the face of pagan alienation and hostility. The primary concern of the Petrine author is therefore religious and theological. In this chapter, I will start my investigation of the manner in which the Petrine theology gives shape to the letter's social behavioural instructions by exploring the author's theological vision.

However, as I also mentioned in the previous chapter, Petrine scholars are not always keen to look for a coherent theological vision in 1 Peter. Petrine scholarship has traditionally focused on form-critical concerns and treated 1 Peter as a collection of earlier traditions clustered together, rather than seeking to understand the author's theological perspective as a whole. This neglect to investigate the author's unique vision is best exemplified by Kelly's comment that only the "generally simple, traditional character" of the letter's theology need be observed.[1] Likewise, Best's failure to include a discussion on theology in his commentary, but using extensive space to argue for the letter's direct literary connection with Romans and Ephesians,[2] is also indicative of scholars' neglect of the letter's overall theological concern.

Another factor contributing to the little progress in giving a better integrated account of the letter's theological vision is that instead of separating the indicative from the imperative to form a more clear-cut section on theology, the Petrine author frequently chooses to lay his ethical

---

1. J. N. D. Kelly, *A Commentary on the Epistles of Peter and of Jude,* BNTC (London: Adam & Charles Black, 1969), 25.
2. Ernest Best, *1 Peter,* NCB (London: Oliphants, 1971), 32–36.

admonitions side by side with their theological rationale. Therefore, while noting the interweaving of the two strands of theology and ethics in 1 Peter, Selwyn remarks, "we may be most true to its message if we do not try to disentangle too much."[3] This view is followed by Dryden who observes that, "This integration of theological and ethical reflections forms an intricate tapestry in 1 Peter that cannot be separated without irreparable damage to the fabric of the epistle."[4] Dryden therefore prefers to adopt a methodology that "does not separate" the theology and ethics of 1 Peter "a priori" in order to gain an understanding of how theology and ethics function *together*,[5] which also results in his failure to offer an account of the coherent theological point of view throughout the letter.

It is my contention that although the Petrine author may not "present anything like a *system* of Christian thought,"[6] it does not follow that he does not have a consistent theological perspective to serve as the conceptual basis for his social behavioural instructions. Likewise, the fact that the author draws upon a variety of earlier traditions does not preclude him from employing these sources to set forth his own unique vision.[7]

In this chapter, I will try to reconstruct the integral theological perspective of 1 Peter by especially taking account of the letter's concentration of OT language and images. I propose that through this appropriation of OT references, the Petrine author actually presents his Christian theological vision in terms of the Jewish eschatological vision. Jesus Christ is thus underscored as the Jewish expected Messiah whose appearance in history has inaugurated the Messianic Age in fulfilment of the OT prophecies and eschatological promises.

It is precisely through the resurrection of Christ the Messiah from the dead (1:3) that Christians are now born again (ἀναγεννήσας, 1:3) and assume the identity and self-understanding of the contemporary people of Israel as "elect exiles of Diaspora" (ἐκλεκτοῖς παρεπιδήμοις διασπορᾶς, 1:1),

---

3. Selwyn, *First Epistle of St. Peter*, 65.
4. Dryden, *Theology*, 4.
5. Ibid., 4.
6. As asserted by Beare, *First Epistle*, 51.
7. Also Peter H. Davids, *The First Epistle of Peter*, NICNT (Grand Rapids, MI: Eerdmans, 1990), 14–15.

inheriting the Jewish eschatological restoration hope as well as their obligations and functions as the holy people of God of Diaspora. What is remarkable is that OT images are at the same time reinterpreted in 1 Peter to highlight Christians' existence as a spiritual temple grounding their existence and experience upon Christ the Messiah as the Cornerstone (2:4–7). It is under these dual influences of christological and ecclesiastical visions that Christians' doing good works (2:12, 15, 20; 3:6, 11, 13, 16, 17; 4:19) and discharging their priestly functions (2:5, 9, 12; 4:16) amidst pagan alienation are perceived as the congruent behavioural expression of their self-understanding as elect exiles of Diaspora, as well as a token of expressing their solidarity with the Messiah-Christ by following his steps.

Therefore, in view of the letter's concerns with Christians' identity and proper conduct in face of pagan alienation, I consider 1 Peter to be essentially christocentric.[8] Although God is the One who determines and initiates everything that comes to pass (cf. 1:2),[9] his salvation plan for humanity is exclusively revealed and accomplished through the suffering and resurrection of Christ the Messiah (1:3, 10–11, 20) through which the Christian elect people of God are "now"[10] (νῦν, 1:12; 2:10, 25; 3:21) called into existence. This "already" dimension of Christian existence has its counterpart as the "not yet," which is to be consummated also in Christ's future revelation (1:7, 13; 4:13; 5:4) when the faithful Christian Diaspora will be rewarded with "glory and honour" (δόξαν καὶ τιμήν, 1:7; δόξης, 5:4) and share in his glory (δόξα, 4:13; 5:1).

Furthermore, being chosen stones constituted into a spiritual temple grounding their existence and experience on Christ as the chosen Cornerstone (2:4–7), and indeed in Christ (ἐν Χριστῷ, 3:16; 5:10, 14),

---

8. Paul J. Achtemeier, "Suffering Servant and Suffering Christ in 1 Peter," in *The Future of Christology: Essays in Honor of Leander E. Keck*, eds. Abraham J. Malherbe and Wayne A. Meeks (Minneapolis, MN: Fortress Press, 1993), 176. My view is supported by Selwyn, *First Epistle*, 76 who, while concluding that the letter is theocentric, nevertheless recognizes "the christocentric orientation which St Peter gives to his idea of the Church." Likewise, Michaels, *1 Peter*, lxviii, observes that Jesus Christ is "the one with whom the theology of 1 Peter is most directly concerned" although he at the same time regards 1 Peter to be God-centered.

9. Cf. Beare, *First Epistle*, 51–52; Andrew Chester and Ralph P. Martin, *The Theology of the Letters of James, Peter, and Jude*, repr. ed. (Cambridge: Cambridge University Press, 1996 [1st published, 1994]), 104–105.

10. All Scripture translations in this work are the author's own.

Christians are to understand their life situations within the contours of Jesus' story. Since Jesus Christ suffered alienation and rejection essentially as a resident-alien and a stranger, human rejection and ostracism are also what the Christians are to expect (εἰς τοῦτο γὰρ ἐκλήθητε, 2:21; μὴ ξενίζεσθε, 4:12) as part of their existence as resident-aliens and exiles (παρεπιδήμοις, 1:1; τῆς παροικίας ὑμῶν, 1:17; ὡς παροίκους καὶ παρεπιδήμους, 2:11) on earth. His manner of social engagement when facing human alienation also constitutes the example (ὑπογραμμόν, 2:21) after which Christians should follow in his steps.

Therefore, in the following discussion of this chapter, I will firstly explore the Petrine perception of Jesus Christ as the Jewish expected Messiah. Christ the Messiah is remarkably underscored as essentially a resident-alien suffering from human rejection on earth rather than as a judge and a warrior (cf. e.g. *2 Bar.* 39.7–40.3; 72.2–6; *4 Ezra* 12.32–33; 13.37–39; *1 En.* 46.3–6), as more commonly was expected in Jewish literature. In the second section, I will explicate the Petrine understanding of Christian existence in terms of the letter's controlling metaphor of Christians as the "elect exiles of Diaspora" (1:1) taking on the self-understanding and eschatological hope of the exilic Jewish Diaspora. In the last section of this chapter, I will then deal with the author's perception of the relationship between Christ the Messiah and the Christian "elect exiles of Diaspora" in terms of (1) the image of the spiritual temple and (2) the existence of the Christian chosen people of God as determined by Christ. It becomes clear that for the Petrine author, Christians' existence and experience as resident-aliens is not something to be lamented or which should turn Christians sullen. On the contrary, their identity as "elect exiles of Diaspora" actually connotes a degree of their commitment and responsibility to the wider pagan world.

2.1 The Christ-Messiah in 1 Peter

As noted by many scholars, the Petrine references to Christ concentrate on Jesus' suffering and his subsequent exaltation.[11] These twin themes of "suffering" and subsequent "glory" of Christ are underscored as the two main

---

11. E.g. Beare, *First Epistle*, 52; Achtemeier, *1 Peter*, 37; John H. Elliott, *1 Peter*, AB 37B (New Haven, CT: Yale University Press, 2000), 110.

subjects testified beforehand (προμαρτυρόμενον, 1:11) by the OT prophets. As Achtemeier remarks, the Christ (Χριστόν) mentioned in 1:11 probably refers to "Jesus of Nazareth rather than the 'messiah' in a general sense" because the subsequent δόξας most likely refers to Christ's resurrection and exaltation.[12] What the prophets in fact foretold, as insisted in 1 Peter, was therefore the passion and resurrection of Jesus of Nazareth, who is thus identified as the Jewish expected Messiah. It is through this identification that the Petrine author further understands Christians, who address the Messiah-Christ as "Lord" (κύριος, 1:3; 3:15; cf. 2:3, 13), as now entitled to claim the Jewish heritage as God's elect people of Diaspora.

In this section, I will explore the Petrine author's choice of OT images to present his understanding of Jesus Christ as the Jewish expected Messiah. This christological reflection of the author is what constitutes the theological/conceptual basis for his further reflection on Christians' existence and their proper mode of social behaviour as God's elect exilic people of Diaspora on earth.

2.1.1 The Suffering Christ-Messiah

Although the suffering of Jesus Christ is only one of the twin themes of the author's christological vision, Jesus is notably understood as the Messiah more by virtue of his suffering than his majestic power and authority. While the terms "suffer" (πάσχω, 2:21, 23; 3:18; 4:1) and "suffering" (πάθημα, 1:11; 4:13; 5:1) are consistently employed to refer to the passion of Jesus Christ, the term ἀποθνήσκω (die; cf. e.g. Rom 5:8; 1 Cor 15:3; Gal 2:21) is not.[13] Only the term θανατωθείς (put to death) is used once in 1 Peter 3:18.

Furthermore, although the cross is the starting point of the Petrine reflection, much emphasis is put on the events prior to Jesus' death. As Michaels observes, "The cross is the basis of Peter's ethics, but not the cross in distinction from the sufferings that preceded it."[14] It is precisely these human sufferings and rejection prior to crucifixion, which render Jesus

---

12. Achtemeier, "Suffering Servant," 182–183.

13. Especially telling is the fact that πάσχω is used in places where ἀποθνήσκω is more commonly expected. This probably gave rise to the various scribal efforts to emend ἀποθνήσκω for πάσχω in 2:21, 3:18 and 4:1.

14. Michaels, *1 Peter*, lxxii.

Christ a stranger and a resident-alien in essence (cf. 1:1, 17; 2:11),[15] that make him the prototype and the theological basis for Christians to understand their own existence as "exilic people of Diaspora" on earth. Jesus Christ's "manner" of responding to human alienation when facing the cross is also the referential behavioural model on which the Petrine author formulates his social strategies for the Christian Diaspora. These are precisely the considerations of the Petrine author when he employs the OT images of the sacrificial Lamb (1:18–19), Rejected Stone (2:4, 7) and the Suffering Servant (2:22–25), to present Jesus Christ as the Messiah.

a) Jesus Christ as the Lamb (1:18–19)

In 1 Peter 1:18–19, Christians' redemption is underscored to have been effected not with perishable things but by the precious blood of Christ as a lamb without blemish or spot. It is on the basis of this origin of Christians' existence that the author derives his ethical exhortations in 1:13–17 as the congruent expression of Christians' new status as the children of God (1:14; cf. 1:3).[16]

Therefore, within the Petrine vision, the source of Christian existence is derived from the sacrificial suffering of Jesus Christ who submitted to human afflictions with meekness like a lamb for a higher cause of accomplishing the salvation plan of God (1:20). The submissiveness and peace-seeking characteristic of the lamb is prominently portrayed in LXX Isaiah 53:7 in which a sheep (ὡς πρόβατον) is viewed as not opening its mouth when led to the slaughter (σφαγήν) and a lamb (ὡς ἀμνός; cf. ὡς ἀμνοῦ, 1 Pet 1:19) is also underscored as remaining silent (ἄφωνος) before its shearer (κείροντος). The reality represented by the metaphor of a lamb is therefore an acceptance of human afflictions in compliance with existing human order. Although Christ is perceived primarily as the Passover lamb in this passage, as I am going to demonstrate, the influence of Isaiah 53:7 on the Petrine author's mind cannot be excluded especially in view of his

---

15. Similar observation of Jesus Christ as "a stranger" on earth is also made by Miroslav Volf, "Soft Difference: Theological Reflections on the Relation between Church and Culture in 1 Peter," *ExAud* 10 (1994): 17; and Christian Blendinger, "Kirche als Fremdlingschaft," *CV* 2–3 (1967): 127, both of whom, however, find support for their idea from other New Testament writings rather than from 1 Peter itself.

16. See also Goppelt, *Commentary*, 114.

notable appropriation of LXX Isaiah 53:4–9 (and possibly also 53:12) to 1 Peter 2:22–25.[17] It is on the basis of this reflection of Christians' origin of existence as derived from the peaceful and submissive sacrificial suffering of Christ that the Petrine author regards submission (ὑποτάσσω, 2:13, 18; 3:1; 5:5), endurance (ὑπομενεῖτε, 2:20), gentleness/humility (πραέως, 3:4; πραΰτητος, 3:16) and peace-seeking (ζητησάτω εἰρήνην καὶ διωξάτω αὐτήν, 3:11) without retaliation (μὴ ἀποδιδόντες κακὸν ἀντὶ κακοῦ ἢ λοιδορίαν ἀντὶ λοιδορίας, 3:9) to be the proper expressions of Christian existence on earth.[18]

I agree with most scholars that the unblemished and spotless lamb (ὡς ἀμνοῦ ἀμώμου καὶ ἀσπίλου, 1:19) in this passage probably alludes to a Passover lamb (cf. Exod 12:5).[19] Although Achtemeier rejects a Passover background on the ground that the blood of the Passover lamb had no redemptive power,[20] the language used and the overall image constructed in the whole 1 Peter 1:13–21 probably points to an Exodus backdrop. Ἀναζωσάμενοι τὰς ὀσφύας τῆς διανοίας ὑμῶν (gird up the loins of your mind) in 1:13 recalls the people of Israel having to eat their first paschal meal with their loins girded (αἱ ὀσφύες ὑμῶν περιεζωσμέναι, LXX Exod 12:11). The exhortation to be holy (ἅγιοι ἔσεσθε, ὅτι ἐγὼ ἅγιός) in 1:16 contains an exact quotation of LXX Leviticus 19:2 in the context of the Exodus. The term λυτρόω (ἐλυτρώθητε, 1 Pet 1:18) is also a term frequently used in the LXX to refer to the deliverance of Israel from the bondage in Egypt (e.g. LXX Exod 6:6; 15:13; LXX Deut 7:8; 9:26; 13:6; LXX 1 Chr 17:21; LXX Mic 6:4).

Although, as Jeremias observes, "The description of the Redeemer as a lamb is unknown to later Judaism,"[21] there is clear evidence that early Christians endowed messianic significance on the Passover lamb and

---

17. So Kelly, *Commentary*, 75; Best, *1 Peter*, 90; Donald Senior, "1 Peter," in *1 Peter, Jude and 2 Peter*, ed. Daniel J. Harrington (Collegeville, MN: Liturgical Press, 2003), 46.

18. These characteristics of the Petrine social ethics will be further explicated in the next chapter.

19. E.g. Selwyn, *First Epistle*, 146; Best, *1 Peter*, 89; Goppelt, *Commentary*, 116; Paul E. Deterding, "Exodus Motifs in First Peter," *Concordia Journal* 7 (1981): 58, 62; Barth L. Campbell, *Honor, Shame, and the Rhetoric of 1 Peter*, SBLDS 160 (Atlanta, GA: Scholars Press, 1998), 73 n.73; Horrell, *1 Peter*, 68.

20. Achtemeier, *1 Peter*, 128–129.

21. Joachim Jeremias, "ἀμνός," *TDNT* 1:338.

applied it to Jesus Christ.[22] Particularly noticeable is that in the Greek version of *T. Jos.*19.11–12, which is commonly recognized as containing a Christian interpolation, the Lamb of God is underlined as the one "who will take away the sin of the world, and will save all the nations, as well as Israel" and "his kingdom is an everlasting kingdom which will not pass away."[23]

Furthermore, the future Messianic Age is envisaged as a New Exodus at least in some pre-Christian Jewish circles.[24] For example, in Isaiah 43, the reference to the Lord "who gives a way in the sea, a path in mighty waters" (43:16) and the themes of "provisions in wilderness," "election" and "the formation of the people of God" (43:19–21) are all resonant with the Exodus motif.[25] Moreover, in Rabbinic traditions, the Passover blood, together with the covenant blood of the circumcision, are referred to as by the merit of which God's people had been redeemed out of Egypt and will be "redeemed at the end of the fourth (Roman) world empire (i.e. in the days of the Messiah)" (*Pirqe R. El.* 29).[26]

Indeed, in LXX, besides liberation of Israel from bondage in Egypt, the term λυτρόω (ἐλυτρώθητε, 1 Pet 1:18) is also used to refer to the eschatological deliverance of Israel from exile. For instance, in LXX Isaiah 51:11, those having been redeemed (λελυτρωμένοις) by the Lord shall return and come to Zion with gladness and everlasting exultation.[27] This observation is aligned with the context of 1 Peter 1:18 that the redemption of Christians is not described as a release from sin or guilt but as a freedom from their former inherited futile way of life. The redemption of the

---

22. E.g. John 1:29–36; 19:36 (cf. Exod 12:46); Rev 5:6. One reason proposed by scholars is that Jesus' crucifixion took place at Passover and was therefore viewed as a Passover victim. See John R. Miles, "Lamb," *ABD* 4 (1992): 133; Jeremias, *TDNT* 1:339.

23. Translation provided in Howard C. Kee, "Testaments of the Twelve Patriarchs," in vol. 1 of *The Old Testament Pseudepigrapha*, ed. James H. Charlesworth (Peabody, MA: Hendrickson, 2009 [1st published, 1983]), 824–825. Kee considers the Christian interpolation to be dated from the early second century CE.

24. See also W. D. Davies, *The Setting of the Sermon on the Mount,* BJS 186 (Atlanta, GA: Scholars Press, 1989), 26.

25. See also Mark Dubis, *Messianic Woes in First Peter: Suffering and Eschatology in 1 Peter 4:12–19,* Studies in Biblical Literature 33 (New York: Peter Lang, 2002), 49.

26. Str-B 4:40. I derive this reference from Joachim Jeremias, *The Eucharistic Words of Jesus,* trans. Normal Perrin, NTL (London: SCM Press, 1966), 225 n. 4.

27. See also e.g. LXX Mic 4:10; Zech 10:8; Isa 43:14; 44:23; Jer 38:11.

Christian people of God is thus presented by the Petrine author as a parallel to the OT promise of deliverance to the people of Israel fulfilled in Christ the Messianic Passover Lamb.

It is important to note that the redemption (ἐλυτρώθητε, 1:18) of Christians accomplished by the sacrificial suffering of Christ is not underscored as from *the wider pagan world* but from the *futile* (ματαίας) way of life they *inherited from their ancestors* (ἀναστροφῆς πατροπαραδότου, 1:18). As Goppelt observes, "This expression elaborates on the image sketched in v. 14 of the pre-Christian situation: μάταιος, 'futile,' elaborates on ἄγνοια, 'ignorance' (of God), and on ἐπιθυμία, 'craving.'"[28] Therefore, τῆς ματαίας ὑμῶν ἀναστροφῆς πατροπαραδότου in 1:18 is actually a parallel to ταῖς πρότερον ἐν τῇ ἀγνοίᾳ ὑμῶν ἐπιθυμίαις (the cravings formerly in your ignorance) in 1:14 to which Christians are exhorted not to conform.

Furthermore, in the LXX, the term μάταιος is "typically connected with idolatry"[29] (e.g. Lev 17:7; 1 Kgs 16:13, 26; 2 Chr 11:15; Isa 44:9; Jer 8:19; 10:15; Jonah 2:9; Wis 15:8; cf. Acts 14:15; ἐματαιώθησαν, Rom 1:21), or else to those who have never known God (e.g. Wis 13:1), or have apostatized from him (e.g. Jer 2:5).[30] The abstention and non-conformity which the Petrine author emphasizes is therefore primarily of religious, rather than social, orientation.[31]

This observation is further supported by van Unnik's comprehensive study of the term πατροπαράδοτος (πατροπαραδότου, 1 Pet 1:18) in which he concludes that the way of life Christians inherited is one that is "strongly stamped by religious rites."[32] Particularly telling is that in Theophilus's *Autol.* 2.34, the terms μάταιος and πατροπαράδοτος are used together in the context of criticism against pagans' worshipping of idols made by human hands.[33] Therefore, by exhorting Christians not to conform to their

---

28. Goppelt, *Commentary*, 117.

29. W. C. van Unnik, "The Critique of Paganism in 1 Peter 1:18," in *Neotestamentica et semitica: Studies in Honour of Matthew Black*, eds. E. Earle Ellis and Max Wilcox (Edinburgh: T&T Clark, 1969), 141.

30. Kelly, *Commentary*, 74.

31. For the examples of connection between pagan ignorance (ἄγνοια) and idolatries, see Wis 14:22–27; Philo, *Decal.* 8.

32. van Unnik, "Critique," 140.

33. I derive this reference from van Unnik, "Critique," 140.

former cravings, and by underscoring Christian existence as having been redeemed from the inherited futile way of life, the Petrine author is not advocating Christians' separation from everything belonging to the pagan way of life but only those aspects which relate to idolatry[34] or otherwise are inconsistent with their religious orientation to God, such as cursing Christ (cf. Pliny, *Ep.* 10.96) or denying God (cf. *Diogn.* 10.7). I hold that this is one major aspect of the Petrine behavioural exhortations to which scholars often fail to pay sufficient attention when studying 1 Peter 1:13–21. This in turn results in their diverse interpretations of this passage.[35]

b) Jesus Christ as the Rejected Stone (2:4, 7)

In 1 Peter 2:4–8, the unity of Christians and Christ is portrayed by way of an image of Christians as living stones of a spiritual house grounding their existence on Christ as the living Cornerstone. The existence and experience of Christians on earth are thus also grounded on, and indeed bound up with, those of Christ.

The idea of Christ being a living stone (λίθον) rejected (ἀποδεδοκι-μασμένον) by human beings (2:4) probably has its origin from λίθον ὃν ἀπεδοκίμασαν οἱ οἰκοδομοῦντες οὗτος ἐγενήθη εἰς κεφαλὴν γωνίας of LXX Psalm 117:22 (MT Ps 118:22)[36] which is more elaborately quoted in 1 Peter 2:7b as λίθος ὃν ἀπεδοκίμασαν οἱ οἰκοδομοῦντες, οὗτος ἐγενήθη εἰς κεφαλὴν γωνίας (a stone which the builders rejected, the same has become the head of the corner). Although LXX Psalm 117:22 speaks of the rejection of the stone by the builders (οἱ οἰκοδομοῦντες) and those who rejected Jesus in the Gospels were the Jewish authorities, the perfect tense ἀποδεδοκιμασμένον in 1 Peter 2:4 probably points to the ongoing rejection of Christ and the Christian faith by the wider hostile world.[37] The author's emphasis is therefore on Christ being continuously treated as a resident-alien and a stranger in the pagan world.

---

34. See also Bechtler, 63.
35. E.g. Davids, *First Epistle*, 67–69, 71–72; Achtemeier, *1 Peter*, 120–128; Elliott, *1 Peter*, 358–359, 370–371; Feldmeier, *First Letter,* 102–105; 116–117; Karen H. Jobes, *1 Peter*, BECNT (Grand Rapids, MI: Baker, 2005), 112–119.
36. Elliott, *1 Peter*, 428.
37. Achtemeier, *1 Peter*, 154.

What is noteworthy is that Jesus Christ the Rejected Stone is understood as none other than the Messiah expected in accordance with the Jewish eschatological vision. The *Targum Psalms* renders Psalm 118:22 a messianic interpretation by reading the cornerstone (לְרֹאשׁ פִּנָּה) as "king and ruler" (למליך ושולטן) to allude to David or the Messiah and reads טליא (child) for אֶבֶן (rock), which child is then further underscored as among the sons of Jesse (בניא דישי), in order to align with this messianic understanding. Likewise, the cornerstone (אֶבֶן אֶבֶן בֹּחַן פִּנַּת יִקְרַת) in Isaiah 28:16 (which 1 Pet 2:6 probably draws from) is also read as "king" (מלך מלך תקיף) in *Jonathan Targum Isaiah*.[38] The concession of Trypho in Justin, *Dial.* 36 that the prophets predicted that Messiah "was to be called *a Stone*"[39] further testifies to the recognition of "the Stone" as a messianic title among the Jews.[40]

This messianic understanding of the rejected stone in Psalm 118:22 is also taken up in the Synoptic traditions with reference to Jesus' crucifixion (Matt 21:42; Mark 12:10; Luke 20:17). For example, in the Markan Gospel, Jesus appropriated this image of the rejected stone to himself in relation to his own cross and subsequent glory (Mark12:10).

It is based on this conviction that Jesus Christ is in fact elected and honoured (ἐκλεκτὸν ἔντιμον) before God (2:4) as the Messiah, but paradoxically had to consistently go through human rejection (ἀποδεδοκιμασμένον, 2:4; ἀπεδοκίμασαν, 2:7), that Christians should also understand their existence as being in similar paradox. Although they have already been elected (ἐκλεκτοῖς, 1:1) before God, they are to continue suffering human rejection as resident-aliens/exiles of Diaspora (παρεπιδήμοις διασπορᾶς, 1:1; ὡς παροίκους καὶ παρεπιδήμους, 2:11) on earth knowing that the Messianic Age has been inaugurated and their vindication in the end is in view (cf. 1:10–11; 1:20–21).[41]

---

38. See also Achtemeier, *1 Peter*, 154 n. 57.

39. Saint Justin Martyr, *Dialogue with Trypho*, trans. Thomas P. Halton, Selections from the Fathers of the Church 3 (Washington, DC: Catholic University of America Press, 2003), 56.

40. See also Norman Hillyer, "'Rock-Stone' Imagery in 1 Peter," *TynBul* 22 (1971): 59.

41. Cf. Achtemeier, *1 Peter*, 154.

c) Jesus Christ as the Suffering Servant (2:22–25)

First Peter 2:21–25 has once been described as a "key passage for understanding the Christology of 1 Peter."[42] Besides its profound reflection on Christ's suffering with reference to the Isaianic Suffering Servant (Isa 53:4–9),[43] it also presents most explicitly the author's perception of Jesus Christ's existence as essentially a resident-alien/stranger on earth in the light of his passion. Christ's social engagement in the face of human afflictions as highlighted in this passage also becomes a paradigm for Christian social strategies/discipleship in the midst of a hostile pagan society.

It is beyond question that 1 Peter 2:22–25 is dependent on LXX Isaiah 53:4–9 (and possibly also 53:12): 1 Peter 2:22 quotes at length from LXX Isaiah 53:9, only with the addition of the relative pronoun ὅς and the substitution of ἁμαρτίαν for ἀνομίαν. Although there is no clue for any direct quotation in 2:23 from Isaiah 53, Achtemeier is probably correct when he argues that "while being reviled, he did not revile in return, while suffering, he did not threaten" (λοιδορούμενος οὐκ ἀντελοιδόρει, πάσχων οὐκ ἠπείλει) is alluding to the silence of the Suffering Servant in Isaiah 53:7.[44] This perception of Christ's suffering in terms of Isaiah 53:7 actually echoes the author's image of a gentle and submissive lamb (1:18–19) in his reflection on Jesus Christ's suffering. Christ's mode of social engagement of non-retaliation and peace-seeking further serves as the basis of his formulation of social ethics for Christians (cf. ἢ λοιδορίαν ἀντὶ λοιδορίας, 3:9; ζητησάτω εἰρήνην καὶ διωξάτω αὐτήν, 3:11).

Furthermore, τὰς ἁμαρτίας ἡμῶν αὐτὸς ἀνήνεγκεν (he himself bore our sins) in 1 Peter 2:24 reflects either οὗτος τὰς ἁμαρτίας ἡμῶν φέρει in LXX Isaiah 53:4 or αὐτὸς ἁμαρτίας πολλῶν ἀνήνεγκεν in LXX Isaiah 53:12.[45] The links of οὗ τῷ μώλωπι ἰάθητε (by whose wound you were healed) in 1 Peter 2:24 to τῷ μώλωπι αὐτοῦ ἡμεῖς ἰάθημεν in LXX Isaiah 53:5 and ἦτε . . . ὡς πρόβατα πλανώμενοι (you were straying as sheep) in 1 Peter 2:25 to ὡς πρόβατα ἐπλανήθημεν in LXX Isaiah 53:6 are also

---

42. Achtemeier, "Suffering Servant," 177.

43. As Horrell, *1 Peter*, 63 remarks, 1 Pet 2:21–25 is "the most extensive and explicit early Christian interpretation of this influential prophetic text."

44. Achtemeier, "Suffering Servant," 179.

45. Ibid., 179–180.

unquestionable. Christ's willing submission to suffering in accordance with human expectation, and without disruption to current societal order, is therefore highlighted by the author as undertaken for a higher cause of redemption of people from sin in accordance with God's divine purpose (cf. 1:20). This observation is supported by the author's further addition of "he kept delivering [himself]⁴⁶to the One who judges justly" (παρεδίδου . . . τῷ κρίνοντι δικαίως,⁴⁷ 2:23), "so that being dead to sins, we might live for righteousness" (ἵνα ταῖς ἁμαρτίαις ἀπογενόμενοι τῇ δικαιοσύνῃ ζήσωμεν, 2:24) and "but now you have been returned to the Shepherd and Guardian of your souls" (ἀλλὰ ἐπεστράφητε νῦν ἐπὶ τὸν ποιμένα καὶ ἐπίσκοπον τῶν ψυχῶν ὑμῶν, 2:25).

In the OT and later Jewish literature, the idea of the "Servant" of God is employed in different senses ranging from the humble self-address of a pious man⁴⁸ to the designation of the Messiah.⁴⁹ In Deutero-Isaiah, the Servant is the one who has been called (49:1) and chosen (42:1; cf. 1 Pet 2:4) by God. He has been endowed with God's Spirit (42:1) and will bring about the restoration and regathering of God's people in exile (49:5–6). Isaiah 52:13–53:12, of which Isaiah 53:4–9 forms a part, points to the rejection and humiliation that this Servant will have to suffer.⁵⁰ The messianic overtone of the Servant is further heightened in *Jonathan Targum Isaiah* 43:10 and 52:13 which read עַבְדִי מְשִׁיחָא for עַבְדִי. It is against this background that the Petrine author perceives the suffering experienced by

---

46. The absence of an object for παρεδίδου creates ambiguity to the text. The insertion of εαυτον in some witnesses, such as two Old Latin versions and Vulgate manuscripts and others, is probably scribal effort to clarify this ambiguity. Nonetheless, this insertion gives a probable sense of the text to posit Christ's manner of enduring suffering an example for Christians to follow (4:19). See also Elliott, *1 Peter*, 531–532.

47. Although some Latin traditions, such as those found in the citations by Clement of Alexandria and Cyprian and the Vulgata, render αδικως to refer to Pilate as the unjust judge, this variant is too weakly attested to receive scholars' acceptance.

48. E.g. Moses in Num 11:11 and Deut 3:24; the young man in 1 Esd 4.59.

49. For details, see W. Zimmerli and J. Jeremias, *The Servant of God*, rev. ed., SBT 20 (London: SCM Press, 1965 [1st published, 1952]), 13–78. See also Richard N. Longenecker, *The Christology of Early Jewish Christianity*, SBT 2nd Series 17 (London: SCM Press, 1970), 104.

50. Zimmerli and Jeremias, *Servant*, 41 actually view the LXX translation of 52:14f as future and in clear deviation from the Hebrew text as evidence of the LXX translator's perception of the Servant as "a messianic figure whose coming he awaits."

Christ as a sign of the appearance of the Messiah in fulfilment of the promise of restoration to the people of God.

It is particularly noticeable that the Petrine author does not stop at underscoring Jesus Christ as fulfilling the Jewish eschatological expectation. The order of the language in Isaiah 53 is indeed restructured in 1 Peter roughly in accordance with the sequence of Jesus' passion story. First Peter 2:22–23 appears to reflect the trial and 1 Peter 2:24, the crucifixion of Jesus. Instead of simply interpreting Jesus' death in the light of Isaiah 53, the focus of the Petrine reflection is, therefore, the *manner/strategies* of Jesus Christ when responding to the rejection by the wider unbelieving world as the Suffering Servant and a resident-alien on earth. While Jesus Christ clearly maintained his own identity and integrity by accepting human rejection without having committed sin (2:22) and preserved his ultimate allegiance to God intact by entrusting himself to God (2:23), the fact that he, for a higher cause (2:24–25), submitted to human afflictions without retaliation (2:22–23) and without disrupting current societal order, is also part of his example (ὑπογραμμόν, 2:21) left for Christians to follow his steps (2:21) during their sojourn (τῆς παροικίας ὑμῶν, 1:17) on earth.[51]

2.1.2 The Exalted Christ-Messiah

While the author's reflection on the suffering of Jesus Christ on the cross provides the theological basis for his understanding of Christians' existence as resident-aliens and exiles on earth, his reflection on Christ's resurrection and ascension further supplies the necessary theological rationale for Christians to hold fast to the grace/salvation of God (1:10–11; 5:12). It is through Christ's resurrection that Christians are now born again to a living hope (1:3; cf. 3:21) for an inheritance (1:4) of salvation made available to Christians through faith (1:5). Just as Christ's suffering is a prelude to his glory (3:18–22), Christians can expect similar reversal of fortune that their existing suffering while doing good (2:20; 3:17) is only a prerequisite for their participating in Christ's glory on the day of visitation (4:13).

What is remarkable is that OT languages and connotations are once again employed to underscore the Petrine author's association of the exalted

---

51. Jesus Christ's social engagement in the face of social alienation and ostracism will be further investigated in the next chapter.

Christ with the Jewish Messiah so that Christians' ultimate redemption and vindication are comprehended within the contours of the restoration of Israel in the days of the Messiah.

a) Christ as the Living Cornerstone and Stone of Stumbling (2:4–8)

As mentioned above in section 2.1.1, the understanding of λίθος as the Messiah is well found in Jewish traditions. Jesus is characterized as the "Living" Stone (λίθον ζῶντα, 1 Pet 2:4), obviously because of his having been made "alive" in the spirit (3:18) (i.e. his resurrection). In 1 Peter 2:4–8, OT stone passages are now extended to encompass Christians as the living stones built into a spiritual house, with Christ as the living Cornerstone.

There is no question that ἰδοὺ τίθημι ἐν Σιὼν λίθον ἀκρογωνιαῖον ἐκλεκτὸν ἔντιμον καὶ ὁ πιστεύων ἐπ' αὐτῷ οὐ μὴ καταισχυνθῇ ("Behold, I am laying in Zion a stone, a cornerstone elect, honoured, and he who believes in him definitely will not be put to shame") in 1 Peter 2:6, comes from LXX Isaiah 28:16 which reads, ἰδοὺ ἐγὼ ἐμβαλῶ εἰς τὰ θεμέλια Σιων λίθον πολυτελῆ ἐκλεκτὸν ἀκρογωνιαῖον ἔντιμον εἰς τὰ θεμέλια αὐτῆς καὶ ὁ πιστεύων ἐπ' αὐτῷ οὐ μὴ καταισχυνθῇ. The quotation in 1 Peter 2:7b, which reads, λίθος ὃν ἀπεδοκίμασαν οἱ οἰκοδομοῦντες, οὗτος ἐγενήθη εἰς κεφαλὴν γωνίας ("a stone which the builders rejected, the same has become the head of the corner"), from λίθον ὃν ἀπεδοκίμασαν οἱ οἰκοδομοῦντες οὗτος ἐγενήθη εἰς κεφαλὴν γωνίας of LXX Psalm 117:22 (MT Ps 118:22) is even more obvious. As for 1 Peter 2:8, although the wording is not identical, scholars commonly agree that λίθος προσκόμματος καὶ πέτρα σκανδάλου (a stone of stumbling and a rock of offence) comes from Isaiah 8:14, which LXX renders λίθου προσκόμματι συναντήσεσθε αὐτῷ οὐδὲ ὡς πέτρας πτώματι.[52] As Jobes observes, 1 Peter 2:4–8 is "the most complete collection of NT references to the stone passages of the OT"[53] (cf. Rom 9:32–33; Matt 21:42; Mark 12:10; Luke 20:17–18; Acts 4:11). The effort of the Petrine author to highlight Jesus Christ as the Jewish expected Messiah is noticeable.

---

52. E.g. Michaels, *1 Peter*, 106; Achtemeier, *1 Peter*, 161; Elliott, *1 Peter*, 430–431.
53. Jobes, *1 Peter*, 153.

Although Jeremias argues that κεφαλὴν γωνίας in LXX Psalm 117:22 (MT Ps 118:22) and ἀκρογωνιαῖον in LXX Isaiah 28:16 should be understood as the topstone rather than a foundation stone,⁵⁴ it is more likely that ἀκρογωνιαῖον in 1 Peter 2:6 and κεφαλὴν γωνίας in 1 Peter 2:7b refer to the foundation stone on the ground level so that one can stumble over it (2:8).⁵⁵ It is in the light of the dramatic reversal of Christ from a Rejected Stone to the Cornerstone and indeed, the touchstone of human destiny, that Christians, though put to shame in the hostile human society (cf. οὐ μὴ καταισχυνθῇ, 2:6) because of their faith, will share his honour (cf. ὑμῖν οὖν ἡ τιμή, 2:7) as the honoured stone (λίθον ἀκρογωνιαῖον . . . ἔντιμον, 2:6) before God. On the other hand, those slanderers of Christians (2:12, 15; 3:16; 4:4), who now appear to be having the upper hand, are doomed to be put to shame before the judgment of God (2:8; cf. καταισχυνθῶσιν, 3:16).

b) *Christ as the Shepherd and Guardian (2:25)*

In 1 Peter 2:25, the dramatic reversal of Christ's experience is underscored as from the Suffering Servant to the Shepherd (ποιμένα) and Guardian (ἐπίσκοπον) of Christians' souls.

Once again, this shepherd motif reflects the OT expectation of Israel's restoration from exile in terms of the eschatological regathering of the children of Israel by God as the Chief Shepherd. In LXX Ezekiel 34:11–13, God is witnessed as promising, "I will seek out my sheep and will care for (ἐπισκέψομαι) them. Just as the shepherd (ὁ ποιμήν) seeks his flock . . . I will bring them away from every place where they were scattered . . . and I will gather them from the countries."

Although the image of the "shepherd" is constantly employed in the OT to refer to God,⁵⁶ it is Jesus Christ who is more frequently described as the shepherd in the NT.⁵⁷ Especially in view of the fact that 1 Peter 2:25 immediately follows οὗ τῷ μώλωπι ἰάθητε (by whose wound you were healed,

---

54. Joachim Jeremias, "Κεφαλὴ γωνίας – Ἀκρογωνιαῖος," *ZNW* 28 (1929): 264–280; "Eckstein – Schlußstein," *ZNW* 36 (1937): 154–157.

55. So Achtemeier, *1 Peter*, 160; Goppelt, *Commentary*, 137–138 n. 16.

56. E.g. Isa 40:11; Jer 31:10 (LXX 38:10); Ezek 34:15.

57. E.g. John 10:11–16; Heb 13:20; Rev 7:17. Cf. Matt 26:31; Mark 14:27; Luke 12:32.

2:24) which clearly refers to the suffering of Christ, it is more likely that τὸν ποιμένα καὶ ἐπίσκοπον in 1 Peter 2:25 is also denoting Jesus Christ.[58]

Especially important for our purpose are the OT passages which describe the promised Messiah in terms of a shepherd over God's people. Micah 5:3, which makes reference to the "ruler in Israel" coming from Bethlehem Ephrathah, reads, ". . . he will shepherd (his flock) in the strength of the Lord, in the exaltation of the name of the Lord his God . . ." Ezekiel 34:23 also witnesses to God's promise, "I will raise up over them one shepherd, my servant David, and he will shepherd them; he will shepherd them and he will be a shepherd to them." This expectation of the Messiah as the shepherd of Israel is also present in other Jewish traditions. In *Pss. Sol*.17.40, the expected Messiah is pictured as "Faithfully and righteously shepherding the Lord's flock."[59]

Therefore, by positing Jesus Christ as the Messianic Shepherd and Guardian of the Christian exilic people of God, the Petrine author is at the same time identifying Christians as inheriting the eschatological promise of the Jewish elect people of Diaspora and looking upon the Messiah for restoration and vindication.

c) *Christ as the Chief Shepherd (5:4)*
Closely related to the image of the Shepherd, Christ is underscored in 1 Peter 5:4 as the ἀρχιποίμενος (Chief Shepherd) who will reappear in the final judgment of God when those elders who have faithfully tended the flock of God will receive their eschatological reward. The fact of the faithful elders receiving the crown of glory is illustrative of how Christians will participate in Christ's glory at the eschaton through following Christ's example and participating in his suffering by standing firm in their faith at the present moment.

Particularly noteworthy for our purpose is that in Jeremiah 23:4–5, after God had indicted the leaders of his people for destroying and scattering his flock, he promised to raise up new shepherds for his people and to

---

58. Also e.g. Kelly, *Commentary*, 124–125; Best, *1 Peter*, 123; Achtemeier, *1 Peter*, 204; Elliott, *1 Peter*, 538–539.

59. Translation provided by R. B. Wright, "Psalms of Solomon," in vol. 2 of *The Old Testament Pseudepigrapha*, ed. James H. Charlesworth, 2 vols. (Peabody, MA: Hendrickson, 2009 [1st published, 1983]), 668.

raise up for David a righteous Branch who will reign as a king. This royal messianic figure is thus also the Chief Shepherd of all the undershepherds. The Petrine association of Christ with the promised Messiah for Israel is again evident.

Section Summary

In this section I demonstrated that the undercurrent beneath the various images of Christ in 1 Peter is the conviction that Christ is the Jewish expected Messiah, whose appearance in history has inaugurated the age of eschatological vindication for the Diaspora people of God. This perception of Jesus Christ in terms of the contemporary Jewish eschatological expectation becomes the conceptual backdrop for the Petrine author's further perception of Christians' existence on earth. They are to identify themselves as part of the holy people of God by stepping into the shoes of Israel so that their religious allegiance and social position are comprehended in terms of the exilic Jewish people of God in the Diaspora (cf. 1:1).

Particularly important for our purpose is that besides positing Christ's exaltation as the theological basis for Christians to stand firm in their faith in the light of their future restoration and deliverance, the Petrine author consciously draws upon OT language to underscore Christ the Messiah as having suffered human rejection essentially as a resident-alien/stranger on earth. The author's concern clearly does not stop at emphasizing the messiahship of Jesus Christ but also falls on the social strategies of Jesus Christ when facing human alienation. It is precisely from the vantage point of the cross that the author proceeds to formulate his social ethics for his Christian readers as their mode of following Christ's steps (2:21) on earth.

2.2 The Christian Elect Exiles of Diaspora in 1 Peter

In this section I will explore the Petrine perception of Christian identity with reference to the letter's controlling metaphor for Christians. As Mbuvi convincingly argues, "A useful heuristic tool, a 'controlling metaphor' is helpful in harnessing the diverse elements found within a writing such as 1

Peter, which, on occasion, may appear disjunctive."⁶⁰ A controlling metaphor is therefore particularly helpful to provide a holistic Petrine vision of Christian identity by bringing the various images and themes in the letter under a unified heading.

As I have shown in the last section, Christian identity in 1 Peter is constructed very much in relation to Jesus Christ as the Jewish expected Messiah. The extensive use of OT images and titles originally applied to Israel further indicates the Petrine perception of Christians as an extension of the Jewish people of God. Therefore, the suggestion of "Israel" by Achtemeier⁶¹ has the merits of recognizing this particular perception of Christian identity in 1 Peter. However, this idea of "Israel" is at the same time too general to highlight the particular historical, geographical and socio-political situations of the people of Israel that the Petrine author understands Christians to be situated.⁶²

Although Pryor's suggestion of "covenant people of God"⁶³ has the merit of highlighting the theological position of Christians before God with reference to Israel, it is difficult to see how the notion of "covenant people" is related to the letter's other metaphors of Christians such as exiles and resident-aliens (παρεπιδήμοις, 1:1; ὡς παροίκους καὶ παρεπιδήμους, 2:11) and Diaspora (διασπορᾶς, 1:1). Indeed, the Petrine Exodus language, which Pryor puts much weight on, can be more aptly explained with reference to the vision of the ultimate deliverance from exile as a New Exodus within Second Temple Judaism.⁶⁴

Therefore, the proposal put forth by Troy Martin to view the controlling metaphor of the whole letter as "the Diaspora"⁶⁵ and, thus, to portray the Petrine perception of Christian existence as "the wandering people of God on an eschatological journey"⁶⁶ has the advantage of representing

---

60. Mbuvi, *Temple*, 23.
61. Achtemeier, *1 Peter*, 69–72 and indeed, also Senior, "1 Peter," 12.
62. See also Mbuvi, *Temple*, 24.
63. John W. Pryor, "First Peter and the New Covenant," *RTR* 45 (1986): 1.
64. See page 24 above.
65. Martin, *Metaphor*, especially 144–161. Martin's suggestion is followed by Philip L. Tite, *Compositional Transitions in 1 Peter: An Analysis of the Letter-Opening* (San Francisco, CA: International Scholars Publications, 1997), 15–17.
66. Martin, *Metaphor*, 152–156.

Christians' existence with specific reference to the socio-historical situation of the exilic Jews in the Diaspora. However, these metaphors of "Diaspora" and "a wandering people" are, on the other hand, too narrow to encompass the other Petrine metaphors under their umbrellas. For example, how the images of Christians as living stones constituting a spiritual house and as a royal priesthood (2:4–10) can be regarded as relating to these metaphors of "Diaspora" and "a wandering people" is far from obvious.[67]

Likewise, "the idea of exile" put forth by Mbuvi as the controlling metaphor of the whole letter,[68] though serving to highlight the social estrangement and eschatological expectations of Christians, is once again too narrow to cover individual Christian metaphors such as "babies longing for pure milk" (2:2) and the "chosen stones of a spiritual building" (2:4–5) in 1 Peter.

In respect of the suggestions of "visiting foreigners and resident-aliens" proposed by Jobes,[69] "strangers" by Feldmeier[70] and "aliens" by Volf,[71] they all have the effect of taking Christians away from the author's identification of Christians with the people of Israel in their specific socio-political situation of exile in the Diaspora (cf. 1:1). In addition, how these suggestions relate to the other Petrine metaphors for Christians such as the children of God (1:14) and the priesthood (2:5, 9) is once again not obvious.

As to Seland's proposal to understand the current social situation of Christians with reference to "proselyte/proselytism,"[72] this suggestion

---

67. See also J. Ramsey Michaels, "Review of Troy W. Martin, *Metaphor and Composition in 1 Peter*," *JBL* 112 (1993): 359.

68. Mbuvi, *Temple*, 22–33. It is remarkable that after positing "the idea of exile" as the controlling metaphor of the whole letter, Mbuvi repeatedly underlines Christians as the "new Israel" in 1 Peter, e.g. on pages 27, 46, 75, 80, 135. Presumably, he understands the Petrine perception of Christians' existence as the "new Israel" within the context of an exile.

69. Jobes, *1 Peter*, 44.

70. Reinhard Feldmeier, *Die Christen als Fremde: die Metapher der Fremde in der antiken Welt, im Urchristentum und im 1. Petrusbrief*, WUNT 70 (Tübingen: Mohr, 1992), 170–192; "The 'Nation' of Strangers: Social Contempt and Its Theological Interpretation in Ancient Judaism and Early Christianity," in *Ethnicity and the Bible*, ed. Mark G. Brett (Leiden: E. J. Brill, 1996), 251–262.

71. Volf, "Soft Difference," 16–17.

72. Seland, *Strangers*, 39–78. The perception of Christians as "proselytes" in 1 Peter has been proposed earlier by W. C. van Unnik, *Sparsa Collecta*, part 2, 3 vols. (Leiden: E. J. Brill, 1980), 71–82; "Christianity according to 1 Peter," *ExpTim* 68 (1956/1957): 81.

appears to be far-fetched in that the idea of "proselyte/proselytism" is neither expressly mentioned nor apparent in the letter. Indeed, the other metaphors for Christians in 1 Peter, such as Diaspora (1:1), holy priesthood (2:5), chosen race (2:9), are designations originally applied to *Israel* itself, rather than *proselytes* only.

One further proposal that needs to be discussed is the "household of God" proposed by Elliott.[73] Much of Elliott's argument is based on his understanding of οἶκος in 2:5 as a "household" rather than its literal meaning of "a house."[74] As I will discuss below, the context of 1 Peter 2:4–10 actually requires the οἶκος constituted by the Christian living stones to refer literally to a house (i.e. a temple), rather than a household. In addition, although Elliott also rests his argument on the Petrine household code as part of the "*household scheme of exhortation* in 1 Peter 2:13–3:9(12) and 5:1–5"[75] which "provided a means for exemplifying and encouraging behavior which would contribute toward internal group cohesion,"[76] the major focus of the Petrine household code (2:18–3:7), except 3:7, is actually Christians' proper behaviour *amidst a non-believing household*, just as 2:13–17 is concerned with Christian engagement in a non-believing society, rather than relationship *within* the Christian community as a household.

In fact, all the proposals mentioned above have overlooked the most prominent designation of Christians in 1 Peter: The readers are simply addressed as "elect exiles of Diaspora" (ἐκλεκτοῖς παρεπιδήμοις διασπορᾶς, 1:1) right at the beginning of the letter which also becomes the controlling metaphor for Christian existence on earth. As Senior comments, this designation signals the "major themes that will be amplified later in the letter."[77]

This Christian identity of "elect exiles of Diaspora" actually underlines two dimensions of the Petrine author's perception of Christian existence on earth. On the one hand, he perceives Christians as identical with the Jewish Diaspora inheriting all the self-definitions and eschatological promises, as well as the responsibilities and social strategies, of the Jewish exilic people

---

73. Elliott, *Home* 200–233. See also Elliott, *1 Peter*, 105–106, 418, 882.
74. Elliott, *Home*, 201–204; *1 Peter*, 415–418.
75. Elliott, *Home*, 205–220.
76. Ibid., 208.
77. Senior, "1 Peter," 25.

of God of Diaspora. As Michaels observes, "the terms ἐκλεκτοί, παρεπίδημοι, and above all διασπορά, appear to be expressions of a Jewish consciousness arising out of the Jewish experience."[78]

On the other hand, this address of "elect exiles of Diaspora" nicely reflects the author's perception of the inherently paradoxical nature of Christian existence on earth. While the term ἐκλεκτοί provides the theological grounding of Christians' identity with reference to their relationship with God as his elect, it is also due to this identity as God's elect that Christians find themselves being strangers and exiles (παρεπίδημοι) in society.[79] Christians' conversion has brought about such dramatic change to their lifestyle and social behaviour that they are constantly ostracized for being "different" from their neighbours (1:14–18; 4:3–4; cf. 3:15; 4:14–16). According to the Petrine author, this paradoxical nature of Christian existence is equivalent to the concrete life situation of the exilic Jews in the Diaspora (διασπορά).

It is also this tension within Christians' identity that occasions the tension in their engagement with the wider world. On the one hand, Christians, as the elect people of God, are to remain steadfast in their faith (5:9) so as to obtain their inheritance of salvation at the end (1:4–9), which necessarily renders them different from the rest of the world. On the other hand, their continuing existence during the in-between time (ὀλίγον, 1:6, 5:10; τὸν ἐπίλοιπον . . . χρόνον, 4:2) also necessitates Christians to cultivate a degree of commitment to the wider society and to do what is "good" also in the eyes of their pagan neighbours to avoid misunderstanding (e.g. 2:12, 14–15) and to proclaim the glory of God (e.g. 2:9, 12). As to be explicated in the next chapter, it is precisely between these two ends of "resistance" and "accommodation" that the author formulates his social behavioural instructions for his readers.

In the following discussion, I will proceed to investigate the three motifs comprised in the author's perception of Christians' existence as "elect exiles of Diaspora," (i.e. ἐκλεκτοί, παρεπίδημοι, and διασπορά), and will explicate how these motifs relate to the individual metaphors of

---

78. Michaels, *1 Peter*, 6.
79. See also Michaels, *1 Peter*, 6; Jobes, *1 Peter*, 59.

Christian identity in the letter. As we shall see, through his understanding of Christians' existence in terms of the self-definition of the Jewish people of Diaspora, the author further perceives Christians' existing social estrangement as part of the Jewish exilic travail so that Christians are also entitled to the salvation hope within the Jewish eschatological vision. This identification of Christians with the Jewish Diaspora further facilitates the Petrine author to draw on the Jewish mode of social engagement in the Diaspora, in addition to that of Jesus Christ, as Christians' social strategy amidst the current inimical environment.

2.2.1 The Christian Elect

With a number of scholars,[80] I hold that both ἐκλεκτοῖς and παρεπιδήμοις of the phrase ἐκλεκτοῖς παρεπιδήμοις διασπορᾶς (1:1) are best understood as substantives. To understand them as parallel, and in apposition, serves to highlight the tension within Christians' existence: They are at same time chosen by God, but estranged in human society. Both theological and sociological realities are equally true, rather than one modifying the other.[81]

It is commonly understood in the OT and other Jewish traditions that Israel is specifically designated as having been "elected" by God as his people.[82] Particularly noticeable is that within the Jewish eschatological vision, the elect are the ones who will survive tribulations and receive God's salvation in the last days. In *1 En.* 1.8, God "will preserve the elect, and kindness shall be upon them. They shall all belong to God and they shall prosper and be blessed."[83] This conviction actually supports the observation of N. T. Wright:

> Faced with national crisis . . . this twin belief, monotheism and election, committed any Jew . . . to a further belief: YHWH, as the creator and covenant god, was irrevocably committed

---

80. Achtemeier, *1 Peter*, 79, 81; Jobes, *1 Peter*, 67; Green, *1 Peter*, 14.

81. This reading is supported by a number of scribes who inserted καί between ἐκλεκτοῖς and παρεπιδήμοις in some manuscripts (א*, manuscripts of the Syriac traditions), obviously to avoid the impression that ἐκλεκτοῖς modifies παρεπιδήμοις.

82. E.g. Deut 4:37; 7:6–7; 14:2; 1 Kgs 3:8; Ps 135:4 (LXX Ps 134:4); Isa 41:8–9; 44:1–2; 65:9; 2 Macc 1:25.

83. Translation provided by E. Isaac, "1 (Ethiopic Apocalypse of) Enoch," *OTP* 1 (2009): 7. See also *1 En.* 38.4; 39.6–7.

to further action of some sort in history, which would bring about the end of Israel's desolation and the vindication of his true people.[84]

Therefore, for the Petrine author, Christians' identity on earth does not primarily depend on their being different or otherwise separate from the wider society, but is understood with reference to their relationship with God as his special elect and their inheriting the privileged self-understanding of the Jewish people of God. It is only due to this special identity before God that Christians have to abstain from any social activities that are inconsistent with their ultimate allegiance to God, (e.g. idolatry), which necessarily make them different from the rest of society. The eschatological vindication hope inherited from the Jewish people of God is where Christians can find encouragement as well as incentive to remain in God's grace/salvation despite pressure to accommodate to the pagan idolatrous culture.

It is in association with this privileged identity of the Jewish people of God and the theological backdrop of their ultimate deliverance that references to the election of Christians form the inclusio (ἐκλεκτοῖς, 1:1 and συνεκλεκτή, 5:13) of 1 Peter. Indeed, this motif of election is further developed by the three prepositional phrases in 1:2[85] which serve to bring the other Petrine metaphors and themes of Christian identity under the umbrella of this motif. I will therefore proceed to investigate these connections in the following discussion.

a) Election according to the Foreknowledge of God the Father

The first prepositional phrase in 1:2 which elaborates ἐκλεκτοῖς in 1:1 is κατὰ πρόγνωσιν θεοῦ πατρός. God's divine initiative and benevolent choice of Christians are effected through his positive act of gracious "calling" the Christian community into existence (1:15; 2:9, 21; 3:9; 5:10). As Goppelt

---

84. N. T. Wright, *The New Testament and the People of God,* Christian Origins and the Question of God 1 (London: SPCK, 1992), 247.

85. With the majority of scholars, I opine that the three phrases κατὰ πρόγνωσιν θεοῦ πατρός, ἐν ἁγιασμῷ πνεύματος and εἰς ὑπακοὴν καὶ ῥαντισμὸν αἵματος Ἰησοῦ Χριστοῦ in 1:2 are governed by ἐκλεκτοῖς rather than ἀπόστολος in 1:1 because these three prepositional phrases are actually closely related to the idea of election. See also Jobes, *1 Peter,* 67–68; Kelly, *Commentary,* 42; Achtemeier, *1 Peter,* 86; Mark Dubis, *1 Peter: A Handbook on the Greek Text* (Waco, TX: Baylor University Press, 2010), 3.

remarks, God's foreknowledge "makes its appearance in history, according to 1 Peter 1:15; 5:10, as in Roman 8:29f., as calling."[86]

It is noticeable that instead of being based on hereditary entitlement as the people of Israel, Christians being foreknown and elected by God are understood in 1 Peter as grounded on God's foreknowledge (προεγνωσμένου) of Christ who has been revealed inaugurating the Messianic Age (ἐπ' ἐσχάτου τῶν χρόνων) and for the sake of Christians (δι' ὑμᾶς) (1:20). It is by virtue of this derivation of their election from that of Christ that Christians find their existence bound up with Christ (2:4–10), and understand their following in Christ's steps, in terms of his social engagement, as an expression of their calling (ἐκλήθητε, 2:21) as God's elect.

b) Election by the Sanctification of the Spirit

The second prepositional phrase elaborating Christians' election is ἐν ἁγιασμῷ πνεύματος (i.e. the work of the Spirit is the means by which Christians are elected and set apart as the holy people of God).[87] This phrase therefore connects Christians' status as God's elect with their holiness. This intertwining of the twin themes of election and holiness is also found in the OT and other Jewish literature as part of Jewish self-understanding. For example, in Deuteronomy 7:6, Israel is described as "a holy people to God" and God has "elected" them "to be a people of his own possession out of all the peoples" on earth. In addition, in 2 Macc. 1:25, God is praised as the One who has elected (ποιήσας . . . ἐκλεκτούς) and sanctified (ἁγιάσας) the ancestors of Israel.[88]

In 1 Peter 1:13–21, the readers are exhorted to be holy in all their conduct as the concrete expression of their having been "called" by God (1:15) into the new existence of the elect (obedient children, 1:14). The basis for this exhortation for holiness is therefore relational rather than doctrinal: Since God is holy, Christians who are called to be his elect should

---

86. Goppelt, *Commentary*, 73. See also Michaels, *1 Peter*, 10.

87. Although Selwyn, *First Epistle*, 119 argues that ἐν is locative meaning "in the sphere of," πνεύματος in the phrase is a genitive and not a dative. The emphasis of this phrase is on the result of the sanctifying action of the Spirit, i.e. Christians become holy as God's elect. So, Achtemeier, *1 Peter*, 86; Jobes, *1 Peter*, 69.

88. Other references in which the twin themes of "election" and "holiness" appear together include e.g. 1 *En.* 48.1; 58.1–5.

demonstrate a similar quality (κατὰ τὸν καλέσαντα ὑμᾶς ἅγιον, 1:15).[89] This relationship between God and his Christian people is analogous to that between God and Israel: ἅγιοι ἔσεσθε, ὅτι ἐγὼ ἅγιός (You shall be holy, because I am holy) (1 Pet 1:16) which is likely to be a direct quotation from LXX Leviticus 19:2.[90] Just as Israel should be holy because they belong to the holy God as his people, Christians are expected to stay holy as a condition of their continuous belonging to him.

This interpretation is consistent with the cultic context in which the term "holy" (קדשׁ) is used in the OT. As Procksch observes, "Anything related to the cultus, whether God, man, things, space or time, can be brought under the term קדשׁ,"[91] and when the verbal form in used in the causative sense "to dedicate," it denotes the "transfer to the possession of God, to whom the person or thing dedicated now exclusively belongs."[92]

Therefore, although as most scholars recognize, "holy" has the root meaning of "marked off," "separated,"[93] "difference,"[94] and "set apart,"[95] the object from which Christians are to be set apart, according to 1 Peter, is not so much everything from the wider pagan world or indiscriminately "commonly accepted norms of behaviour"[96] or "ways of the world"[97] as scholars have proposed. Rather, Christians are to be set apart from those parts of the pagan culture that have *cultic* connotations and, thus, may jeopardize their "belonging" to God (e.g. idolatry and any social activities, festivals and common meals that take place in a cultic context).[98]

This observation is consistent with my interpretation of 1 Peter 1:14 and 1:18 which form the context of the Petrine exhortation of holiness in 1 Peter 1:15–16. As I argued in section 2.1.1 above, the cravings which

---

89. Cf. Cranfield, *First Epistle*, 35–36; Feldmeier, *First Letter*, 58.
90. Michaels, *1 Peter*, 59; Achtemeier, *1 Peter*, 122.
91. Procksch, "ἅγιος," *TDNT* 1:89.
92. Procksch, *TDNT* 1:91. Cf. Kelly, *Commentary*, 70.
93. Kelly, *Commentary*, 69; Cranfield, *First Epistle*, 35.
94. Jo Bailey Wells, *God's Holy People: A Theme in Biblical Theology*, JSOTSup 305 (Sheffield: Sheffield Academic Press, 2000), 229.
95. Achtemeier, *1 Peter*, 121.
96. Kelly, *Commentary*, 26.
97. Jobes, *1 Peter*, 112.
98. See the examples of Israel in e.g. Deut 7:3–6; Josh 24:19–20; Jer 2:3–5.

Christians formerly had in their ignorance (ταῖς πρότερον ἐν τῇ ἀγνοίᾳ ὑμῶν ἐπιθυμίαις, 1:14) and the futile (ματαίας, 1:18) way of life Christians inherited from their ancestors should be understood as of religious, rather than social, orientation. The non-conformity called for by the author is also directed primarily to those aspects of pagan way of life which mark them as non-believers of God (i.e. idolatry or other practices which are inconsistent with Christians' religious allegiance to God). The Petrine exhortation on holiness should be understood likewise within this context.

c) Election unto Obedience and the Sprinkling of the Blood of Jesus Christ

The third phrase modifying ἐκλεκτοῖς (1:1) is εἰς ὑπακοὴν καὶ ῥαντισμὸν αἵματος Ἰησοῦ Χριστοῦ (1:2), that is, the orientations of God's election of Christians include (i) Christians' obedience (ὑπακοήν)[99] and (ii) the sprinkling of Christ's blood (ῥαντισμὸν αἵματος Ἰησοῦ Χριστοῦ) on them.

i. Elected unto Obedience

The first orientation of God's election is Christians' obedience (εἰς ὑπακοήν) which serves to connect the image of Christians as "the elect" with the other metaphors and themes of Christian identity in the letter. The destiny of Christians being elected unto obedience (εἰς ὑπακοήν) is none other than to become obedient children (τέκνα ὑπακοῆς, 1:14) of God the Father (πατήρ, 1:2, 17) by accepting the gospel.[100] It is also this obedience to the truth (τῇ ὑπακοῇ τῆς ἀληθείας, 1:22) that facilitates the Christian children of God to enter into a distinctive community of sincere "brotherly" love to each other (εἰς φιλαδελφίαν ἀνυπόκριτον, 1:22; cf. φιλάδελφοι, 3:8; ἀδελφότης, 2:17; 5:9).

This transformation of Christian elect into the new status of obedient children is further linked to the image of "being born again" (ἀναγεννήσας,

---

99. I agree with a number of scholars that ὑπακοήν should be taken as independent of Ἰησοῦ Χριστοῦ so that Ἰησοῦ Χριστοῦ need not be both a subjective and an objective genitive at the same time. This obedience of Christians is related to their obedience to the truth (1:22) and their new existence as the obedient children of God (1:14). So, Kelly, *Commentary*, 43–44; Goppelt, *Commentary*, 74; Michaels, *1 Peter*, 11–12; Achtemeier, *1 Peter*, 87–88.

100. Michaels, *1 Peter*, 56.

1:3; cf. ἀναγεγεννημένοι, 1:23)¹⁰¹ which appears immediately after 1:2 and introduces another metaphor of Christians as "newborn babies longing for pure milk of the word" (ἀρτιγέννητα βρέφη τὸ λογικὸν ἄδολον γάλα ἐπιποθήσατε, 2:2). As McCartney convincingly argues, the term λογικός is closely related to the term λόγος and should mean "having to do with [the] word."¹⁰² This image of "newborn babies longing for milk," therefore, should probably be read together with 1:23 in which Christians are perceived to have been born anew (ἀναγεγεννημένοι) through the word of God (διὰ λόγου . . . θεοῦ) which word is the gospel proclaimed to them (ῥῆμα, 1:25).¹⁰³ The idea of the author is that Christians having been born anew through the word of God, should continue to crave the milk of God's word, so that they may grow to fully experience salvation (αὐξηθῆτε εἰς σωτηρίαν, 2:2) at the consummation of the Messianic Age (1:5).¹⁰⁴

Especially noticeable for our purpose is that the abiding nature of God's word is highlighted by διότι πᾶσα σὰρξ ὡς χόρτος καὶ πᾶσα δόξα αὐτῆς ὡς ἄνθος χόρτου· ἐξηράνθη ὁ χόρτος καὶ τὸ ἄνθος ἐξέπεσεν· τὸ δὲ ῥῆμα κυρίου μένει εἰς τὸν αἰῶνα ("For all flesh is like grass and all its glory is like the flower of grass. The grass withers and the flower falls off but the word of the Lord remains forever") (1 Pet 1:24–25a), which is a clear allusion to πᾶσα σὰρξ χόρτος καὶ πᾶσα δόξα ἀνθρώπου ὡς ἄνθος χόρτου ἐξηράνθη ὁ χόρτος καὶ τὸ ἄνθος ἐξέπεσεν τὸ δὲ ῥῆμα τοῦ θεοῦ ἡμῶν μένει εἰς τὸν αἰῶνα of LXX Isaiah 40:6–8. Isaiah 40:6–8 is situated amidst God's promises to restore and regather his exilic people. In LXX Isaiah 40:11, God, "like a shepherd, will shepherd his flock and, with his arms, will gather the lambs . . ." while in LXX Isaiah 40:31, "those who hold on God will renew strength; they will grow feathers like eagles."

Therefore, the word (ῥῆμα, 1 Pet 1:25) which calls Christians into new existence as the elect children of God is the same word (ῥῆμα, LXX Isa

---

101. Senior, "1 Peter," 40.
102. Dan G. McCartney, "λογικός," *ZNW* 82 (1991): 131. See also Elliott, *1 Peter*, 400–401.
103. See also Goppelt, *Commentary*, 131; Davids, *First Epistle*, 82–83; Achtemeier, *1 Peter*, 146–147.
104. See also Davids, *First Epistle*, 82–83; Achtemeier, *1 Peter*, 147; David G. Horrell, *The Epistles of Peter and Jude,* Epworth Commentaries (Peterborough: Epworth Press, 1998), 37.

40:8) which promises the eventual deliverance and restoration of Israel in exile.¹⁰⁵ The expectation of ultimate salvation (εἰς σωτηρίαν, 2:2) of the Christian elect children of Diaspora is also perceived as an extension of the eschatological hope of the contemporary Jewish Diaspora. Indeed, within the vision of Second Temple Judaism, God's children (sons) of Israel are those who will be vindicated and renewed in the last days. In *1 En.* 62.11, vengeance shall be executed on the "oppressors of his children and his elect ones."¹⁰⁶ Likewise, in *Pss. Sol.* 17.26–7, the messianic son of David "will gather a holy people whom he will lead in righteousness" and "will know them that they are all children of their God."¹⁰⁷

It is in association with this eschatological hope promised to God's elect children that Christians' ultimate salvation (εἰς σωτηρίαν, 1:5) and blessing (εὐλογίαν, 3:9) are also understood by the Petrine author in terms of the Jewish vision of the eschatological blessing of God's elect as an inheritance (κληρονομίαν, 1 Pet 1:4; κληρονομήσητε, 3:9; cf. συγκληρονόμοις χάριτος ζωῆς, 3:7). In the OT and other Jewish literature, Israel understands itself as an heir to the land of Canaan "which the Lord your God is giving you as an inheritance to possess" (Deut 15:4).¹⁰⁸ After the exile, this inheritance of their homeland becomes part of the Jewish eschatological restoration hope.¹⁰⁹ Furthermore, κληρονομία and its verb form κληρονομέω are also used in post-exilic Jewish literature to refer to the entitlement of God's elect children as heirs to eschatological salvation and blessing. In *Pss. Sol.* 12.6, the salvation (ἡ σωτηρία) of Israel is the promise that the Lord's devout inherit (κληρονομήσαισαν), and in *Pss. Sol.* 14.10, the devout of the Lord are also expected to inherit (κληρονομήσουσιν) life in gladness.¹¹⁰ For the Petrine author, Christians are sharing with the Jewish exilic people

---

105. The deliberate shift from λόγου . . . θεοῦ (1 Pet 1:23) to ῥῆμα κυρίου (1 Pet 1:25) is telling of the author's placing Christians' salvation hope within the eschatological restoration hope of Israel promised in Isaiah 40.

106. Translation provided by Isaac, *OTP* 1:43.

107. Translation provided by R. B. Wright, *OTP* 2:667. See also e.g. *Jub.* 1.24–25; *T. Mos.* 10.3.

108. See also e.g. Num 34:2; Lev 20:24; Deut 19:10; 25:19; 2 Chr 6:27; Jer 3:18–19; Jdt 8:22; 2 Macc 2:4.

109. E.g. Isa 49:8; 60:21; Ezek 47:14; Cf. *Pss. Sol.* 17.23.

110. See also LXX Isa 54:17.

of Diaspora the same identity as the elect children of God, as well as their eschatological hope of salvation as an inheritance.

ii. Elected unto the Sprinkling of Christ's Blood

The other orientation of God's election is the "sprinkling of the blood of Jesus Christ" (εἰς . . . ῥαντισμὸν αἵματος Ἰησοῦ Χριστοῦ). Scholars generally agree that the whole imagery is taken from Exodus 24:3–8 when the blood of the offerings was used to seal the covenant between God and his people.[111] In Exodus 24:7, after Moses had sprinkled the blood on the altar and read the book of covenant to the people, the Israelite children responded with a promise of obedience, "All that the Lord has spoken, we will do and we will hear (obey)." (Exod 24:7; cf. ὑπακοήν, 1:2). The remaining blood was then sprinkled on the people (Exod 24:8). For the Petrine author, the Christian elect have now entered into a new covenantal relationship with God in the same way as the people of Israel, not through the blood of other offerings but the sacrificial blood of Christ. The whole sense is collective: By participating in this new covenant, all Christians become members of a new community of the elect people of God.[112] This collective dimension of Christian existence, in terms of OT covenantal language, is climaxed in 1 Peter 2:4–10, in which the Christian elect people of God is underscored as an elect race, a royal priesthood and a holy nation, as I will discuss in greater length in the following section.

At the same time, by underlining Christians' covenant with God as effected by the sprinkling of the blood of Jesus Christ, the Petrine author is also reinterpreting the OT notions of divine election and covenant in the light of the historical appearance of Jesus Christ the Messiah. Christians are now entitled to the same privileged identity as the people of Israel no longer by virtue of a hereditary link but through the blood of Jesus Christ the Messiah. It is based on this reflection on Christian existence as inheriting "the identity of the Jewish elect people of Diaspora" through "the sacrificial suffering of Jesus Christ the Messiah" that the social engagements of both "Jesus Christ" and "the Jewish elect people of Diaspora" become the twin

---

111. E.g. Beare, *First Epistle*, 77; Best, *I Peter*, 71–72; Kelly, *Commentary*, 44; Senior, "1 Peter," 26, 29; Achtemeier, *1 Peter*, 88.

112. Kelly, *Commentary*, 44; Senior, "1 Peter," 27; Michaels, *1 Peter*, 12–13.

2.2.2 The Christian Exiles

The second component of the Petrine controlling metaphor of Christian identity is "exiles" (παρεπίδημοι). Although παρεπίδημοι and its related terms πάροικοι and παροικία only appear in a total of three verses (1:1, 1:17 and 2:11) in 1 Peter, the theme of Christians sojourning in the wider society runs through the whole letter. Besides highlighting Christians' existing social situation as παρεπίδημοι right at the beginning of the letter (1:1), "the time of your sojourn" (τὸν τῆς παροικίας ὑμῶν χρόνον) in 1:17 further underlines the thematic characteristic of Christians' life in society. The author's teachings on Christian social engagement in society are also introduced by 2:11 which underscores Christians' existence as "resident-aliens and exiles" (παροίκους καὶ παρεπιδήμους).

The metaphorical understanding of Christians' identity as exiles/resident-aliens has been challenged by Elliott, who argues that these terms παρεπίδημοι, πάροικοι, and παροικία should be taken literally to describe the social condition of the addressees who were "actual resident-aliens and visiting strangers within their Asia Minor society"[113] even prior to their conversion.[114] The addressees of 1 Peter, according to Elliott, may well have been members of the rural population and villagers "who had been relocated to city territories and assigned inferior status to the citizenry"[115] and who after their conversion, "still find themselves estranged from any place of belonging."[116]

Although Elliott's proposal serves to bring scholars' attention to the sociological implications of Christians' existence on earth as resident-aliens and exiles, his understanding of παρεπίδημοι and πάροικοι as referring literally to the addressees' pre-conversion social condition appears shaky. On the one hand, according to Pliny, Christians in Pontus and Bithynia included "Persons of all ranks and ages, and of both sexes" and Christianity

---

113. Elliott, *Home*, 42.
114. Ibid., 49; Elliott, *1 Peter*, 481.
115. Elliott, *Home*, 48.
116. Ibid., 49. See also Elliott, *1 Peter*, 481–482.

"is not confined to the cities only, but has spread through the villages and rural districts."[117] Such observation precludes any understanding of Christians in Asia Minor as enclosed to one particular socio-legal stratum of resident-aliens in society. On the other hand, the Petrine author actually highlights Christians' existing estrangement as stemming from their conversion: they (the Gentiles) "are surprised that you no longer go with (them) in the same excess of dissipation, they slander (you)" (1 Pet 4:4). This remark seems to suggest that the addressees were by no means in an alienated social situation prior to their conversion.[118]

Παρεπίδημος, literally "visiting stranger,"[119] is a rare word in the Bible. Besides the two occurrences in 1 Peter, another NT occurrence of this word is found in Hebrew 11:13, in which the patriarchs of faith are referred to as having died in faith after having been strangers and exiles (ξένοι καὶ παρεπίδημοι) on earth. As for the LXX, παρεπίδημος appears only twice (LXX Gen 23:4, LXX Ps 38:13[MT 39:13]) and in both instances, it appears together with πάροικος just as 1 Peter 2:11. In any event, it is commonly accepted that the essential characteristic of παρεπίδημος is the "temporary nature" of the stranger's stay in the foreign land.[120]

As for the term πάροικος, literally "neighbour,"[121] it refers to a "resident-alien" having his "domicile with or among natives, having no civic rights but living under the common protection."[122] Instead of living in the foreign place *only for a short time* like παρεπίδημος, πάροικος is a "'resident-alien' who dwelled *permanently* in a foreign locale, and one who was permitted only limited political, economic, and social rights and status."[123]

---

117. Pliny, *Ep.*10.96 (Melmoth, LCL).

118. So, Senior, "1 Peter," 9. For other arguments against Elliott's view, see Paul J. Achtemeier, "Newborn Babes and Living Stones: Literal and Figurative in 1 Peter," in *To Touch the Text: Biblical and Related Studies in Honor of Joseph A. Fitzmyer, SJ*, eds. Maurya P. Horgan and Paul J. Kobelski (New York: Crossroad, 1989), 217; Frederick W. Danker, "Review of John Elliott, *A Home for the Homeless: A Sociological Exegesis of 1 Peter, Its Situation and Strategy*," *Int* 37 (1983): 87–88.

119. Elliott, *1 Peter*, 312.

120. E.g. Grundmann, "παρεπίδημος," *TDNT* 2:64–65; "παρεπίδημος," BDAG, 775; Selwyn, *First Epistle*, 118; Goppelt, *Commentary*, 66; Michaels, *1 Peter*, 7; Elliott, *1 Peter*, 312.

121. K. L. Schmidt and M. A. Schmidt, "πάροικος," *TDNT* 5:842.

122. Ibid.

123. Elliott, *1 Peter*, 312.

Therefore, although scholars tend to regard 1 Peter to be using the two terms interchangeably and without differentiation,[124] the fact that the two terms παρεπίδημοι and πάροικοι, connoting two different temporal modes of stay in the foreign land, are used together in 1 Peter 2:11 requires more profound consideration.

I propose that the placing of παρεπίδημοι and πάροικοι side by side actually reflects the two dialectical dimensions of the Petrine understanding of Christians' existence during the in-between time before the ultimate revelation of their salvation in the last time. On the one hand, if Christians' earthly existence is viewed from the perspective of their heading towards their inheritance of salvation (εἰς σωτηρίαν, 1:5; 2:2) kept in heaven (1:4), Christians' stay as exiles/strangers (παρεπίδημοι) on earth is "temporary" and "transitory" in contrast to their ultimate belonging in heaven. This is also the sense παρεπίδημος is employed in Hebrews 11:13 to denote the life of the exile as a sojourning "awaiting repatriation to their heavenly home."[125] On the other hand, the Petrine author also recognizes that Christians still need to stay as resident-aliens (πάροικοι) in the current world for an indeterminate period of time before the final revelation of their salvation. Therefore, Christians are underscored as having to suffer trials and, thus, further alienation "for a little while" (ὀλίγον, 1:6; 5:10) which hinted at a duration.[126] In 1 Peter 1:17, the existence of Christians is highlighted as τὸν τῆς παροικίας ὑμῶν χρόνον in which χρόνον is also an accusative (cf. τὸν ἐπίλοιπον . . . χρόνον, 4:2) and expresses "an extent" or "duration" of time.[127] As Delling observes, the term χρόνος means mostly "span of time" in the NT.[128] Although many scholars tend of focus only on the *temporary and transitory* dimension of Christians' existence to understand the

---

124. E.g. Beare, *First Epistle*, 135; Best, *1 Peter*, 110; Michaels, *1 Peter*, 7; Moses Chin, "A Heavenly Home for the Homeless: Aliens and Stranger in 1 Peter," *TynBul* 42 (1991): 100, 110; Green, *1 Peter*, 67.

125. Harold W. Attridge, *The Epistle to the Hebrews: A Commentary on the Epistle to the Hebrews*, Hermeneia (Philadelphia, PA: Fortress Press, 1989), 330. See also the use of παρεπιδημέω in Philo, *Agr.* 65; *Conf.* 76.

126. Achtemeier, *1 Peter*, 101.

127. Daniel B. Wallace, *Greek Grammar Beyond the Basics: An Exegetical Syntax of the New Testament* (Grand Rapids, MI: Zondervan, 1996), 201–203.

128. Delling, "χρόνος," *TDNT* 9:591.

Petrine metaphor of Christians as "exiles and resident-aliens,"[129] the *more permanent* dimension of Christians' sojourn as πάροικοι (cf. τῆς παροικίας ὑμῶν, 1:17) is actually an aspect of the Petrine perception of Christian existence on earth that cannot be overlooked.

Indeed, this degree of permanence (though not eternal) within Christian existence is what gives shape to one important aspect of Petrine Christian social ethics. Although the longing for the eternal inheritance in heaven requires Christians to hold fast to their exclusive allegiance to God so as not to jeopardize their eschatological reward, the fact that they still have to "stay" in the current world for an indeterminate period of time, also necessitates Christians to cultivate a sense of belonging to their current habitat and to negotiate room to uphold their ultimate allegiance to God in their interaction with the larger world. Therefore, although Christians have to set themselves apart from any pagan activities that may have religious/cultic connotations (idolatry, for example), they also have to stay within the existing socio-political system and discharge their roles with commitment and due diligence as citizens (1 Pet 2:13–17), slaves (2:18–25), husbands and wives (3:1–7) and members of society. As Wolff judiciously observes, although πάροικοι

> indeed lacked political rights, such as the right to vote and to stand for election, they had the right of abode as well as the capacity to carry on trade and business and could be requisitioned to military service.[130]

Christians are not just considered as temporary strangers (παρεπίδημοι), "but also as people, who in spite of their foreignness have discerned rights and responsibilities in the world."[131]

---

129. E.g. Kelly, *Commentary*, 41, 103; Beare, *First Epistle*, 75, 135; Best, *1 Peter*, 70, 110; Victor Paul Furnish, "Elect Sojourners in Christ: An Approach to the Theology of 1 Peter," *PSTJ* 28 (1975): 3–4; Davids, *First Epistle*, 46, 71, 95.

130. "Ihnen fehlten zwar die politischen Rechte wie aktives und passives Wahlrecht, aber sie hatten das Wohnrecht sowie die Befugnis, Handel und Gewerbe auszuüben und konnten zum Kriegsdienst herangezogen werden." Christian Wolff, "Christ und Welt im 1. Petrusbrief," *TLZ* 100 (1975): 338.

131. "sondern auch als Menschen, die trotz ihrer Fremdheit Rechte und Pflichten in der Welt wahrzunehmen haben." Wolff, "Christ," 338.

Indeed, although many scholars nowadays prefer to understand the Petrine metaphors of παρεπίδημοι and πάροικοι as denoting Christians' current sociological situation of being estranged by the larger world,[132] rather than in terms of the cosmological view of contrasting Christians' stay "on earth" with their true home "in heaven,"[133] *both* the theological *and* the sociological understandings of Christians' sojourn are actually present in 1 Peter. Theologically speaking, Christians are sojourning on earth awaiting the revelation of their inheritance of salvation now kept in heaven (1:4–5). Sociologically speaking, their new status as God's elect people brings with it animosity and social ostracism such that they are no longer accepted as full members (citizens) of the wider society (4:4, 14–16).

Particularly noteworthy for our purpose is that in 1 Peter 1:1, παρεπιδήμοις is modified by διασπορᾶς which provides a concrete socio-historical connotation to Christians' existence as strangers on earth – their sojourning is perceived as that of an "exile" and equivalent to the exilic experience of the Jewish Diaspora. Indeed, the term παροικία (cf. 1 Pet 1:17) is also used in the LXX (e.g. 1 Esd 5:7; 3 Macc 6:36; 7:19) to describe the exilic experience of the Jewish Diaspora in the foreign land.

More importantly, in the only two occurrences of παρεπίδημος in the LXX (i.e. LXX Gen 23:4; Ps 38:13 [MT 39:13]), the Diaspora translators employed the two terms πάροικος and παρεπίδημος (cf. παροίκους καὶ παρεπιδήμους, 2:11) to translate the Hebrew terms גֵּר and תּוֹשָׁב so as to underscore the self-understanding of the Israelite patriarchs.[134] In LXX Genesis 23:4, Abraham recognized himself as a resident-alien and visiting stranger (πάροικος καὶ παρεπίδημος ἐγώ εἰμι) among the Hittites. As K. L. and M. A. Schmidt observe, "the patriarch as a resident-alien is a τόπος in whom the people of Israel sees its own true nature reflected."[135] Therefore,

---

132. E.g. Goppelt, *Commentary*, 67–69; Senior, "1 Peter," 28; Jobes, *1 Peter*, 168–169; Achtemeier, *1 Peter*, 174–175.

133. E.g. Cranfield, *First Epistle*, 52–54; Kelly, *Commentary*, 103; Beare, *First Epistle*, 75; Best, *1 Peter*, 70; Davids, *First Epistle*, 95.

134. In the other instances where גֵּר appears together with תּוֹשָׁב, the LXX renders προσήλυτος and πάροικος in Lev 25:23, 35, 47; Num 35:15. In the remaining instances (Lev 25:6, 45; 1 Chr 29:15), πάροικος alone is used. I derive these references from Chin, "Heavenly Home," 99.

135. Schmidt and Schmidt, "πάροικος," 846.

for the Diaspora Septuagint translators, the existence of Israel throughout history is marked by the same dual theological and sociological dimensions as 1 Peter of *both* a longing for the promised land (inheritance) *and* the existing sojourn as πάροικοι among foreigners. It is also due to this recognition of God's sovereignty over the land (their inheritance) and towards his people that the Diaspora Septuagint translators understand Israel as resident-aliens and exiles before God: ὅτι πάροικος ἐγώ εἰμι παρὰ σοὶ καὶ παρεπίδημος καθὼς πάντες οἱ πατέρες μου, LXX Psalm 38:13.¹³⁶

Therefore, by underlining Christians as παροίκους καὶ παρεπιδήμους (1 Pet 2:11), the Petrine author also appropriates to them the same self-understanding of the Jewish Diaspora, whether before God or amidst the wider pagan world. Just as the Jewish elect exiles of Diaspora, who recognized the sovereignty of God and negotiated their exilic existence among foreigners with the same faith and obedience as the Abraham typology,¹³⁷ the Christian elect people of Diaspora are to accept their existence as exiles and resident-aliens with the same exclusive allegiance to God and the same faith for a promised inheritance (1 Pet 1:4–5) of salvation and deliverance at the end.

2.2.3 The Christian Elect Exiles of Diaspora

The Petrine appropriation of the Jewish identity to Christians is further reinforced by διασπορᾶς (1:1) which represents Christians' existence as "elect exiles" with reference to the concrete socio-historical context of the Jewish Diaspora. As Schmidt asserts, διασπορά is "a technical term" in the LXX "for the 'dispersion of the Jews among the Gentiles,'" meaning in concrete terms "the Jews as thus scattered"¹³⁸ outside Palestine (e.g. Deut 28:25; 30:4; 2 Macc 1:27; *Pss. Sol.* 8.28; Isa 49:6; Jer 41:17[MT 34:17]). It is therefore preferable to understand διασπορᾶς in 1 Peter 1:1 as epexegetical and constituted by the Christian readers themselves.¹³⁹

---

136. Ibid., 846–847.

137. Ibid., 846. See also Philo's repeating Abraham's self-address as πάροικος καὶ παρεπίδημος in *Conf.* 79.

138. Karl Ludwig Schmidt, " διασπορά," *TDNT* 2: 99. See also Kelly, *Commentary*, 40; Goppelt, *Commentary*, 65 n. 18; John M. G. Barclay, "Introduction: Diaspora Negotiations," in *Negotiating Diaspora: Jewish Strategies in the Roman Empire*, ed. John M. G. Barclay, Library of Second Temple Studies 45 (London: T&T Clark, 2004), 1.

139. See also Michaels, *1 Peter*, 8; Jobes, *1 Peter*, 63.

"Diaspora" serves very well as the third component of the controlling metaphor of Christian identity in 1 Peter. Echoing διασπορᾶς in 1:1, Βαβυλῶνι (Babylon) in 5:13 completes the inclusio which renders Christians' dispersion in an estranged world a major theme of the whole letter. In addition, the linkage of συνεκλεκτή, to ἐν Βαβυλῶνι in 5:13 further connects the motif of the "elect" to that of "Diaspora" and, thus, "exiles" to form the unique controlling metaphor for Christians in 1 Peter.

More crucial for our investigation is that by specifically identifying Christians with the Jewish Diaspora, the Petrine author at the same time appropriates to Christians the same deliverance hope (e.g. LXX Neh 1:9; Isa 49:5–6; Ps 146:2 [MT 147:2]) as well as the same strategies of the Jewish scattered people in engaging with the wider Gentile world (ἔθνεσιν, 1 Pet 2:12; ἐθνῶν, 1 Pet 4:3). As Martin comments: "The author of 1 Peter took images and concepts from the Jewish Diaspora and applied them to his readers in order to describe their ontological status and their moral obligations."[140] This total transference of the theological as well as socio-historical identity of Diaspora Jews to Christians probably accounts for the total absence of any reference to Jews in the letter,[141] which would otherwise have been remarkable in view of the prominence of the Jewish communities around the Christian readers in Asia Minor.[142]

Therefore, the Petrine identification of Christians' life experience with that of the Jewish Diaspora actually posits the "Jewish way of life" as the frame of reference by which the author's social behavioural instructions should be understood. Regrettably, when interpreting the metaphor of "exiles of Diaspora" in 1 Peter, scholars, without going into the actual social engagement of the Jewish Diaspora, tend to lay emphasis on the transience and displacement of Christian existence in this world. For example, Martin asserts that the basic conception of Diaspora is a journey so that Christians are perceived as "the wandering people of God on an eschatological

---

140. Martin, *Metaphor*, 148.
141. Cf. Achtemeier, *1 Peter*, 72.
142. Paul R. Trebilco, *Jewish Communities in Asia Minor*, SNTSMS 69 (Cambridge: Cambridge University Press, 1991), 189, observes, "In interpreting the NT and patristic sources, the likely presence of Jewish communities in the 'foreground' of the Christian communities must certainly be taken more seriously than has been normal hitherto."

journey."¹⁴³ Although Mbuvi prefers to take "the idea of exile" as the controlling metaphor of the letter, he once again holds that "exile" represents a period of "instability and homelessness" in the history of Israel.¹⁴⁴ What follows is that since the exilic people of Diaspora regard their present state of affairs as transitory and do not have any sense of belonging to their present place of residence, they must resist assimilation and remain different from the surrounding world.¹⁴⁵ Their sole task is to get prepared to return to their true home at the eschaton.

Since I will explore the social strategies and the Diaspora consciousness of the Jewish exilic people of God in greater depth in chapter 4, it is sufficient for me at this stage to refer to Barclay's observations that the Diaspora communities "retain a sense of belonging elsewhere (in memory, myth or longing to return), but also typically develop strong attachments to their present place of belonging."¹⁴⁶ This tension within the Diaspora consciousness actually allows for corresponding complexity among the Diaspora Jews to negotiate between "*both* cultural integration *and* cultural critique."¹⁴⁷ It is also this tension within the Diaspora mentality and its corresponding mode of social engagement that forms the basis on which the Petrine author formulates his social behavioural instructions for Christians whom he understands also as "elect exiles of Diaspora."

Section Summary

In this section, I explored the Petrine perception of Christians' existence on earth with reference to the controlling metaphor of "elect exiles of Diaspora" and explained how this designation relates to the other metaphors and themes of Christian existence in 1 Peter.

Through this investigation, it becomes clear that for the Petrine author, Christian identity is not derived primarily from any special strategy to keep

---

143. Martin, *Metaphor*, 154. Martin's idea is followed by Joel B. Green, "Identity and Engagement in a Diverse World: Pluralism and Holiness in 1 Peter," *AsTJ* 55 (2000): 87, 89.

144. Mbuvi, *Temple*, 24.

145. E.g. Martin, *Metaphor*, 156–160; Green, "Identity," 90–91; Cranfield, *First Epistle*, 52–54.

146. Barclay, Introduction, 2.

147. Ibid.

Christians "separate" or "different" from the wider culture. The sequence should actually be reversed, that it is Christians' new relationship with God and their unique identity as his elect that necessarily renders Christians different from the surrounding idolatrous culture. Since the author's primary concern is Christians holding fast to their inheritance of salvation, he is not preoccupied with Christians setting themselves apart from everything from the surrounding culture, but primarily from those things which may jeopardize their belonging to God. His perception of Christians inheriting the self-understanding and eschatological promise of Jewish elect people of God actually provides an appropriate frame of reference for him to formulate his social ethics for Christians based on the experience of the Jewish Diaspora as I will elucidate in chapter 4.

On the other hand, Christians succeeding to the privileged identity of the Jewish Diaspora are not derived from hereditary entitlement but from the sacrificial suffering of Jesus Christ the Messiah on the cross. Steadfast faith and participation in the existence and experience of the Messiah-Christ also become crucial for the maintenance of Christians' identity and elect status before God, as I am going to explore in the next section.

2.3 Christ-Christians Unity in 1 Peter

After considering the Petrine vision of Christ and Christian existence on earth, I now proceed to explore the correlation between the notions of Christ as "the Jewish expected Messiah" and Christians as "elect exiles of Diaspora" in 1 Peter.

One particular feature of the Petrine vision of the relationship between Christians and their Christ is that Christians are understood as the elect people of God who are "in Christ" (ἐν Χριστῷ, 3:16; 5:10; 5:14). Of the three occurrences of ἐν Χριστῷ in the letter, one concerns Christians' behaviour in society (3:16), one their relationship with God (5:10) and the remaining one appears in the context of Christians' relationship with each other (5:14). Christians are thus God's people who have their whole existence orientated in the Messiah-Christ.

This dependence of the Christian community on Christ is actually the corollary of the unity and close existential identification between Christians and their Messiah-Christ as expounded in 2:4–10. In this passage, the election of Christians is understood as founded upon the prior election of Christ by God. Christians, portrayed as living stones (λίθοι ζῶντες, 2:5), are identified with Christ the living stone (λίθον ζῶντα, 2:4), and indeed built into a spiritual house upon Christ as the first elect and honoured Cornerstone (λίθον ἀκρογωνιαῖον ἐκλεκτὸν ἔντιμον, 2:6; ἐκλεκτὸν ἔντιμον, 2:4). In addition, membership in the elect priestly community of God (εἰς ἱεράτευμα ἅγιον, 2:5; βασίλειον ἱεράτευμα, 2:9) is possible only through faith in the Messiah-Christ (cf. ὑμῖν . . . τοῖς πιστεύουσιν, 2:7; ὑμεῖς δέ, 2:9).

Indeed, 1 Peter 2:4–10 occupies a pivotal position in the letter. On the one hand, it concludes the author's exposition in 1:3–2:3 in relation to Christians' new existence as the new born elect people of God through Christ. On the other hand, the close link of 2:4–10 to ὡς παροίκους καὶ παρεπιδήμους in 2:11 introduces the dual images of Christians as both "God's elect" and "resident-aliens and exiles" to shape their corresponding way of life in Christ amidst pagan alienation as appears in the rest of the letter.

In this section, I will investigate the Petrine perception of Christians' collective existence as God's elect people with reference to the Messiah-Christ as expressed in 2:4–10. It is once again noticeable that pagan hatred and ostracism does not necessarily make early Christians sullen or withdrawn to their own exclusive community. According to the Petrine author, Christians' identity is derived from their conviction of having exalted status before God grounded on the Messiah-Christ, and which they have inherited from the Jewish people of God. Instead of viewing themselves as a close sectarian community,[148] Christians' continuing interaction with the wider society is perceived as the service of the Christian priestly community to God by offering spiritual sacrifices and proclaiming his glory.

As the two overriding visions of Christians in 2:4–10 are (1) chosen living stones built into a spiritual temple (2:4–8) and (2) an elect people of God (2:9–10), I will also devote my discussion to these two themes.

---

148. Contra Elliott, *Home*, 101–150.

2.3.1 The Christ-Christian Spiritual House

In 1 Peter 2:4–8, Christians, having tasted that Christ is good (χρηστός, 2:3),[149] become individual living stones of a spiritual house by coming to him (2:4–5). The parity between Christians and Christ is underscored by the designation of Christians as λίθοι ζῶντες (2:5) in correspondence to Christ the "Living Stone" (λίθον ζῶντα, 2:4). The grounding of Christians' existence and experience is further reinforced by the image of the Messiah-Christ being the elect, honoured (ἐκλεκτὸν ἔντιμον, 2:6) Cornerstone of the spiritual house. Since Christians' existence is so derived from the Messiah-Christ, their distinctively exalted identity of being God's elect is also derived from Christ who is "elect and precious before God" (παρὰ . . . θεῷ ἐκλεκτὸν ἔντιμον, 2:4).

Since Christ as the Cornerstone is "the starting point from which the edifice of a new humanity is erected,"[150] Christians are to frame their social behaviour also following his model of social engagement. As Senior remarks, "The Christians are invited to base their life of discipleship on Jesus himself and thereby to share completely in his destiny."[151]

The edifice, into which the Christian living stones are to be built, is a spiritual house (οἶκος πνευματικός, 2:5). Although Elliott argues that οἶκος in 2:5 should mean "household,"[152] this οἶκος image is placed together with those of "living stones" (λίθοι ζῶντες), "holy priesthood" (εἰς ἱεράτευμα ἅγιον) and "spiritual sacrifices" (πνευματικὰς θυσίας) as a group, which renders the connotation of "a temple" difficult to avoid.[153] Indeed, it is in correspondence with this architectural imagery of the Christian community that the author puts forth his trust that God will restore, establish, strengthen and provide them with a firm foundation (καταρτίσει, στηρίξει,

---

149. As ὅν in 2:4 refers to the Living Stone who is clearly Christ, its antecedent ὁ κύριος in 2:3 should naturally refer to Christ rather than God. Also Achtemeier, *1 Peter*, 153; Elliott, *1 Peter*, 403.

150. Goppelt, *Commentary*, 146.

151. Senior, "1 Peter," 59.

152. Elliott, *Home*, 167–170, 200–205; *1 Peter*, 415–418.

153. Also Kelly, *Commentary*, 89–90; Goppelt, *Commentary*, 141; Senior, "1 Peter," 54; Wells, *Holy People*, 216–217.

σθενώσει, θεμελιώσει, 5:10)[154] so that they will stand firm to endure the hostility and alienation from the pagan world.

The background of this temple image may be what Gärtner observes as "the belief, common among the Jews at that time, that the temple would be restored and re-established in the last days. The old temple would be replaced by a new one, of quite new dimensions."[155]

In Tob 14:5, it is envisaged that after the times of the age are fulfilled, the people of Israel will return to Jerusalem from their captivity and "the house of God will be built in it with a glorious building for all generations for ever." As N. T. Wright observes, "None of these wonderful things had come to pass in the first century; even the rebuilding of the temple by Herod would hardly count . . ., since the other signs of the real return had not yet taken place."[156]

With this background, the Christian community, who are addressed as "elect exiles of Diaspora," are now perceived as "the temple" in fulfilment of the eschatological restoration hope among the exilic communities. Just as the present form (indicative or imperative) οἰκοδομεῖσθε is used in 1 Peter 2:5,[157] the Christian Diaspora is now "being built up" in the in-between time as the eschatological temple awaiting its eventual completion upon the future revelation of Jesus Christ. What is distinctive about this Christian temple is that it can be established as the ideal eschatological dwelling place of God among men only because it is grounded on Christ as its foundation Cornerstone.[158] On the basis of this close-knit unity with their Messiah-Christ, the Christian temple community is at the same time built towards its destination of "a holy priesthood" (εἰς ἱεράτευμα ἅγιον, 2:5) so that

---

154. Howard Clark Kee, *Who Are the People of God?: Early Christian Models of Community* (New Haven, CT: Yale University Press, 1995), 125.

155. Bertil Gärtner, *The Temple and the Community in Qumran and the New Testament: A Comparative Study in the Temple Symbolism of the Qumran Texts and the New Testament*, SNTSMS 1 (Cambridge: University Press, 1965), 16.

156. Wright, *People*, 270. Cf. *Sib. Or.* 3.282–294.

157. In which way the verb should be interpreted does not affect my discussion.

158. It is actually from this theological conviction of the corporate solidarity and identity of Christians that the author's exhortations on the fraternity and unity "within" the Christian community (1:22; 2:17; 3:8; 4:7–11; 5:1–5) are derived. Since my focus is on the author's "social" behavioural instructions, I do not intend to devote my discussion further to these exhortations on the internal solidarity of Christians.

they are to offer true worship and authentic sacrifices to God (ἀνενέγκαι πνευματικὰς θυσίας, 2:5). Once again, these spiritual sacrifices can be acceptable to God only through Jesus Christ (διὰ Ἰησοῦ Χριστοῦ, 2:5).

Therefore, although the Petrine author does not clarify what he means by "spiritual sacrifices," they should be understood with reference to Christ himself as first of all the Passover lamb (1:18–19) and the covenant-sealing sacrifice (1:2). The spiritual sacrifices offered by Christians are no more than their way of following the steps of Jesus Christ (2:21) to dedicate themselves in the service of God. As McKelvey remarks, "imitating Christ is to the author's way of thinking the sacrifice that is well-pleasing to God."[159] Cultic language is here used to highlight the theological footing for the letter's instructions on Christians' proper conduct in the wider culture. Based on Christians' close-knit unity with their Messiah-Christ who himself is the first sacrifice and who suffered human rejection as a resident-alien on earth, Christians' proper social engagement based on Christ's model is perceived as none other than their offering spiritual sacrifices to God.

2.3.2 The Christian Elect Diaspora Determined by Christ

In 1 Peter 2:9–10, a list of honorific titles is appropriated to the Christian community to highlight their corporate identity in Christ. Scholars generally agree that these titles are originally ascribed to Israel as God's special people in the OT. The four adjectives modifying these titles; namely, elect (ἐκλεκτός), royal (βασίλειος),[160] holy (ἅγιος) and for possession (εἰς περιποίησιν), all point to Christians' special relationship with God as his elect, thus reverberating the controlling metaphor for Christians in the letter.

What deserves close attention is that 1 Peter 2:9 starts with an adversative ὑμεῖς δέ. It is here that the Petrine author is drawing what he truly considers to be the boundary between Christians and "the others": While

---

159. R. J. McKelvey, *The New Temple: The Church in the New Testament*, Oxford Theological Monographs (London: Oxford University Press, 1969), 129–130.

160. I agree with most translators that βασίλειον is adjectival to ἱεράτευμα and not a substantive. The main reason is that all the other titles in 2:9 are also modified by adjectives. Furthermore, ἱεράτευμα should be interpreted as a substantive and not modifying βασίλειον because ἱεράτευμα in 2:5 is clearly a substantive. Neither does the fact that the adjectival βασίλειον is placed before rather than following the substantive ἱεράτευμα as in the case of the other three titles affect my judgment. Achtemeier, *1 Peter*, 164 is probably correct in observing that this order is just to follow βασίλειον ἱεράτευμα in LXX Exod 19:6. Also Michaels, *1 Peter*, 108–109.

Christians are marked by their belief in Christ (πιστεύουσιν, 2:7), the "others" are underscored as "non-believers" (ἀπιστοῦσιν, 2:7; cf. τοῖς ἔθνεσιν, 2:12; τῶν ἐθνῶν, 4:3), namely, those who do not stand in the salvation of God. As Jobes remarks, "Christ has become the touchstone of one's destiny."[161] For those who disobey (ἀπειθοῦντες) the gospel (τῷ λόγῳ, 2:8; cf. τὸ ῥῆμα τὸ εὐαγγελισθὲν εἰς ὑμᾶς, 1:25), their destiny is condemnation and thus "shame."

But for Christians (ὑμεῖς δέ) who believe, their destiny is honour and thus the exalted status in 2:9–10. Therefore, Christians' identity is once again seen in 1 Peter as primarily determined and defined by their faith in Christ (i.e. their religious conviction), rather than by maintaining their distinctiveness in society for its own sake. Indeed, it is only through their faith in Christ the Messiah that Christians are entitled to the self-identity and privileged status of the Jewish Diaspora as God's elect.

There is no dispute that the four Christian titles in 1 Peter 2:9 are taken from LXX Exodus 19:6 and LXX Isaiah 43:20–21. The first (γένος ἐκλεκτόν) and the last (λαὸς εἰς περιποίησιν) items of the list are from LXX Isaiah 43:20–21 (τὸ γένος μου τὸ ἐκλεκτόν, 43:20 and λαόν μου ὃν περιεποιησάμην, 43:21) while inside these bracketing terms, the second (βασίλειον ἱεράτευμα) and the third (ἔθνος ἅγιον) are from βασίλειον ἱεράτευμα καὶ ἔθνος ἅγιον of LXX Exodus 19:6. More importantly, Exodus 19:6 forms part of God's promise that Israel was to be exalted into special relationship with him, and the emphasis of Isaiah 43:20–21 falls on the New Exodus when God will deliver his people from exile. This interweaving of the Exodus and Isaianic texts aptly reflects Christians' existence as "elect exiles of Diaspora." Their succession to Israel as God's elect nation and royal priesthood is placed and comprehended in the eschatological context of the deliverance of the exilic Diaspora. This restoration event has now been triggered by the coming of the Messiah-Christ through whom Christians' privileged relationship with God becomes an existing reality.

Although Christians are at present subject to constant alienations, their religious conviction actually directs them to another reality of their "true" status and identity in society. Though apparently exiles and resident-aliens

---

161. Jobes, *1 Peter*, 78.

in dispersion, Christians are in fact a new "race" (γένος), "priesthood" (ἱεράτευμα), "nation" (ἔθνος) and a unique people (λαός) belonging to God and entitled to the future deliverance hope inherited from the Jewish Diaspora. As Horrell observes, the occurrence of the three terms, γένος, ἔθνος and λαός, "suggests an almost deliberate attempt to pack the verse with ethnic identity labels."[162] Therefore, the author's Christian theological self-perception as an extension of the exilic elect people of God actually generates a unique sense of identity expressed in ethnoracial terms grounded, not on ancestral or hereditary links, but on their newborn status before God through the Messiah-Christ.

This unique sense of identity generated by Christians' own theological self-understanding is further underscored in 2:10 that Christians are those "who once were no people, but now are a people of God; who once had not received mercy, but now have received mercy" (οἵ ποτε οὐ λαὸς νῦν δὲ λαὸς θεοῦ, οἱ οὐκ ἠλεημένοι νῦν δὲ ἐλεηθέντες). Taken loosely from LXX Hosea 2:25, ". . . ἐλεήσω τὴν Οὐκ-ἠλεημένην καὶ ἐρῶ τῷ Οὐ λαῷ μου λαός μου εἶ σύ . . .," the distinctive status of Christians expressed in 1 Peter 2:10 is once again derived from the Petrine conviction of Christians' entitlement to God's promise to regather his children in exile and renew his covenant with Israel, which is now made available to Christians through the universal salvation accomplished by the Messiah-Christ.

Based on this self-understanding of their unique exalted status before God, the author does not understand Christians as a sectarian group in society despite contrary assessment by their neighbours from an outsider viewpoint. Indeed, Christians' privileged status carries with it corresponding responsibility of positive social engagement with the surrounding hostile world. God is the One who himself acts and intervenes in human history by calling Christians "out of darkness into his marvelous light" (ἐκ σκότους . . . εἰς τὸ θαυμαστὸν αὐτοῦ φῶς, 2:9), that is, from unbelieving to believing. Christians' good conduct, derived from their unique relationship with God, should also be conspicuously recognizable by the mundane world. Therefore, in 1 Peter 2:9, the purpose (ὅπως) of the Christians being

---

162. David G. Horrell, "'Race', 'Nation', 'People': Ethnic Identity-Construction in 1 Peter 2.9," *NTS* 58 (2012): 129.

constituted into an elect exalted people of God is to "proclaim the excellencies (τὰς ἀρετάς) of God."

Given the appropriation of γένος ἐκλεκτόν and λαὸς εἰς περιποίησιν from Isaiah 43:20–21, ὅπως τὰς ἀρετὰς ἐξαγγείλητε (2:9) probably comes from τὰς ἀρετάς μου διηγεῖσθαι of LXX Isaiah 43:21. As Michaels asserts, the term ἐξαγγέλλω "belongs in the category of worship, not missionary activity"[163] which should also be regarded as the basic connotation for τὰς ἀρετὰς ἐξαγγείλητε in 1 Peter 2:9:[164] The establishment of Christians as a people uniquely belonging to God has the purpose of Christians proclaiming the praises to God through their proper social conduct among the Gentiles (cf. τὴν ἀναστροφὴν ὑμῶν ἐν τοῖς ἔθνεσιν, 2:12) by doing good (καλός, 2:12; ἀγαθοποιός, 2:14; ἀγαθοποιέω, 2:15, 20; 3:6, 17; ἀγαθός, 3:11, 13, 16; ἀγαθοποιΐα, 4:19). These "good deeds" are to bring about the praises of pagans to glorify God (δοξάσωσιν, 2:12; cf. δοξάζηται, 4:11; δοξαζέτω, 4:16) at the *end*. This notion of Christians worshipping and glorifying God through their behaviour is actually in line with 2:5, in which Christians' "spiritual sacrifices" also denotes their dedication of their lives in the service of God.

Therefore, although Christians are subject to constant animosity and alienation which render them resident-aliens and strangers in the pagan world, the Petrine author is not keen to paint a gloomy picture of their existence on earth. Instead of a sullen people finding consolation only from their own enclosed community, Christians are underscored as an esteemed elect people of God engaging a life of service and worship by bringing about the praises of pagans and, thus, glory to God. Their unique identity is again seen as derived primarily from their religious conviction of what Jesus Christ accomplished on the cross, rather than any special strategy of distancing or deliberate differentiation from the larger society. The value of reading the text from an insider viewpoint is therefore evidenced.

---

163. Michaels, *1 Peter*, 110.

164. See also Balch, *Let Wives*, 133 who shows that among the occurrences of ἐξαγγέλλω in the LXX (e.g. LXX Ps 55:9 [MT 56:9]; 70:15 [MT 71:15]; 106:22 [MT 107:22]), "there is no Septuagint text where this verb is used to refer to mission preaching."

Section Summary

In this section, I explicate how the Petrine vision of Christians' identity finds its root from the author's religious conviction of Christians' special relationship with God brought about by their belief in Christ (τοῖς πιστεύουσιν, 2:7). It is also through their faith in Christ (ὑμεῖς δέ, 2:9) that Christians are entitled to the honorific titles and eschatological hope of deliverance of the Jewish Diaspora.

Indeed, through the theological perception in terms of the spiritual temple in 2:4–8, Christians' election is grounded on the prior election of the Messiah-Christ who paradoxically has been rejected by human beings essentially as a resident-alien on earth and whose experience is now also the necessary experience of Christians. This christological-ecclesiastical unity between Christians and Christ is also the theological grounding for Christians to shape their social behaviour in the face of pagan rejection, following Christ's example by offering spiritual sacrifices of their lives in "doing good," as I will further investigate in the next chapter.

2.4 Chapter Conclusion

In this chapter, I explored the consistent theological perspective of the Petrine author which gives shape to his strategies on Christian social engagement with the surrounding hostile world.

I argued that through his extensive use of OT images and language, the author's theological perspective is expressed mainly in terms of the Jewish eschatological vision. Against the backdrop of the historical appearance of Jesus Christ inaugurating the Messianic Age, Christians' existence on earth is underscored by the metaphor "elect exiles of Diaspora," inheriting the privileged self-definitions as well as eschatological vision of the Jewish Diaspora. The total appropriation of the Jewish identity and self-understanding actually facilitates the author's formulation of Christian social strategy with reference to the example and experience of the Jewish exilic people of Diaspora.

At the same time, this self-understanding of elect exilic people of Diaspora actually underscores the necessity for Christians to negotiate their existence amidst the pagan culture with both resistance and accommodation. On the one hand, Christians' exalted status as God's elect and their inheritance of salvation calls upon their holding fast to their faith and rejecting anything from the pagan culture that may vitiate their ultimate allegiance and belonging to God, such as idolatry. On the other hand, Christians' continuing existence during the indeterminate in-between period of sojourn on earth as resident-aliens also necessitates their cultivating some sense of belonging and responsibility to the world of their present abode, and to do what is also acknowledged as good in the eyes of their pagan neighbours to gain room to uphold their ultimate allegiance to God.

Therefore, for the Petrine author, Christians' identity is primarily dependent on their special relationship with God brought about by Christ on the cross. It is only due to this religious conviction of their unique status and exclusive relationship with God that necessarily renders Christians different from the surrounding idolatrous world. Likewise, the Christian social ethics devised by the author are understood not as any strategy for Christians' survival or protection of Christians' social distinctiveness for its own sake. Instead, the Petrine Christian social strategy is underscored as the congruent behavioural expression of Christians' identity as "elect exiles of Diaspora" and their solidary with Christ who himself suffered human alienation essentially as a resident-alien and stranger on earth. This perception of the Petrine social behavioural instructions is what I will discuss in the next chapter.

CHAPTER 3

Social Behavioural Instructions in 1 Peter

In the last chapter, I argued that the Petrine perception of Christians' identity is derived from the author's theological perspective presented in terms of the eschatological vision of the Jewish Diaspora. Jesus Christ is underscored as the expected Messiah whose historical appearance has inaugurated the Messianic Age of restoration for the exilic people of God. Christians, born again through the resurrection of the Messiah-Christ (1:3), are thus viewed as "elect exiles of Diaspora" inheriting the exalted identity as well as the eschatological hope of the Jewish Diaspora. This metaphor of "elect exiles of Diaspora" aptly reflects the tension within Christians' existence in the contemporary hostile environment. While being God's elect and longing for their inheritance of salvation requires Christians to resist anything that may jeopardize their exclusive allegiance to God, being resident-aliens having to stay on earth for an indeterminate period of time also demands Christians to live out a degree of belonging and commitment to their place of abode and to gain room to uphold their ultimate allegiance to God.

I also demonstrated in the last chapter that the existence of the Christian Diaspora as an extension to the Jewish one is interpreted in 1 Peter in the light of Jesus Christ. The christological-ecclesiastical unity between Christians and Christ is highlighted by the image of the spiritual temple so that Christians' exalted status as God's elect is grounded on and determined by the Messiah-Christ. Since Christ is the first covenantal sacrifice who himself faces human alienation essentially as a resident-alien on earth, Christians dedicating themselves to proper social behaviour and in following Christ's steps, is also perceived as spiritual sacrifices and proclamation of God's excellencies.

In this and the next chapters, I will proceed to investigate how these eschatological, christological and ecclesiastical dimensions of the Petrine theological vision serve as the basic frame of reference that gives shape to the author's instructions on Christians' social engagement with the outside world. As I mentioned in chapter 1, this question of Christians' relation with the larger world was the focus of the Balch-Elliott debate. The main concern of this debate lies in the Petrine Christian social strategy amidst pagan hostility: "Does the author aim at reinforcing the internal cohesion and, thus, the identity of the Christian community?" or "Is he encouraging Christian social acculturation in order to reduce the tension between the church and the wider world?"

In his study to trace the origin and function of the Petrine household code,[1] Balch argues that the pattern of submissiveness stressed in the NT household codes originates from the Aristotelian topos "concerning household management" in *Politics* I.[2] This Aristotelian form was also widely used and developed by philosophers contemporary with the NT writers.[3] Balch then concludes that the Petrine household code was adopted in 1 Peter with a view to encourage Christians to reduce tension with the larger society[4] and to contradict slanders by acculturating to the Roman society.[5] The purpose of the Petrine household code is therefore apologetic.[6] In his subsequent dialogue with Elliott, Balch further maintains that such proposed Christian acculturation implies the acceptance of Hellenistic social values in tension with those of the Jewish tradition and even "in tension with the early Jesus movement, changes that raise questions about continuity and identity in early Christianity."[7]

---

1. Balch, *Let Wives*.
2. Ibid., 33, 34, 109.
3. Ibid., 51.
4. Ibid., 87–88.
5. Ibid., 119.
6. Ibid., 109.
7. Balch, "Hellenization/Acculturation, 81.

On the other hand, Elliott, in his work on the situation and strategy of 1 Peter as a whole, proposes that the Petrine strategy is to avert the forces of social disintegration "through a reinforcement of the distinctive identity of the Christian community and of its socioreligious cohesion."[8] Characterizing the church as a "conversionist sect,"[9] set apart and "disengaged from the routine affairs of civic and social life,"[10] Elliott argues that the Petrine author accentuates the conflict between the church and the world so as to foster Christians' resistance against outside pressure and to solidify their distinctive identity and social cohesion.[11] He also criticizes Balch for failing to account for the letter's "repeated call for Christian separation from the world" and understating its "missionary interests."[12] In his later dialogue with Balch, Elliott further contends that "nothing in 1 Peter . . . indicates an interest in promoting social assimilation."[13] It is precisely "a temptation to assimilate" that the letter intends to counteract.[14]

The fact that both Balch and Elliott manage to locate a sound base from the text for their proposals on the one hand, but arrive at significantly different conclusions about the letter's purpose on the other, actually warrants another possibility: The Petrine social ethical exhortations are containing *both* elements of accommodation *and* resistance to the wider pagan culture. Indeed, when one looks at the arguments of Balch and Elliott closely, their views are not so opposed to each other as their debate presupposes.

On the one hand, Balch also recognizes that the Petrine exhortation on Christians' conformity is subject to their holding fast to their *religious*

---

8. Elliott, *Home*, 217.

9. Elliott, *Home*, 73–78. Elliott's idea is developed from the sociological studies of Bryan R. Wilson, *Sects and Society: A Sociological Study of the Elim Tabernacle, Christian Science, and Christadelphians* (Berkeley, CA: University of California Press, 1961) and *Magic and the Millennium: A Sociological Study of Religious Movements of Protest among Tribal and Third-World Peoples* (London: Heinemann, 1973).

10. Elliott, *Home*, 79.

11. Ibid., 112–118.

12. Ibid., 111.

13. Elliott, "Situation, 72.

14. Elliott, "Situation," 73. Similar view is shared by Achtemeier, "Newborn Babes," 219, who asserts that "the farthest thing from the author's mind is accommodation to Hellenistic culture."

attitudes[15] and refusing to worship the pagan gods.[16] However, by restricting his study to the Petrine household code (which for Balch includes 1 Pet 2:13–3:9), Balch has not sufficiently dealt with a substantial part of the Petrine social instructions (i.e. 3:10–4:19), which actually underscores the more resistant elements of the Petrine social ethics. This partial treatment is what seems to contribute to his overstating that the author was writing to advise Christians "about how they might become socially-politically acceptable to their society."[17] Indeed, by neglecting the author's theological/religious conviction as his primary concern, Balch has further overstated his case by asserting that the accommodating elements within the Petrine instructions implies "tension with the early Jesus movement"[18] which at its core is actually *a religious movement*. As I will argue in this chapter, the accommodating aspect of the Petrine social ethics is not so much to render Christians "socially-politically acceptable to their society" as to *gain some room for Christians to maintain their ultimate allegiance to God in their various vulnerable situations*.

On the other hand, Elliott also recognizes that there is certain overlap between Petrine and pagan ethics. He, however, ascribes this overlap to the letter's missionary concern.[19] In another instance, he simply recognizes that the "avoidance of evil and the doing of good is behavior consonant with both societal and divine norms (2:1, 12, 14–16; 3:10–12, 13–17; 4:12–19)."[20] If this is the case, the boundary between the church and the world imposed by 1 Peter is not so marked as Elliott has been insisting. Indeed, there is only one instance in 1 Peter (3:1–2) where "conversion of unbelievers" is unambiguously in view.[21] Elliott seems to have overstated the missionary interest of the Petrine author.[22]

---

15. Balch, *Wives*, 88; cf. 121.
16. Ibid., 90, 119.
17. Ibid., 88.
18. Balch, "Hellenization/Acculturation," 81.
19. Elliott, "Situation," 72, 78.
20. Ibid., 73. Cf. 66.
21. Also Bechtler, *Following*, 166.
22. Contra also e.g. Volf, "Soft Difference," 15–30; Christoph Stenschke, "Reading First Peter in the Context of Early Christian Mission," *TynBul* 60 (2009): 107–126.

Therefore, both Balch and Elliott actually suffer from the same problem of arguing from their own stance without admitting the dialectical tension within the Petrine social strategy. Both elements of resistance and accommodation are present in the Petrine social ethics, which does not allow the exclusion of one from the other.

This tension within the author's instructions is recognized by Bechtler who proposes that the author perceives Christian life as a liminal existence: Followers of Christ find themselves in both the old aeon and the new "but not completely engaged in either"[23] and they are supposed to occupy a place that is "neither here nor there, neither fully within society nor completely removed from it."[24] However, Bechtler's explanation is unconvincing. Since the author's purpose is to encourage the readers to stand firm in God's grace/salvation (1 Pet 5:12), it is improbable that the author would encourage the readers to accept such an ambiguous identity. To request Christians to behave as if they were "*neither* here *nor* there" could hardly do service in empowering them to go through the present fiery ordeal and test (πυρώσει πρὸς πειρασμόν, 4:12; ποικίλοις πειρασμοῖς, 1:6) of social ostracism.

In view of the difficulty with Bechtler's proposal, Talbert's view deserves serious attention. Instead of "*neither . . . nor,*" Talbert holds that 1 Peter is *both* emphasizing the social cohesion and, thus, the identity of the Christian groups *and* advising Christians to behave "in terms of the highest social and cultural conventions of their time and place" in so far as avoiding the excess of the worst in pagan society.[25] Talbert's conclusion is derived from the pragmatic consideration of Christians' survival in a hostile environment following the model furnished by Homans's sociological study on group behaviour.[26] However, as the Petrine author clearly states in 1 Peter 5:12, the purpose of his instructions is primarily to facilitate Christians standing firm in God's grace (i.e. their holding fast to the Christian faith), rather than the survival of the Christian community in society. Talbert's

---

23. Bechtler, *Following*, 21.
24. Ibid., 118. See also 155–156 and 177.
25. Talbert, "Once Again," 146–148.
26. Ibid., 146. Homans's study can be found in George Caspar Homans, *The Human Group*, International Library of Sociology and Social Reconstruction (London: Routledge & Kegan Paul, 1975).

observation seems to be more an effort to fit the Petrine text into his theory, than an interpretation of the letter's social ethics with reference to what is expressed in the text.[27]

Another suggestion which requires attention is that put forth by Feldmeier who argues that Christians are addressed "*absolutely*" as "strangers and sojourners"[28] and that being "strangers" in society "*is precisely their vocation.*"[29] "Non-identity" in society is thus the characteristic of Christian existence.[30] If one reads Feldmeier's previous work, *Die Christen als Fremde: die Metapher der Fremde in der antiken Welt, im Urchristentum und im 1. Petrusbrief*, alone, Bechtler is probably correct to categorize Feldmeier's view as that 1 Peter advocates *neither* a sectarian existence *nor* acculturation.[31] However, Feldmeier's position is much more ambiguous than it first appears. In his later essay, he states that Christians' self-understanding as "strangers" implies *both* "distinction and encounter, loyalty to one's own belief and coming to terms with the foreign,"[32] although he also remarks that 1 Peter "does not go the way of sectarian self-isolation which rubbishes everything else. . . . At the same time, however, this primitive Christian pastoral letter sharply distinguishes itself from any religious overexaltation of this 'human creation.'"[33]

This ambiguity within Feldmeier's view actually betrays the fact that the Petrine social behavioural instructions are too complex to allow such simplistic categorization as "either . . . or," "both . . . and" or "neither . . .

---

27. Another scholar who recognizes the ambivalence in the Petrine ethical instructions is Lauri Thurén, *The Rhetorical Strategy of 1 Peter: With Special Regard to Ambiguous Expressions* (Åbo, Finland: Åbo Akademis Forlag, 1990). He argues that 1 Peter is written to a "composite audience." To the type of audience who are tempted to assimilate to society, the letter seeks to strengthen their religious identity and alienate them from society, but to those who are tempted to resist the social pressure in an improper way, its aim is to make them avoid conflict and to acculturate them to their social setting to some degree. The problem with Thurén's proposal is that there is nothing in 1 Peter which indicates that the author is writing to two different groups of readers. Without such indications, the author would have no way to ensure that his different instructions could be brought home to the relevant supposed targeted group of audience.

28. Feldmeier, "Nation," 256.

29. Ibid. See also Feldmeier, *Christen*, 174.

30. Feldmeier, "Nation," 259. See also Feldmeier, *Christen*, 180.

31. Bechtler, *Following*, 116. See Feldmeier, *Christen*, 189.

32. Feldmeier, "Nation," 269.

33. Ibid.

nor." A more profound explication of the Petrine social strategies is necessary to let the author's voice heard.

Maybe the major problem with Feldmeier's proposal is that the idea of Christians having their "vocation" as "strangers in society" does not appear a judicious reading of 1 Peter. As I explicated in the last chapter,[34] the "calling" (vocation) of Christians, according to 1 Peter, is to be "God's elect people" rather than "strangers in society." Indeed, in both 2:21 and 3:9 where the phrase εἰς τοῦτο . . . ἐκλήθητε appears, Christians' calling is linked to their maintaining proper social relationship as far as possible within the larger society. Christians are actually exhorted to stay within the existing social structure, rather than regard themselves as strangers in society.

In the light of the inadequacy of the simplistic articulation of the Petrine social ethics in terms of "either . . . or," "both . . . and," or "neither . . . nor," Volf's attempt to explicate "how the processes" of both difference and accommodation "were combined"[35] is a step forward in understanding the Petrine social behavioural instructions. Volf argues that Christians are under a "mission to proclaim the mighty deeds of God for the salvation of the world."[36] They are to live out their missionary distance of "soft difference" by way of joining their belief in the truth of their own convictions "with a respect for the convictions of others."[37] However, Volf's assessment seems to have neglected the fact that on matters going to Christians' ultimate and exclusive allegiance to God, the Petrine author actually calls upon Christians' "hard difference"[38] from the surrounding idolatrous culture. Christians are to gird up the loins (ἀναζωσάμενοι τὰς ὀσφύας) of their mind and be sober (νήφοντες) (1:13), and not to conform to the cravings formerly in their ignorance (1:14); they are to arm themselves (ὁπλίσασθε) with the same thought of Christ (4:1) and be ready to undergo suffering for doing good (3:17; cf. 3:13–14). In the face of the attack of their adversary

---

34. See pages 40–41 above.
35. Volf, "Soft Difference," 22.
36. Ibid., 27.
37. Ibid., 25.
38. "Hard difference" is defined by Volf, "Soft Difference," 24, as presenting "the other with a choice: either submit or be rejected."

the devil (5:8), Christians are once again exhorted to resist (ἀντίστητε) and be firm (στερεοί) in their faith (5:9).

In fact, Volf's idea suffers from the common problem among Petrine scholarship in not taking into account of the extensive references to the OT and the larger theological and historical contexts of 1 Peter. By neglecting the Petrine perception of Christians as the Diaspora in extension to the Jewish one, Volf also fails to appreciate the dynamics within the Petrine social ethics of "differentiated resistance" as I will also explicate in this and the next chapters.

Similar criticism also applies to the proposal of Seland who adopts a "modified form"[39] of the model of Gordon[40] and concludes that 1 Peter argues for a modified acculturation, a rather low form of structural assimilation, a modified marital assimilation, very low identificational assimilation, and very low, close to non-existent attitude-, behavioural relational- and civic assimilation.[41] Besides the fact that Seland's proposal fails to take into account of the historical and theological contexts of 1 Peter, it is also doubtful how a short text like 1 Peter can support such complicated proposal as put forth by Seland.

Horrell's proposal to adopt a "post-colonial reading" of 1 Peter[42] has the merit of understanding the Petrine Christian social engagement with reference to its historical imperial context of the colonial rule by the Roman Empire. Viewing Christians as a subordinate group negotiating their existence under the domination of the empire between conformity and resistance, Horrell labels the Petrine social strategy as "polite resistance." Behind the author's exhortations "to conform as far as possible to the standards of goodnesss expected by the powerful,"[43] there is "a kind of hidden and alternative transcript" in his narrative of Christian identity and the author's

---

39. Seland, *Strangers*, 165.

40. Milton Myron Gordon, *Assimilation in American Life: The Role of Race, Religion, and National Origins* (New York: Oxford University Press, 1964).

41. Seland, *Strangers*, 188–189.

42. Horrell, "Between Conformity," 110–143.

43. Ibid., 141.

resistance "comes clearly and publicly into view" in certain contexts and on certain points.[44]

Horrell's proposal is helpful in bringing scholars' attention back to the imperial context of the Petrine social instructions and the vulnerability of Christians in expressing their exclusive allegiance to God in the face of imperial domination. However, while a post-colonial reading may be helpful to throw light on the delicate relationship between Christians and the Roman Empire, it remains doubtful whether a post-colonial reading is equally helpful to clarify the Petrine strategy in relation to Christians' ostracism by their neighbours in society (e.g. 4:3–4) which was hostility from *the colonized themselves* rather than domination from *the colonizer*. As Horrell judiciously observes, it is a combination of both public and imperial hostility that rendered the socio-political situation of Christians particularly precarious (e.g. Pliny, *Ep.* 10.96–7).[45] This complexity in the sources of alienation against Christians actually requires an explication of the Petrine social strategy that can give an account for the author's (differentiated) treatments of Christians' relationship with the ruling authorities, as well as their neighbours in day-to-day interactions.

In this and the next chapters, I wish to add one more perspective to the current discussions of the Petrine social strategies by placing the letter's social behavioural instructions within its theological context and understanding these instructions from the author's own religious concern of Christians standing fast in God's grace/salvation. As I mentioned in chapter 1, 1 Peter is a correspondence from a member of the Christian community to the others and so, theology/religious convictions should play a primary and pivotal role in making intelligible the author's social strategy. Indeed, it is precisely this primary concern with theology/religion that accounts for the author's firm rejection of the pagan idolatrous culture while allowing Christians to adopt those societal norms which are not incompatible with their ultimate allegiance to God.

In the next chapter, I will look into the actual experience of the Jewish Diaspora in their daily interactions with the pagan culture especially in

---

44. Ibid., 142–143.
45. Ibid., 139–140.

Rome and Asia Minor, and explicate how the Jewish strategy for engaging their social existence among pagans, while maintaining their ultimate allegiance to God, is also reflected in the Petrine social ethical exhortations to the Christian Diaspora. The Petrine perception of Christian existence as "elect exiles of Diaspora" actually carries with it the experience and tactics of the Jewish Diaspora, which facilitate the author's formulation of his own teachings for the infant Christian communities in Asia Minor.

In this chapter, I will firstly conduct an exegetical study of 1 Peter 2:11—4:19, and engage in the Balch-Elliott debate by explicating how the Petrine behavioural instructions reflect the shape of the author's eschatological and christological-ecclesiastical convictions as explored in the last chapter. I will look into those individual units of 1 Peter 2:11—4:19 which deal with the readers' social engagement and elucidate the author's strategy in relation to four areas of Christians' life; namely, (1) civil life; (2) household life; (3) daily social life; and (4) when facing suffering for the name of Christ. My focus is on how these instructions are derived from the author's unique eschatological worldview and his perception of Christians as the elect exilic people of God in extension to the Jewish Diaspora. The Petrine understanding of Christ's social engagement, as exemplified by the cross, and his union with Christians, as represented by the image of the spiritual temple, will also be taken into account.

Instead of asking "whether or how accommodating" or "how accommodation combines with resistance," I will seek an empathic understanding of the author's own theological conviction by exploring "when" and "to what" Christians are exhorted to resist or accommodate to the pagan culture. The Petrine social strategy actually represents a form of what I would call "differentiated resistance." Subject to the overriding boundary of ultimate allegiance to God to facilitate Christians standing firm in salvation, which gives rise to the "resistance" aspect of his exhortations, the Petrine author actually has no problem advising Christians to be the best citizens following the current societal order and moral ideals of the larger society.

Indeed, the passage of 1 Peter 2:11—4:19, comprising the Petrine exhortation section of 2:11—4:11 and an introductory unit of 4:12—19 to the final section of the letter, is characteristically marked by the inclusio of exhortation to do good (τὴν ἀναστροφὴν . . . καλήν; τῶν καλῶν ἔργων,

2:12 and ἐν ἀγαθοποιΐᾳ, 4:19). In addition, there are ten times in this passage when the author features his ideal Christian social conduct as "good."[46] The idea of "doing good" is therefore the unifying thread that runs through the whole passage. It is however noticeable that although there are a number of incidences where Christians' "good works" are seen as Christians responsibly performing their societal roles and subjecting themselves to societal order in compliance with contemporary expectations, there are also a number of places where "good works" actually results in Christians suffering for resisting the pagans' demand to accommodate. To understand the author's strategy as "differentiated resistance" actually serves to explain this ambiguity of what amounts to "good work" within the author's perception.

Furthermore, although the Petrine notion of "good works" comprises elements of accommodation,[47] Christians' identity does not primarily depend on whether Christians are socially distinctive from the wider culture. For the Petrine author, the reverse is the case. Christians' "good works" are merely the congruent expression of their identity as "elect exiles of Diaspora" and in solidarity with their Messiah-Christ. His primary concern in formulating his Christian social strategy is therefore primarily religious rather than social.

---

46. Καλός, twice in 2:12; ἀγαθοποιέω in 2:15, 20, 3:6, 17; ἀγαθός in 3:11, 13, 16; ἀγαθοποιΐα in 4:19. Cf. ἀγαθοποιός, 2:14.

47. For "accommodation," I would follow, with some modifications, the definition of John M. G. Barclay, *Jews in the Mediterranean Diaspora: From Alexander to Trajan (323 BCE–117 CE.)* (Edinburgh: T&T Clark, 1996), 96–97 when he describes the process in which the Diaspora Jews make use of the Greek cultural heritage. This definition includes "imitation of Hellenistic culture, its internalization and its employment in reinterpreting the Jewish tradition." Since accommodation is already an integration process and for simplicity of language, I would include in my definition the material aspects of social integration and assume that "accommodation" includes "social assimilation" which is defined by Rogers Brubaker, "The Return of Assimilation? Changing Perspectives on Immigration and Its Sequels in France, Germany, and the United States," in *Ethnic and Racial Studies* 24 (2001): 534 as "the process of becoming similar or of making similar or treating as similar." Therefore, by "accommodation," I mean the phenomena wherein the Christian Diaspora internalize the norms, values and practices of the wider Greco-Roman world and, at the same time, reinterpret their original values and practices to form an integral harmonious set of Christian ethics.

3.1 The Governing Principle (2:11–12)

The Petrine exhortation section of 2:11–4:11 is introduced by 2:11–12 as the governing principle of Christians' social engagement. It is noticeable that both elements of "resistance" and "accommodation" within the Petrine social ethics are already present in these two verses.[48]

Right at the beginning of the exhortation section, the readers are addressed as παροίκους καὶ παρεπιδήμους (2:11) living amidst "the Gentiles" (τοῖς ἔθνεσιν, 2:12). As I explained in section 2.2 of the last chapter,[49] in the only two occasions in the LXX where the two terms πάροικος and παρεπίδημος are found together (LXX Gen 23:4 and LXX Ps 38:13), the phrase "πάροικος καὶ παρεπίδημος" is employed by the Jewish Diaspora translators to underscore the self-understanding of the Israelite patriarchs, which also became that of the Diaspora translators on earth. "Παροίκους καὶ παρεπιδήμους" in 1 Peter 2:11 therefore recalls the letter's controlling metaphor of Christians as the continuing "elect exiles of Diaspora." Indeed, along with the contrast of τοῖς πιστεύουσιν and ἀπιστοῦσιν in 2:7, παροίκους καὶ παρεπιδήμους is now further adopted as the identity marker for Christians in contrast to the Gentiles (τοῖς ἔθνεσιν, 2:12; cf. τῶν ἐθνῶν, 4:3), that is, the unbelievers as against the elect people of God.

As I also argued in the last chapter,[50] the combined use of πάροικος and παρεπίδημος in 1 Peter 2:11 underscores Christians' existence on earth during the in-between time before the ultimate revelation of their salvation. When viewed against their eternal salvation and ultimate belonging to heaven, Christians are exiles/strangers (παρεπίδημοι) "temporarily" staying on earth. At the same time, the need for Christians to stay for an indeterminate period of time before the arrival of the eschaton also renders them resident-aliens (πάροικοι) having their domicile in the current world. It is also this *duality of time* which requires Christians to negotiate their existence with both "resistance" and "accommodation." Although the *longing for the eternal inheritance of salvation* necessitates Christians' resistance to anything that may jeopardize their eschatological entitlement, subject to

---

48. See also Horrell, "Between Conformity," 133.
49. See pages 51–52 above.
50. See pages 48–51 above.

this boundary of accommodation, the *need to stay* for an indeterminate period of time also requires Christians to remain in the larger socio-political system and discharge their societal roles with due diligence. This mode of "differentiated resistance" is also reflected in 1 Peter 2:11–12 as the governing principle of Christian social engagement amidst the pagan world.

The Petrine teaching of "resistance" is underlined by the exhortation to "abstain from fleshly cravings" (ἀπέχεσθαι τῶν σαρκικῶν ἐπιθυμιῶν, 2:11). These cravings are notably underscored as "fleshly" and warring against the soul (στρατεύονται κατὰ τῆς ψυχῆς), that is, Christians' new life reborn through the death and resurrection in Christ (1:3).[51] Therefore, instead of teaching Christians to abstain unselectively from anything belonging to the wider culture, the author only encourages Christians to resist those cravings that "can jeopardize their salvation" through Christ (i.e. their belonging and allegiance to God). Consistent with my interpretation of τῆς ματαίας ὑμῶν ἀναστροφῆς πατροπαραδότου (1:18) and ταῖς πρότερον ἐν τῇ ἀγνοίᾳ ὑμῶν ἐπιθυμίαις (1:14) in the last chapter,[52] the resistance which the Petrine author emphasizes is of religious, rather than social, orientation: Christians are to abstain from everything from the pagan culture that relates to idolatry, including any collateral social and sexual activities, or that otherwise jeopardizes their ultimate allegiance to God such as cursing Christ before the authorities (cf. Pliny, *Ep.* 10.96) or denying God (cf. *Diogn.* 10.7).

Indeed, this resistance to the wider idolatrous culture is sufficient to result in Christians being slandered (καταλαλοῦσιν) as evildoers (κακοποιῶν) (2:12). Why Christians were abused as "evildoers" is clarified in 4:1–4. After their conversion, Christians had given up their former Gentile way of life which was driven by human cravings (ἀνθρώπων ἐπιθυμίαις, 4:2; cf. ταῖς πρότερον ἐν τῇ ἀγνοίᾳ ὑμῶν ἐπιθυμίαις, 1:14; τῶν σαρκικῶν

---

51. I agree with most commentators that ψυχή in 2:11 does not refer to the immaterial part of the human nature as opposed to the "body" within the Greek thought but to the whole Christian being destined for salvation through Christ that transcends the human earthly life.

52. See pages 25–26 above.

ἐπιθυμιῶν, 2:11). This new behaviour driven by religious conviction is what leads to blasphemies (βλασφημοῦντες, 4:4) from their neighbours.[53]

Therefore, when the Petrine author exhorts Christians to maintain "good works" (τὴν ἀναστροφὴν . . . καλήν and τῶν καλῶν ἔργων, 2:12) to contradict pagan accusation of evildoing (κακοποιῶν), what is intended to be "good" cannot be too distinct from the current social norms. The Petrine author obviously envisages a certain overlap between Christians' ethics and what is also recognized as "good" in the eyes of the wider culture.[54] In so far as it is not inconsistent with their faith and ultimate allegiance to God, Christians have no problem doing what is good in accordance with the pagan moral ideals. This is how the Petrine "differentiated resistance" should be understood.

The purpose of the Christians' "good works" is to bring about their slanderers' glorifying God in the "day of visitation" (ἐν ἡμέρᾳ ἐπισκοπῆς, 2:12). Although, as van Unnik observes, the term ἐπισκοπή "is typical for the LXX where it can have a general meaning of visitation, care, searching,"[55] the only instance where "the day" of visitation appears in LXX is Isaiah 10:3 (ἐν τῇ ἡμέρᾳ τῆς ἐπισκοπῆς) and in the context of a prophetic declaration of God's judgment.[56] Indeed, the vision of non-believers regretting having slandered believers and recognizing the glory of God at the eschaton is also present in post-exilic Jewish literature. Wis 5:1–7 states:

> Then the righteous man will stand with great boldness in the presence of those who have oppressed him, and those who make light of his labours. When they see him, they will be

---

53. Most illustrative are the accounts of Suetonius and Tacitus when they recorded Nero's persecutions of Christians. Suetonius underscores Christians as "a class of men given to a new and mischievous superstition" (Suetonius, *Vit.* 6.16.2 [Rolfe, LCL]) while Tacitus also describes Christians as "a class of men, loathed for their vices, whom the crowd styled Christians" (Tacitus, *Ann.* 15.44 [Jackson, LCL]).

54. See also W. C van Unnik, "Christianity according to 1 Peter," *ExpTim* 68 (1956/1957): 82–83; Michaels, *1 Peter*, 117.

55. W. C. van Unnik, "The Teaching of Good Works in 1 Peter," *NTS* 1 (1954/1955): 104.

56. The "time" of visitation appears in Wis 3:7 is a time of vindication for the righteous, whereas in Jer 6:15 and 10:15, it refers to a time of God's judgment (cf. Luke 19:44). Besides these references, the "hour" of visitation in Sir 18:20 is a time of judgment when he, who has examined himself before, will find forgiveness. See also *1 En.* 63.

troubled with terrible fear, and they will be amazed at the wonder of [his] salvation. They will speak to one another in repentance, and will groan in anguish of spirit, and say, "This is the one whom we once held in derision and made a figure of reproach – we fools! . . . How has he been reckoned among the sons of God? . . . So we strayed from the way of truth, . . . but the way of the Lord we have not known."[57]

Therefore, instead of expressing concern for conversion of pagans as asserted by scholars such as Elliott,[58] Volf,[59] and Green,[60] it is likely that the Petrine author is applying to the Christian Diaspora the Jewish eschatological expectation of God's ultimate vindication of his own elect people at the consummation of history. This interpretation is also more aligned with the author's expectation of the ultimate punishment of those who cause Christians' sufferings at the present time as expressed in the rest of the letter (3:16; 4:5; 4:17).[61]

Indeed, this notion of pagans praising and glorifying (δοξάσωσιν) God recalls the cultic language in 2:4–10, in which Christians dedicating themselves to proper social behaviour is perceived as their way of offering spiritual sacrifices following the steps of Christ as the first sacrifice, and proclaiming the excellencies of God as I explored in the last chapter.[62] Christians' good works are therefore perceived in 1 Peter as the Christian "elect exiles of Diaspora" discharging their function as the holy priesthood and the spiritual temple to offer spiritual sacrifices following the model and in union with Christ, their Messiah-Cornerstone.

It is precisely the eschatological and christological-ecclesiastical convictions already laid down in 2:11–12 that run through the whole fabric of the Petrine behavioural instructions, as I will further explicate in my discussions of the other units.

---

57. I derive this reference from Green, *1 Peter*, 69, but my conclusion is different from Green who still considers 1 Pet 2:12 to have evangelical import.

58. Elliott, *1 Peter*, 471.

59. Volf, "Soft Difference," 25.

60. Green, *1 Peter*, 70.

61. Also e.g. van Unnik, "Teaching," 104–105; Ernest Best, *1 Peter*, 112; Achtemeier, *1 Peter*, 178; Bechtler, *Following*, 160.

62. See pages 62 above.

3.2 Christian Engagement in Civil Life (2:13–17)

After outlining the governing principle of Christian social behaviour in 2:11–12, the Petrine author proceeds to deal with Christians' engagement with the civil authorities in 2:13–17.

Although Balch chooses to include this unit as part of the Petrine household code,[63] 1 Peter 2:13–17 mainly deals with Christians' role as citizens of the state, whereas both of the other typical household codes found in the NT, namely, Colossians 3:18–4:1 and Ephesians 5:22–6:9, only deal with members under the same roof of the house. In addition, different members occupying different roles of the household are directly addressed in a typical household code, such as αἱ γυναῖκες (Col 3:18, Eph 5:22) and οἱ δοῦλοι (Col 3:22, Eph 6:5). This feature is also found in the proper Petrine household code of 2:18–3:7 (αἱ[64] γυναῖκες in 3:1; οἱ οἰκέται in 2:18). However, the whole passage of 2:13–17 is addressed to all the readers generally without singling out any group and without specifying their individual roles. I therefore consider 1 Peter 2:13–17 a separate unit independent of the Petrine household code.

It is understandable why Balch chooses to include 1 Peter 2:13–17 as part of the Petrine household code. References to Christians' "good works" (ἀγαθοποιοῦντας, 2:15; cf. ἀγαθοποιῶν, 2:14), expressed in this unit as subjecting themselves to every human creature (institution) (ὑποτάγητε πάσῃ ἀνθρωπίνῃ κτίσει, 2:13), apparently gives the impression that the author is exhorting Christians to conform to the demands of society. As Sanders comments, "our author in effect endorses a society that supports submission institutionally."[65] Likewise, Munro also argues that the idea represented by the term ἀγαθοποεῖν "fully accords with Hellenistic ideas of

---

63. Balch, *Wives*, 81. Other scholars who treat 2:13–17 as part of the Petrine Household Code include e.g. Beare, *First Epistle*, 139; Green, *1 Peter*, 70–72; Edgar Krentz, "Order in the "House" of God: The Haustafel in 1 Peter 2:11–3:12," in *Common Life in the Early Church: Essays Honoring Graydon F. Snyder*, ed. Graydon F. Snyder et. al. (Harrisburg, PA: Trinity Press International, 1998), 281.

64. For a reading to include the article αἱ due to its inclusion in P[72] ℵ[2] C Ψ and other manuscripts and despite its absence from P[81] ℵ*A B and others manuscripts, see Bruce M. Metzger, *A Textual Commentary on the Greek New Testament*, 2nd ed. (London: United Bible Societies, 1994 [1st published, 1971]), 620.

65. Jack T. Sanders, *Ethics in the New Testament: Change and Development* (London: SCM Press, 1975), 85.

citizenship to find the state referred to as giving recognition and credit to those who do good."⁶⁶

Indeed, the idea of being subject to the existing social order and responsibly performing one's role as a citizen of society is also present in Hellenistic moral teachings. For Epictetus, "a god-fearing man, a philosopher and a diligent student" is supposed to know his duty towards the gods, towards parents, towards brothers, towards his country and towards strangers.⁶⁷ Xenophon also states that, "the city in which the citizens are most obedient to the laws has the best time in peace and is irresistible in war"⁶⁸ and that, "agreement is deemed the greatest blessing for cities."⁶⁹ Therefore, it is likely that there is substantial overlap between the good works intended in this unit and the pagan ideal of good citizenship, so as to command the praise of human authorities (ἔπαινον . . . ἀγαθοποιῶν, 2:14). As van Unnik argues, good works must refer to those deeds that can qualify Christians as "first-class citizens" so that they can stop slanders against them (2:15).⁷⁰

What is remarkable is that for the Petrine author, Christians accommodating to pagan norms does not necessarily mean loss of identity. These commonly accepted norms are now perceived with a theological orientation. The ultimate motivation for Christians subjecting themselves to existing social order is "for the Lord's sake" (διὰ τὸν κύριον, 2:13). In view of the fact that except for two Old Testament citations (1 Pet 1:25; 3:12) which necessarily relate to God,⁷¹ κύριος unambiguously refers to Christ in other instances (1:3; 2:3; 3:15), it is likely that Christ is also referred to in 2:13,⁷² (i.e. it is because of Christ that Christians submit to the current societal order). As Michaels observes, the author probably has in mind "Jesus' behavior toward his detractors and toward Jewish and Roman authority at

---

66. Winsome Munro, *Authority in Paul and Peter: The Identification of a Pastoral Stratum in the Pauline Corpus and 1 Peter*, SNTSMS 45 (Cambridge: Cambridge University Press, 1983), 53.
67. *Diatr*, 17.31 (Oldfather, LCL).
68. *Mem.* 4.4.15 (Marchant, LCL).
69. *Mem.* 4.4.16 (Marchant, LCL).
70. van Unnik, "The Teaching," 99.
71. And except 3:6 where κύριον refers to Abraham.
72. Also Feldmeier, *First Letter*, 131.

the time of his arrest and trial."⁷³ Christians living out their civil responsibility in accordance with societal order is therefore perceived by the author as a token of their following the steps of Christ their Cornerstone, who accepted suffering essentially as a resident-alien and submitted to human authorities in compliance with societal expectations. It is also with this vision of following Christ's step in complying with the "will of God" (ἐστὶν τὸ θέλημα τοῦ θεοῦ, 2:15; cf. παρεδίδου . . . τῷ κρίνοντι δικαίως, 2:23) that, by doing good, Christians are to silence the ignorance of the foolish men (i.e. the unbelieving slanderers), and even their accusations before the ruling authorities (2:15).⁷⁴

Indeed, this compliance with societal order to silence the slanders of others is closely related to the author's perception of Christians living in the in-between time as πάροικοι on earth. Since Christians have to stay at their existing place of domicile for an indeterminate period of time, it becomes necessary for them to remain within the wider socio-political system, and minimize the tension from their neighbours and the ruling authorities, so as to make room for their continuing exclusive worship of God. Hence, contrary to Davids' observation that 1 Peter betrays "clearly a "Christ against culture" type of relationship,"⁷⁵ the author actually recognizes the capacity of the emperor and his delegates to differentiate those who do good (ἀγαθοποιῶν) from those who do evil (κακοποιῶν) (2:14). This optimism is consistent with the fact that when the devil is mentioned in 5:8–9 as the enemy to Christians' faith, he is not posited as the evil force behind the ruling authorities as is noticeable in Revelation (e.g. Rev 13:4). Instead, human institutions are actually underscored in 1 Peter as part of God's creation (κτίσει, 2:13). Therefore, for the Petrine author, following the demands of the ruling authorities is not inherently incompatible with Christians' faith in God *per se*.

On the other hand, the Petrine author also differentiates Christians' loyalty to God from that to the empire, so that he is not calling for Christians' unlimited accommodation to the expectations of the wider culture. Although the notion of the emperor and his representatives being

---

73. Michaels, *1 Peter*, 124. See also Selwyn, *St. Peter*, 172; Davids, *First Epistle*, 99.
74. Cf. Michaels, *1 Peter*, 127.
75. Davids, *First Epistle*, 21.

part of God's creation (κτίσει, 2:13) provides an avenue for Christians to submit to the rule of human authorities, it also sets the boundary for Christians following the demands of the empire. Κτίσις, literally "creature," "which is created," meticulously subordinates the king and his delegates to the sovereignty of God the Creator (πιστῷ κτίστῃ, 4:19).

This distinction between the divinity of God and the humanity of the emperor is further reinforced by the concluding remark in 2:17. Whereas the emperor is to be "honoured" (τὸν βασιλέα τιμᾶτε) just as everyone else (πάντας τιμήσατε),[76] God is to be "feared" (τὸν θεὸν φοβεῖσθε). Here, φοβεῖσθε (recalling ἐν φόβῳ in 1:17) represents man's appropriate responses of reverence and worship that are exclusively reserved to the only God.[77] Particularly relevant for our purpose is *Act Scil.* 9 in which Donato, when required to swear by the genius of the emperor, actually said, "Pay honour to Caesar as Caesar; but it is God we fear."[78] In similar fashion, Tatian also remarks, "Man is entitled to honour to the degree appropriate for humanity, but only God is to be feared" (*Orat.* 4).[79] Especially in view of the fact that the vitality of imperial cult actually continued in Asia Minor throughout the first and the second centuries CE,[80] the author's effort to subtly deny the claim of divinity for the emperor is remarkable.

We thus arrive at the Petrine strategy of "differentiated resistance" in this unit. Although the author has no problem instructing Christians to subject themselves to the current socio-political system and to honour the emperor, such as to offer prayers to God for the empire and the emperor[81]

---

76. This observation actually renders the arguments of Warren Carter, "Going," 14–33 and. Bird, *Abuse,* 82 that 1 Peter is advocating Christians' cultic participation in emperor worship unlikely.

77. So, Horrell, *1 Peter*, 87; Achtemeier, *1 Peter*, 188.

78. Translation provided in Herbert Musurillo, *The Acts of the Christian Martyrs, Introduction, Texts and Translations* (Oxford: Clarendon Press, 1972), 89. See also Deut 6:13–14; 13:3–5; Josh 24:14; 2 Kgs 17:38–39; Tob 14:6; *Act Scil.* 8.

79. Tatian, *Oratio Ad Graecos and Fragments,* trans. Molly Whittaker (Oxford: Clarendon, 1982), 9.

80. S. R. F. Price, *Rituals and Power: The Roman Imperial Cult in Asia Minor* (Cambridge: Cambridge University Press, 1984), 58–62. More discussions on the imperial cult in Asia Minor will be provided in ch. 5.

81. Cf. Tertullian, *Scap* 4; *Apol.* 39.2.

or to participate in some public benefactions for the well-being of the city,[82] these instructions clearly do not apply when the emperor claims the status of god (imperial cults), or when contributions to benefaction are supposed to be made in relation to the pagan cults.[83] Christians are to resist the demands of the wider society when their ultimate allegiance to God is at stake.

It is noticeable that when expressing the concern for the necessity of Christians to resist the demands of the empire in some circumstances, the Petrine author does it with obvious subtlety, and in such a way as reflecting what Horrell calls "polite resistance."[84] Furthermore, the theme of "Christians' suffering," which pervades the letter, is notably absent in this unit. Besides differentiating "what" and "when" to resist, it appears that the Petrine author is also devising differentiated treatment between Christians' engagement with the Roman authorities and their neighbours at municipal level. Christians are to maintain, as far as possible, normal relationship with the Roman authorities, so that they can concentrate their effort on dealing with the slanders and ostracism of their neighbours at provincial level, which is actually the primary source of hostility against them (4:3–4). As I will further explicate in the next chapter, this was actually the social strategy adopted by the Jewish Diaspora in Asia Minor and Rome, and which the Petrine author appropriated to Christians as a result of his understanding of Christians' existence on earth as "elect exiles of Diaspora."

Indeed, in 2:16, the Petrine author underscores Christians' good works of subjecting themselves to the current socio-political system as merely part of their expressing their identity as the slaves of God (ὡς θεοῦ δοῦλοι, 2:16), which recalls Christians' continuity with the Jewish Diaspora. In

---

82. Bruce W. Winter, "The Public Honouring of Christian Benefactors," *Journal for the Study of the New Testament* 34 (1988): 92–97. One of the inscriptions cited by Winter concerns the selling of a quantity of wheat cheaper than that which was being sold in the market (88).

83. As described in Stephen Mitchell, *Anatolia: Land, Men, and Gods in Asia Minor*, vol. 1, 2 vols. (Oxford: Clarendon, 1993), 109–111, benefactions provided for the imperial cult could take the forms of statues of the emperors, provision of oil for the use in the gymnasium, multiple sacrifice of animals, holding of public feasts, organization of gladiatorial shows and related forms of public entertainment, and even distribution of grains, etc.

84. Horrell, "Between Conformity,"143.

the LXX, δοῦλοι is also a self-designation of the people of Israel with reference to God, and underscores "the relation of dependence and service" in which the elect people stand to him.[85] Good works (ἀγαθοποιοῦντας, 2:15) performed by the Christian slaves of God, therefore, represents the collective effort of the Christian Diaspora to serve God among the nations, and is reminiscent of the spiritual sacrifices Christians offer to God (2:5). It is based on this theological understanding of good works as an expression of their service to God, as elect exiles of Diaspora and in solidarity with Christ, that Christians themselves do not consider their adopting the norms and values of the wider culture to a certain degree as losing their unique sense of identity before God.

Section Summary

In 1 Peter 2:13–17, the Petrine social strategy of "differentiated resistance" is seen at work in relation to Christian civil life. Subject to the overriding boundary to resist everything that may jeopardize their ultimate allegiance to God, such as cultic participation in emperor worship, Christians are actually exhorted to be the best citizens by subjecting themselves to the current socio-political system. The author's differentiated treatments between Christians' engagement with the Roman authorities and with their neighbours in the cities also begin to emerge: Christians are to preserve, as far as possible, a normalized relationship with the Roman authorities so that they can concentrate their energy on dealing with hostility and slanders at municipal level.

It is due to the understanding of good works as the befitting behavioural expressions of Christians' identity as elect exiles of Diaspora, and representing their collective offering of service to God that the author has no problem allowing Christians to adopt those norms and values of the wider culture that are not inconsistent with their allegiance to God. Once again, for the Petrine author, Christians' identity does not primarily depend on their being socially distinctive from the rest of society.

---

85. Rengstorf, "δοῦλος" *TDNT* 2.267–268. E.g. LXX 2 Chr 6:23; Neh 1:6; Ps 78:10 (MT 79:10); Jer 3:22; 2 Macc 7:33.

3.3 Christian Engagement in Household Life (2:18–3:7)

After dealing with Christians' civil life, the author proceeds to the specific roles within the household in 1 Peter 2:18–3:7. As mentioned in my review of scholarship above, the Petrine household code is the source of argument giving rise to the Balch-Elliott debate. As Balch argues, the Petrine household code conforms to the form of moral teachings adopted by contemporary philosophers, and this set of rules also seems to represent the ideals of the current culture. However, this overlap between the Petrine household code and current Greek moral teachings does not necessarily have the effect of raising (in Balch's words) "questions about continuity and identity in early Christianity."[86]

In this section, I will explore how the Petrine social strategy of "differentiated resistance" is at work in the letter's household code. "Ultimate allegiance to God" is still what Christians are expected not to forego. Subject to this boundary of accommodation, Christians are exhorted to stay within the current societal order and negotiate their existence with the same meekness and humility as their civil life, which is underscored by the same exhortation of "being subject" (ὑποτάγητε, 2:13; ὑποτασσόμενοι, 2:18; ὑποτασσόμεναι, 3:1, 5). It is noticeable that Christians subjecting themselves to the norms of the wider world is not regarded as implying loss of their sense of identity but is, again, merely part of the congruent behavioural expression of their identity as "elect exiles of Diaspora" and in solidarity with their Messiah-Christ.

Indeed, when compared with the three pairs of relations addressed in the Ephesian and Colossian Household Codes, only the slaves, but not the masters, are addressed in 1 Peter (2:18–25) and the children-fathers pair is absent altogether. Even when both wives and husbands are mentioned (3:1–7), the attention is focused on the wives (3:1–6) with only a brief note to the husbands (3:7). Since "Christians' suffering and social estrangement" is the core subject that the Petrine author is dealing with, his instructions to the most vulnerable members of the non-believing households (i.e.

---

86. Balch, "Hellenization/Acculturation," 81.

slaves and wives), probably serve as a paradigm of proper behaviour for all Christian elect exiles in their own situations.[87]

3.3.1 Exhortations to Slaves (2:18–25)

Although slaves (οἱ οἰκέται) are directly addressed in 2:18 and the instructions in 2:18–20 are particularly relevant to them, 2:21–25, especially the reference to Jesus' exemplary suffering, is likely intended to include the entire Christian community as well.[88] In addition, as Christians are mentioned as God's slaves (θεοῦ δοῦλοι) in 2:16, the exhortations to Christian slaves, who suffer unjustly (2:19), are paradigmatic generally for proper Christian response to outside ostracism and pressure to accommodate.[89]

Indeed, when one considers the particularly precarious situation of Christian slaves in a pagan household, it becomes clear why the author's strategy of "differentiated resistance," rather than "total dismissal," is particularly seemly for Christians' engagement amidst the predominantly idolatrous host culture. In the Greco-Roman world, slaves were expected to worship the gods of the masters' households. For example, Columella once asserted that a slave "shall offer no sacrifice except by direction of the master."[90]

At the same time, as Joshel succinctly observes, "The *familia* as a group was formally expressed in cult."[91] In Rome, for example, every household had at least one shrine called a *lararium* dedicated to the deities that protected the house, household, and owner. The shrine was the focus for religious worship by the whole *familia* and was frequently entrusted to the slaves for administration.[92] Particularly in view of the fact that loyalty and obedience were commonly expected from slaves in antiquity,[93] severe

---

87. So, e.g. Senior, "1 Peter," 77; Achtemeier, "Newborn Babes," 220.

88. Senior, "1 Peter," 77; Cf. Michaels, *1 Peter*, 135, 145–146.

89. See also Achtemeier, *1 Peter*, 54; Elliott, *1 Peter*, 522–523; Campbell, *Honor*, 143; Horrell, *1 Peter*, 66.

90. *Rust.* 1.8.5–6 (Boyd, LCL). See also Balch, *Wives*, 68–69, 85.

91. Sandra R. Joshel, *Slavery in the Roman World*, Cambridge Introduction to Roman Civilization (New York: Cambridge University Press, 2010), 144. See also Isaeus 8.15–16.

92. Joshel, *Slavery*, 144.

93. E.g. Columella, *Rust.* 1.8; Tacitus, *Ann.* 14.60. See also K. R. Bradley, *Slaves and Masters in the Roman Empire: A Study in Social Control*, Collection Latomus 185 (Bruxelles: Latomus, 1984), 21–45.

punishment "apparently often exceeding the transgression"⁹⁴ could be expected if slaves refused the orders of their owners.

Therefore, the price that Christian slaves had to pay for upholding their ultimate allegiance to God, by refusing to attend to the household shrine or participate in the household cult, could only be huge. Not only could they be seen as lazy or idle, they could also be accused of subjecting the master and indeed, the whole household, to the risk of revenge by the deities. The cruelties which slaves could receive from their masters were most tellingly reported by Galen when he saw his friends having "bruised their hands by hitting their slaves on the mouth," and that "There are other people who don't just hit their slaves, but kick them and gouge out their eyes and strike them with a pen if they happen to be holding one."⁹⁵

Christian slaves' "holding fast to their own faith in the pagan households" and "negotiating their existence in the households in fear (ἐν παντὶ φόβῳ, 2:18; cf. τὸν θεὸν φοβεῖσθε, 2:17), and with consciousness of God (συνείδησιν θεοῦ, 2:19)" may be all that could be expected from them. It is further noteworthy that the author emphatically underscores the readers' following his instructions as the way to remain in God's grace (τοῦτο γὰρ χάρις, 2:19; τοῦτο χάρις παρὰ θεῷ, 2:20; cf. ταύτην εἶναι ἀληθῆ χάριν τοῦ θεοῦ, 5:12)

It is against this demand of "ultimate allegiance to God" that the author's exhortations of subordination in 2:18 should be understood. Although the Christian slaves are now free men (ὡς ἐλεύθεροι, 2:16) for having been redeemed (ἐλυτρώθητε, 1:18) by the blood of Christ, they are instructed to remain within the existing social order, and subject themselves (ὑποτασσόμενοι) to their masters even if their masters are unscrupulous and perverted (σκολιοῖς, 2:18) or even unjust (cf. ἀδίκως, 2:19).⁹⁶ Here, Christians' "doing good and enduring suffering" (ἀγαθοποιοῦντες καὶ πάσχοντες ὑπομενεῖτε, 2:20) can actually be viewed from *both* perspectives of "resistance" *and* "accommodation." On the one hand, living in a world

---

94. Bradley, *Slaves*, 122.

95. Galen, *The Diseases of the Mind*, 4. Translation provided in Thomas Wiedemann, *Greek and Roman Slavery* (London: Croom Helm, 1981), 180. Other examples can also be found in Seneca, *Ira* 3.32; Xenophon, *Mem.* 2.1.16–17.

96. Goppelt, *Commentary*, 194.

where slaves could be beaten simply because they had "irritated a crabby master" or become "outlets for an owner's frustration,"[97] slaves subjected to a perverted master could only imply faithfully submitting to the beating, insults, tortures and even sexual demands[98] of the masters.[99] On the other hand, if the Christian slaves resisted the commands of the masters to attend the household shrine or to participate in the household cult, "doing good" would be viewed as their upholding allegiance to God and willing acceptance of the punishments and cruelties from their masters. In either case, unjust sufferings and harsh treatments would be the only outcome.

What is important to note is that "being obedient members of the household" is understood in 1 Peter as the identity expression of Christians as members of the exilic elect people of God. Traditional Greco-Roman household form is now viewed from a theological perspective. Christians doing good and enduring suffering for it (ἀγαθοποιοῦντες καὶ πάσχοντες ὑπομενεῖτε, 2:20) are perceived as fulfilment of their calling (εἰς τοῦτο γὰρ ἐκλήθητε, 2:21) and, thus, the vocation of the Christian elect people of God. In fact, "fear of the Lord" (ἐν παντὶ φόβῳ, 2:18; cf. τὸν θεὸν φοβεῖσθε, 2:17; ἐν φόβῳ, 1:17; 3:2; μετὰ . . . φόβου, 3:16) is a well-known expression in the OT and second temple Jewish literature to denote the proper attitude of Israel before God, and to ensure that God's will is followed by his people. In LXX Exodus 20:20, the purpose of the fear of God (ὁ φόβος αὐτοῦ) is to keep Israel from sinning. *T.Gad* 5.3–4 also asserts, "Righteousness expels hatred; . . . He will not denounce a fellow men, since fear of the Most High overcomes hatred."[100] Christians' submission to their human masters as slaves (οἰκέται, 2:18) is in fact submission ultimately

---

97. Joshel, *Slavery*, 40.
98. Cf. Plutarch, *Mor.* 140B (Babbitt, LCL).
99. See also Goppelt, *Commentary*, 195; Campbell, *Honor*, 143–144,
100. Translation provided by H. C. Kee, "Testaments of the Twelve Patriarchs," *OTP* 1.815. This reference likely belongs to the Jewish stratum of the text since no Christian interpolation is obvious. Those parts of the book which Emil Schürer, *The History of the Jewish People in the Age of Jesus Christ (175 BC–AD 135)*, vol. 3, 3 vols. rev. Eng. ed, eds. Fergus Millar et al. (Edinburgh: T&T Clark, 1973–1986), 768 and 768 n. 6 regards as containing Christian interpolations include *T. Sim.* 6.5, 7; *T. of Levi* 4.1; *T. Iss.* 7.7; *T. Zeb.* 9.8; *T. Dan* 5.13; *T. Naph.* 8.3; *T. Ash.* 7.3; *T. Benj.* 10.7–9; 11. Those bracketed out by H. C. Kee, *OTP* 1:775–828 further include *T. of Sim.* 7.1, 2; *T. Levi* 2.11; 4.4; 10.2, 3; 14.2; 18.7; *T. Dan.* 6.8; *T. Jos.* 19. 8–12; *T. Ben.* 3.8; 9.3. See also e.g. LXX 2 Chr 19:7; 26:5; Neh 5:9; Prov 1:7; 9:10; 10:29; Sir 1:30; 23:27.

directed to God the divine master as his elect slaves (cf. θεοῦ δοῦλοι, 2:16) and, therefore, an expression of their identity of God's new elect people of Diaspora.

Furthermore, besides the behavioural expression of Christians' common identity, "do good and endure suffering" (ἀγαθοποιοῦντες καὶ πάσχοντες ὑπομενεῖτε) is also the mode of social existence which the author understands as what Jesus Christ exemplified on the cross and, thus, a way for Christians to find solidarity with their Messiah-Christ (2:21–25). As I mentioned in the last chapter, 1 Peter 2:21–25 is not just a mechanical transportation of LXX Isaiah 53:4–9 to understand Jesus Christ as the messianic Suffering Servant, but is a Petrine reworking of OT text to reflect the author's understanding of Jesus Christ's passion.[101] Although Jesus was actually put to death, the author's focus is obviously more on his suffering (ἔπαθεν,[102] 2:21). For the Petrine author, the example (ὑπογραμμόν, 2:21) Jesus Christ left for Christians on the cross is indeed that of a resident-alien rejected by society at large.[103]

It is therefore important to note that the example of Jesus Christ understood by the Petrine author is not merely of "unjust sufferings," but rather "doing good and enduring suffering" (ἀγαθοποιοῦντες καὶ πάσχοντες ὑπομενεῖτε, 2:20), which also reflects the form of "differentiated resistance" in his response to human alienation. The element of resistance is seen from his confronting the rejection by his contemporaries without having committed any sin (2:22), and entrusting himself to God while suffering (2:23). Subject to this allegiance to God, the fact that Jesus Christ did not revile in return and did not threaten when suffered (2:23) also posits him an obedient member of society, subjecting himself to societal rules, in order to achieve a higher cause of accomplishing the eternal salvation

---

101. See page 30 above.

102. Although P⁸¹ ℵ Ψ and some other manuscripts read ἀπέθανεν instead of ἔπαθεν rendered in P⁷² A B C P and many other manuscripts, it is likely that this reading of ἀπέθανεν is affected by the Pauline formulation of ἀπέθανεν + ὑπέρ such as Rom 5:8; 1 Cor 15:3; 2 Cor 5:14, 15; cf. τοῦ ἀποθανόντος ὑπὲρ ἡμῶν in 1 Thess 5:10. The stress of Christ's suffering actually suits the context better. See e.g. Kelly, *Commentary*, 119; Achtemeier, *1 Peter*, 189. Also Thomas P. Osborne, "Guide Lines for Christian Suffering: A Source-Critical and Theological Study of 1 Peter 2:21–25," *Bib* 64 (1983): 386, 390–391; Michaels, *1 Peter*, 134.

103. See section 2.1.1 above.

purpose of God (2:24). Therefore, instead of reducing his Christology as "functional" to facilitate the author's own intended Christians' response to sufferings,[104] the sequence should be reversed. It is the author's convictions of what the cross denotes, and what constitutes Christians' solidarity with their Christ-Messiah, that give rise to his teachings on Christians' engagement amidst pagan hostility.

Just as the submission of Jesus Christ on the cross is understood as for the higher purpose of accomplishing God's salvation plan so that Christians "being dead to sin, might live to righteousness" (2:24), Christians submitting to existing social order is also for a higher purpose to strive for some room to hold fast to their ultimate allegiance to God by refusing to participate in the pagan idolatrous practices (and the household cults in the situation of the Christian slaves).

Hence, "do good and endure suffering" is perceived by the author as Christians' mode of following Christ's example of "differentiated resistance" in following his steps (ἐπακολουθήσητε τοῖς ἴχνεσιν αὐτοῦ, 2:21), that is, the way of following Christ. This path becomes the distinctive shape of the exilic life of the Christian flock (2:25) on their way to restoration, understood in terms of the Jewish eschatological expectations. Entering into fellowship with their Messiah-Shepherd and participating in his suffering, the Christian Diaspora flock understand their present suffering as an unavoidable prelude to their ultimate salvation. Here, the Petrine author is once again seen as understanding the Jewish eschatological worldview afresh, in the light of Jesus Christ, to form the theological basis of his Christian social ethics. The relationship between the exilic people of God and their Messiah is now reinterpreted as Christians following the steps of their Christ-Shepherd by adopting his mode of social engagement as their own.

Therefore, for the Petrine author, his concern is ultimately religious. Although from an outsider point of view, the Petrine instructions may be regarded as accommodating or "collusive" with the existing kyriarchal structures in the oppression of the outcast,[105] such social concern is actually not the question the author himself is addressing. Indeed, as one of the

---

104. Contra Bechtler, *Following*, esp. 1, 38–40, 179–204.
105. Bird, *Abuse*, 89–94. See also Kathleen E. Corley, "1 Peter," in *Searching the Scriptures*, vol. 2, 2 vols., ed. Elisabeth Schüssler Fiorenza (London: SCM, 1994), 356,

Christians who is himself being oppressed rather than an oppressor, the author's primary concern is still how Christians can remain in the grace/salvation of God (5:12) during the period of their stay on earth amidst the surrounding aversive situation. This is precisely the value of reading the text from the author's own point of view, which should also be borne in mind to understand the Petrine exhortation to Christian wives.

3.3.2 Exhortations to Wives (3:1–6)

The exhortations in 3:1–6 are primarily directed to those households in which Christian wives were married to unbelieving husbands. Ἀπειθοῦσιν τῷ λόγῳ in 3:1 probably connotes the husbands' hostility to the Christian faith rather than mere refusal to believe.[106] This actually places the Christian wives in a most difficult situation. According to the traditional Greco-Roman culture, wives were also expected to adopt the social circle and assume the religion of their husbands. Plutarch's instruction is most illuminating:

> A wife ought not to make friends of her own, but to enjoy her husband's friends in common with him. The gods are the first and most important friends. Wherefore it is becoming for a wife to worship and to know only the gods that her husband believes in, and to shut the front door tight upon all queer rituals and outlandish superstitions.[107]

The tension created by the wives' adopting their own religion is particularly imaginable when one considers that venerating the household gods was a daily activity of family life in the Greco-Roman world. As I mentioned in the last section, each household had its domestic shrines. In Roman religion, "the whole household gathered daily to invoke the protection of its special deities and ancestors."[108] Once she got married, a

---

who asserts that the Petrine author "reinforces that oppression at the expense of women and slaves."

106. So also Achtemeier, *1 Peter*, 210; Senior, "1 Peter," 82.

107. Plutarch, *Mor.* 140D (Babbitt, LCL).

108. Carolyn Osiek and David L. Balch, *Families in the New Testament World: Households and House Churches* (Louisville, KY: Westminster John Knox Press, 1997), 83.

Christian wife was supposed to preside "as materfamilias" over the household worship.[109] In addition to the fact that a Greco-Roman household was composed not just of the nuclear family but was "an intergenerational social unit that included other relatives and any slaves as well,"[110] the reproaches directed to Christian wives for abstaining from the domestic cult could only be considerable.

Furthermore, living in a culture where increasing honour and avoiding shame were the chief motivating factors in influencing behaviour, having a good (obedient) wife was a matter of social virtue and respectability for a man in the Mediterranean world.[111] The refusal of Christian wives to worship the household gods could only dishonour their pagan husbands. The disgust that the pagans may have for the "disobedience" of Christian wives is most blatantly evinced by Apuleius when he underscores the baker's wife as "the worst and by far the most depraved woman in the world" because she, among others, "scorned and spurned all the gods in heaven, and, instead of holding a definite faith, she used the false sacrilegious presumption of a god, whom she would call 'one and only' (*Metam.* 9.14 [Hanson, LCL])."[112]

Therefore, the mere fact that the author structures his admonitions from a Christian point of view is by itself evidence of the author's concern for the believing wives to remain in faith and uphold their ultimate allegiance to God by resisting the pressure to participate in the household idolatrous cults. Balch's argument that 1 Peter implies the acceptance of Hellenistic social values "in tension with the early Jesus movement"[113] is hardly an accurate assessment of the text. Bird's complaint that, "In choosing to elevate the roles of the household, the author makes an accommodation to Empire. Collusion with the exploitative system precludes seeking justice for those who are exploited *by* the system"[114] is again only

---

109. Osiek and Balch, *Families*, 83.

110. Moyer V. Hubbard, *Christianity in the Greco-Roman World: A Narrative Introduction* (Peabody, MA: Hendrickson, 2010), 179.

111. Lynn H. Cohick, *Women in the World of the Earliest Christians: Illuminating Ancient Ways of Life* (Grand Rapids, MI: Baker Academic, 2009), 86.

112. As Michaels, *1 Peter*, 157 observes, the mentioned wife was probably a Christian.

113. Balch, "Hellenization/Acculturation," 81.

114. Bird, *Abuse*, 102.

an outsider viewpoint in addressing a question which is actually not the author's primary concern. The author's primary concern is still to facilitate Christians standing fast in God's grace (5:12) rather than to subvert the existing socio-political system. To subvert the current order would only attract pagan accusations of being evildoers (κακοποιῶν, 2:12; κακοποιός, 4:15) and would only hinder their effort to gain room to uphold their own exclusive allegiance to God. Indeed, the fact that the author is presupposing the wives' sheer disobedience in rejecting the household gods clearly rebuts any suggestion of collusion with the existing socio-political structure.

Indeed, this unit is linked to the previous one by ὁμοίως which shows that the Christian wives' subordinating to existing familial order has the same christological basis as slaves' submission. As Thompson asserts, "the order of the ancient society is assumed in 1 Peter, but the ancient order is transformed by the story of the cross."[115] While Jesus Christ rejected "the pursuit of power and the will to dominate"[116] for the higher purpose of bringing about the salvation and righteousness of humanity (2:24), wives' "fear" and "chastity" (τὴν ἐν φόβῳ ἁγνὴν ἀναστροφήν, 3:2) is also directed to a higher purpose of bringing about the salvation of their husbands (κερδηθήσονται, 3:1).[117] Instead of facilitating Christians' unreserved *fitting in to the existing system*, Christian wives' subordination in compliance with highly prized social values is once again viewed from a religious perspective to reverse the direction of participation for *winning unbelievers to the Christian community*.

Likewise, although priority of inward virtue over outward beauty is also widespread in the Greco-Roman world,[118] the exhortations on adornment with "a gentle and quiet spirit" (τοῦ πραέως καὶ ἡσυχίου πνεύματος) rather than with extravagant clothing and ornamentation (3:3–4) are grounded not merely on social acceptability, but on what is precious in the sight of God (ὅ ἐστιν ἐνώπιον τοῦ θεοῦ πολυτελές, 3:4). Although Bird

---

115. James W. Thompson, "The Submission of Wives in 1 Peter," in *Essays on Women in Earliest Christianity*, vol. 1, 2 vols., ed. Carroll D. Osburn (Joplin, MI: College Press, 1993), 392.
116. I borrow these words from Thompson, "The Submission," 392.
117. See David Daube, "Κερδαίνω as a Missionary Term," *HTR* 40 (1947): 109–120.
118. E.g. Seneca, *Mar.* 3.3–4; Plutarch, *Mor.*141D–E; Epictetus, *Ench.* 40.

views this admonition for "a gentle and quiet spirit" as the author's effort to circumscribe wives to "silent positions of submission . . . roles that support kyriarchal power structures,"[119] it should be noted that this exhortation of "gentleness" (πραΰτητος, 3:16; cf. ταπεινώθητε, 5:6) and "not to return revile when being reviled" (3:9) is also found in the author's exhortation to *all the members* of the Christian community. The exhortations of keeping "a gentle and quiet spirit," therefore, can hardly be seen as oppression on the wives alone but is actually consistent with the general tenor of the Petrine concern for Christians subjecting themselves to the existing societal order in solidary with Jesus Christ by following his steps.

Therefore, good works in this unit (ἀγαθοποιοῦσαι, 3:6) once again reflects the shape of "differentiated resistance." The primary concern is still the wives' staying in the grace of God by retaining their own religious faith within the household and resisting any pressure to accommodate to the household cults. Subject to this overriding boundary, they are to stay within the familial system and subordinate themselves to the demands of the larger society for the higher purpose of winning their husbands to faith. Christian wives do not submit to their husbands just because they are terrified. They are actually not to be frightened (μὴ φοβούμεναι, 3:6) by any intimidation, which is an exegetical key to ἐν φόβῳ in 3:2 that their fear in good behaviour is not directed to their husbands but to God. As I explained above, "fear of the Lord" is regarded as the proper attitude of the exilic people of God within Second Temple Judaism. The good works of Christian wives are once again posited as the unique identity expression of the Christian Diaspora.

This understanding of good works as the congruent behavioural expression of Christians' identity as the elect exilic people of God is further made explicit when the author relates the subordination (ὑποτασσόμεναι, 3:1) and adornment (κόσμος, 3:3) of the Christian wives to those of the holy women (ἐκόσμουν . . . ὑποτασσόμεναι, 3:5) of the Jewish Scripture. Christian wives are now viewed as claiming their heritage from the matriarchs of the Jewish Diaspora[120] "who have travelled the same path of

---

119. Bird, *Abuse*, 96.
120. Both Achtemeier and Michael propose that these holy women include Sarah, Rebecca, Rachel, and Leah, Achtemeier, *1 Peter*, 214; Michaels, *1 Peter*, 164.

hoping faith."[121] Following the example of the holy women who hoped in God (ἐλπίζουσαι εἰς θεόν, 3:5), Christians wives, through their hope in God (ἐλπίδα . . . εἰς θεόν, 1:21), are therefore perceived as travelling the same path of the flock of God's holy people following their Shepherd-Messiah toward ultimate restoration and salvation (cf. 2:25, 3:1).

This identification of Christians with the Jewish elect exilic people of God is further reinforced by the author's underscoring the Christian wives as the children of Sarah (ἧς ἐγενήθητε τέκνα) when doing good (ἀγαθοποιοῦσαι) (3:6). "Doing good" is therefore once again understood as the proper social expression of Christians' identity as "elect exiles of Diaspora." What is remarkable is that Christian wives become the children of Sarah not *by birth* like the Jewish Diaspora. Their hereditary link to the matriarchs stems from their being born again from God (ἀναγεννήσας, 1:3, ἀναγεγεννημένοι, 1:23) through the resurrection of the Messiah-Christ, which entitles them to the same promise of eschatological vindication and restoration (1:10–12) as the Jewish exilic people of Diaspora.[122]

3.3.3 Exhortations to Husbands (3:7)

Although the exhortations to Christian husbands only receive a brief treatment in 3:7, the author is once again seen adopting widely accepted social values but with a Christian perspective. This verse is connected to 3:6 by the same term ὁμοίως. Just like the Christian wives, Christian husbands are exhorted in the same capacity as the children of the continuing Israel (τέκνα, 3:6), and the instructions in 3:7 continue to represent "good works" (ἀγαθοποιοῦσαι, 3:6) as congruent behavioural expression of their identity as continuing exilic people of God.

As the householder of the whole family, a Christian husband in the Greco-Roman world was likely to be at liberty to have his own religion and could expect his wife to follow his Christian faith. It is remarkable that although women were commonly regarded as the weaker sex[123] in the Greco-Roman culture, the recognition of the wife as the weaker vessel (ἀσθενεστέρῳ σκεύει, 3:7) is no longer the basis for the dominance

---

121. Goppelt, *Commentary*, 223.
122. Ibid., 224.
123. Plato, *Leg.* 6.781A; Plato, *Resp.* 5.455–456; Tacitus, *Ann.* 3.33.

and control of the husband but rather, actually requires his living with his wife with consideration and understanding (κατὰ γνῶσιν). Husbands are to bestow honour (ἀπονέμοντες τιμήν) on their wives because wives are their "co-heirs of the grace of life" (συγκληρονόμοις χάριτος ζωῆς; cf. 5:12). All Christians, having been born again through the resurrection of Christ (1:3), are now children of God (τέκνα ὑπακοῆς, 1:14) awaiting the realization of their hope for the inheritance of salvation in the last time (1:4–5).

Although Christians are to remain within the current familial order, their relationship within the households is no longer determined by human expectations but their relationship with God. Just as the submission of the slaves and the wives is perceived as what entitles them to God's grace (τοῦτο γὰρ χάρις, 2:19; τοῦτο χάρις παρὰ θεῷ, 2:20) and is precious before God (ἐνώπιον τοῦ θεοῦ πολυτελές, 3:4), the relationship between Christian husbands and their wives is also no longer understood in terms of "power relations"[124] but "fraternal love" (cf. τὴν ἀδελφότητα ἀγαπᾶτε, 2:17) owing to their new existence as elect children of God. It is the continuing relationship with God (μὴ ἐγκόπτεσθαι τὰς προσευχὰς ὑμῶν) rather than the calculation of ruling and being ruled that counts. "Ultimate allegiance to God" is still the author's primary concern in formulating his exhortations for Christian husbands.

Section Summary

The Petrine household code once again witnesses the Petrine social strategy of "differentiated resistance" at work. Christians holding fast to their ultimate allegiance to God in their different life situations is still the author's primary concern. Within the boundary of resistance to participate in the household cults, the author has no problem in Christians staying within the familial order and subjecting themselves to societal expectations for the higher purpose of holding fast to their loyalty to God. This mode of Christians' good works is understood as the congruent expression of their identity as the "elect exiles of Diaspora" and a token of their solidarity with Jesus Christ the Messiah, who subjected himself to human sufferings also for a higher purpose, and in his case, of accomplishing the eternal salvation plan of God.

---

124. Contra Bird, *Abuse*, 99–100.

It is precisely seen through the theological lens of their identity before God as slaves and elect children of God that Christians' relationship within the household is no longer articulated in terms of power relations or control. It is now understood afresh as marked by respect and love (cf. πάντας τιμήσατε; τὴν ἀδελφότητα ἀγαπᾶτε, 2:17), whether in terms of the subordination of the slaves and wives, or the husbands' living with their wives with understanding and respect.

3.4 Christian Engagement in Daily Social Life (3:9–4:6)

After dealing with the internal fraternity and solidarity within the Christian community in 3:8, the author returns to the subject of Christian relationship with outsiders in 3:9–4:6. Since no specific area of Christian life is addressed, these instructions are directed to Christians' daily interactions with their neighbours in general. It is remarkable that different from the exhortations on Christians' relationship with the official authorities in 2:13–17 in which suffering was not mentioned, Christians' response to suffering and abuses becomes the focus of the author's teachings. The need for Christians to hold fast to their exclusive faith and ultimate allegiance to God is also much more blatantly amplified. At the same time, "differentiated resistance" remains the main thrust of the Petrine social strategies. In so far as Christians are not required to get involved in any activities which may be inconsistent with their exclusive loyalty to God, the author has no problem with Christians seeking peace and complying with current societal order for the higher purpose of defending their faith in the face of pagan accusations and slanders.

Although similar themes and language run through the whole passage, I will divide the passage into individual units according to the different foci of good works being exhorted, hoping that my readers can follow my discussion with greater ease.

3.4.1 Do Not Return Evil for Evil (3:9–12)

In the face of neighbours' abuses, Christians are instructed in this unit not to return evil for evil, or reviling for reviling, but instead to bless (εὐλογοῦντες, 3:9). Similar to the exhortation to subordination in the previous units, gentleness and humility remains the tenor of the author's social strategies for Christians. In addition, enduring unjust suffering without retaliation, but with blessing, is again taken as an integral part of Christians' calling (εἰς τοῦτο ἐκλήθητε, 3:9; cf. εἰς τοῦτο . . . ἐκλήθητε, 2:21)[125] as the elect people of God who are entitled to inherit (κληρονομήσητε; cf. εἰς κληρονομίαν, 1:4) their eschatological blessing (εὐλογίαν) (3:9).

The exhortation is then followed by a reference to the OT to serve as its theological basis. 1 Peter 3:10–12, ὁ γὰρ θέλων ζωὴν ἀγαπᾶν καὶ ἰδεῖν ἡμέρας ἀγαθὰς παυσάτω τὴν γλῶσσαν ἀπὸ κακοῦ καὶ χείλη τοῦ μὴ λαλῆσαι δόλον, ἐκκλινάτω δὲ ἀπὸ κακοῦ καὶ ποιησάτω ἀγαθόν, ζητησάτω εἰρήνην καὶ διωξάτω αὐτήν· ὅτι ὀφθαλμοὶ κυρίου ἐπὶ δικαίους καὶ ὦτα αὐτοῦ εἰς δέησιν αὐτῶν, πρόσωπον δὲ κυρίου ἐπὶ ποιοῦντας κακά, largely follows LXX Psalm 33: 13–17a (MT 34:13–34:17a): τίς ἐστιν ἄνθρωπος ὁ θέλων ζωὴν ἀγαπῶν ἡμέρας ἰδεῖν ἀγαθάς παῦσον τὴν γλῶσσάν σου ἀπὸ κακοῦ καὶ χείλη σου τοῦ μὴ λαλῆσαι δόλον ἔκκλινον ἀπὸ κακοῦ καὶ ποίησον ἀγαθόν ζήτησον εἰρήνην καὶ δίωξον αὐτήν ὀφθαλμοὶ κυρίου ἐπὶ δικαίους καὶ ὦτα αὐτοῦ εἰς δέησιν αὐτῶν πρόσωπον δὲ κυρίου ἐπὶ ποιοῦντας κακά, with a few exceptions.[126] Here, "doing good" is again taken as antithetical to "doing evil" (ἐκκλινάτω . . . ἀπὸ κακοῦ καὶ ποιησάτω ἀγαθόν, 3:11; cf. 2:12).

It is important to note that "good works" (cf. ποίησον ἀγαθόν, LXX Ps 33:15) as quoted from the LXX text are now placed in 1 Peter as a parallel to the example of Christ underscored in 1 Peter 2:22–23. Keeping the tongue from evil and the lip from speaking guile (παῦσον τὴν γλῶσσάν σου ἀπὸ κακοῦ καὶ χείλη σου τοῦ μὴ λαλῆσαι δόλον, LXX Ps 33:14; cf. 3:10) is reminiscent of Jesus Christ's not reviling in return while being reviled, and not threatening while suffering (2:23), as well as no guile having been found in his mouth (οὐδὲ εὑρέθη δόλος ἐν τῷ στόματι αὐτοῦ, 2:22). The assurance of God's care and ultimate vindication in LXX Psalm 33:16–17a

---

125. For the argument that εἰς τοῦτο refers to what precedes rather than what follows, see John Piper, "Hope as the Motivation of Love: 1 Peter 3:9–12," *NTS* 26 (1979/80): 212–231.

126. The Petrine adaptations include changing from the second person of the LXX text to the third person, modifying the question in LXX Ps 33:13 into a noun clause to fit in the context of the exhortations, and the addition of ὅτι to align with the Petrine pattern of the theological rationale following the preceding imperative.

(1 Pet 3:12) also recalls Jesus Christ's entrusting himself to God who judges justly (2:23). Since the context of LXX Psalm 33 is God's deliverance of the righteous from persecutions, Christ's example of non-retaliation is now understood in 1 Peter as realizing the Jewish ideal of doing good and seeking peace (ζήτησον εἰρήνην, LXX Ps 33:15; cf. ζητησάτω εἰρήνην, 1 Pet 3:11) when facing abuses. It is based on this identification of Christ's example with the Jewish ideal that Christians' strategy of seeking peace without returning abuses is understood by the author as *both* a token of their solidarity with Christ in following his steps *and* a congruent expression of their existence as the continuing elect people of Diaspora.[127]

Indeed, the Petrine strategy of "differentiated resistance" is again at work in this unit. Although Christians' resistance to pagan religion render them different and result in slanders and hostility from their neighbours, Christians do not mind complying with current societal order and seeking peace by submitting to human abuses without subversion. Once again, Christians' subordination and humility in society is perceived as a concrete expression of their identity as the continuing "elect exiles of Diaspora" and their solidarity with Christ.

3.4.2 Suffer for the Sake of Righteousness (3:13–22)

The Petrine strategy of "differentiated resistance" is also the theme of Christian good works explicated in 1 Peter 3:13–22. The passage 3:13–17 is characterized by the repeated occurrence of terms relating to the notion of "good" (τοῦ ἀγαθοῦ, 3:13; συνείδησιν . . . ἀγαθήν, 3:16; τὴν ἀγαθὴν ἐν Χριστῷ ἀναστροφήν, 3:16; ἀγαθοποιοῦντας, 3:17). Doing good is once again pronounced as antithetical to doing evil (κρεῖττον . . . ἀγαθοποιοῦντας . . . πάσχειν ἢ κακοποιοῦντας, 3:17).

As I have been explaining throughout this chapter, the Petrine idea of Christians "suffering for doing good" (ἀγαθοποιοῦντας . . . πάσχειν, 3:17; πάσχοιτε διὰ δικαιοσύνην, 3:14) actually includes *both* aspects of suffering

---

127. Although Gordon M. Zerbe, *Non-Retaliation in Early Jewish and New Testament Texts: Ethical Themes in Social Contexts*, JSPSup 13 (Sheffield: JSOT Press, 1993), 294 considers the Petrine non-retaliatory ethics to be "different" from those of early Judaism due to this appeal to the example of Jesus, I would rather regard this appeal to the example of Jesus Christ the Messiah as the Petrine perception of Christians at the same time "fulfilling" the ideal of the second temple Judaism as the continuing exilic people of Diaspora.

for upholding their ultimate allegiance to God (i.e. resistance) *and* submitting to societal order and responsibly discharging one's societal role according to common expectations (i.e. accommodation). Indeed, "differentiated resistance" as the mode of Christians' good works is again expressed in the exhortations in 3:15–16, where Christians are instructed to demonstrate "gentleness and fear" (μετὰ πραΰτητος καὶ φόβου, 3:16) when making defence for their salvation hope (τῆς ἐν ὑμῖν ἐλπίδος, 3:15; cf. εἰς ἐλπίδα, 1:3).[128] On the one hand, Christians are to hold fast to their ultimate allegiance to God by defending their faith so that their good conscience/consciousness of God (συνείδησιν . . . ἀγαθήν, 3:16; cf. συνείδησιν θεοῦ, 2:19) must be kept intact, and their fear (φόβου, 3:16) is directed to God and not to men (τὸν . . . φόβον αὐτῶν μὴ φοβηθῆτε, 3:14; cf. 2:18; 3:2). On the other hand, within the overriding boundary of their ultimate allegiance to God, Christians are to conduct their defence with the same tenor of seeking peace and with the same gentleness and meekness (πραΰτητος, 3:16; πραέως, 3:4) as appear in other units, which in effect exclude any attempt to disrupt the existing social order. In so far as Christians are not required to participate in the pagan religions or to do anything inconsistent with their exclusive loyalty to God, they are to behave as good and proper citizens as expected by the larger society.

It is important to note for our purpose that by positing "good works" (ἀγαθοποιοῦντας . . . πάσχειν, 3:17) as in parallel with "righteousness" (πάσχοιτε . . . δικαιοσύνην, 3:14), "good works" is once again featured as the necessary attribute of Christians as the continuing elect exiles of Diaspora. "Righteousness" in the LXX denotes one's "observance of the will of God which is well-pleasing to Him"[129] (cf. θέλοι τὸ θέλημα τοῦ θεοῦ, 3:17).

---

128. As mentioned on page 14 note 66 above, I agree with the view commonly held by scholars such as Selwyn, *First Epistle*, 193; Kelly, *Commentary*, 143; Goppelt, *Commentary*, 243–244; Michaels, *1 Peter*, 188; Achtemeier, *1 Peter*, 233; Jobes, *1 Peter*, 230 that ἀπολογίαν in 3:15 refers to Christians' defense of their faith primarily in informal inquiries happened in the daily social life (cf. 1 Cor 9:3 and 2 Cor 7:11). This observation is consistent with the author's exhorting the readers to "always" (ἀεί) be prepared to make a defence to "everyone who asks" (παντὶ τῷ αἰτοῦντι). Since private accusations can also result in formal court proceedings as is shown in Pliny's letters (*Ep.*10.96–97) and the term ἀπολογία can also refer to the defence in a legal action (cf. Acts 25:16; Phil 1:7, 16 and 2 Tim 4:16), it is probable that the author is not excluding the possibility of the readers having to make defence in formal judicial inquiries.

129. Schrenk, "δικαιοσύνη," *TDNT* 2:196.

Thus, in Tobit (e.g. 4:5; 13:8; 14:7), δικαιοσύνη is understood as the ideal way of life of the Jewish Diaspora appropriate for their special relationship with God.[130] Likewise, in LXX Ezekiel 18:5–24 and 33:12–20, it is righteousness in the conduct of the exilic people that enables them to survive God's judgment. Christians' persistence in righteousness in accordance with God's will is therefore also viewed in 1 Peter as the seemly demonstration of their piety to God as his elect exilic people during their sojourn on earth.

Furthermore, immediately following the assurance of God's vindication of the suffering righteous in 3:10–12 with the quotation of LXX Psalm 33:16–17a, the passage of 1 Peter 3:13–17 also presents the vindication of the Christian righteous in terms of the eschatological hope of vindication of the Jewish Diaspora. The blessedness expected by Christian sufferers (μακάριοι, 3:14) is something to be fully realized at the final day of judgment when those who revile them now will be put to shame (καταισχυνθῶσιν, 3:16). The promise of eschatological blessing for the suffering righteous is also present in the exilic Jewish literature. For example, in 4 Macc. 7:22, it is blessed (μακάριον) to endure every pain for the sake of moral excellence, which blessing is regarded as transcending death (7:19).

Particularly pertinent to the Petrine vision of the eschatological blessing for Christian righteous sufferers is Wis 5:1–2 which states that "Then the righteous man will stand with great boldness in the presence of those who have oppressed him" (τότε στήσεται ἐν παρρησίᾳ πολλῇ ὁ δίκαιος κατὰ πρόσωπον τῶν θλιψάντων αὐτόν) and that the unrighteous "will be troubled with terrible fear, and they will be amazed at the wonder of the salvation" (ταραχθήσονται φόβῳ δεινῷ καὶ ἐκστήσονται ἐπὶ τῷ παραδόξῳ τῆς σωτηρίας) of the righteous. It is precisely against this theological backdrop of the hope for an eschatological reversal of fortune that the Christian righteous are pronounced as being blessed (3:14), and their oppressors may be "put to shame" (3:16), and that it is better (κρεῖττον) to suffer for doing good (ἀγαθοποιοῦντας) *now* than to suffer for doing evil (κακοποιοῦντας) *at the end time* (3:17).[131]

---

130. See also *Let. Aris.* 141–171.

131. I agree with scholars such as Michaels, *1 Peter*, 191–192; Jobes, *1 Peter*, 232; Green, *1 Peter*, 113–115 who understand κρεῖττον in 3:17 to mean "better at eschaton"

Therefore, although Christians enduring suffering without retaliation and subversion necessarily involves certain accommodation to the existing societal order, "good works" are still perceived in this unit as the means of expressing Christians' unique identity as the continuing elect exiles of Diaspora by living out the highest ideal of righteousness, and their unique eschatological hope of vindication inherited from the Jewish Diaspora.

On the other hand, Jewish visions are again understood afresh to take into account the historical appearance of Jesus Christ. Since Christians living for righteousness is made possible by Christ suffering for righteousness himself (2:24), Christians are to sanctify Christ as Lord (3:15). Quoting from τὸν δὲ φόβον αὐτοῦ οὐ μὴ φοβηθῆτε οὐδὲ μὴ ταραχθῆτε κύριον αὐτὸν ἁγιάσατε in LXX Isaiah 8:12b–13a, τὸν δὲ φόβον αὐτῶν μὴ φοβηθῆτε μηδὲ ταραχθῆτε, κύριον δὲ τὸν Χριστὸν ἁγιάσατε ἐν ταῖς καρδίαις ὑμῶν in 1 Peter 3:14b–15a notably introduces a christological overtone by inserting τὸν Χριστόν.[132] While God is the object of sanctification by the people of Israel in the Isaianic text, it is now Christ who is to be sanctified by the Christian people of God. The relationship between the holy God and the people of Israel in the OT is now drawn upon and appropriated to the relationship between the Christ-Messiah and the Christian continuing exilic people of God.

Moreover, this quotation from Isaiah 8 recalls 1 Peter 2:4–10 in which another verse of Isaiah 8; namely, 8:14 is alluded to. As I discussed in the last chapter,[133] Christ is underscored in 1 Peter 2:4–10 as the elect Cornerstone of the spiritual temple of which individual Christian elect stones form part. This vivid depiction of the unity between Christ and Christians now finds concrete expression in Christians' "good conduct in Christ" (τὴν ἀγαθὴν ἐν Χριστῷ ἀναστροφήν) in 1 Peter 3:16. It is through following the steps of Christ (2:21) in doing good and enduring unmerited suffering for the sake

---

rather than to distinguish between good and bad citizenship in Roman society. Christians' eschatological blessing and reversal of fortune have been the focus of the author's discussion throughout this unit.

132. Although a majority of the later manuscripts insert θεόν for Χριστόν probably to align with Isa 8:13, the superior witness of the early manuscripts including P[72] ℵ A B C Ψ and others decisively supports the more difficult Χριστόν to be the more probable reading. So, Michaels, *1 Peter*, 183; Achtemeier, *1 Peter*, 228; Elliott, *1 Peter*, 625.

133. See pages 57–59 above.

of righteousness that Christians find close identification with the Messiah-Christ. Once again, the question for the author is not whether or how far Christians are accommodating to the pagan culture, but rather, whether Christians are faithful in expressing their identification with Christ by living out his example demonstrated on the cross. As Davids observes, for the Petrine author, "good conduct flows out of and is determined by the Christian's relationship to Christ, that is, his or her union with Christ."[134]

This connotation of ἐν Χριστῷ is actually the exegetical key to the following unit, 1 Peter 3:18–22. By understanding Christ as the model righteous sufferer, who has suffered for the sake of righteousness (δίκαιος ὑπὲρ ἀδίκων, 3:18; cf. ἵνα . . . τῇ δικαιοσύνῃ ζήσωμεν, 2:24) but now exalted before God (3:19–22), the author is providing a theological basis for Christians to be assured that no one will harm them for persisting in doing good and enduring suffering for the sake of righteousness (3:13–14), and that it is better to suffer for doing good than for doing evil (3:17).

It is now accepted by most scholars that the notion of Christ "going and proclaiming to the spirits in prison who formerly did not obey" in 1 Peter 3:19–20a probably derives from the Enoch tradition in Jewish apocalyptic literature[135] rather than the traditional connection with the doctrine of *descensus ad inferos* that Christ descended to the underworld and preached the good news of salvation between the time of his death and resurrection.[136] According to the Enoch legend, the spirits are the rebellious sons of God (fallen angels) who took human daughters as their wives (Gen 6:2) and have offspring that led humanity to sin and, thus, the flood.[137] Enoch was then sent to proclaim condemnation rather than good news to these spirits. Furthermore, in 2 *En.* 7, Enoch was "taken up" (cf. πορευθείς,

---

134. Davids, *First Epistle*, 133.

135. This view is cogently argued by William J. Dalton, *Christ's Proclamation to the Spirits: A Study of 1 Peter 3:18–4:6*, AnBib 23 (Rome: Pontifical Biblical Institute, 1965) and is more or less adopted by scholars such as Davids, *First Epistle*, 138–141; Michaels, *1 Peter*, 207–211; Achtemeier, *1 Peter*, 252–262; Richard Bauckham, "Spirits in Prison," ABD 6:177–178; Horrell, *1 Peter*, 34–35; Jobes, *1 Peter*, 242–245. See also Barnabas Lindars, "Enoch and Christology," *ExTim* 92 (1981): 295–299.

136. This view is maintained by scholars such as Beare, *First Epistle*, 172; Goppelt, *Commentary*, 255–263; Anthony Hanson, "Salvation Proclaimed, 1 Peter 318–22," *ExTim* 93 (1981/82): 100–105.

137. Gen 6:1–7; 1 *En.* 15.2–12; 106.13–17. See also e.g. 1 *En.* 6; 7; 12.4–6; 16.

3:19) to the second heaven, on which the prison of the condemned angels is located.[138] Accordingly, Christ's proclamation in 1 Peter 3:19 probably took place in the course of his ascension after resurrection, and was a proclamation of the condemnation and, thus, his victory over the disobedient powers and spirits. This declaration of victory is also consistent with 3:22 that angels, authorities, and powers are also subject to Christ.[139]

This line of interpretation actually harmonizes very well with my analysis of the coherence between the theology and social ethics in this unit. The main thrust of the Petrine notion of Christ proclaiming to the spirits is not so much the universality of Christ's salvation or the "saving effectiveness" of his suffering[140] as his ultimate exaltation after suffering for the sake of righteousness. The pattern of Christ's present victory over the source of evil following his suffering constitutes the paradigmatic basis for Christians' experience as the continuing righteous sufferers. Deriving their existence and experience "in Christ" (cf. 3:16) as their Cornerstone, the Christian elect stones are confident that their persistence in suffering actually marks the continuous defeat of the evil powers who will be decisively conquered in the final day when Christians will also be exalted following the example of Christ.

Reading 1 Peter 3:19 in this light, the reference to Noah and his family in 3:20 becomes intelligible. Closely connected with the Enoch story, the flood is now underscored as the water (δι' ὕδατος) through which Noah and his family are saved *in contrast to the destruction of their surrounding unbelieving world*.[141] Likewise, baptism, being the antitype (ἀντίτυπον, 3:21) of the flood, is accordingly the water through which Christians' deliverance *from their surrounding unbelieving world* is ensured. What must be pointed out is that just as in the Synoptic traditions in which "the days of Noah" (ἡμέραις Νῶε, 1 Pet 3:20) is given an eschatological connotation and linked to the parousia (Matt 24:37) and the days (Luke 17:26) of the messianic Son of Man, the deliverance of Christians through baptism

---

138. Cf. *1 En* 10.13; 21.6–10.

139. So Dalton, *Proclamation*, 186, 236–237; Achtemeier, *1 Peter*, 260–261; Senior, "1 Peter," 103–104; Jobes, *1 Peter*, 244.

140. Contra Goppelt, *Commentary*, 259.

141. So Dalton, *Proclamation*, 112.

is also perceived in 1 Peter as the vindication of the exilic people of God expected within the Jewish eschatological hope.

The Jewish eschatological overtone is further heightened in 3:22 where Christ is declared as now "at the right hand of God" (ἐστιν ἐν δεξιᾷ [τοῦ][142] θεοῦ). Taken from Psalm 110:1 [LXX Ps 109:1] which also received a messianic interpretation in rabbinical circles,[143] the exaltation of the resurrected Christ to the right hand of God was received by the early Christians as the sign of his messiahship.[144] This Petrine linkage of Christ's messiahship to the Noah story actually forms a coherent vision in terms of the Jewish eschatological expectation. In view of the historical appearance of the Messiah-Christ who has inaugurated the fulfilment of the eschatological hope of the exilic people of God, Christians as the continuing Diaspora are armed with the motivation to persist in doing good, knowing that their present suffering will not be in vain as their ultimate victory over evils is already underway.

We therefore witness the same conviction of the Petrine author: Christians subjecting themselves to the existing societal order and accepting suffering for holding fast to their ultimate allegiance to God is perceived as an opportunity for them to find identification in their Messiah-Christ (ἐν Χριστῷ), and to live up to their distinctive eschatological hope as the continuing elect exiles of Diaspora. The major question is still religious rather than whether Christians should be socially distinctive from the wider culture.

3.4.3 Do Not Accomplish the Will of the Gentiles (4:1–6)

In 4:1–6, the reason for Christians' estrangement in society comes to the surface. Christians become exiles and resident-aliens (1:1, 17; 2:11) in society because they have converted to live for "God's will" (θελήματι θεοῦ, 4:2). Having abandoned their former unbelieving idolatrous way of life,

---

142. Elliott, *1 Peter*, 682 n. 341 is probably correct to observe that the absence of the definite article for θεοῦ in manuscripts such as ℵ* B Ψ is due to haplography. The manuscripts having the article include P⁷² ℵ² A C P and others. Contra Michaels, *1 Peter*, 196.

143. For example, it is stated in Midr. Ps 18 § 29 (79ᵃ), "In the future, God will let the king, the Messiah, sit at his right, as Ps 110:1 states, 'Saying of Yahweh to my Lord: Sit at my right'" (Str-B 4:457).

144. Lindars, "Enoch," 298.

they are no longer sharing the same lifestyle as their neighbours, which is featured as "the will of the Gentiles" (τὸ βούλημα τῶν ἐθνῶν, 4:3). As a result, their neighbours are surprised (ξενίζονται) that Christians "no longer go with (them) in the same excess of dissipation" (μὴ συντρεχόντων . . . εἰς τὴν αὐτὴν τῆς ἀσωτίας ἀνάχυσιν, 4:4) which results in pagan slanders and hostility against Christians. It is immediately noticeable that good works in this unit involve a certain tension with the customs of the wider society.

At the same time, it must also be stressed that the author's teaching by no means represents total resistance to the wider culture. As I have been arguing, although the Petrine exhortation unavoidably involves difference from the wider world, the separation that the author emphasizes is not so much synchronically from the wider culture, as diachronically from Christians' former way of life (ὁ παρεληλυθὼς χρόνος, 4:3), which distinguishes believers from non-believing ones (cf. τοῖς πιστεύουσιν, ἀπιστοῦσιν δέ, 2:7). The difference that concerns the author is once again religious rather than social. This observation is supported by 4:2 in which Christians are exhorted not to live for the "cravings of human beings" (ἀνθρώπων ἐπιθυμίαις) any longer. Ἀνθρώπων ἐπιθυμίαις recalls ταῖς πρότερον ἐν τῇ ἀγνοίᾳ ὑμῶν ἐπιθυμίαις in 1:14 and τῶν σαρκικῶν ἐπιθυμιῶν in 2:11, and should be interpreted in similar vein as the cravings that can pervert Christians from salvation and belonging to God.[145] Ἀνθρώπων ἐπιθυμίαις are thus the character traits that mark unbelievers as such and thus parallel to the will of "the Gentiles" (τῶν ἐθνῶν, 4:3; cf. τοῖς ἔθνεσιν, 2:12), that is, those who are antithetical to Christians as the elect people of God. Therefore, what Christians should renounce is not everything from the wider culture, but those norms and practices that have religious implications and, thus, jeopardize their entitlement to be the people of God, e.g. idolatry, imperial cults and any festivals and activities that may vitiate their exclusive worship to God. "Differentiated resistance" is still the theme of the Petrine social behavioural instructions.

Indeed, an overlap between the Petrine social ethics and those of the wider world is actually reflected in the vice list in 4:3b. It has been observed by scholars that the literary form of a vice list can also be found

---

145. See pages 25–26, 77 above.

in contemporary Greco-Roman moral teachings. As Schweizer observes: "Lists of vices and house-tables are traditional patterns of the Jewish and heathen world in the first century AD. The New Testament took them up, selecting and reshaping, but basically accepting them."[146]

A similar observation also applies to the individual vices on the Petrine list. The combination of ἀσέλγεια (licentiousness, immorality) and ἐπιθυμία (craving) likely points to excessive sexual indulgence[147] while οἰνοφλυγία (drunkenness), κῶμος (revel) and πότος (drinking party) can also be summed up as excessive drinking and feasting. This kind of condemnation of lack of self-control, excessive sexual lusts and drunkenness is also present in Greco-Roman moral teachings. Particularly pertinent to our discussion is Plutarch, *Mor.* 12B, in which items in a similar list of "unlimited gluttony, theft of parents' money, gambling, revels (κῶμοι), drinking-bouts (πότοι), love affairs with young girls, and corruption of married women" are regarded as "iniquities of early manhood" and "often monstrous and wicked"[148] Likewise, Seneca also comments, "Drunkenness inflames and lays bare every vice, stripping away the reserve that acts as a check on wrong endeavour" (*Ep.* 83.19).[149] Therefore, the Petrine behavioural instructions may not be so "different" from the pagan culture as scholars frequently emphasize although Christians' insistence on living out the best of current moral ideals and even outdo the pagans in fulfilling these ideals, may also be a cause of ostracism from their neighbours.

The real difference that the author wants Christians to make from the wider world is in fact underlined by his addition of ἀθεμίτοις εἰδωλολατρίαις (lawless idolatries) as the last item to his vice list. This notion of idolatry is hardly found in the pagan contemporary literature nor will the pagan polytheistic culture regard any religion as idolatry.[150] To abstain from

---

146. E. Schweizer, "Traditional Ethical Patterns in the Pauline and Post-Pauline Letters and Their Development (Lists of Vices and House-Tables)," in *Text and Interpretation: Studies in the New Testament Presented to Matthew Black*, eds. Ernest Best and Robert McLachlan Wilson (Cambridge: Cambridge University Press, 1979), 207.

147. So, Michaels, *1 Peter*, 231.

148. Babbitt, LCL.

149. Translation provided in Seneca, *Seneca's Letters to Lucilius*, vol. 2, 2 vols., trans. Edward Phillips Barker (Oxford: Clarendon, 1932), 24.

150. Achtemeier, *1 Peter*, 282.

idolatry and maintain their exclusive worship of God is what truly marks Christians from the rest of society and from their pre-conversion state as Gentiles. Indeed, as scholars recognize,[151] pagan idolatrous cults were often connected with sexual immoralities, feastings and drinking parties as represented by the other items of the Petrine vice list.[152] As Tertullian mocks the activities of imperial festivals, "it is a splendid ceremony . . . to dine in the streets, to make the city smell like a tavern, to make mud with their wine, to chase around in bands in order to commit crimes, effrontery, and the seductive pleasures of lust" (*Apol.* 35.2).[153]

It is here that "differentiated resistance" of the Petrine social ethics is at work. The Petrine author's real concern is still Christians' "religious difference" rather than their maintaining a socially distinctive lifestyle just for sake of being different.

At the same time, it has to be stressed that Christians' religious difference was not just a matter of internal piety, but had to be translated into concrete social behaviour in the Greco-Roman world in which, social concord was regarded as of paramount importance and religious activities actually constituted a dominant part of people's social life. As Wilken asserts, "Piety toward the gods was thought to insure the well-being of the city, to promote a spirit of kinship and mutual responsibility, indeed, to bind together the citizenry."[154]

For example, according to Tacitus, the rebuilding of the temple was an event that involved different strata of the society, including "the magistrates, the priests, senators, knights, and a great part of the people."[155] Likewise, Cicero also asserts that, "the disappearance of piety towards the

---

151. Selwyn, *First Epistle*, 211; Michaels, *1 Peter*, 232; Davids, *First Epistle*, 151; Elliott, *1 Peter*, 724.

152. See also Wis 14:12–27; 1 Cor 8:7–10; 10:14–22.

153. Translation provided in Tertullian and Minucius Felix, *Tertullian Apologetical Works and Minucius Felix Octavius*, trans. Rudolph Arbesmann et al. FC 10 (Washington, DC: Catholic University of America Press, 1950), 91.

154. Robert L. Wilken, *The Christians as the Romans Saw Them* (New Haven, CT: Yale University Press, 1984), 58.

155. Tacitus, *Hist.* 4.53 (Moore, LCL).

gods will entail the disappearance of loyalty and social union among men as well, and of justice itself, the queen of all the virtues."[156]

On the other hand, Christians' abstention from idolatry and pagan cults actually involved a wide range of activities as complained by their critics:

> [Y]ou do not frequent the theatres; you do not take part in the processions; the public banquets are held without you; you shun the sacred games, the viands set apart for the altars and the drinks poured in libation upon them.[157]

Particularly in view of the fact that their polytheistic neighbours were accustomed to be tolerant with the other religions, the intolerant Christians actually appeared out of place in a tolerant society,[158] and could only be regarded as a socially deviant group having the reputation of "being atheists"[159] and "hating the human race"[160] in the eyes of pagans.

In addition, the pagan gods were thought to bring advantage to the citizens.[161] Trivial details of religious ceremonies (such as the feeding of the sacred chickens and the taking note of the ill-omened cry of a bird) were regarded as relevant to bring about the well-being and success of the Roman Republic.[162] Christians' refusal to reverence the pagan gods could only be viewed as injuring the goodwill of the gods and jeopardizing the harmonious relationship between gods and human beings.[163] As Tertullian complains, "they consider that the Christians are the cause of every public calamity and every misfortune of the people" (*Apol.* 40.1).[164]

Furthermore, Christians' renunciation of idolatry also brought about economic consequences. As exemplified by the account in Acts 19:23–40

---

156. Cicero, *Nat. d.* 1.2.4 (Rackham, LCL).

157. Minucius Felix, *Oct.* 12.5. Translation provided in Tertullian and Felix, *Apologetical Works*, 342.

158. Walter Woodburn Hyde, *Paganism to Christianity in the Roman Empire* (New York: Octagon Books, 1970), 102.

159. E.g. Minucius Felix, *Oct.* 8.2; *Mart. Pol.* 9.2.

160. E.g. Tacitus, *Ann.* 15.44.

161. Cf. Augustine, *Civ.* 3.4.

162. Livy, 6.41.8 (Foster, LCL). See Wilken, *Christians*, 59.

163. G. E. M. de Ste. Croix, "Why Were the Early Christians Persecuted?" *Past & Present* 26 (1963): 24.

164. Translation provided in Tertullian and Felix, *Apologetical Works*, 102.

of the city mob in Ephesus, Christians' missionary activities were viewed as a serious threat to the livelihood of a significant portion of the population whose trades and professions were related to the pagan cults. This account was further attested by Pliny's letter that the spread of Christianity in Pontus and Bithynia led to the desertion of the temples, interruption of the sacred festivals and drop in sales of sacrificial animals (*Ep.* 10.96).

Therefore, abstention from idolatry was actually the primary cause of pagan hostility and alienation that rendered Christians strangers and resident-aliens on earth. As Tertullian testifies:

> "You do not worship the gods," you say, "and you do not offer sacrifice for the emperors." . . . Consequently, we are considered guilty of sacrilege and treason. This is the chief accusation against us – in fact, it is the whole case . . ." (*Apol.* 10.1).[165]

It is precisely against this background that the Petrine author exhorts Christians not to accomplish the will of the Gentiles (τὸ βούλημα τῶν ἐθνῶν, 4:3), and which accounts for his primary concern for Christians to stand firm in God's grace/salvation.

It is noteworthy that the christological-ecclesiological and eschatological bases of Christian good works appeared in the preceding units applies once again to the author's exhortation in this unit. Following the reflection of Christians suffering "in Christ" in 3:18–22, Christians' solidarity with Christ is now understood as "arming" (ὁπλίσασθε) with "the same thought" (τὴν αὐτὴν ἔννοιαν, 4:1) of Christ (i.e. sharing his mindset and worldview). The insight Christians derive from the cross (i.e. Christ's enduring suffering in the flesh unto death [θανατωθεὶς . . . σαρκί, 3:18]) and subsequent conquering of evils "in His spiritual mode of existence, as spirit"[166] (πνεύματι, 3:18; ἐν ᾧ, 3:19), leads Christians to conclude that their present suffering in the flesh (ὁ παθὼν σαρκί, 4:1) in fact denotes a similar victory over evils, as signified by their having nothing more to do with sin (πέπαυται ἁμαρτίας, 4:1). It is precisely this perception of sharing Christ's victory over sin that empowers the readers to persist in doing good through differentiated

---

165. Ibid., 35.
166. Kelly, *Commentary*, 152. Also Davids, *First Epistle*, 138.

resistance, even if it means continuous alienation and abuse from the pagan neighbours.

Furthermore, Christians sharing the thought of Christ, who entrusted himself to God the righteous judge (2:23), means that they can also count on God's judgment which is at the doorstep (ἑτοίμως, 4:5) although the author at the same time reveals the necessity for Christians to stay in their earthly life for a certain period of time (τὸν ἐπίλοιπον ἐν σαρκὶ . . . χρόνον, 4:2). Christians' expected reversal of fortune, which is subtly pronounced as their abusers "being put to shame" (καταισχυνθῶσιν) and Christians finding themselves "better off" (κρεῖττον) than their opponents in 3:16–17, is now concretized as God's universal judgment of both the living and the dead (κρῖναι ζῶντας καὶ νεκρούς, 4:5) at the eschaton when their abusers will have to give an account (λόγον, 4:5; cf. 3:15) to God.

This reversal of fortune Christians expect at God's final judgment actually provides a befitting lens through which to understand the Petrine notion of "the gospel having been preached to the dead" (νεκροῖς εὐηγγελίσθη, 4:6). The author's focus is not so much on the universal proclamation of Christ's gospel as God's universal judgment even to the dead.[167] Νεκροί in 4:6 are thus those Christian righteous sufferers who have died before the final time of visitation.[168] Whereas death may be viewed by their abusers as condemnation in the human existence of the flesh (κριθῶσι . . . σαρκί), Christians having received the gospel and persisted in doing good are assured of the same experience as Christ of living in spiritual existence (ζῶσι . . . πνεύματι, cf. θανατωθεὶς . . . σαρκὶ ζωοποιηθεὶς . . . πνεύματι, 3:18) in the Day of God's judgment.

This vision of the vindication of the righteous dead is also present in the Jewish exilic worldview and aptly applied by the Petrine author to the Christian continuing Diaspora. In Wis 3:2–5, the righteous,

> seemed to have died in the eyes of the foolish, and their departure was taken to be a disaster . . . but they are in peace. For though they be punished in the sight of human beings, their

---

167. Contra Beare, *First Epistle*, 182; Goppelt, *Commentary*, 289, 291.
168. So Dalton, *Proclamation*, 14, 49–51, 270–277. Also Senior, "1 Peter," 116, 118; Achtemeier, *1 Peter*, 290; Davids, *First Epistle*, 154–155.

hope is full of immortality. Having been disciplined a little, they will receive great benefit because God tested them and found them worthy of himself.

It is against this expectation of the vindication of the righteous dead that the Christian righteous sufferers, though abused for doing good and even having died before God's final visitation, are assured of receiving favourable final judgment as expected within Jewish eschatological vision.

Section Summary

In this section on Christians' engagement in daily social life, "differentiated resistance" remains the theme of good works, whether in terms of non-retaliation, enduring suffering for the sake of righteousness or refusal to accomplish the will of the Gentiles. The real concern of the author is still Christians' resistance to any practices or activities with pagan idolatrous connotations that may jeopardize their remaining in God's grace/salvation. Subject to the overriding boundary of ultimate allegiance to God, the author's exhortations virtually render Christians ideal citizens complying with the current moral ideals even better than their pagan neighbours.

On the other hand, Jewish ideals and eschatological visions are also freshly understood by the Petrine author in the light of Christ the Messiah. Besides signalling the inauguration of the Messianic Age and, thus, the vindication for the Christian Diaspora, Christ is also viewed as having fulfilled the Jewish ideal of righteous suffering and seeking peace without returning abuses. Christians following Christ's steps in doing good and enduring suffering is therefore understood as *both* fulfilling the ideal of the elect exiles of Diaspora, *and* manifesting their close-knit unity with Christ as their Cornerstone (ἐν Χριστῷ, 3:16).

It is noticeable that the author's differentiated treatments of Christians' engagement with the ruling authorities and with their neighbours at provincial level become apparent. Whereas Christians are to retain comparatively normal relations with the ruling authorities, and keep their differentiated loyalty to God and the emperor subtle (2:13–17), they are now blatantly exhorted to defend their faith (3:15–16), armed with the same mindset of Christ not to go with the way of the Gentiles (4:1–3), and to endure suffering for it. Since the primary source of hostility and pressure comes from their neighbours (4:4), Christians are in essence exhorted to concentrate their effort on resisting their neighbours' demand so as to stand firm in God's grace (5:12). Their religious faith is still the primary concern of the author.

3.5 Christian Engagement in Suffering for the Name of Christ (4:12–4:19)

Immediately following the doxology in 4:11, 1 Peter 4:12–19 introduces the last section (4:12–5:11) of the body of the whole letter. This passage 1 Peter 4:12–19 therefore does not form part of the exhortation section of 2:11–4:11 in terms of literary structure. This section division is supported by the address ἀγαπητοί which is also the introductory address in 2:11. However, I include this unit in my discussion because it recapitulates most of the themes that the author has discussed, and indeed develops them to the full.

Indeed, the core reason for Christians' alienation, and the author's real concern, is now finally and unambiguously unveiled as Christians suffering "as a Christian" (ὡς Χριστιανός, 4:16; cf. ἐν ὀνόματι Χριστοῦ, 4:14). As commonly agreed by scholars, "Christian" was not a self-designation, but a title conferred with contempt by unbelieving contemporaries to denote Christians belonging to the faith of Christ. This is evidenced by Tacitus' description of Christians as "a class of men ... whom the crowd styled Christians."[169] The fact that Christians were persecuted not because of any specific wrongdoings, but merely for the name "Christian," is frequently complained of in early Christian writings.[170] Pliny's Letters further betray that bearing the name of "Christian" alone was sufficient for Christians to be executed by the official authorities (*Ep.*10. 96–7). The label "Christian" (Χριστιανός, 4:16) is therefore a social stigma that marks Christians out from the rest of society.[171]

---

169. Tacitus, *Ann.* 15.44 (Jackson, LCL).
170. Tertullian, *Apol.* 1–3; Justin, *1 Apol.* 4; *Mart. Pol.* 12.1.
171. Cf. David G. Horrell, "The Label Χριστιανός: 1 Peter 4:16 and the Formation of Christian Identity," *JBL* 126 (2007): 376–378.

Hence, we once again witness the author's strategy of "differentiated resistance" at work. When facing persecutions, Christians may be under pressure to deny their name. As Pliny's reports:

> Those who denied they were, or had ever been, Christians, who repeated after me an invocation to the Gods, and offered adoration, with wine and frankincense, to your image, which I had ordered to be brought for that purpose, together with those of the Gods, and who finally cursed Christ . . . these I thought it proper to discharge.[172]

However, the author asserts that if one suffers as a Christian, "let him not be ashamed, but glorify God in this name" (μὴ αἰσχυνέσθω, δοξαζέτω δὲ τὸν θεὸν ἐν τῷ ὀνόματι[173] τούτῳ, 4:16). This resistance is no longer "soft" or subtle, but "hard" and definite. Christians' unyielding resistance to pagan pressure to renounce their allegiance to God/Christ and, thus, enduring suffering is once again understood with cultic connotations as offering spiritual sacrifices (2:5) and proclaiming the excellencies of God (2:9) by "glorifying" him as the spiritual temple and holy priesthood (cf. 2:12, δοξάσωσιν).

Subject to this overriding boundary of ultimate allegiance to God, the Petrine author once again has no problem exhorting his readers to follow the current societal order – "let none of you suffer as a murderer, or a thief, or an evildoer, or as a meddler" (μὴ . . . τις ὑμῶν πασχέτω ὡς φονεὺς ἢ κλέπτης ἢ κακοποιὸς ἢ ὡς ἀλλοτριεπίσκοπος,[174] 4:15).[175] Therefore, doing good (ἀγαθοποιΐᾳ, 4:19) in this unit is having the same form of "differentiated difference" as in other units. In so far as they are not required to overstep the overriding boundary of ultimate allegiance to God, Christians

---

172. Pliny, *Ep.* 10.96 (Melmoth, LCL).

173. Although the majority of the later manuscripts (including P 049) read μέρει (with regard to, in the matter of) instead of ὀνόματι, the superior witness of the best manuscripts including P72 ℵ A B Ψ 33, 323 and others renders the reading of ὀνόματι the much more probable one. So, Achtemeier, *1 Peter*, 303–304; Kelly, *Commentary*, 191.

174. For the idea that ἀλλοτριεπίσκοπος refers to an inappropriate movement outside one's assigned role in subversion to the fabric of society, see Jeannine K. Brown, "Just a Busybody? A Look at the Greco-Roman Topos of Meddling for Defining ἀλλοτριεπίσκοπος in 1 Peter 4:15," *JBL* 3 (2006): 549–568.

175. See also Horrell, *1 Peter*, 83–84.

are to remain as ideal citizens and comply with societal norms and order, even if this means submitting to unjust suffering in accordance with common expectations.

At the same time, the solidarity with Christ that Christians experience from their suffering is most fully encompassed in this unit. Deriving their name from Christ (cf. 4:14), Christians suffering for their name is now underscored as participating in the sufferings of Christ (κοινωνεῖτε τοῖς τοῦ Χριστοῦ παθήμασιν, 4:13), that is, bound with Christ in what he himself underwent. It is just because of this mystical union with their Messiah-Christ that Christians should rejoice (χαίρετε, 4:13). This joy is enduring until its perfection (χαρῆτε ἀγαλλιώμενοι) at the eschaton when Christ's glory is revealed (ἐν τῇ ἀποκαλύψει τῆς δόξης αὐτοῦ, 4:13; cf. 1:5–6) and when Christians become also the partakers of his glory (ὁ . . . τῆς μελλούσης ἀποκαλύπτεσθαι δόξης κοινωνός, 5:1). This union with Christ, both in his suffering and his glory, is the most pertinent implication of the Petrine image of the Christian spiritual temple grounded on the Christ-Cornerstone.

Furthermore, this eschatological glory for Christians is once again envisioned in terms of the realization of the final vindication of the people of God as expected within the Jewish eschatological vison. The Jewish conception that "a period of special distress and affliction must precede the dawn of salvation"[176] is also alluded to in other NT writings.[177] This period, often referred to by scholars as the "Messianic Woes," is likely to be the background of 1 Peter 4:12,[178] so that the readers are exhorted not to be surprised by the fiery ordeal (πυρώσει) that comes for testing (πειρασμόν) them.[179]

On the other hand, while the Messianic Woes are perceived within the Jewish vision *as a prelude* to the revelation of the Messiah, who will gather

---

176. Schürer, *History*, vol. 2, 514. See e.g. Dan 7:21–22; 12:1; Joel 3:3–5; *Jub.* 23.22–31; 2 *Bar.* 70.

177. E.g. Matt 24:6–31; Mark 13:7–27; Rev 7:14.

178. For a comprehensive discussion of the motif of the Messianic Woes in 1 Pet 4:12–19, see Dubis, *Messianic Woes*. Also Best, *1 Peter*, 162–163; Martin, *Metaphor*, 245–248.

179. For the Jewish perception of suffering as testing (πειρασμός, πειράζω) through fire so that the people of God are to be approved (δοκιμάζω; cf. 1 Pet 1:7) by God, see e.g. LXX Ps 65:10 (MT 66:10); Wis 3:5–6; Sir 2:1–5; Jdt 8:25–27.

the elect people of God and put an end to their exile,[180] the Christian Diaspora derives their social alienation *from* Jesus Christ the Messiah who himself was rejected and suffered as a resident-alien in essence. The Messianic Woes are for Christians during the present in-between period in which they suffer in union with Christ (4:13), while awaiting their final salvation (1:4–5) and restoration at the second coming of Christ.

This reshaping of the Jewish eschatological vision is further witnessed in 4:14. The eschatological blessing (μακάριοι) available for Christians, for being insulted for the name of Christ, is here perceived as the resting of God's Spirit of Glory (τὸ τῆς δόξης καὶ τὸ τοῦ θεοῦ πνεῦμα ἐφ' ὑμᾶς ἀναπαύεται) on them. It is commonly recognized that this image of the resting of God's Spirit owes its background to ἀναπαύσεται ἐπ' αὐτὸν πνεῦμα τοῦ θεοῦ of LXX Isaiah 11:2. Whereas Isaiah 11:2 envisions the Spirit of God as resting on an individual figure who is understood as the Messiah in other NT writings,[181] it is now applied in 1 Peter 4:14 corporately to the whole Christian exilic people *as the spiritual temple* grounded on Christ the Cornerstone. The present resting of God's Spirit of Glory becomes the basis of Christians' assurance of their future partaking in Christ's glory at his second coming (5:1).

This image of the Christian Diaspora as the spiritual temple continues to dominate in 1 Peter 4:17. Here, the final judgment is said to begin with the house of God (τοῦ ἄρξασθαι τὸ κρίμα ἀπὸ τοῦ οἴκου τοῦ θεοῦ). Although other OT backgrounds have been suggested,[182] the verbal resonance of καὶ <u>ἀπὸ τῶν ἁγίων μου ἄρξασθε</u> καὶ <u>ἤρξαντο ἀπὸ</u> τῶν ἀνδρῶν τῶν πρεσβυτέρων οἳ ἦσαν ἔσω <u>ἐν τῷ οἴκῳ</u> in LXX Ezekiel 9:6 can hardly go unnoticed.[183] Particularly pertinent to our discussion is that while in the context of Ezekiel 9, the Shekinah is said to be *withdrawn* from the temple when the judgment begins (9:3), God's Spirit of Glory is now said *to rest on* the Christian temple community (1 Pet 4:14). Instead of being deprived

---

180. E.g. *4 Ezra* 13.29–32; *Pss. Sol.* 17.11–25; *2 Bar.* 70.

181. E.g. Matt 3:16; John 1:32.

182. LXX Jer 32:29 (MT 25:29); Mal 3:1–5, 19. For the reasons provided by scholars, see Dubis, *Messianic Woes*, 150–4.

183. Also Dubis, *Messianic Woes*, 153; Schutter, *Hermeneutic*, 156–164; Michaels, *1 Peter*, 271.

of God's presence and, thus, doomed as in the Ezekiel text, the Christian spiritual temple is now viewed as privileged with God's glorious presence and, thus, assured of their ultimate salvation. Their suffering is no more than the first act of the drama of God's final judgment so that they entrust their souls to God (πιστῷ κτίστῃ παρατιθέσθωσαν τὰς ψυχὰς αὐτῶν, 4:19) following the step of Christ (cf. παρεδίδου . . . τῷ κρίνοντι δικαίως, 2:23), knowing that the reversal of fortune that Christians expect with their abusers (4:17–18) is already underway.

Section Summary

In this section, the author's social strategy of "differentiated resistance" is once again shown as derived from his theological conviction. Christians are to persevere in keeping their name even though it means suffering for the name of Christ. It is here that Christians' resistance is to be hard and unyielding; otherwise, they are in effect the best law-abiding citizens in society.

Although from an outsider point of view, the label "Christians" is a social stigma and carries shame with it, suffering for this name becomes a sign of blessedness and a reason for joy from the insider point of view of the author's religious convictions. Christians suffering for the name of Christ is no more than an expression of their solidarity and closeness with Christ, which is now intensified as a mystical union with him in his suffering and glory. At the same time, the eschatological expectation of the Jewish Diaspora remains the background of the theological basis of the Petrine social ethics and indeed, continues to be reshaped in the light of the historical appearance of Jesus Christ and his relationship with the Christian spiritual temple.

3.6 Chapter Conclusion

In this chapter, I sought an empathic understanding of the Petrine text by investigating the author's instructions on Christians' social engagement from an insider's viewpoint of his theological convictions and, especially, his christoloigcal-ecclesiological and eschatological visions. Instead of asking whether the Petrine social ethics are "identity maintaining" or "accommodating," this approach serves to answer the questions of "when" and "to what" Christians are exhorted to resist in the face of pagan pressure to accommodate to the wider idolatrous culture. I demonstrated that the overriding shape of the Petrine "good works" is "differentiated resistance."

The distance which the author wishes Christians to maintain is not just for the sake of being socially distinctive *per se*. His real concern is rather Christians' steadfastness in their exclusive faith and allegiance to God. In so far as they are not required to get involved in activities and practices that may jeopardize their standing in God's grace/salvation, such as idolatry, Christians are actually the best citizens, seeking peace and complying with current societal order, even at the expense of submitting to unmerited sufferings in accordance with common expectations. This aspect of accommodation is not just for the practical purpose of survival *for its own sake* but, rather, is borne out of the religious concern to silence the slanders of Gentiles (2:15), cause them to glorify God at eschaton (2:12; cf. 4:16), and even win them to Christ (3:1).

Although Christians' refusal to participate in a substantial part of the pagan social life may be regarded by outsiders as sectarian, the Petrine author himself actually does not regard Christians as a closed community. Christians remaining in the current socio-political system, and in continuous engagement with the pagan world, is just part of their offering spiritual sacrifices and proclaiming the praise of God (2:5, 9). More positive relations with the pagan neighbours also serve to gain room for Christians to uphold their exclusive allegiance to God. An investigation of the Petrine social strategies from the perspective of the author's religious conviction, therefore, serves to avoid posing questions on the text which are actually not the author's primary concern or which he is not addressing.

In addition, by following the author's own concern as expressed in the text, I demonstrated that the Petrine theology is not merely "functional" in providing a rationale to serve the author's paranetic purpose. The reverse is the case, that Christians' "good works," with their elements of both "resistance" and "accommodation," are perceived as the congruent behavioural expression of their self-understanding as the continuing elect exiles of the Diaspora, as well as a token of their finding solidarity with the Messiah-Christ as their Cornerstone.

The elements of Greco-Roman values and practices within the Petrine "good works" are merely what the author understands as what Jesus Christ demonstrated on the cross in submitting to societal order for a higher purpose of accomplishing the salvation plan of God. On the other hand, exilic Jewish visions are also reshaped and reinterpreted from a Christian perspective to take into account the historical appearance of the Messiah-Christ and the new existence of Christians as the new people of God, so that "good works" are now securely anchored to the eschatological visions of the exilic people of Diaspora.

Therefore, the reference point for understanding the Petrine social strategy is designated by the Petrine author himself when he addresses Christians as "elect exiles of Diaspora" (1:1). Through this theological self-understanding of Christian existence on earth as the continuing elect people of Diaspora, the experience of Jewish elect exiles of Diaspora in negotiating their social existence also becomes the frame of reference that inspires the Petrine behavioural instructions. The strategy of "differentiated resistance" adopted by the exilic Jewish Diaspora in a similar socio-political milieu is therefore also the pertinent resource and an "entrance to understand imaginatively"[184] the dynamics within the Petrine teachings. This is what I am going to engage in the next chapter.

---

184. See pages 8–9 in chapter 1.

CHAPTER 4

The Jewish Elect Exiles of Diaspora

In my exegetical study of the Petrine social behavioural instructions in the last chapter, I demonstrated that "differentiated resistance" represents the form of Christian "good works" in 1 Peter. In so far as Christians are not required to participate in pagan customs and practices that may have religious implications, Christians are in essence exhorted to be the ideal citizens seeking peace and complying with societal order in accordance with current social expectations. This mode of "good works" is perceived by the author as the congruent expression of Christians' identity as the continuing "elect exiles of Diaspora," and a token of their solidarity with Christ by following his steps as exemplified by the cross.

I also argued in the last chapter that although the Petrine social behavioural instructions are grounded on the Jewish eschatological hope inherited by Christians as the continuing exilic people of God, Jewish eschatological visions and images are understood afresh in the light of Jesus Christ. Besides sharing the same hope of ultimate vindication with the Jewish Diaspora, Christians' present suffering for doing good and future glory are respectively understood as participating in Christ's suffering and partaking in his glory. This mystical union of Christians with Christ is further derived from the author's vision of the Christians as a spiritual temple deriving its existence and experience from those of their Christ-Cornerstone.

In this chapter, I will conduct a historical study on the strategies of Diaspora Jewish social engagement in the Gentile world as an entrance to gain a concrete understanding of the Petrine "good works" of "differentiated resistance" with reference to the Jewish experience. As I mentioned in chapter 2, διασπορά is a "technical term" in the LXX for the Jews living outside Palestine among the Gentiles.¹ By understanding his Christian readers as the continuing "elect exiles of Diaspora" (1 Pet 1:1) and indeed, perceiving their identity in terms of the honorific titles and self-definitions specifically applied to the people of Israel in the OT (e.g. 2:9–10), the Petrine author is also positing the Diaspora Jewish social engagement as the frame of reference with which his social ethics should be understood. As Achtemeier asserts, "In 1 Peter, the language and hence the reality of Israel pass without remainder into the language and hence the reality of the new people of God,"[2] although Achtemeier's observation must be qualified in that it is not the reality of "Israel in general" but, specifically, "the exilic Jewish Diaspora" that is appropriated to Christians in 1 Peter.

As a matter of fact, it is commonly recognized among scholars that the Petrine author alludes to Jewish identity and experience when presenting his vision of Christian existence amidst pagan alienation. However, current Petrine scholarship generally fails to proceed to understand the Petrine social behavioural instructions with reference to Jewish strategies. Hence, although Troy Martin observes, "The author of 1 Peter took images and concepts from the Jewish Diaspora and applied them to his readers in order to describe their ontological status and their moral obligations,"[3] and whereas Michaels also concludes, "The author sees himself and his readers as a community situated in the world in much the same way the Jews are situated, and sharing with the Jews a common past,"[4] neither of them goes further to investigate specifically how these allusions to the Jewish status and experience affect the Petrine teaching on Christian social ethics, and how Jewish strategies can throw light on the tension and dynamics within the letter's social behavioural instructions.

Indeed, the Jewish Diaspora were living in a strikingly similar sociopolitical milieu to the early Christians. Being a people banished from their homeland, the Jewish exiles of Diaspora were also resident-aliens living in

---

1. See page 52 above.
2. Achtemeier, *1 Peter*, 69.
3. Martin, *Metaphor*, 148.
4. Michaels, *1 Peter*, l.

cities which were "not their own"[5] (cf. παρεπιδήμοις in 1 Pet 1:1; παροίκους καὶ παρεπιδήμους in 1 Pet 2:11). Their stay in the foreign land is also described as παροικία (cf. 1 Pet 1:17) in Diaspora Jewish literature (e.g. 3 Macc. 6:36 and 7:19).[6] However, they flourished in different parts of the Diaspora.[7] They grew to a significant number[8] and their presence was influential enough to obtain the necessary official protection to resist the pressure from their neighbours in the polis to abandon their ancestral laws.[9] At the same time, the Diaspora Jews were able to maintain their identity[10] and had their "undisguised" distinctiveness[11] noticeable by pagan intellectuals. This successful experience of the *actual* Jewish elect exiles of Diaspora is therefore a valuable resource for the Petrine author to draw on when

---

5. In his letter to the Alexandrians in 41 CE, Claudius regarded the Jews of Alexandria as living "in a city which is not their own" (ἐν ἀλλοτρίᾳ πόλει) (*CPJ*, 2, no. 153).

6. Likewise, the Jews of Rome were recorded to have been expelled from the city probably in 139 BCE (Valerius Maximus, *Facta et Dicta Memorabilia* 1.3.3), 19 CE (Josephus, *Ant.* 18.65–84; Tacitus, *Ann.* 2.85.4; Suetonius, *Tib.* 36; Cassius Dio, *Historia Romana* 57.18.5a) and 49 CE (Suetonius, *Claud.* 25.4; Acts 18:2). As David Noy, *Foreigners at Rome: Citizens and Strangers* (London: Duckworth, 2000), 258 observes, "The fact that there were three expulsions of Jews from Rome up to the time of Claudius . . . shows that they were perceived as 'foreign' at least until that date, since expulsions were only practised against groups which were in some sense foreign."

7. As recognized by scholars such as Étan Levine, "The Jews in Time and Space," in *Diaspora: Exile and the Jewish Condition*, ed. Étan Levine (New York: J. Aronson, 1983), 1. For the prosperity of Jewish communities in Asia, see Barclay, *Jews*, 266–269. The fact that Flaccus managed to confiscate more than a hundred pounds of gold from the Jewish communities in Asia Minor is indicative of the wealth enjoyed by these communities (Cicero, *Flac.* 28.68).

8. Philo asserts that the nation of Jews "is diffused throughout every continent, and over every island, so that everywhere it appears but little inferior in number to the original native population of the country" (*Legat.* 214) (Translation provided in Philo, *The Works of Philo: Complete and Unabridged*, trans. C. D. Yonge, new updated ed. [Peabody, MA: Hendrickson, 1993], 777). Similar fact was noted by pagan writers such as Strabo who observes, "This people has already made its way into every city, and it is not easy to find any place in the habitable world which has not received this nation and in which it has not made its power felt" (apud: Josephus, *Ant.* 14.115 [Marcus, LCL]). The significant size of the Jewish community in Rome was noted by Cicero despite possible exaggeration in *Flac.* 28.66. See also Philo, *Legat.* 245.

9. See also the remarks by Barclay, *Jews*, 296 that, "the Jews are noticed as a social body able to pressurize others, with perhaps religious, but also social (and political?) consequences."

10. As commonly recognized by scholars such as Carol Bakhos, "Introduction," in *Ancient Judaism in Its Hellenistic Context*, ed. Carol Bakhos (Leiden: Brill, 2005), 2; Michael Grant, *The Jews in the Roman World* (London: Phoenix Giant, 1999 [1st pub., 1973]), 18.

11. Erich S. Gruen, *Diaspora: Jews amidst Greeks and Romans* (Cambridge, MA: Harvard University Press, 2002), 6.

formulating his social ethics for the *metaphorical* Christian elect exiles of Diaspora and, thus, the appropriate lens through which the Petrine good works of "differentiated resistance" can be seen to be worked out in reality.

Furthermore, an appreciation of Diaspora Jewish experience also provides a pertinent answer to those scholars who reject the view that *both* "resistance" *and* "accommodation" can be advocated *at the same time* in the Petrine social strategy. When criticizing Talbert's proposal of *both* Christian social cohension *and* social adaptability,[12] Thurén casts doubt on whether it is plausible that "the same group is simultaneously tempted both to assimilate and to dissimilate, so that the author has to emphasize both problems in the same short letter,"[13] while Bechtler rejects the proposals of both Thurén[14] and Talbert regarding them as "overly complicated."[15] The experience of the Jewish Diaspora in reality actually betrays the need for the resident-aliens to negotiate their boundary somewhere between the two poles of total resistance and unqualified accommodation to the host culture. It also warns scholars that the real life situation is too complex to allow for unrealistically simplistic interpretations.

In the following discussion, I will firstly look into the social strategies of the Jewish Diaspora especially in the cities of Asia Minor and Rome from the late Roman Republic up to the end of the first century CE and demonstrate how these strategies are appropriated for the Christian Diaspora in 1 Peter. Evidence from the other parts of the Diaspora will be adduced when certain characteristics of the Diaspora life in Asia Minor and Rome are seen to be commonly found elsewhere. Since 1 Peter is a letter from Rome (ἐν Βαβυλῶνι, 5:13) to the Christian Diaspora in Asia Minor (1:1),[16] the experiences of the Jewish Diaspora in these areas are particularly pertinent for our investigation.[17] As in my study of the Petrine behavioural

---

12. For Talbert's proposal, see pages 69–70 above.
13. Thurén, *Rhetorical Strategy*, 37–38.
14. For Thurén's argument of "composite audience," see page 70 note 27 above.
15. Bechtler, *Following*, 117.
16. See my discussion in chapter 1 on pages 11–12 above.
17. Therefore, I am not overlooking the fact that different Jewish communities at different times and in different parts of the Diaspora may adopt different approaches to engage with the surrounding world as has been judiciously demonstrated by Barclay's *Jews in the Mediterranean Diaspora*. Since I am only focusing on the aspects of Diaspora life at

The Jewish Elect Exiles of Diaspora 125

instructions in the last chapter, I will particularly focus on the question of "where" the Jews placed the boundary of their accommodation (i.e. "when" and "to what" they resisted the pagan culture). While the real concern of the Petrine author is Christians standing fast in the grace/salvation of God and thus their "ultimate allegiance to God,"[18] this same boundary was also what the Jewish communities adhered to. Since "Jews" is an *ethnic* as well as a *religious* label for the elect people of God,[19] complying with the will of God, expressed by the observance of their ancestral laws of the Torah,[20] remained the fundamental concern of the Jewish Diaspora; otherwise, they were prepared to participate in and even adapt to the pagan culture in other aspects of life.

In the second section of this chapter, I will proceed to analyse what constitutes a "Diaspora consciousness" and how the exilic Jews in the Second Temple period understood their Diaspora existence. I will demonstrate that the dual dimensions of "a longing for the eschatological homeland" and "an existential belonging to the cities in which they settled" were always at work together when the Jewish communities formulated their Diaspora self-understanding in the foreign land. It was precisely these dual dimensions of the Diaspora consciousness that required the Jewish Diaspora to resist pagan pressure to abandon their ancestral laws of God on the one hand *and* allow a degree of normality in their day-to-day social life in the cities of their residence on the other. I will also argue that these dual dimensions of "longing" *and* "belonging" within the Diaspora consciousness are what is present in the vision of the Petrine author when he designates his Christian readers as the elect exiles of Diaspora (1:1), and which frame his instructions of "differentiated resistance" for the readers.

---

the "particular" time and place that the "Petrine author himself" probably perceived and encountered and, thus, appropriates to formulate his instructions (i.e. in Rome and Asia Minor by the end of the first century CE), some general features of the Jewish Diasporic social strategies in these particular localities and during this particular period can still be derived.

18. Please refer to my discussions in the last chapter.
19. Noy, *Foreigners*, 255.
20. Note Paul's observation of the Jews' equating "the laws" with "the will of God" in Rom 2:17–18. Philo, *Virt.* 108 also identifies the act of listening to "the divine words" as "being instructed in the will of God" (Translation provided in Philo, *Works*, trans. Yonge, 650. See also e.g. Deut 30:9–10; Ps 40:9 (LXX 39:9); 1 Esd 9:7–9.

4.1 Social Engagement of the Jewish Elect Exiles of Diaspora

Just as the Elliott-Balch debate has continued to fascinate Petrine scholarship, the question of whether or how the Jewish Diaspora accommodated to their alien environment has also attracted extensive scholarly attention. In the past, scholarship on the Jewish Diaspora tended to stress the "separatist and exclusive" characteristic of Jewish existence among the Gentiles. Hence, Grant observes, "Jewish settlers in these countries did not assimilate very extensively with the native populations, which therefore regarded them as separate, a conclusion that they themselves were happy to accept,"[21] while Tcherikover also concludes that "a form of public life was created which gave the people of Israel the strength to resist assimilation."[22]

Nowadays, scholars generally recognize the "'irreducible complexities' that both Judaism and Hellenism present in the ancient world,"[23] and that the Diaspora Jewish communities adopted *both* identity maintainence/resistance *and* accommodation as the twin themes of their social engagement.[24] However, the focus of current scholarship usually concentrates on "how assimilating or accommodating" the Jewish communities were,[25] and the conclusion one can obtain can be quite vague. Whether the relevant community is "more assimilating/accommodating" or "less assimilating/accommodating" is often a matter of individual judgment and does not tell much about the actual strategies and boundary employed by the community.

---

21. Grant, *Jews*, 18.

22. Victor Tcherikover, *Hellenistic Civilization and the Jews,* trans. Shimon Applebaum (New York: Atheneum, 1970), 297. See also E. Mary Smallwood, *The Jews under Roman Rule: From Pompey to Diocletian*, SJLA 20 (Leiden: Brill, 1976), 123–124.

23. Bakhos, "Introduction," 2.

24. E.g. Trebilco, *Jewish Communities,* 186–190; Barclay, "Introduction," 2–3; Gruen, *Diaspora*, 6; Tessa Rajak, "The Jewish Community and Its Boundaries," in *The Jews among Pagans and Christians in the Roman Empire,* eds. John A. North et al. (London: Routledge, 1992), 9–28.

25. For example, Barclay, *Jews*, 92–102 categorizes the various socio-cultural responses of a given Jewish community into a spectrum of "high, medium and low assimilation" and scales of "acculturation" and "accommodation." For a critique of Barclay's categorization, see Leonard Victor Rutgers, *The Hidden Heritage of Diaspora Judaism*, CBET 20 (Leuven: Peeters, 1998), 34–39.

Therefore, in this section, besides asking the question of *"how"* accommodating or *"how much"* assimilation, I will explore *"when"* the Jewish Diaspora, especially in Asia Minor and Rome, were prepared to embrace the culture of the host city, and *"when"* and *"to what"* they would resist the pressure to blend with the dominant culture with greatest vigour (i.e. *"where"* they placed their boundary of accommodation). "Ultimate allegiance to God" was also their boundary. It was for the sake of the higher course of complying with the will of God, expressed in terms of persistent observance of their ancestral laws, that the Diaspora Jews in these areas did their best to maintain positive interactions with the Roman authorities so that they could focus their attention to resist their neighbours' pressure to abandon their ancestral customs in the local cities. This form of "differentiated resistance" is what 1 Peter appropriates for the Christian Diaspora as their social strategy.

For the ease of comparison with the Petrine social behavioural instructions, I will discuss the Jewish strategies in relation to the following areas of their Diaspora existence; namely, their (1) civil life; (2) household life; and (3) daily social life.

4.1.1 Jewish Diaspora Engagement in Civil Life

In 1 Peter 2:13–17, the Christian Diaspora are exhorted to subject themselves to every human creature (institution) whether to the emperor or his government officials. As I argued in the last chapter, Christians discharging their commonly expected civil duties is subtly emphasized in 1 Peter as always subject to their absolute obedience to God.[26] Whereas the emperor was to be "honoured," "fear" (i.e. reverence and worship) is exclusively reserved to God (1 Pet 2:17). The experience of the Jewish Diaspora in Asia Minor and Rome is actually the concrete model of how these Petrine instructions can be practised in reality.

Since the reign of Julius Caesar in 48–44 BCE, Jews had managed to obtain noticeable favours from the Roman emperors and officials. As a token of gratitude for the support of Hyrcanus II[27] and Antipater[28] in

---

26. See pages 82–84 above.
27. Josephus, *Ant.* 14.192–193 (Marcus, LCL).
28. Ibid., 16.52–53.

his war against Egypt,[29] Julius Caesar issued a series of decrees benefitting Hyrcanus and Judaea, as well as the Diaspora in Rome and Asia Minor.[30] According to Josephus' record of the relevant decree in *Ant.* 14. 213–216, the Jews in Asia were permitted "to assemble and feast in accordance with their native customs and ordinances."[31] In the same decree, it was also mentioned that the Jews in Rome were not forbidden "to live in accordance with their customs and to contribute money to common meals and sacred rites."[32] When Caesar's decree was followed and applied by subsequent emperors and Roman officials to Asia, the Jews' privileges were extended to "exemption from military service,"[33] "the right to Sabbath observance,"[34] "exemption from court attendance on Sabbath,"[35] "freedom to hold religious meeting,"[36] "manage their own funds"[37] and "protection of their funds and sacred books from being stolen from their synagogues."[38]

Besides following the benevolence of Julius Caesar, Augustus also showed favour for the Roman Jews by ordering that if the monthly distributions of corn for the needy took place on the Sabbath, the dispensers were to reserve a portion of the dole to the next day so that the Jews would be at liberty to receive them.[39] Those eligible for the dole were likely to be

---

29. Ibid., 14.127–139.

30. Barclay, *Jews*, 277. Scholars today commonly accept that despite their apologetic purpose and the errors and deficiencies found in the contents, Josephus' records of the decrees, edicts and rescripts in *Ant.* 14.185–267 and 16.160–78, in relation to the privileges granted to the Jews, are not forgeries and can be taken as evidence of relevant historical happenings for further investigations. See e.g. Tcherikover, *Hellenistic Civilization*, 306; Philip A. Harland, *Associations, Synagogues, and Congregations: Claiming a Place in Ancient Mediterranean Society* (Minneapolis, MN: Fortress Press, 2003), 304, n. 7; Gruen, *Diaspora*, 85–86; Leonard Victor Rutgers, "Roman Policy toward the Jews: Expulsions from the City of Rome during the First Century C.E.," in *Judaism and Christianity in First-Century Rome*, eds. Karl P. Donfried and Peter Richardson (Grand Rapids, MI: Eerdmans, 1998), 95–96.

31. Josephus, *Ant.* 14. 213–216.

32. Ibid.

33. Ibid., 14.225–227. Cf. 14.228–232.

34. Ibid., 14.241–246, 262–264.

35. Ibid., 16.162–165.

36. Ibid., 14.227, 244–246, 259–261.

37. Ibid., 14.244–246; 16.162–168, 171–173.

38. Ibid., 16.162–168. See also Grant, *Jews*, 59.

39. Philo, *Legat.* 158.

Roman citizens[40] and there must be a significant number of Jewish Roman citizens whose interests were at stake before Augustus's concern could be aroused. These Jewish Roman citizens were in fact an integral part of the wider social landscape but they were so persistent in obeying God's commandments that they would rather give up the monthly entitlement to their food in order to observe the Sabbath.[41]

It was against this background of imperial benefactions that the Diaspora Jews in Asia Minor and Rome were seen positively integrated into the wider socio-political context. Many of them indeed obtained the status of Roman citizens including well-known individuals such as the Apostle Paul from Asia Minor[42] and Josephus in Rome.[43] As I mentioned in the last paragraph, the number of Jewish Roman citizens in Rome must have been significant enough to arouse Augustus' attention to their interest. According to Philo, the Jews in Rome were mostly Roman citizens who had been emancipated from being slaves and war captives to Italy (*Legat.* 155). However, as Philo was already writing a century after Pompey,[44] Gabinius,[45] and Cassius[46] brought these Jewish war captives to Rome in the series of wars in Judaea in 60s–50s BCE, it was likely that the Jews of Rome obtained Roman citizenship also through other means such as individual grants from Roman patrons, rewards for public services, attainment of high office or discharge after serving as auxiliary troops.[47] What is noticeable is that, according to Philo, living as Roman citizens was not incompatible with the Jewish practice of ancestral laws as the holy people

---

40. So, Jan Nicolaas Sevenster, *The Roots of Pagan Anti-Semitism in the Ancient World*, NovTSup 41 (Leiden: Brill, 1975), 80–81; Barclay, *Jews*, 292–293; Gruen, *Diaspora*, 29; Rutgers, "Roman Policy," 97.

41. See also Barclay, *Jews*, 293.

42. Acts 16:37–38; 22:25–29; 23:27.

43. Josephus, *Life*. 423. It is also remarkable that a number of Herod's sons, Alexander, Aristobulus, Antipas, Archelaus and Philip, were actually brought up in Rome (Josephus, *Ant.* 15.342–343; 17.20–21) while another of his sons Antipater was also sent to Agrippa to take him along to Rome to become a friend of Augustus (Josephus, *Ant.* 16.86–87; 17.52–53).

44. Josephus, *Ant.* 14.71, 79; 20.244; *J. W.* 1.154.

45. Josephus, *Ant.* 14.83–85, 95–97.

46. Josephus, *Ant.* 14.120, 275; *J. W.* 1.180.

47. So, Gruen, *Diaspora*, 22–23, 131. See also Trebilco, *Jewish Communities*, 258 n. 20.

of God: they were able to obtain Roman citizenship "without ever having been compelled to alter any of their hereditary or national observances" (*Legat*. 155).[48]

Besides the Jews in Rome, there were also Jews in Ephesus "who were citizens of Rome" (πολίτας 'Ρωμαίων, *Ant*. 14.228) and were recorded to be exempted from military service by the consul, Lucius Lentulus.[49] Similar decrees were issued in Sardis and Delos as well.[50] Although Smallwood argues that the number of Jews affected by Lentulus' decree must have been "infinitesimally small,"[51] it is unlikely that different decrees from different cities would have been issued if virtually no one would be affected by them. It is more probable that the presence of Jews with Roman citizenship was not something extraordinary in Asia Minor.[52]

Therefore, the Diaspora Jewish communities at least in Rome and Asia Minor were by no means exclusivist or separatist. Instead, they managed to find a place in the political scene and many of them even obtained Roman citizenship through positive interactions with some distinguished patrons, participation in public services or the like. It was also likely that they were a people who generally would not attempt to subvert the Roman rule. Besides the absence of any record of Jewish civil disobedience in Asia Minor or in Rome,[53] there is also no record of the Jewish communities

---

48. Translation provided in Philo, *Works*, trans. Yonge, 771.
49. Josephus, *Ant*.14.228, 234, 240.
50. Ibid., 14.231–232.
51. Smallwood, *Jews*, 127–128.
52. So, Gruen, *Diaspora*, 131. For the view that a notable number of Jewish Roman citizens in Asia were covered by these decrees, see M. Stern, "The Jewish Diaspora," in *The Jewish People in the First Century: Historical Geography, Political History, Social, Cultural and Religious Life and Institutions*, vol. 1, 2 vols., eds. S. Safrai and M. Stern (Assen: Van Gorcum, 1974), 152; Schürer, *History*, 120–121.
53. Although the Jews in Rome were recorded to have been expelled twice during the period of our present investigation (i.e. 19 CE and 49 CE), it should be noted that whatever motive behind the Roman action may be, none of the records attributes the cause of these expulsions to any Jewish disobedience to the Empire or antagonism to their pagan neighbours. Among the diverse records of the expulsion in 19 CE, both Tacitus, *Ann*. 2.85.4 and Suetonius, *Tib*. 36 report the expulsion as a Roman suppression of the Jewish rites together with the others, while Cassius Dio 57.18.5a refers to the Jews converting the others to their religion. On the other hand, Josephus, *Ant*. 18.65–84 relates the event to the embezzlement of several Jewish impostors in appropriating the gifts of a Roman proselyte to the Jerusalem Temple for their own use. As for the expulsion in 49 CE, Suetonius, *Claud*. 25.4 reports that the disturbances of the Jews were made at the instigation of

in these areas giving support to the Great Revolt in Judaea of 66–73 CE despite their consistent attachment to Jerusalem. I hold that this non-antagonistic stance towards pagan rule is probably what the Petrine author envisions Christians to inherit when he exhorts the Christian Diaspora to be "subject to every human creature (institution)" (ὑποτάγητε πάσῃ ἀνθρωπίνῃ κτίσει) (1 Pet 2:13).

In addition, the Petrine exhortation to "honour the emperor" (1 Pet 2:17) can also locate its root in the Jewish Diaspora in Asia Minor and Rome who had no reluctance in expressing their loyalty and honour to the Roman emperors publicly in accordance with Greco-Roman conventions. Although Suetonius was not at all friendly to the Jews, he nevertheless reported that at the assassination of Julius Caesar when large crowds of foreigners in Rome gathered to express their public grief, the Jews "above all" "even flocked to the funeral-pyre for several successive nights" (*Jul.* 84.5).[54] Augustus also mentioned in his edict that the Jewish community in Asia had given a resolution to his honour (τὸ δοθέν μοι) on account of his piety (εὐσεβείας) which he had towards all mankind, and he thus ordered this Jewish resolution be set up with his edict in the most prominent place assigned to him at Ancyra.[55] Therefore, when the Petrine exhortation of "honouring the emperor" is understood with reference to the Jewish Diaspora, it becomes clear that such "honouring" does not stop at passively accepting "as a given" the authority of emperor and governors as Elliott observes.[56] A positive display of appreciation and respect in accordance with Greco-Roman conventions can be included as the appropriate conduct of the Diaspora.

In fact, besides public display of gratitude, demonstration of honour to the emperors was also part of the cultic life of the Jewish Diaspora. Although the Jewish exclusive worship of Yahweh rendered emperor worship or any

---

"*Chrestus*" which is commonly recognized by scholars as a synonym for Christianity. Since the expulsion happened at a time when Christians were still a part of the Jewish community, the disturbances should be seen more as unrests "within" the Roman Jewish community (Rutgers, "Roman Policy," 106) than any subversive activity of the Roman Jews against the Roman rule or any Jewish retaliation against pagan hostility.

54. *GLAJJ*, 2, no. 302.
55. Josephus, *Ant.* 16.165.
56. Elliott, *1 Peter*, 502.

erection of the emperors' images out of question, the Jewish communities would offer sacrifices and prayers for the emperors and their imperial families, as a gesture of their loyalty to the empire. Philo argues that his people were inferior to none whatever in Asia or in Europe,

> whether it be in respect of prayers, or of the supply of sacred offerings, or in the abundance of its sacrifices, not merely of such as are offered on occasions of the public festivals, but in those which are continually offered day after day; by which means they show their loyalty and fidelity. (*Legat.* 280)[57]

Likewise, when claiming that the Jews offered perpetual sacrifices for the emperors and the people of Rome, Josephus further states that,

> not only do we perform these ceremonies daily, at the expense of the whole Jewish community, but, while we offer no other victims in our corporate capacity, . . . we jointly accord to the emperors alone this signal honour which we pay to no other individual.[58]

It must be noted, however, that Josephus at the same time admits that the Jewish legislator (Moses) allows the Jews to confer honours on the emperors and the people of Rome only in so far as it is a "payment of homage of another sort, secondary to that paid to God."[59] Therefore, Josephus is actually expressing the same hierarchy of reverences as that appears in 1 Peter 2:13–17: While the emperor is to be "honoured," "fear" is to be reserved to God. The holy people of God can express their honour and loyalty to the emperors in accordance with current societal conventions provided that such expression must be of a different kind. The emperor cannot be the object of worship, and the honour endowed on the emperor must be inferior to God. Ultimate allegiance to God is still the boundary of their accommodation. This is how the Jewish Diaspora provide inspirations for the Petrine social ethics, and how the Petrine good works of "differentiated resistance" should be understood.

---

57. Philo, *Works*, trans. Yonge, 782. See also *Legat.* 157, 232, 356.
58. Josephus, *Ag. Ap.* 2.77 (Thackeray, LCL); cf. *J.W.* 2.197.
59. Josephus, *Ag. Ap.* 2.76 (Thackeray, LCL).

A similar boundary of accommodation is also found from the honour granted to the emperors by the Jewish synagogues. On the funerary epitaphs found in the Jewish catacombs in Rome, the names of at least eleven synagogues have been found. Particularly relevant for our purpose is the name Augustesioi (Αὐγουστησίων)[60] which is commonly agreed to relate to the emperor Augustus. This synagogue was therefore probably founded during the reign of Augustus (27 BCE–14 CE) and named to express the congregation's gratitude for his benefaction.[61] However, no matter in what manner the Jewish communities were prepared to honour the emperors, it was unlikely that they would construct any images and statues of the emperors in their synagogues which is explicitly forbidden in the Jewish Scriptures. This phenomenon was notable even by pagan outsiders such as Tacitus who observes amidst his contempt of the Jewish religion,

> they regard as impious those who make from perishable materials representations of gods in man's image; that supreme and eternal being is to them incapable of representation and without end. Therefore, they set up no statues in their cities, still less in their temples; this flattery is not paid their kings, nor this honour given to the Caesars. (*Hist.* 5.5.4)[62]

Likewise, when Philo argues that the Jews of Alexandria did follow the societal expectations of paying honour to the emperor in the synagogues, he mentioned that such honour was expressed in the forms of ornaments "such as gilded shields, and gilded crowns, and pillars, and inscriptions" (*Legat.* 133).[63] The noticeable absence of statues and images in Philo's portrayal of the Alexandrian synagogues is consistent with Tacitus' observations,

---

60. *CII*, 1, no. 284 = *JIWE*, 2, no. 547; *CII*, 1, no. 301 = *JIWE*, 2, no. 96; *CII*, 1, no. 338 = *JIWE*, 2, no. 169; *CII*, 1, no. 368 = *JIWE*, 2, no. 189; *CII*, 1, no. 416 = *JIWE*, 2, no. 194; *CII*, 1, no. 496 = *JIWE*, 2, no. 542.

61. So, Harry J. Leon, *The Jews of Ancient Rome,* The Morris Loeb Series (Philadelphia, PA: Jewish Publication Society of America, 1960), 142; Peter Richardson, "Augustan-Era Synagogues in Rome," in *Judaism and Christianity in First-Century Rome*, ed. Karl P. Donfried and Peter Richardson (Grand Rapids, MI: Eerdmans), 20–21; Barclay, *Jews*, 293, 306 n. 59; Gruen, *Diaspora*, 112, 266–267 n. 85.

62. *GLAJJ*, 2, no. 281.

63. Translation provided in Philo, *Works*, trans. Yonge, 769.

and probably reflects the general practice of the Jewish Diaspora. As Harland concludes,

> granting special honors to emperors and members of the imperial family was common among many Jewish groups in the Roman Empire, though this clearly and understandably stopped short of cultic honors or the dedication of images or statues, which would be considered idolatry or "fornication" by virtually all Jews. (cf. Wis 14)[64]

Here, the Jewish creativity in negotiating their Diaspora existence is distinctly manifested. Although God's commandments prohibit the construction of images and statues which the Jews were not prepared to transgress, they nevertheless located a common ground with the pagan culture by paying honour to the emperors through other media they could devise within the boundary imposed by their ancestral laws (i.e. the will of God).

However, it was also this insistence on observing God's laws that led to the Jews' continuous tension with their pagan neighbours in the cities, at least in Asia Minor. Although Josephus states that his purpose of recording the decrees and rescripts in favour of the Jews was "to reconcile the other nations to us and to remove the causes for hatred which have taken root in thoughtless persons among us as well as among them,"[65] his records actually betray the general reluctance of the Greek cities to recognize the rights of the Jewish group to observe their ancestral laws and customs.[66] Hence, Julius Caesar is said to have issued his edict allowing the Jews to practise their ancestral customs only as a result of the petition from the Jews of Delos, complaining about the denial of their rights by the city of Paros.[67] The report letter from the magistrates of the Laodiceans to the Roman consul also reveals that the Trallians had denied the Jews the rights to observe their ancestral laws, which led to the intervention of the consul.[68] Similarly, Philo says that Augustus issued his decree to the Asian governors,

---

64. Harland, *Associations*, 217.
65. Josephus, *Ant.* 16.175 (Marcus, LCL).
66. Barclay, *Jews*, 275–276.
67. Josephus, *Ant.* 14.213.
68. Josephus, *Ant.* 14.242.

granting the Jews the rights of assembly and to send their temple contributions to Jerusalem, only "because he heard that the sacred first fruits were neglected" (*Legat.* 311–2).[69]

Especially important for our purpose is that although the Diaspora Jews in Asia Minor were usually prepared to seek peace and to submit to the existing societal order, it was when their continuous compliance with the laws (will) of God was at stake that they would become contentious and resist the harassment and pressure from the cities to abandon their ancestral laws.[70] Therefore, we have Josephus recording that when Agrippa, Augustus' son-in-law, was in Ionia with Herod, "a great multitude" (πολὺ πλῆθος) of Ionian Jews came to him and complained of not being allowed to observe their own laws in the city. Their complaints included being compelled to appear in court on the Sabbath, deprived of the sacred money sent to Jerusalem as temple contributions, forced into the army and public services (liturgies), and compelled to spend their sacred money on them.[71] This incident betrays that the Asian Jewish communities were in fact maintaining a degree of normality in their Diaspora life. They were involved in day-to-day transactions with the pagans which sometimes resulted in court proceedings, and these proceedings were not rare occurrences so that some of them had to take place on the Sabbath. It also suggests that the presence of Ionian Jews in the social scene was so prominent that some of them were required to take up certain military and civic responsibilities in the city.[72]

---

69. Translation provided in Philo, *Works*, trans. Yonge, 785.

70. I agree with the view generally held by scholars today that the edict of Julius Caesar, as reviewed and applied by subsequent decrees of Roman rulers, did not constitute a "Magna Carta" of Jewish rights which elevated Judaism to the status of *religio licita*. The Diaspora Jewish communities had to lodge their complaints and petitioned to the authorities from time to time to secure the protection from the Roman authorities which then acceded to their requests on an ad hoc and case-to-case basis. See Tessa Rajak, "Was There a Roman Charter for the Jews?" *JRS* 74 (1984): 107–123; Trebilco, *Jewish Communities*, 8–11; Barclay, *Jews*, 278; Harland, *Associations*, 221–222.

71. Josephus, *Ant.* 16.27–28. Other Jewish communities in Asia Minor recorded to have lodged similar complaints included those of Sardis (*Ant.* 14.235, 259–260) and Ephesus (*Ant.* 14.262–264, 16.172–173). As for Miletus, although it is not very clear whether Prytanes, the one who brought the pagan mistreatment of the Jews to the notice of the proconsul, was a Jew or a pagan patron, the fact that the proconsul heard arguments "from both sides," indicates that the Jewish community was also taking a contentious role in securing the rights to observe their ancestral practices (*Ant.* 14.244–246).

72. See also Barclay, *Jews*, 328.

It was only when they were required to go over the boundary prescribed by the Torah (μήτε νόμοις οἰκείοις ἐώμενοι χρῆσθαι, *Ant.* 16.27), that is, not observing the Sabbath, not sending their temple contributions to Jerusalem, etc., that the Jewish Diaspora found it necessary to resist the expectations of the larger society. "Differentiated resistance" is again seen as the Diaspora Jewish strategy in the engagement with the wider pagan world with "ultimate allegiance to God," their boundary of accommodation.

This Jewish ultimate allegiance to God, expressed in the form of persistent observance of the Torah, is also evidenced from Cicero's famous defence of Flaccus, the governor of Asia. This governor had promulgated a decree forbidding the export of gold from Asia in 62 BCE. Cicero mentions that over a hundred pounds of gold intended as temple contributions to Jerusalem was confiscated from the Jews at Apamea, Laodicea, Adramyttium and Pergamum.[73] For generations, the Diaspora Jews had been following the Torah to bring their "first fruits" to the temple.[74] It is remarkable that Flaccus was allegedly acting in pursuance of an earlier decision of the Senate to ban the export of gold from the provinces.[75] Although scholars have different views as whether this senatorial resolution applied to the Jews in Asia Minor and whether Flaccus' action was legal,[76] this incident still indicates that the Asian Jewish Diaspora were so resolute in complying with God's commandment that they were prepared to ignore the current social and political pressure to abandon the practice of sending temple contributions to Jerusalem.[77]

---

73. Cicero, *Flac.* 28.68.

74. Philo, *Spec. Laws* 1.76–78; *Legat.* 156. This contribution involved an annual payment of a half-shekel by every male Jew (Exod 30:12–16; *Ant.* 18.312. Cf. Neh 10:32–34) while Josephus also mentions that the amount of annual contribution was two drachmae when the Temple was destroyed in 70 CE (*J.W.* 7.218). See also Trebilco, *Jewish Communities*, 13.

75. Cicero, *Flac.* 28.67.

76. For the view that the Jews were exempted from the senatorial resolution and Flaccus's action was illegal, see Smallwood, *Jews*, 126. For the view that Flaccus's edict was legal, see Trebilco, *Jewish Communities*, 14–15. Bilhah Wardy, "Jewish Religion in Pagan Literature During the Late Republic and Early Empire," in *Aufstieg Und Niedergang der römischen Welt: Geschichte und Kultur Roms im Spiegel der neueren Forschung, Principat* 19.1, ed. Wolfgang Haase (Berlin: Walter de Gruyter, 1979), 603 simply asserts that the senatorial resolution was not a law but Flaccus was acting within his power as the provincial governor.

77. See Trebilco, *Jewish Communities*, 15.

Even more noteworthy is the fact that the Jews of Asia Minor were not alone in having zealous loyalty to God's laws. When Flaccus was tried in Rome, a multitude of Roman Jews gathered in the vicinity of the place in which the trial took place. Thus Cicero remarks, "You know what a big crowd it is, how they stick together, how influential they are in informal assembles" (*Flac.* 28.66).⁷⁸ Obviously, the Jews of Rome were sharing the same zeal with their fellow-countrymen in Asia Minor for the continuous export of the temple contributions to Jerusalem. Although the Jewish communities of Rome did not normally cause troubles to the city just like their compatriots in Asia Minor, they would nevertheless demonstrate their solidarity and make their presence felt by the pagan public when the continuous observance of the ancestral laws from God was at stake.

These incidents of tension actually testify to the anomalous situation of the Jewish Diaspora especially in Asia Minor and Rome amidst the Gentile world. Although the Jewish exilic people of God managed to receive tolerations and privileges from the Roman emperors for the continuous observance of their ancestral laws, they were often ostracized by their pagan neighbours at the provincial level.⁷⁹ This pagan hostility was due to the fact that the Jewish life style as prescribed by the Torah was simply "too different" to align with current societal expectations. Whereas the Jews constantly requested their neighbours to recognize their rights to observe their own laws, their neighbours could only see that the Jews were not taking up corresponding civic duties in return: they refused to take up military services⁸⁰ and public services, and even refused to contribute to their pay-

---

78. *GLAJJ*, 1, no. 68.

79. Although Gruen maintains that these incidents of Gentile harassment were episodic and infrequent (Gruen, *Diaspora*, 86–104), the fact that a series of such persecutions are mentioned in Josephus' *Jewish Antiquities* actually betrays the otherwise. If Josephus's purpose in relating these happenings was to show the Greeks that "in former times we were treated with all respect and were not prevented by our rulers from practising any of our ancestral customs" (*Ant.* 16.174 [Marcus, LCL]) and "to reconcile the other nations to us and to remove the causes for hatred which have taken root in thoughtless persons among us as well as among them" (*Ant.* 16.175 [Marcus, LCL]) but he turns out revealing a series of Greek resentment cases, one can imagine that there could only be many more such cases in reality. So Barclay, *Jews*, 275–276.

80. The reluctance of the Jews to go into the armies was explained in the decree of Dolabella that they were not allowed to bear arms or to march on the Sabbath, and they could not obtain the native food to which they were accustomed (Josephus, *Ant.* 14.226).

ments despite their means to do so.[81] They would rather send their funds to the Jerusalem temple and in disregard of the current financial drains in their own cities.[82] Although many Diaspora Jews acceded to the status of Roman citizens, they continued to embarrass the emperors by refusing to take part in the imperial cult and declined sharing the same gods with the cities. Their failure to engage in any business or other transactions on the Sabbath could only cause further nuisance to their fellow-townsmen.

It is against this socio-political backdrop that the Jewish strategies of civil engagement in Rome and Asia Minor become intelligible. At a time when the Jewish Diaspora had to resist the pressure from their neighbours at provincial level to abandon their ancestral laws and worship the pagan gods, it is of critical importance that they had access to the support from the Roman authorities, especially from the emperors, so that they could draw up their resources to face antagonism only from one front. Therefore, the Jewish Diaspora adopted the Greco-Roman conventions of submitting to the Roman authorities and honouring the emperor within the boundary of ultimate allegiance to God while at the same time, they focused their attention to resist the pressure and harassment from the cities.[83] Although Josephus' record of the Roman concessions dries up after the decree of Claudius,[84] the fact that his *Jewish Antiquities* was published with its apologetic purpose in the 90s CE, shows that this mode of Jewish civil engagement was likely to be still in force by that time.[85] As Rajak concludes, "It shows that specific rights were still (or perhaps even more) important in the aftermath of the fall of the temple. It reveals the Jewish population clinging

---

81. The large amount of gold confiscated by Flaccus from the Asian Jewish communities actually betrays their wealth.

82. For a comprehensive introduction to the financial drains in the Greek cities of Asia Minor from the mid-first century BCE up to the time of Augustus, see David Magie, *Roman Rule in Asia Minor: To the End of the Third Century after Christ*, vol. 1, 2 vols. (Princeton, NJ: Princeton University Press, 1950), 405–441; Barclay, *Jews*, 266–269.

83. As Shaye J. D. Cohen, *From the Maccabees to the Mishnah*, LEC 7 (Philadelphia, PA: Westminster Press, 1987), 59 also observes, "A Jew might, say, be quite accommodating in the political sphere, wholeheartedly supporting the ruling power, but quite unyielding in the cultural or social sphere."

84. Josephus, *Ant.* 19.280–291.

85. It is notable how Josephus, *Ant.* 12.119–128 emphasizes that the privileges and exemption enjoyed by the Jews remained in the reigns of Vespasian and Titus despite the Great Revolt in Judea in 66–73 CE. See also Josephus, *J.W.* 7.110–111.

desperately to a small privilege which had evidently come to represent security for them."[86]

All these observations serve to explain why the Diaspora Jewish experience and social strategies were relevant to inspire the Petrine author to formulate his mode of social engagement for Christian Diaspora. As I demonstrated in the last chapter, Christians become exiles (resident-aliens) in society because they also become "different" from their neighbours after conversion: "They are surprised that you no longer go with (them) in the same excess of dissipation, they slander (you)" (1 Pet 4:4). Christians' estrangement originates primarily from the provincial level just as with the Diaspora Jews. By perceiving Christians' existence on earth also as "elect exiles of Diaspora," the Petrine author is at the same time arming them with similar strategies to the Jewish Diaspora in Asia Minor and Rome, who managed to survive similar pagan estrangement with their primary allegiance to God kept intact. We therefore witness the Petrine author exhorting Christians to "be subject to every human institution (creature)" (1 Pet 2:13) and to "honour the emperor" at the imperial level while subtly differentiating the hierarchy of reverence due to the emperor from that to God (2:17). On the other hand, and in the face of their neighbours' pressure to accommodate, Christians are blatantly exhorted to defend their salvation hope with a good consciousness toward God (3:15–16), arm themselves with the mindset of Christ and not to go with the way of the Gentiles (4:1–3), and endure suffering as a Christian (4:15–16; cf. 4:14). Their resistance in these situations is to be hard and definite.

The Diaspora Jewish engagement in daily social life will be discussed further in section 4.1.3 below.

4.1.2 Jewish Engagement in Household Life

In the Petrine household code of 1 Peter 2:18–3:7, the author deals with three specific roles within the household: slaves (2:18–25), wives (3:1–6) and husbands (3:7). Although records of the Diaspora Jewish household engagement are scanty, ultimate allegiance to God can still be seen as their fundamental concern in the conduct of their household life.

---

86. Rajak, "Roman Charter," 121.

Evidence from various sources testify that there were a notable number of Jewish slaves in Rome whether in the slave markets or in ordinary households. For example, Cicero repeatedly refers to the Jews as a nation of slaves. In *Flac.* 28.69, he expresses his contempt of the Jews by pronouncing that their nation "has been conquered, let out for taxes, made a slave"[87] while in *Prov. cons.* 5.10, he further ridicules them as a people "born to be slaves."[88] As mentioned in section 4.1.1 above, a large number of Jews were reported to have been taken by Pompey, Gabinius, and Cassius as war captives and arrived at Rome as slaves. These records are consistent with the observations of Philo that most of Jews in Rome were Roman citizens who had been brought to Italy as war captives and manumitted by their masters.[89] It was likely that many of these Jewish slaves would serve in pagan households.

Regrettably, we do not have comprehensive records showing the strategies of these slaves in negotiating their existence in the households of their Gentile masters. It is however reasonable to expect that life in the pagan households must not have been easy for them if they wanted to preserve their Jewish identity. As Cohick asserts, if a Jewish slave woman was in a Gentile house, "gone was her freedom to worship God, to rest on the Sabbath, to eat only food prescribed in the law."[90] These must be accompanied by the hardship of being compelled to participate or help out in the household cults, and making herself available to satisfy the sexual appetite of her master.[91] The same of course applies to male Jewish slaves as well. If they refused to submit to the orders of the Gentile masters, it would mean exposing themselves to bodily abuses as I mentioned in chapter 3 above.[92] As also explained by Hubbard with insight, "The reliance on physical punishment was due, in part, to the fact that slaves had no property that could

---

87. *GLAJJ*, 1, no. 68.
88. Ibid., no. 70.
89. Philo, *Legat.* 155. Cf. Tacitus, *Ann.* 2.85.4. The Jewish War in 66–73 CE also contributed to the notable number of Jewish war captives around the Mediterranean (Barclay, *Jews*, 325).
90. Cohick, *Women*, 275.
91. Hubbard, *Christianity*, 193–194; Cohick, *Women*, 275.
92. See pages 87–88 above.

be confiscated or money to surrender. Their bodies became the focal point of a master's discipline."[93]

Although we know very little about how these Jewish slaves actually dealt with their difficulties in the Gentile households, Smallwood may be too optimistic when she conjectures, "Manumission may have come very quickly to some of the Jews sold as slaves in Rome, if their purchasers found them to be more trouble than they were worth because of their dietary and other laws and their disinclination to work one day in seven."[94]

As slaves were treated as mere chattel or property of their owners, it was more likely that their Gentile masters would use every means including violence to subdue the Jewish slaves into compliance with their wishes.

From the sporadic records of different sources, it seems that the Diaspora Jewish slaves were negotiating somewhere between the two poles of resistance and accommodation. On an epitaph probably from Naples and dated 70–95 CE, a captive from Jerusalem called Claudia Aster was mentioned.[95] This epitaph was obviously put up by an imperial freedman, Tiberius Claudius Proculus, who was probably the master of this Jewish slave. What is remarkable is that there was an appeal on this epitaph from this Proculus to the public that they must take care that no one cast down his inscription contrary to the law. Although the epitaph gives too little information to render it absolutely certain that this Proculus was a Gentile, it is probable that this Jewish slave girl had managed to assimilate into the household very well and discharged her duties to the satisfaction of Proculus so as to win tremendous favour from a master.[96] She thus can be viewed as an example of a Jewish slave adopting "utmost subordination" (cf. 1 Pet 2:18–19) as the mode of her engagement within the pagan household which could possibly have practical value in reality.

On the other hand, no matter how far individual Jewish slaves were prepared to submit to their pagan masters, there is also evidence showing

---

93. Hubbard, *Christianity*, 193.

94. Smallwood, *Jews*, 131.

95. *CII*, 1. no. 556. It is believed that she was one of the Jews who had been captured to Rome at the fall of Jerusalem in 70 CE. See *JIWE*, 1, no. 26.

96. Barclay regards this Proculus as a pagan master and includes this Jewish slave girl in his discussions of Jewish assimilation in the pagan world. See Barclay, *Jews*, 326.

that ultimate allegiance to God, expressed in terms of persistent observance of the Torah, was still put forth as the ideal mode of engagement by the Diaspora slaves in the pagan households. Philo, when mentioning the emancipation of the Jewish slaves in Italy, did not forget to stress that these Jews had been manumitted and became Roman citizens "without ever having been compelled to alter any of their hereditary or national observances" (*Legat.* 155).[97] Regardless of whether Philo may have exaggerated for rhetorical purpose, his account at least reveals that "persistent observance of the ancestral laws," implying abstention from the Gentile household cults, was still the ideal for the Diaspora Jewish slaves despite the practical difficulties in reality. This Jewish ideal of slaves' household engagement may also include enduring suffering (cf. 1 Pet 2:19–20) for resisting their masters' request to abandon practising the commandments of God.

It is against this backdrop of Diaspora Jewish household engagement that the dynamics within the Petrine exhortations to Christian slaves come to light. Although the Christian Diaspora no longer needed to observe the Torah, they in fact faced the same challenge as the Jewish slaves to hold fast to their faith by refusing to participate in the idolatrous household cults or to disown God. The Petrine author is actually positing the Jewish ideal as his frame of reference when he instructs Christian slaves to subject themselves to their masters with "all fear" (2:18) and "conscience" (2:19) toward God. It is within this overriding boundary and with the same strategy of "differentiated resistance" that Christians are to subordinate themselves to their masters even if they are unscrupulous, perverse and even unjust (2:18–19) hoping that they may win some favour from their masters as exemplified by the Jewish slave girl mentioned on the epitaph in Italy and, thus, have some room to uphold their faith and stand firm in the salvation of God.

In respect of the engagement of the wives and husbands with their spouses, the situation of the Jewish Diaspora was somewhat different from Christians because the Jewish people of God were not supposed to marry anyone not belonging to them. In Deuteronomy 7:3–4, Israel is forbidden to intermarry with the Gentiles because it will turn the nation away

---

97. Translation provided in Philo, *Works*, trans. Yonge, 771.

from God and draw them into idolatry (cf. Exod 34:16; Num 25:1–2). Mixed marriages with the nations continued to be regarded as transgression of God's laws in Diaspora Jewish literature.[98] Ultimate and exclusive allegiance to God remains the rationale for this prohibition.

Although it can be expected that there were cases in which some Diaspora Jews did marry Gentiles,[99] these must not be regarded as the norm. At least, what can be observable by an outsider such as Tacitus was that the Jews "abstain from intercourse with foreign women" (*Hist.* 5.5.2).[100] After having settled in Rome in 71 CE, Josephus himself also took a Jewess from Crete as his wife.[101] It is likely that a majority of the Diaspora Jews would follow their ancestral laws to marry within their nation.[102]

Particularly pertinent for our investigation is Josephus' assertion that a woman should be submissive to her husband so that she may be directed, for "the authority has been given by God to the man."[103] This assertion is actually part of his defence for the Jewish laws which he claims to teach that a woman "is in all things inferior to the man."[104] Scholars however note that nowhere is this reference found in the present versions of the OT.[105] Balch is probably justified to conclude that, "Aristotle's outline of household submissiveness was adapted by Hellenistic rhetoric; and Josephus and Philo assimilated it to the extent that it was used to praise Moses' laws!"[106]

We therefore once again witness the presence of "differentiated resistance" within the Diaspora social engagement. Whereas the ancestral law of endogamy was what the Jewish Diaspora were not prepared to give up,

---

98. Philo, *Spec.* 3.29; *T. Levi.* 9.10. Cf. Tob 4:12–13.

99. E.g. although Timothy's mother was a Jew in Derbe or Lystra, her husband was a Greek and Timothy had never received circumcision before meeting Paul (Acts 16:1–3).

100. *GLAJJ*, 2. no. 281.

101. Josephus, *Life*, 427.

102. Also Cohen, *Maccabees*, 51; Louis H. Feldman, *Jew and Gentile in the Ancient World: Attitudes and Interactions from Alexander to Justinian* (Princeton, NJ: Princeton University Press, 1993), 79.

103. Josephus, *Ag. Ap.* 2.201 (Thackeray, LCL).

104. Ibid.

105. E.g. Whiston's comment in Josephus, *The New Complete Works of Josephus*, trans. William Whiston; rev. ed. (Grand Rapids, MI: Kregel, 1999), 980 n. 24.

106. Balch, *Wives*, 55, followed by Cohick, *Women*, 79.

they found themselves also at liberty to appropriate the values and norms from the wider culture to form parts of their own ethics.

This framework of household engagement is also what the Petrine author adopts for Christian wives. While he also instructs wives to subject themselves to their husbands in accordance with societal expectations (1 Pet 3:1), this subordination is also subject to Christians' fear (3:2) to God and doing what is precious in his sight (3:4). Since most of the Petrine readers were Gentiles,[107] many Christian wives must have the extra dilemma of having husbands of different religious commitments. "Submission" actually serves an extra function of easing tension within the household to allow room for the Christian wives to hold fast to their exclusive allegiance to God.

It therefore becomes understandable why the Petrine author regards his vision of "good works" as the congruent identity expression of the Christian elect exiles of Diaspora. Besides serving as the conceptual framework of Christians' self-understanding and existence on earth, the Jewish elect exiles of Diaspora further provide the proper form of identity expression for the Petrine author to formulate his social ethics for his Christian readers. The value of investigating the social strategies of the Jewish Diaspora as the reference point to understand the dynamics within the Petrine good works is therefore evidenced.

4.1.3 Jewish Engagement in Daily Social Life

When I discussed the Petrine instructions on Christian engagement in daily social life in the last chapter,[108] I argued that in the face of surrounding social estrangement, the author's primary concern is Christians standing fast in the grace/salvation of God, expressed in particular by their refusal of idolatry (1 Pet 4:3). It is precisely this insistence on living by the will of God (4:2), and not according to that of the Gentiles (4:3), that leads to ostracism and hostility from their neighbours (4:4). It is remarkable that "religious exclusivism" is also the primary source of pagan hostility against the Diaspora Jews in the cities, which renders the experience and strategies of the Jewish Diaspora particularly relevant for the Christian Diaspora.

---

107. See my discussion on page 11 in chapter 1.
108. See pages 108–111 above.

Indeed, the Jewish exclusive worship of Yahweh (i.e. their refusal to honour the gods of the cities), was what fundamentally marked them out from the pagan society.[109] Although Greco-Roman polytheism had no problem in accepting the Jewish God, it was the intolerant Jewish God that the Gentiles found annoying: "The gods of Greece could easily compromise with the God of Israel, but He could not compromise with them."[110] It was this religious exclusivism of the Jewish Diaspora that had earned them the reputation of "a race remarkable for their contempt for the divine powers" (Pliny the Elder, *Nat.* 13.46).[111]

When viewed against the centrality of religion in the life of the cities, it is understandable how this Jewish exclusivism attracted the hostility from their neighbours. As I demonstrated in the last chapter, religion ran through each and every fabric of city life.[112] What I wish to add here is that at a time when the local autonomy of the cities were declining, study of old myths, building of new temples, instituting new festivals and setting up commemorative or celebrative inscriptions were taken as the necessary media for the cities to recover their past glories.[113] Refusal to participate in the civic cults was naturally viewed as destructive to the common bond and an insult to the dignity of the cities.[114] The significance of the civic cult to the honour of the city is concretely testified by the agitation in Ephesus recorded in Acts 19:23–40. Particularly telling about the incident is the connecting of Artemis the city god with the honour of the citizens when the crowd cried, "Great is Artemis of the Ephesians!" (19:28).

When this sort of fervour for the city gods met the refusal of Jews to participate in the city liturgies, to contribute to the needs of the gymnasia, the organization of the athletic games and the building of the temples, which were generally associated with the cultic rites,[115] there is no wonder

---

109. See also John M. G. Barclay, "Snarling Sweetly: Josephus on Images and Idolatry," in *Idolatry: False Worship in the Bible, Early Judaism, and Christianity*, ed. Stephen C. Barton (London: T&T Clark, 2007), 73.
110. Tcherikover, *Hellenistic Civilization*, 374.
111. *GLAJJ*, 1, no. 214. See also Josephus, *Ant.* 3.179.
112. See pages 109–111 above.
113. E. Ferguson, "Religion, Greco-Roman," *DLNT*: 1007.
114. Feldman, *Jew and Gentile*, 151; Tcherikover, *Hellenistic Civilization*, 28.
115. Tcherikover, *Hellenistic Civilization*, 374.

that the Jews were continuously alienated in the cities. Such ostracism was most blatantly expressed by the claim of the Ionians that if the Jews were to be their fellows (συγγενεῖς), "they should worship the Ionians' gods."[116] Similar disgust was also expressed by Apion when he asked, "why, then, if they are citizens, do they not worship the same gods as the Alexandrians?"[117]

Particularly relevant for our discussion is that pagan hostility towards the Jewish religious exclusivism was often translated into accusations against them for being "misanthropic"[118] which was remarkably the same as those which Christians had to face.[119] For the pagan intellectuals, the Jews were an exclusive people who could not accept anyone having a different concept of God, and who would refuse to have fellowship with anyone having a different lifestyle.[120] The outlandish laws introduced by Moses only endowed them with an "unsocial and intolerant mode of life" (Hecataeus of Abdera, *Aegyptiaca*, apud: Diodorus, *Bib. Hist.* 40.3.4).[121] When things went to the extreme, these pagan neighbours even concluded that the Jews "sit apart at meals and they sleep apart, and although as a race, they are prone to lust, they abstain from intercourse with foreign women; yet among themselves nothing is unlawful (Tacitus, *Hist.* 5.5.2)."[122] It therefore appears that the major source of pagan hostility arose from the Jews' insistence on being "distinct" through persistent observance of their ancestral practices.[123]

---

116. Josephus, *Ant.* 12.126 (Marcus, LCL).

117. Josephus, *Ag. Ap.* 2.65 (Thackeray, LCL).

118. Apollonius Molon *apud.* Josephus, *Ag. Ap.* 2.148; Diodorus, *Bib. Hist.* 34.1.2–3; Tacitus, *Hist.* 5.5.1.

119. E.g. When recording Nero's punishment of Christians for arson, Tacitus, *Ann.* 15.44 observes that Christians were convicted not so much on the count of arson as "for hatred of the human race" (Jackson, LCL).

120. Apollonius Molon, apud: Josephus, *Ag. Ap.* 2.258. See also Diodorus, *Bib. Hist.* 34.1.1.

121. *GLAJJ*, 1, no. 11. Cf. Diodorus, *Bib. Hist.* 34.1.2. See also the satire of Juvenal, *Sat.* 40.101–104 that the Jewish law handed down by Moses forbade the Jews "to point out the way to any not worshipping the same rites, and conducting none but the circumcised to the desired fountain" (*GLAJJ*, 2, no. 301).

122. *GLAJJ*, 2, no. 281.

123. E.g. Tacitus *Hist.* 5.4.1 asserts that "Moses introduced new religious practices, quite opposed to those of all other religions. The Jews regard as profane all that we hold sacred; on the other hand, they permit all that we abhor" (*GLAJJ*, 2, no. 281). See also Sevenster, *Roots*, 89, 108.

However, further investigation into the Greco-Roman culture reveals that except for the refusal to participate in the pagan cults, the Jewish ancestral practices were actually not so "strange" or "depraved" as to attract such gravity of antagonism. As recognized by scholars, the Jews were not the only people in the Roman Empire who practised circumcision and abstained from certain food.[124] Although the Jewish observance of the Sabbath may have caused inconvenience to the others, there is nothing shameful or immoral in the practice itself which warranted extensive hostility. Records of various ancient writers actually betray that pagan adoption of the Jewish practices especially the Sabbath and the dietary laws was far from a rare occurrence.[125] Therefore, the root of pagan antagonism still lay in the Jews refusing to honour the gods of the cities. It is only after the hatred to the Jews became deeply rooted that each and every institution of Jewish practice was automatically viewed with malice and contempt.[126] The real difference between the Jewish Diaspora and the pagan world was therefore once again primarily religious rather than social. The fundamental concern of the Jewish Diaspora in persistently observing the ancestral laws was also not so much to keep themselves "distinct" from the rest of society as maintaining their "ultimate allegiance to God" intact.

This task of the Diaspora to hold fast to the ultimate allegiance to God is what the Petrine author captures when he exhorts Christians to separate themselves from those cravings which mark unbelievers as such, that is, those who do not stand in the grace/salvation of God (ἐπιθυμία, 1 Pet 1:14, 2:11, 4:2).[127] Exclusive worship to God, including refusal of lawless idolatries (ἀθεμίτοις εἰδωλολατρίαις, 4:3) and enduring suffering as a Christian (ὡς Χριστιανός, 4:16; cf. ἐν ὀνόματι Χριστοῦ, 4:14), is also the basic concern of Christians which necessary renders them different; otherwise, the

---

124. For peoples who practised circumcision, see e.g. Jer 9:24–25; Philo, *Spec.* 1.2. For peoples who abstained from certain food, see e.g. Sextus Empiricus, *Pyr*, 3.222–223; Epictetus, apud: Arrian, *Epict. diss.*1.11.12–13.

125. E.g. Horace, *Sat.* 1.9.67–72; Seneca, *De Superstitione*, apud. Augustine, *Civ.* 6.11; Josephus, *Ag. Ap.* 2.282. See also Leon, *Jews*, 250–251.

126. Tcherikover, *Hellenistic Civilization*, 376. For pagan contempt of the Sabbath, see e.g. Juvenal, *Sat.* 14.105–106; Seneca, *De Superstitione*, apud: Augustine, *Civ*, 6.11; Tacitus, *Hist.* 5.4.3, of Jewish dietary laws, e.g.Tacitus, *Hist.* 5.5.1–2; Epictetus, apud: Arrian, *Epict. diss.*1.11.12–13; of Jewish circumcision, e.g. Martial, *Epigrammata* 7.82; 11.94.

127. Please see my analysis of these verses on pages 25–26, 77 and 107 above.

Diaspora people of God are to seek peace and submit to current societal order just like the best citizens in society.

Therefore, unyielding observance of God's commandments remained the overriding theme of Jewish social engagement. The Diaspora Jews, whether in Asia Minor, Rome or elsewhere, continued practising circumcision although it was "turned into ridicule by people in general" (Philo, *Spec.* 1.1.1).[128] They were also willing to risk their business prospects,[129] abandon their legal claims[130] and even give up their entitlement to the public dole[131] so that the Sabbath could be properly observed.

Of special relevance for Christians is the Jewish perseverance in keeping their dietary laws because in the Greco-Roman world, pagan food was frequently associated with idolatry whether in relation to meals in temples, pagan festivals or even sacrifices in private domestic cults.[132] If the Diaspora Jews were to eat with the Gentiles, they would have to think of ways not to transgress the laws[133] including sitting at separate tables,[134] bringing their own food to Gentile homes,[135] or the Gentile hosts providing only such food as acceptable to their dietary laws and let the Jews say their own prayers over the food.[136] No matter which options the Jews adopted, it was inevitable that they would be viewed as antisocial and misanthropic for

---

128. Translation provided in Philo, *The Works*, trans. Yonge, 534. Pagans' disgust towards circumcised Jews is best exemplified by Martial, *Epigrammata*, 7.82; 11.94.

129. Philo, *Migr.* 91 mentions that on the Sabbath, the Jews were not allowed to "light a fire, or till land, or carry burdens, or bring accusations, or conduct suits at law, or demand a restoration of a deposit, or exact the repayment of a debt, or do any other of the things which are usually permitted at times which are not days of festival" (Philo, *Works*, trans. Yonge, 262).

130. From the zeal for Sabbath observance as expressed by the Ionian Jews, it was likely that many of them did abandon their legal rights by failing to appear in court on the Sabbath (Josephus, *Ant.* 16.27). See Barclay, *Jews*, 442.

131. Philo, *Legat.* 158.

132. A similar problem was also encountered by the early Christians as evidenced by Paul having to engage in extensive discussion on Christians' eating food offered to idols in 1 Cor 8–11:1.

133. See Barclay, *Jews*, 435; Mark Bonnington, "Fleeing Idolatry: Social Embodiment of Anti-Idolatry in the First Century," in *Idolatry: False Worship in the Bible, Early Judaism, and Christianity*, 117–118.

134. E.g. *Jos. Asen.* 7.1.

135. E.g. Jdt 12.2, 19.

136. E.g. *Let. Aris.* 180–181, 184 (cf. Josephus, *Ant.* 12.94–98).

refusing "to break bread with any other race" (Diodorus, *Bib. Hist.* 34.1.2),[137] and sitting apart at meals (Tacitus, *Hist.* 5.5.2).[138] Although it cannot be excluded that some Diaspora Jews may not have followed the dietary laws to the full, it is likely that a majority of them did observe the laws so that it actually formed an impression on the pagan writers such as Diodorus and Tacitus.[139]

It is particularly noteworthy that when defending the Jewish dietary laws, *Letter of Aristeas* indeed explains that these laws were complied with "for the sake of righteousness" (*Let. Aris.*144, 147, 151, 159, 168, 169; cf. 1 Pet 2:24, 3:12, 14; 4:18) and "in fear of God" (*Let. Aris.* 159; cf. 168; cf. 1 Pet 1:17; 2:18; 3:2, 16), which are the same motifs repeatedly emphasized in the Petrine social behavioural instructions. The ostracism experienced by the Jews as a result of their abstention from sharing meals with the Gentiles, is possibly a concrete example of what is covered by the Petrine vision of Christians suffering "for the sake of righteousness" (πάσχοιτε διὰ δικαιοσύνην, 1 Pet 3:14). Although the Christian Diaspora are no longer required to observe the Torah, living in accordance with "the will of God" (1 Pet 2:15; 3:17; 4:2; 4:19)[140] still demands concrete behavioural expression from Christians, including abstention from sharing with pagans meals that may have religious or idolatrous connotations (cf. ἀθεμίτοις εἰδωλολατρίαις, 4:3) such as participating in temple feasts or eating in cultic settings. Especially in view of the fact that ἀθεμίτοις εἰδωλολατρίαις is placed after οἰνοφλυγίαις (drunkenness), κώμοις (revel) and πότοις (drinking party) in the vice list of 1 Peter 4:3, the criticism that may result if Christians refuse

---

137. *GLAJJ*, 1, no. 63.

138. *GLAJJ*, 2, no. 281.

139. See also Barclay, *Jews*, 436–437. Likewise, although there are records of individual Jews concealing or abandoning their Jewish origin or practices and which Barclay categorizes as cases of high assimilation (Barclay, *Jews*, 321–326), the fact that various pagan writers formed similar impression of the Jewish idiosyncratic customs actually indicates that a majority of Diaspora Jews did persist in observing their ancestral laws and customs. See also Tcherikover, *Hellenistic Civilization*, 352–353; Margaret Williams, "Jews and Jewish Communities in the Roman Empire," in *Experiencing Rome: Culture, Identity and Power in the Roman Empire*, ed. Janet Huskinson (London: Routledge in association with the Open University, 2000), 323–324.

140. See n. 20 above.

to participate in common meals, public festivals, athletic games,[141] guild gatherings,[142] etc., is probably one of the scenarios envisioned when the Petrine author exhorts Christians to endure suffering.

Indeed, the major reason why the Jewish Diaspora managed to maintain the continuous observance of their ancestral laws of God was the widespread distribution of the synagogues in various parts of the Roman Empire where there was a Jewish concentration. In Asia Minor, Paul was said to have entered the synagogues in Antioch of Pisidia (Acts 13:14), Iconium (Acts 14:1) and Ephesus (Acts 18:19; 19:8). A place was also said to be set aside for the Jewish community to build a synagogue in Sardis.[143] Likewise in Rome, besides the synagogue dedicated to Augustus mentioned in section 4.1.1 above,[144] synagogues named probably after Augustus' chief lieutenant and heir, Marcus Vipsanius Agrippa (Ἀγριππησίων),[145] and one Volumnesius (Βολουμνησίων, Βολυμνησίων)[146] were also discovered in the Monteverde catacomb. In addition, a synagogue named "of the Hebrews (Ἑβρέων)"[147] is believed to be the earliest one of all that are mentioned in the inscriptions found in the catacomb.[148] All these synagogues were probably founded in the period of our present investigation.[149] It is noticeable

---

141. For the notion that the athletic games in antiquity were actually pagan religious festivals, see Feldman, *Jew and Gentile*, 59.

142. I will discuss the cultic overtone of the guild gatherings in Greco-Roman world in the next chapter.

143. Josephus, *Ant.* 14.235, 259–261.

144. See page 133 above.

145. *CII*, 1, no. 365 = *JIWE*, 2, no. 170; *CII*, 1, no. 425 = *JIWE*, 2, no. 130 (cf. *CII*, 1, no. 503 = *JIWE*, 2, no. 549 whose provenance of Monteverde is regarded by Noy as doubtful). It is also possible that this Agrippa refers to one of the Jewish kings Agrippa I and II. In any case, this synagogue falls within the period of my present study.

146. *CII*, 1, no. 343 = *JIWE*, 2, no. 167; *CII*, 1, no. 402 = *JIWE*, 2, no. 100, *CII*, 1, no. 417 = *JIWE*, 2, no. 163 (Cf. *CII*, 1, no.523 = *JIWE*, 2, no. 577 the provenance of which Noy classifies as unknown). It is noticeable that one Volumnius is mentioned in the records of Josephus (*J.W.* 1.535–542; *Ant.* 16.277–283, 344–369) as one connected with the Jewish communities although nothing with absolute certainty can be said.

147. *CII*, no. 291= *JIWE*, 2, no. 33; *CII*, no. 317= *JIWE*, 2, no. 2 (cf. *CII*, no. 510 = *JIWE*, 2, no. 578; *CII*, no. 535= *JIWE*, 2, no. 579 the provenance of which Noy once again regards as unknown).

148. Leon, *Jews*, 148–149; Richardson, "Augustan-Era Synagogues," 20, 22.

149. Another synagogue that probably belonged to the late 1st century BCE or the beginning of the 1st century CE is the one seemed to be named after Herod the Great (*CII*. no. 173= *JIWE*, 2, no. 292). See the argument in Richardson, "Augustan-Era

that both Josephus (*Ag. Ap* 2.175; Cf. *Ant.* 16.43) and Philo (*Somn.* 2.127; *Prob.* 81–83; *Mos.* 2.216) have emphasized the prominence of Torah reading, instructions and discussions in the synagogues on every Sabbath (Cf. Acts 13:14–15; 15:21). Josephus even claims, probably with exaggeration, that the Jewish people could repeat the laws "all more readily than his own name" and had the laws engraven on their souls.[150]

As Gruen observes, these synagogues were actually "a prime signal of Jewish existence"[151] which helped to preserve the visibility and identity of the Jewish communities in the pagan world. According to the decree recorded by Josephus in *Ant.* 14.259–261, the synagogue in Sardis was to be a place where the Jews could assemble and conduct life together (συνάγωνται καὶ πολιτεύωνται) and adjudicate suits among themselves. The activities within it may include assemblies on Sabbaths, prayers and other sacral rites to God.[152] As the special arrangement of food was also mentioned in the decree, it is likely that festival celebrations and common meals would also be held in the synagogues. Hence, the widespread presence of Jewish synagogues throughout the Roman Empire provided the Jews with the necessary venue to express their religious as well as ethnic identity whether among themselves or before the surrounding world.[153]

It must be stressed, however, that the Diaspora Jewish communities had never lived in separatist seclusion. They were in fact an integral fabric of the Greco-Roman social world[154] and prepared to maintain positive

---

Synagogues," 23–28. The relevant inscription is, however, too fragmentary to allow any definite conclusion.

150. Josephus, *Ag. Ap* 2.178 (Thackeray, LCL).

151. Gruen, *Diaspora*, 105.

152. Scholars agree that θυσίας in *Ant.* 14.260 should not be understood literally as "sacrifices" as those which took place in the Jerusalem temple. Ralph Marcus understands this term in its larger sense of "offerings" (Josephus, *Jewish Antiquities*, vol. 7, 9 vols., trans. Ralph Marcus, LCL [London: William Heinemann, 1933–1963], 589 n.d.) while Tcherikover takes it to refer to "worship in a general sense" (Tcherikover, *Hellenistic Civilization*, 509 n. 34).

153. For the other functions of synagogues, Gruen, *Diaspora*, 119 suggests that they also constituted "asylum for the refugee" and "housed records, displayed offerings, held sacred funds, and supplied a setting for assemblies to promulgate measures and tribunals to pass judgment."

154. For the variety of professions and occupations taken up by the Jewish Diaspora in the larger society, see Tcherikover, *Hellenistic Civilization*, 343; Grant, *Jews*, 62; Sevenster, *Roots*, 81, 86–87.

daily interactions with their neighbours, in so far as the continuous observance of their ancestral laws was not affected. As can be implied from the various decrees mentioned in section 4.1.1 above, the Jews in Asia Minor and Rome were parties to business transactions and court litigations, potential contributors to public services and even among the needy entitled to public dole.

Particularly noteworthy is that despite consistent antagonism from their neighbours, the Jews, at least in Asia Minor and Rome, notably did not seek to disrupt public order by resorting to violent retaliation measures against their neighbours in the cities.[155] Even Flaccus' confiscation of the huge amount of gold from the Asian Jewish communities was not said to have met any drastic resistance.[156] The decrees recorded by Josephus also indicate that when the Diaspora Jews had any grievances, they would choose to have them redressed through proper legal process rather than by way of violent or subversive measures.

This pacifist and somewhat docile response towards pagan hostility is another example of Diaspora Jewish behaviour reflected in the Petrine ethics, especially when the author instructs Christians "not to return evil for evil, or reviling for reviling" (1 Pet 3:9) and to "seek peace and pursue it" (1 Pet 3:11). As I explained in the last chapter,[157] Christ's own experience of "not reviling in return while being reviled, and not threatening while suffering" (1 Pet 2:23) is perceived by the Petrine author as "fulfilling" the Jewish ideal of seeking peace without returning abuses. Hence, Christians suffering abuse without retaliation nicely falls within the Petrine author's perception as *both* an expression of their identity as the continuing elect exiles of Diaspora, *and* a token of their solidarity with the Messiah-Christ by following his steps as exemplified on the cross.

Indeed, Diaspora Jewish communities both in Rome and Asia Minor did not stop at passively enduring alienations from their neighbours, but positively followed the Greco-Roman convention to express their sociability

---

155. As for the expulsions of the Jews in Rome in 19 CE and 49 CE, neither of them was caused by Jewish hostility against their pagan neighbours. See my discussion in n. 53 on pages 130–131 above.

156. If the Diaspora Jews had made any dramatic or violent resistance, Cicero would not have missed the chance to mention it in his defence for Flaccus.

157. See pages 99–100 above.

in so far as the overriding boundary of ultimate allegiance to God was not overstepped. Besides naming their synagogues after some beneficent figures, they may also accept gifts from some distinguished pagan patrons and adopt the Greco-Roman reciprocal system of granting honours to them in return.[158] Hence, on an inscription dealing with the restoration of a synagogue in Acmonia of Asia Minor,[159] it is mentioned that this synagogue was originally constructed by one Julia Severa. She was actually a famous priestess of the imperial cult at Acmonia during the reign of Nero and appeared on the city coinage.[160] This inscription reveals that the Asian Jewish communities did maintain consistent friendship with the other members of the pagan society, some of whom could be wealthy aristocrats and even of different religious orientations.[161]

What the Jewish communities would however insist was that they would not honour the patrons' statues. As Rajak asserts, "Statues in honor of individuals were common currency in the honors system of the Roman empire and in euergetistic transactions; but there is absolutely no evidence to suggest that even the laxest of Diaspora Jews countenanced the erection of images of living beings."[162] "Differentiated resistance," now expressed through avoidance of erecting any images to uphold the ultimate allegiance to God, is once again seen as the Diaspora strategy of social engagement.

Besides distinguished figures of the cities, there is also evidence indicating that the Jewish Diaspora did manage to win sympathy and support from different strata of the wider society. Particularly noticeable is the presence of an impressive group of proselytes (e.g. Acts 13:43) and sympathizers (God-fearers) (e.g. Acts 13:16, 50; cf. 14:1) at the synagogue assemblies in

---

158. Tessa Rajak, "The Synagogue within the Greco-Roman City," in *Jews, Christians, and Polytheists in the Ancient Synagogue: Cultural Interaction During the Greco-Roman Period*, ed. Steven Fine (London: Routledge, 1999), 164, 166–167. Cf. Harland, *Associations*, 219.

159. *CII*, 2, no. 766.

160. Rajak, "Synagogue," 162–163; Trebilco, *Jewish Communities*, 59.

161. As Anne Fitzpatrick-McKinley, "Synagogue Communities in the Graeco-Roman Cities," in *Jews in the Hellenistic and Roman Cities*, ed. John R. Bartlett (London: Routledge, 2002), 68 observes, the purposes of the Diaspora Jews in cultivating such patronage among the Roman elites were to "protect their rights, possibly also to express their sense of belonging to the city and sometimes to ensure their safety."

162. Rajak, "Synagogue," 170.

Asia Minor.¹⁶³ Although most scholars recognize that the Diaspora Jewish communities did not have missionary activities in the Christian sense of sending out missionaries or propaganda for mass conversion, the fact that numbers of pagans were attracted to the Jewish religion bespeaks the synagogues' openness in maintaining positive interactions with different sectors of the cities. Gentiles who expressed an interest in Judaism were likely to be received with the warmest enthusiasm.¹⁶⁴

Indeed, the Jewish Diaspora were likely capable of attracting pagans to their religion through day-to-day interactions. As Sevenster observes, "Many were impressed by the great age of Judaism, by its proclamation of one God, by the exceptional standard of life and society in accordance with the Jewish laws, by the fixed line in their way of thinking and living, by their courage in life and in death."¹⁶⁵ Therefore, besides following their distinctive ancestral laws at all costs, the Jewish communities must have adopted a lifestyle which was also recognized as virtuous according to commonly expected standards, before they could win the sympathy and even conversions of their pagan neighbours.

Once again, this Jewish way of witnessing to God through daily good conduct is probably the Petrine author's frame of reference when he asserts that Christians' "good works" (ἀγαθοποιοῦντας) can silence the ignorance of their unbelieving slanderers (1 Pet 2:15), and that unbelieving husbands

---

163. Although A. Thomas, Kraabel, and Robert S. MacLennan, "The God-Fearers – a Literary and Theological Invention," in *Diaspora Jews and Judaism: Essays in Honor of, and in Dialogue with, A. Thomas Kraabel*, eds. J. Andrew Overman and Robert S. MacLennan (Atlanta, GA: Scholars Press, 1992), 134, argue that God-fearers were "a figment of the scholarly imagination," many scholars nowadays accept the presence of a notable group of sympathizers with differing degree of involvement in the synagogues, although this group might fall short of a formal and universally recognized category. See e.g. Tessa Rajak, *Translation and Survival: The Greek Bible of the Ancient Jewish Diaspora* (Oxford: Oxford University Press, 2009), 118; Judith Lieu, *Neither Jew nor Greek?: Constructing Early Christianity* (London: T&T Clark, 2002), 50–51; J. Andrew Overman, "The God-Fearers: Some Neglected Features," in *Diaspora Jews and Judaism: Essays in Honor of, and in Dialogue with, A. Thomas Kraabel*, eds. J. Andrew Overman and Robert S. MacLennan (Atlanta, GA: Scholars Press, 1992), 145–152.

164. Shaye J. D. Cohen, "Was Judaism in Antiquity a Missionary Religion?" in *Jewish Assimilation, Acculturation and Accommodation: Past Traditions, Current Issues and Future Prospects*, ed. Menahem Mor (Lanham, MD: University Press of America, 1992), 15, 20–21. For the view that Judaism was a missionary religion, see Feldman, *Jew and Gentile*, 288–334.

165. Sevenster, *Root*, 217.

may be won to faith by the conduct (ἀναστροφῆς) of their believing wives (1 Pet 3:1–2). As I argued in chapter 3,[166] 1 Peter 3:1–2 is actually the only place in the letter where a concern for the conversion of pagans is unambiguously expressed. In the face of surrounding ostracism, the primary concern of the Diaspora people of God was not so much to make converts, as to gain room to uphold their ultimate allegiance to God, although pagan conversion to Christ is most welcomed. Through this reading of 1 Peter with the proper lens of the Jewish Diaspora, the absence of keen missionary interest in 1 Peter can be accounted for, and a judicious assessment of the Petrine concern for pagan conversion can be obtained.

Section Summary: Jewish Resonances in 1 Peter

In my above analysis of Jewish engagement in their civil, household and daily social life, I demonstrated how the theme of "differentiated resistance" within the Petrine social behavioural instructions can be concretely understood with reference to the strategies and experience of the Jewish Diaspora especially in Asia Minor and Rome.[167] The estrangement undergone by the Diaspora Jews is strikingly similar to the Petrine Christian readers, which renders it particularly pertinent for Christians to understand their existence on earth as the continuing exilic people of God of Diaspora, and to draw upon the experience of the Jewish elect exiles of Diaspora as the appropriate resource for the formulation of their own social ethics.

As I also demonstrated in this section, the primary concern of the Jewish Diaspora was to preserve intact their exclusive worship of Yahweh in the midst of the host idolatrous culture. Ultimate allegiance to God, expressed in terms of persistent observance of the Torah, was also the boundary of their accommodation. In so far as God's commandments were not transgressed, the Jews, at least in Asia Minor and in Rome, were prepared to adopt the current societal conventions and to take up their roles as ordinary members of the wider society. This theme of "differentiated resistance"

---

166. See page 68 above.
167. It is noticeable that Tessa Rajak underlines the Jewish social strategy also as a process of "selective appropriation." See Tessa Rajak, "Benefactors in the Greco-Jewish Diaspora," in *Geschichte–Tradition–Reflexion: Festschrift für Martin Hengel zum 70. Geburtstag*, vol. 1, 3 vols., ed. Peter Schäfer (Tübingen: J.C.B. Mohr [Paul Siebeck], 1996), 318.

is captured in 1 Peter as the Christian social strategy. Although Christians are no longer required to observe the Laws, the gist of Torah observance (i.e. living in accordance with the will of God), is still taken up by Christians (1 Pet 2:15; 3:17; 4:2, 19). As long as this boundary is not overstepped, they are also expected to live responsibly according to their societal roles, and to behave as the best citizens in accordance with the wider societal order.

On the other hand, in view of the prominence of religion in every facet of city life, the rejection of the pagan rituals by the Diaspora people of God could lead to frequent hatred and ostracism from their pagan neighbours. The Jewish strategy of "differentiated resistance" actually facilitates the Diaspora people of God to make an effort to maintain positive relationships with the emperors and other Roman authorities, so that they could concentrate their efforts on resisting pressure to give up their ancestral laws at provincial level. At the same time, the Jewish attitude towards their hostile neighbours, at least in Asia Minor and Rome, was by no means antagonistic or sullen. They maintained, as far as possible, positive interactions with different sectors of the cities, and properly discharged their social functions whether in the households or in their daily social life.

This strategy of "differentiated resistance" is what the Petrine author understood as applicable to the Christian Diaspora. Thus, Christians are to subject themselves to every human creature (institution) (2:13) and to honour the emperor with fear reserved to God (2:17) in their civil life, while at the same time enduring suffering for the sake of righteousness without fear or being disturbed (3:14), making defence to their neighbours (3:15), and not submitting to the will of the Gentiles (4:3) in their daily social life. Just like the effort of the Jewish Diaspora to gain room to hold fast to their exclusive allegiance to God, accommodation understood in terms of following societal order through subordination in the households (2:18–20; 3:1–4), seeking peace without returning abuses (3:9–11), and abstention from wrongdoing which are also recognized by society as such (4:15; cf. 2:12) are also encouraged so that the Christian Diaspora do not unnecessarily aggravate their already precarious situation. Since the Jewish Diaspora at least in Asia Minor and Rome were already implementing the strategy of "differentiated resistance," it is only natural that the Petrine "good works" in the form of "differentiated resistance" is also regarded by the Petrine author as the appropriate identity expression of Christians as the continuing elect exiles of Diaspora.[168]

With the Jewish strategies as the frame of reference, we can now understand how the Petrine strategy of "differentiated resistance" may be practised in reality. Taking the Diaspora Jews as the example, honouring the emperors (2:17) can be carried out by the Christian Diaspora through offering prayers for the emperors or even establishing certain inscriptions commemorating the beneficence of the imperial court. Seeking peace (3:11) in the cities can also be fulfilled through responsibly discharging their societal roles as business partners, court litigants, slaves, wives etc., and contributing to public services in accordance with societal expectations.

On the other hand, to uphold the overriding boundary of ultimate allegiance to God, honouring the emperors must not include taking them as the objects of worship. Subordination within the household whether as slaves (2:18) or wives (3:1) must also exclude any participation in the household cults. In addition, the Christian Diaspora are to follow the Jewish example in staying apart from anything related to the pagan cults including abstaining from public festivals and common meals in cultic settings, and refusing to contribute to any public works or activities that may associate with idolatry. Whereas abuses and ostracism in the form of deprivation of civil rights and slanderous attacks can be anticipated, Christians should still follow the Jewish ideal to pursue peace (3:11) in the cities.

What is remarkable is that the Diaspora Jews managed to prosper and took root in the pagan world for centuries without losing their religious and ethnic identity. The notable number of proselytes and God-fearers found in the synagogues testified that it was not impossible to have positive interactions with the outside world while remaining "different." This Diaspora Jewish mode of witnessing through virtuous conduct in daily life actually serves to throw light on scholars' debate on the missionary interest of 1 Peter. With 1 Peter 3:1–2 the only reference having conversion of unbelievers unambiguously in view, 1 Peter actually reflects a Diaspora Jewish attitude on Gentile conversion and does not demonstrate such a central missionary interest as some scholars are inclined to see.

---

168. Please refer to my analysis in chapter 3.

In fact, besides social strategies, the Petrine understanding of Christian identity in terms of the elect exilic people of Diaspora also carries with it the Jewish Diaspora consciousness, which in fact accounts for the dual elements of "resistance" and "accommodation" within the Petrine social strategies.

4.2 Diaspora Consciousness of the Jewish Exilic People of God

In chapter 2, I have mentioned that when interpreting the metaphor of "exiles of Diaspora (παρεπιδήμοις διασπορᾶς, 1:1)" in 1 Peter, scholars tend to lay emphasis on the transience and displacement of Christian existence in this world.[169] Hence, Martin advocates that the Petrine author perceives the existence of Christian as "the wandering people of God on an eschatological journey."[170] Mbuvi also understands the image of an "exile" to represent a period of "instability and homelessness" in the history of Israel.[171] What follows is that the exilic people of Diaspora regard their present state of affairs as soon to pass and so must resist assimilation and remain different from the surrounding world. Their sole task is to get prepared to return to their inheritance of the true home at the eschaton so that any attachment to the place of their present residence is not necessary.

Regrettably, this simplistic line of interpretation is far from adequate to account for the complexities of Diaspora life. Even in the Jewish Scriptures, although Psalm 137 expresses the melancholic sentiment of a deep yearning for Jerusalem and a burning desire for the destruction of Babylon, their existing land of residence, we also have Jeremiah exhorting the Babylonian exiles to settle down in the Diaspora by building houses, getting married and having offspring (MT Jer 29:5–6 [LXX Jer 36:5–6]). Particularly important to note is that LXX Jeremiah 36:7 encourages the exiles to seek peace (ζητήσατε εἰς εἰρήνην; cf. ζητησάτω εἰρήνην, 1 Pet 3:11) of the land

---

169. Please refer to pages 53–54 above.

170. Martin, *Metaphor*, 154. See also Troy W. Martin, "The Rehabilitation of a Rhetorical Step-Child: First Peter and Classical Rhetorical Criticism," in *Reading First Peter with New Eyes: Methodological Reassessments of the Letter of First Peter*, eds. Robert L. Webb and Betsy Bauman-Martin (London: T&T Clark, 2007), 57–58.

171. Mbuvi, *Temple*, 24.

in which they settle, because the host land in its peace (ἐν εἰρήνῃ αὐτῆς) "will be" (ἔσται) peace to them. This identification of interest and destiny with the surrounding environment necessarily assumes some adoption of the norms and values of the host cities by the exilic Diaspora.

Indeed, although the forced exile to Babylon in 586 BCE constituted the bleakest phase of the ancient Israelite history and continued to haunt the memory of the Jewish Diaspora for centuries, it is equally true that when they had the chance to return to their homeland during the reign of Cyrus, a majority of them actually did not choose to have this supposed "longing" for Jerusalem "fulfilled" by going back.[172] Especially in the first century CE when millions of Jews had already lived in the foreign land for generations, it seems unrealistic to suppose that they only lingered on in the traditional hope of returning without having cultivated any sense of belonging to the local city, in which many of them in fact had been living since birth. As Gruen argues, "Respect and awe paid to the Holy Land could coincide with commitment to local community and allegiance to Gentile governance."[173]

In my following analysis of the Jewish Diaspora consciousness, I will demonstrate how the Diaspora Jewish communities, including those in Rome and Asia Minor, fell squarely into what Barclay ascribes to them: They "retain a sense of belonging elsewhere (in memory, myth or longing to return), but also typically develop strong attachments to their present place of belonging,"[174] and were "neither a wandering body of people, nor simply a community of 'immigrants' absorbed into a new home."[175] It was precisely this complexity within the Diaspora consciousness that accounted for the presence of both elements of "resistance" and "accommodation" within the Jewish social strategies. I will also argue that this tension of *both* "longing" for an eschatological home elsewhere *and* existentially "belonging" to the present place of abode is what the Petrine author understands

---

172. Jacob Neusner, "Exile and Return as the History of Judaism," in *Exile: Old Testament, Jewish and Christian Conceptions*, ed. James M. Scott (Leiden: Brill, 1997), 226.

173. Gruen, *Diaspora*, 11.

174. Barclay, "Introduction," 2.

175. Ibid.

Christian Diaspora existence to be in this world, which in turn gives shape to his Christian social ethics.

4.2.1 Diaspora's Longing for Return

It is commonly found in the Jewish literature that the Jewish exile and dispersion throughout the foreign land was God's punishment for the sins of Israel. Besides repeated appearance of this understanding in the Jewish Scriptures,[176] the Diaspora novels of Tobit and Judith also interpret the exile and dispersion as the result of Israelites' transgression of God's commandments.[177] Similar comprehension is also expressed in the literature believed to be written in the Diaspora such as the *Testaments of the Twelve Patriarchs*[178] and *Sybilline Oracles*, Book 3.[179] This painful memory of God's punishment had not washed away with time and was still in force after the destruction of the temple in 70 CE.[180]

One factor that held the integrity of the Jewish Diaspora intact was the hope that one day, God would end their exilic travail, regather them and bring them back to the land that he had promised to their patriarchs. This expectation of a return is also prominently reiterated in the Jewish Scriptures,[181] Diaspora novels[182] and pseudepigrapha of probable Diaspora provenance.[183] Even up to the time of Philo, this desire for a return was still current among the Jewish Diaspora.[184] One prominent image forming part of this expectation is God, as the shepherd, gathering his people as the flock, bringing them back, and feeding them with the goodness of the land

---

176. E.g. Lev 26:27–33; Deut 28:58–64; Jer 5:19; 9:12–15; Zech 7:12–14; Ezek 12:8–15; 36:17–20; Dan 9:7.

177. E.g. Tob 3:3–4; Jdt 5:18.

178. E.g. *T. Dan* 5.7–8; *T. Ash* 7.5–6. These references likely belong to the Jewish substratum of *T. 12 Patr*. See page 89 n. 100 above.

179. E.g. *Syb. Or.* 3.265–279.

180. See e.g. *2 Bar.* 1.2–4.

181. E.g. Deut 30:4–5; Isa 11:11–12; Jer 12:15; 16:15; 23:7–8; 29:14; 31:8–9 (LXX 38:8–9); Ezek 11:17; 34:13–14; 36:8, 12, 24; 37:21–22; 39:25–28.

182. E.g. Tob 13:5; 14:5.

183. E.g. *T. of Ash.* 7.7.

184. *Praem.* 162–172. See Barclay, *Jews*, 422.

of Israel.¹⁸⁵ In Ezekiel 37:24, this role of the shepherd of the Israelite flock is further said to be taken up by a future king David.

Another vision related to the restoration of Israel as a nation is the restoration of Jerusalem and the Temple to their glory and splendour.¹⁸⁶ In Tob 13:17, Jerusalem is envisioned to be rebuilt elaborately with sapphire, emerald, precious stones, pure gold, beryl, ruby and stones of Ophir, while *Syb. Or.* 3.290–292 also foretells the rebuilding of the temple with "gold and bronze and much-wrought iron"¹⁸⁷ contributed by pagan kings. Particularly relevant for our investigation is the fervour expressed in Isaiah 2:2–3 that the future Jerusalem will be the centre of the world when "all the nations will stream to it." The law will go out from Zion while the word of God will also go out from Jerusalem. Similarly pertinent is the expectation that Jerusalem will be a joy to both God and humanity (Isa 65:18–19).

It is against this backdrop of an ultimate return and restoration that Jerusalem and the Temple continued to capture the nationalistic imagination of the Diaspora Jews. As Philo observes, the Jews of Europe and Asia, whether islands or continents, all looked upon "the holy city as their metropolis¹⁸⁸ in which is erected the sacred temple of the most high God" (*Flacc.* 46).¹⁸⁹ Indeed, both Philo and Josephus recognize that the temple in Jerusalem was the only legitimate temple of God in which sacrifices to God could be performed.¹⁹⁰ Especially at a time when the Jews of Diaspora experienced hostility and ostracism from the cities, this sentimental attachment to the mother city, Jerusalem, actually offered them a homeland to hold on to their faith. As Fitzpatrick-McKinley comments, Jerusalem "provided them with an inspiring and universal symbol of an alternative *polis*, a symbol which they turned to especially when their situation in the cities of Diaspora deteriorated."¹⁹¹ A conviction of the existence of a "homeland"

---

185. Jer 31:10 (LXX 38:10); Ezek 34:12–16; Isa 40:10–11. Cf. Ezek 36:37–38.
186. Tob 14:5.
187. Translation provided by J. J. Collins, "Sibylline Oracles," *OTP* 1:368.
188. The Greek term employed by Philo is μητρόπολιν, i.e. mother city; cf. μητρόπολις, Philo, *Legat.* 281; μητρόπολιν, Josephus, *Ant.* 3.245; μητρόπολις, Josephus, *J.W.* 7.375.
189. Translation provided in Philo, *The Works*, trans. Yonge, 729.
190. Philo, *Spec.* 1.67–68; Josephus, *Ag. Ap.* 2.193.
191. Fitzpatrick-McKinley, "Synagogue Communities," 75.

elsewhere was therefore a "compensation" for the alienation suffered by Diaspora Jews in the cities of their residence.[192]

This aspiration for an alternative reality (homeland), in compensation for the present estrangement, is also what the Petrine author adopts when he understands Christians' existence on earth as "elect exiles of Diaspora." Just as the land of Israel was regarded as the inheritance (κληρονομία; κληρονομέω in its verb form) of the Jews,[193] the Christian Diaspora is also longing for (εἰς ἐλπίδα, 1 Pet 1:3; ἐλπίσατε, 1:13; cf. 1:21; 3:15) an inheritance (εἰς κληρονομίαν) now being kept in heaven (ἐν οὐρανοῖς)(1:4), that is, their salvation (εἰς σωτηρίαν, 1:5, cf. 2:2) to be revealed in the last time. What is unique for the Christian Diaspora is that this revelation (ἀποκαλυφθῆναι, 1:5) of the eschatological salvation will take place together with the revelation (ἀποκαλύψει, 1:7) of Jesus Christ, who has also gone into heaven (εἰς οὐρανόν, 3:22). This alternative reality of an eschatological salvation is the basis on which the Christian Diaspora can continue to rejoice (ἀγαλλιᾶσθε, 1:6, 8; cf. χαίρετε; χαρῆτε ἀγαλλιώμενοι, 4:13) despite their present alienation, and to hold on to their faith (1:5, 7, 8, 9, 21; 2:6, 7; 5:9) to God. For the Petrine author, Christians obtaining their ultimate salvation is the end (τὸ τέλος) of their faith (1:9).

The significance of this longing for an alternative reality is that the exilic Diaspora community would forge their lifestyle in a way as to accord with this longing, which necessarily renders them "different" from their pagan neighbours. The Jewish Diaspora had never shrunk from their attachment and loyalty to Jerusalem. As evidenced by Flaccus' trial,[194] the Asian Jewish communities did insist on sending a considerable amount of gold as temple contributions to Jerusalem regardless of political and social pressure to abandon the practice.[195] Besides Cicero,[196] both Josephus and Philo also attest to the readiness of the Diaspora Jews of different cities in

---

192. Ibid., 72.

193. See pages 45–46 above.

194. See pages 136–138 above.

195. Cicero, *Flac.* 28.67. Cf. Josephus *Ant.* 16.28, 45; Philo, *Leg.* 311. Both Barclay, *Jews*, 417 and Fitzpatrick-McKinley, "Synagogue Communities," 71 observe that the pressure experienced by the Asian Minor Jewish communities is also implied in the accounts of Josephus, *Ant.* 16.162–168, 171–173.

196. Cicero, *Flac.* 28.67.

making the contributions,[197] including Rome[198] and Asia.[199] Such a practice of sending contributions to Jerusalem was so prominent that even a pagan writer like Tacitus took notice of it.[200] Since every male adult of the Jewish communities was expected to make the contributions every year,[201] this practice was actually a constant reminder to each Diaspora Jew of the continuous connection between Jerusalem and the Diaspora.

Another way through which the Jews could express their aspiration for the homeland was through pilgrimages to Jerusalem, especially for festivals. That thousands of Jews from different parts of the Diaspora flocked to Jerusalem served to foreshadow the eschatological regathering of the scattered people of God when Jerusalem will once again be the centre of the world. Although we do not know the exact number of the Diaspora Jews who visited Jerusalem each year, the statement in Acts 2:9–11 that there were a multitude of Jews from Parthia, Media, Elam, Mesopotamia, Cappadocia, Pontus, Asia, Phrygia, Pamphylia, Egypt, Cyrene, Rome, Crete and Arabia present in Jerusalem at the time of Pentecost is very telling. Although this account may have been exaggerated, it is still sufficient to testify the presence of a sizable number of Diaspora Jews in Jerusalem, especially at festival times.[202]

In fact, what particularly marked the Diaspora Jewish longing for the ultimate homeland was their ardour for observing their ancestral laws. As the Diaspora Jews understood their national catastrophe of the exile as the result of their fathers' transgression of the commandments of God, it was of cardinal importance that they did not tread the same path as their ancestors. Hence, Tobit commanded his son to "keep the law and commandments" (Tob 14:9) in the light of the expected gathering and return of Israel to the promised land (Tob 14:5).[203] This faithful compliance with God's commandments foreshadowed the way of life of God's

---

197. Philo, *Spec.* 1.77–78. Cf. *Legat.* 216; Josephus, *Ant.* 18.312.
198. Philo, *Legat.* 156.
199. Josephus, *Ant.* 14.245; 16.172–173.
200. Tacitus, *Hist.* 5.5.1.
201. Philo, *Spec.* 1.77.
202. Furthermore, according to Josephus, *J. W.* 5.199, a court was reserved in the Jerusalem temple for all Jewish women including "visitors from abroad" (Thackeray, LCL).
203. Cf. *T. Ash.* 7.4–7; *Sib. Or.* 3.282–288.

people after their future return to their homeland. As Ezekiel envisions, they will be clean from all detestable things and idols and will walk in the statutes of God.[204]

Therefore, although the Jewish Diaspora became distinctive and visible through zealous observance of their ancestral laws, they did not preserve their difference just for the sake of being different or for the pragmatic consideration to resist being engulfed by an alien host culture. As the holy people of God, Diaspora Jews led a lifestyle distinct from their pagan neighbours because of their theological vision of a final regathering and return to their promised homeland under the lead of their shepherd God. Religious conviction came before pragmatic consideration of social or political necessities to remain different. As Neusner observes, "it is the Jews' religion, Judaism, that has formed their world and framed their realities, and not the world of politics, culture, society, that has made their religion."[205]

The primacy of theological vision in the shaping of corresponding behaviour is also prominent in the shaping of Petrine social ethics. Since the Christian Diaspora are also longing for an inheritance kept in heaven, which is their salvation (1:5) to be fully revealed with the future revelation of Jesus Christ (1:7), they must stand firm in the grace of God (5:12) and be prepared and sober (1:13),[206] and not be conformed to the cravings which marked them as non-believers in the past (cravings formerly in their ignorance, ταῖς πρότερον ἐν τῇ ἀγνοίᾳ ὑμῶν ἐπιθυμίαις, 1:14). It is this abstention from the fleshly cravings (τῶν σαρκικῶν ἐπιθυμιῶν), which war against the soul (στρατεύονται κατὰ τῆς ψυχῆς), i.e. which jeopardize their salvation,[207] that marks the lifestyle of Christians as resident-aliens and exiles (ὡς παροίκους καὶ παρεπιδήμους, 2:11) among Gentiles (2:12). This abstention from human cravings (ἀνθρώπων ἐπιθυμίαις) (4:2) and refusal to do the will of the Gentiles (4:3) is also what makes them "different" from their neighbours and attracts slanders (4:4).

---

204. Ezek 36:24–27; 37:23.

205. Neusner, "Exile and Return," 225.

206. Whether the participles ἀναζωσάμενοι and νήφοντες are taken to have an indicative or an imperative force renders the same implication.

207. See page 77 above.

What is unique for the Christian Diaspora is that whereas the Jewish Diaspora abstained from sins and zealously observed God's commandments (will) in order not to tread the same path as their fathers, the rationale provided by 1 Peter for Christians to abstain from the cravings of non-believers is that they have been redeemed from the futile (ματαίας) idolatrous[208] way of life inherited from their ancestors by the blood of Christ (1:18–19). Through the resurrection of Jesus Christ from the dead, Christians have been born again (1:3) into a new existence as obedient children (1:14) and, thus, entitled to the "inheritance" of salvation to be revealed at the end time. As God the Father (1:17) judges everyone impartially according to his work and he himself is holy, Christians must be holy in their conduct (1:15) and abstain from anything of the idolatrous culture that may profane their holiness and, thus, their belonging to the people of God. It is with this concern for the inheritance of ultimate salvation that the Christian Diaspora must stand firm in the grace of God (5:12) by holding fast to their ultimate allegiance to God, and conduct themselves in fear (ἐν φόβῳ) during their sojourn (1:17) on earth.

Just as the Jewish Diaspora, the Christian Diaspora do not remain different only for the sake of being different. Their distinctiveness (resistance) arises from their commitment to conduct their life on earth in accordance with their theological (eschatological) conviction. Other than this, there is actually an element of normality (accommodation) within Christians' lifestyle which arises from an existential sense of belonging to their native place of birth and nurture.

4.2.2 Diaspora's Belonging to the Native Country

While the longing for an ultimate return was kept alive through concrete behaviour, assemblies and scripture readings in the synagogues week after week throughout their Diaspora life, it also holds true that Jewish literature of Diaspora origin at the same time betrays an understanding of a certain "duration" in their Diaspora existence in the foreign land.

As a matter of fact, the traditionally-held concept of a forced exile and the following distressful dislocation did not necessarily apply to the experience of every Diaspora Jew. At least, in Josephus' record of the letter

---

208. See my analysis of μάταιος on pages 25–26 above.

by Antiochus III to Zeuxis about the first Jewish settlement in Asia Minor (*Ant.* 12.148–153), it is mentioned that 2,000 Jewish families were to be transferred from Mesopotamia and Babylonia to Lydia and Phrygia to carry out military service and to keep a fortress there. Especially worth notice is that each of these families was given "a place to build a house and land to cultivate and plant with vines."[209] A series of tax concessions and provisions was then ordered so that the Jews "may show themselves the more eager" for such emigration.[210] Although this transfer necessarily constituted compulsory dislocation in some sense, these arrangements also foresaw "settlement" and "rootedness" of the Jews in the Asian land, which was likely to be realized afterwards when the family possession of the land was passed on from generations to generations.

A similar sense of rootedness in the foreign land was evidently present among Roman Jews as well. Although many Jews in Rome were originally brought to Italy as war captives, it is remarkable that after they had been emancipated, they did not choose to return to the promised land of Judea but, instead, continued to remain in Rome and even became Roman citizens.[211] Indeed, Cicero actually witnessed a significantly sizable Jewish crowd nearby during the trial of Flaccus in 61 BCE, mentioning that such Jewish communities stuck together and were influential in informal assemblies.[212] It is quite possible that such a large number of Jews in Rome did not all come from war captives. Since the period from Alexander the Great up to the Roman Empire was marked by political expansions and mass movements of peoples,[213] it is probable that many Jews had migrated to Rome genuinely out of their own volition.[214] Although the Diaspora Jews were truly expecting a time when God would lead his flock of holy people

---

209. Josephus, *Ant.* 12.151 (Marcus, LCL).

210. Josephus, *Ant.* 12.152 (Marcus, LCL). For the genuineness of this letter, see Tcherikover, *Hellenistic Civilization*, 287–288.

211. See Philo, *Legat.* 155.

212. Cicero, *Flac.* 28.66.

213. James M. Scott, "Exile and the Self-Understanding of Diaspora Jews in the Greco-Roman Period," in *Exile: Old Testament, Jewish, and Christian Conceptions*, ed. James M. Scott (Leiden: Brill, 1997), 176.

214. Gruen, *Diaspora*, 22 suggests that the possible purposes for the Jews' migrating to Rome and Italy included those of "commerce, to join families, to seek employment, or to enjoy the advantages of attachment to the center of power in the Mediterranean."

to the ultimate homeland, they nevertheless settled and took root in the present environment, regardless of the estrangement they experienced from the host cities.[215]

This Jewish sense of "duration" in their Diaspora existence is also betokened by the fact that the Jewish Diaspora actually understood themselves to be living as "colonies" and "settlements" (ἀποικία, μετοικεσία, κατοικία) rather than in exile and banishment (φυγή).[216] When describing the Jews' existence as exiles, the Septuagint preferred to use the terms ἀποικία[217] (and its related terms ἀποικεσία[218]) and μετοικεσία[219] to represent the Hebrew term גּוֹלָה, although the term αἰχμαλωσία[220] (and its related term αἰχμάλωτος[221]), meaning captives, captivity, were also employed. When dealing with the other Hebrew term גָּלוּת for exile or exiles, the same terms ἀποικία[222] (and its related terms ἀποικεσία[223] and ἀποικίζω[224]), μετοικεσία,[225] and αἰχμαλωσία[226] were again employed.[227] Therefore, in the translations of the Scriptures meant to be read by the Jewish Diaspora, their existence in the foreign land was perceived more as a "settlement" which implies a certain degree of permanence.

Likewise, Josephus also uses the term ἀποικία when he argues that the Jews of Alexandria constituted a colony (εἰς ἀποικίαν) and were entitled to be called Alexandrians (*Ag. Ap.* 2.38) just like their neighbours. When he described the event of the exile, he employed the term κατοικία (*Ag. Ap.*

---

215. See also Roy A. Rosenberg, "Exile, Mysticism, and Reality," in *Diaspora: Exile and the Jewish Condition*, ed. Étan Levine (New York: Jason Aronson, 1983), 44–45.

216. See also Louis H. Feldman, "The Concept of Exile in Josephus," in *Exile: Old Testament, Jewish, and Christian Conception*, ed. James M. Scott (Leiden: Brill, 1997), 145–172.

217. LXX Ezra 1:11; 2:1; 4:1; 9:4; 10:6, 7, 8, 16; Neh 7:6; Jer 35:6 (MT 28:6); 36:4 (MT 29:4); 36:31 (MT 29:31). Cf. Jer 36: 1 (MT 29:1).

218. LXX 2 Kgs 24:15; Ezra 6:19, 20, 21.

219. LXX 2 Kgs 24:16; 1 Chr 5:22; Ezek 12:11; Nah 3:10.

220. LXX Ezek 1:1; 3:11, 15; 11:24, 25; 12:3, 4, 7; 25:3; Zech 6:10; 14:2.

221. Esth 2:6.

222. LXX Jer 35:4 (MT 28:4); 36:22 (MT 29:22); 47:1 (MT 40:1).

223. LXX 2 Kgs 25:27.

224. LXX Jer 24:5; LXX Jer 52:31.

225. LXX Obad 1:20.

226. Isa 45:13; Ezek 1:2; 33:21; 40:1.

227. See also Feldman, "Concept," 145–146.

1.138), also meaning "colony," "settlement," and ἀποικία (*Ant.* 10.223) to refer to the Jewish settlement in Babylon. In similar vein, the verb μετοικίζω, meaning "to remove to another place of habitation, resettle,"[228] is used to describe Shalmaneser's "transferring" the ten tribes of Israelites to Media and Persia (*Ant.* 9.278) and Nebuchadnezzar's "transferring" the people of Judah to Babylon (*Ant.* 11.91; *Ag. Ap.* 1.132).[229] Indeed, Josephus' perception of Diaspora existence is most revealing in his version of Balaam's oracle, in which he claims that "the habitable world, be sure, lies before you as an eternal habitation."[230] As Josephus was writing at a time when the memory of the Roman suppression of the Jewish Revolt and destruction of the temple was still fresh, it is understandable that Josephus expected the Jewish habitation in the foreign land to go on for some more time.

Indeed, Josephus is not alone in understanding the Diaspora existence as a continuous sojourn. Philo also understands the Jewish settlements as "colonies (ἀποικία)" sent out from the land of their mother city (Jerusalem) to settle throughout the Roman Empire.[231] Particularly remarkable is that in *Flacc.* 46, Philo states that the Diaspora Jews, while regarding the holy city (i.e. Jerusalem) as their mother city (μητρόπολιν), also counted the native countries which the Jewish inhabitants had occupied since "their fathers, and grandfathers, and great grandfathers, and still more remote ancestors, and in which they have been born and brought up"[232] as their "fatherlands" (πατρίδας). For Philo, the Jewish Diaspora did not regard their host cities merely as a place of temporary residence but, instead, their native land to which they felt themselves belong.[233]

Therefore, although the Jewish Diaspora constantly faced alienation and exclusion from their neighbours in the cities, they nevertheless considered themselves "at home" in the land of their sojourn. In a petition to the prefect of Egypt dated by Tcherikover to 5–4 BCE,[234] a Jew of Alexandria,

---

228. "μετοικίζω," BDAG, 643.
229. So, Feldman, "Concept," 147–154.
230. Josephus, *Ant.* 4.116 (Thackeray, LCL).
231. Philo, *Mos.* 2.232; *Legat.* 281–282.
232. Translation provided in Philo, *Works*, trans. Yonge, 729.
233. See also Gruen, *Diaspora*, 243.
234. *CPJ*, 2, no. 151.

called Helenos, lodged a complaint, apparently for having been required to pay the poll tax. It is noticeable that he at first styled himself as "an Alexandrian" which was subsequently crossed out by himself, or by a scribe, and amended to "a Jew from Alexandria." This incident clearly indicates that the Diaspora Jews genuinely considered themselves as members of their local cities, although they may not be regarded as such by the cities or in accordance with the prevailing rules. Hence Philo would identify his city of residence as "our Alexandria" (τὴν ἡμετέραν Ἀλεξάνδρειαν)[235] while Josephus also argues that the Jews of Alexandria should be entitled to be called "Alexandrians," just like those Jews who were called "Antiochians" as well as the Jewish inhabitants of Ephesus and other cities of Ionia and, thus, to enjoy the right to be called after the names of their cities of habitation.[236]

Hence, side by side with the religious conviction of an ultimate return to the promised land, there was still an existential dimension within the Diaspora mentality (i.e. a belonging to the local place in which one was brought up and nurtured). As indicated in the petition of Helenos mentioned in the last paragraph, his father was an Alexandrian citizen and he had always lived in Alexandria where he had received appropriate education. It was only natural that he felt at home in the local environment and regarded himself as "an Alexandrian." For the Jewish Diaspora, they regarded themselves as part of the local social landscape and were prepared for a degree of permanence in their Diaspora existence before their final restoration and return. This attachment to their usual habitat was not affected by the antagonism they from time to time had to face from their neighbours.

It is especially noticeable that the Diaspora Jews had no problem in understanding themselves as *both* settling in colonies (ἀποικία) *and* in the course of a sojourn (παροικία) (cf. τὸν τῆς παροικίας ὑμῶν χρόνον, 1 Pet 1:17). In the LXX, whereas ἀποικία is used to represent the Hebrew terms גּוֹלָה and גָּלוּת for exile, παροικία is also rendered as a translation for גּוֹלָה in LXX Ezra 8:35 (τῆς παροικίας). Since the translators of the LXX understood the Jewish Diaspora existence to last for a certain duration of time as evidenced by their use of the terms ἀποικία and μετοικεσία which denotes

---

235. Philo, *Legat*. 150.
236. Josephus, *Ag. Ap*. 2.38–39.

settlement, it is clear that they did not take "transience" or "instability" to be the essence of the term παροικία. Likewise, in 3 Macc, both terms ἀποικία (6:10) and παροικία (6:36; 7:19) are used to refer to Jewish Diaspora existence in the foreign land. Particularly telling is that in 3 Macc 6:36, the common rite was set up for the παροικία "for generations" (εἰς γενεάς).

I hold that this Diaspora Jewish understanding of παροικία as a form of "settlement in the mundane world (the foreign land)" is what the Petrine author envisages when he designates Christians as παροίκους καὶ παρεπιδήμους (1 Pet 2:11), and their existence on earth as τῆς παροικίας (1:17). As I argued in chapter 2,[237] the Petrine designation of Christians as παροίκους καὶ παρεπιδήμους denotes the two dimensions of Christians' existence during the in-between time before the ultimate revelation of their inheritance of salvation in the last time (1 Pet 1:5; cf. 2:2). On the one hand, Christians' stay as παρεπίδημοι on earth can be said to be "temporary" when compared with their ultimate eternal belonging in heaven, so that the final judgment of God lies ahead at the doorstep (4:5), the end of all things is imminent (4:7) and the judgment of God has already begun with his own people (4:17). On the other hand, the Petrine author sees the whole process as taking an indeterminate period of time before its final consummation, so that Christians still need to stay in the current world as resident-aliens (πάροικοι). Therefore, Christians have to live the rest of the time in the flesh (τὸν ἐπίλοιπον ἐν σαρκὶ ... χρόνον) by the will of God (4:2), and still need to suffer various trials "for a little while" (ὀλίγον, 1:6; 5:10). Their existence on earth is highlighted as τὸν τῆς παροικίας ὑμῶν χρόνον (1:17) in which χρόνον is also an accusative and expresses "an extent" or "duration" of time.

Therefore, besides the eschatological dimension of a "longing" for the inheritance of their ultimate salvation, there is within the Christian Diaspora consciousness, as expressed in 1 Peter, also an existential dimension of a "belonging" to this existing world in which they need to "settle" during the in-between time before the final consummation of history. This settlement necessarily involves a certain sense of "at-homeness" and a degree of "normality" (and thus accommodation) in their Diaspora life, in so

---

237. See pages 48–50 in chapter 2 above.

far as the overriding boundary of ultimate allegiance to God is not jeopardized. This existential dimension of Diaspora consciousness is particularly fitting for the Gentile readers of 1 Peter (cf. 1 Pet 1:14, 18; 4:3) who were born in and nurtured by the culture of this world before their conversion. "Accommodation" for them is not so much "adoption" of foreign norms and values as "continuing" what they have been used to since birth.[238] The confinement of Christians' resistance only to matters which may jeopardize their religious allegiance actually serves to avoid unnecessary disorientation to the Gentile readers in requiring a complete uprooting after Christian conversion.

It must of course be stressed, at the same time, that this Diaspora belonging and settlement in a foreign land does not necessarily involve a thorough endorsement and identification with pagan values and practices. It only means what Gafni observes as relating "to their place of residence in the proper manner, by evincing the requisite degree of loyalty and devotion to the well-being and security of the 'patris.'"[239] This "proper manner" in relating to their place of residence is best exemplified by Jeremiah's exhortation to the Babylonian exiles to "build houses and dwell in them," "plant gardens and eat their fruits," "get married and multiply" and "seek peace of the host land and identify this peace as their own" (LXX Jer 36:5–7 [MT 29:5–7]).

In respect of the Jewish Diaspora, besides being continuously involved in the normal civil, social and economic life of their native cities as I mentioned in section 4.1 above, they could also make their sense of belonging visible to their neighbours through some media. For example, on a Jewish inscription from the Phrygian city of Acmonia, it is stated "ὑπὲρ εὐχῆ[ς] πάσῃ τῇ πατρίδι"[240] ("for the sake of a vow for the whole πατρίδι"). This inscription is presumably part of a gift and it is commonly accepted that πατρίδι of this inscription probably refers to "the city of Acmonia."[241] This

---

238. See also Seland, *Strangers*, 148, 172–173.

239. Isaiah Gafni, *Land, Center and Diaspora: Jewish Constructs in Late Antiquity*, JSPSup 21 (Sheffield: Sheffield Academic, 1997), 47.

240. *CII*, ii. no. 771. The inscription is undated but Trebilco, *Jewish Communities*, 221 n. 112 believes it to be dated probably after 135 CE.

241. Trebilco, *Jewish Communities*, 81–82; Fitzpatrick-McKinley, "Synagogue Communities," 70; Gafni, *Land*, 49–50; Gruen, *Diaspora*, 243.

inscription indicates that a Jew or Jewish community expressed their attachment to the host city by acknowledging it once again as the father city and indeed, contributed to its welfare by donating a gift for some public purposes.[242]

Likewise, the Petrine author also formulates his social behavioural instructions to express the Christian sense of belonging and settlement in the local place of residence, which allows for a degree of accommodation and normality in Christian Diaspora life. Christians are to follow current societal order and behave as best citizens by subjecting themselves to every human institution (2:13) and honouring everyone including the emperor (2:17); they are to continue building up families on earth and keep their proper roles within the household (2:18–3:7); they are to seek peace (3:11) and endure suffering for doing good (2:20; 3:14, 17) without retaliation (3:9).

Understanding themselves as "exiles of Diaspora" does not render Christians a separatist melancholic sect, feeling detached from the wider world, and putting every bit of their attention to a future reality as the means of escape from the existing hostile surroundings. To face the alienation from their unbelieving neighbours, the Petrine readers are exhorted to express their innate belonging to their native place of residence by contributing to the well-being of the wider world, and behaving as ordinary members of society. Besides gaining room to hold fast to their exclusive allegiance to God by silencing the slanders of hostile neighbours (2:15) and opening the way for pagan conversion (3:1–2), this allowance for some normality in Christian social life also helps to avoid unnecessary hardships on the Gentile converts which may result from an undifferentiated uprooting from their former connections and lifestyle.

Section Summary: Jewish Resonances in 1 Peter

By designating his readers as "elect exiles of Diaspora" in continuation to the Diaspora Jews, the Petrine author at the same time equips Christians with the two dimensions of the Jewish Diaspora consciousness. On the one hand, the Christian Diaspora are sharing with the Jews a similar "longing" for an eschatological alternative reality to their existing alienation.

---

242. See also Gruen, *Diaspora*, 243.

While the Jewish Diaspora longed for the return to their inheritance of the promised land, the Christian Diaspora are longing for their inheritance of ultimate salvation already accomplished by Jesus Christ. On the other hand, the Christian Diaspora also develop a sense of "belonging" to the native land to which they have to settle during the indeterminate in-between duration before the final consummation of human history. The essence of Diaspora existence is not simply "instability" or "transience" as often too one-sidedly emphasized by Petrine scholars.[243]

It is remarkable that *both* of these dimensions of a longing for an "eschatological" inheritance *and* an "existential" belonging to the local cities actually coexisted within the mentality of the Diaspora Jews in reality,[244] although probably in different proportions among different individuals.[245] This coexistence of *both* "longing" *and* "belonging" within the Diaspora consciousness is what the Petrine author appropriates as the ideological basis, on which to shape his social behavioural instructions comprising *both* elements of resistance *and* accommodation as proper Christian response to surrounding hostility.

The eschatological dimension of a longing for the ultimate salvation calls upon Christians to lead a life on earth conducive to the attainment of this inheritance. The Christian Diaspora must resist any parts of the pagan culture that have religious connotations and, thus, may jeopardize their exclusive allegiance to God, which necessarily makes them "different" from the rest of society. At the same time, the existential dimension of a belonging to the local place of residence also occasions a certain degree of normality to Christian Diaspora life, which renders them "similar" to the outside world in other aspects of Diaspora life.

It is precisely the co-working of these dimensions of "longing" and "belonging" that enables Christians to gain room to hold fast to their faith

---

243. E.g. Martin, *Metaphor*; Green, "Identity," 85–92; Mbuvi, *Temple*, 24.

244. See also Fitzpatrick-McKinley, "Synagogue Communities," 70; Barclay, *Jews*, 422.

245. As Scott, "Exile," 182 comments, "Jews living in foreign lands represented a whole spectrum of different perspectives on their Diaspora situation, dependent in part on time, place and circumstances" while he at the same time reckons that they "to some degree nevertheless have a common identity."

in God while settling in their existing place of residence pending the final revelation of their inheritance of salvation.

4.3 Chapter Conclusion

In this chapter, I demonstrated how the Petrine "good works" of "differentiated resistance" can be concretely understood and practised in reality with reference to the strategies and experience of the Jewish Diaspora especially in Asia Minor and Rome. The necessary link is established by the Petrine author addressing his readers as "elect exiles of Diaspora" (1:1), and appropriating the titles and self-definitions specifically applied to the people of Israel (e.g. 2:9–10) as Christian identity on earth.

As a matter of fact, the theme of "differentiated resistance" was also present in the social strategies of the Jewish Diaspora in Asia Minor and Rome, who adopted the same principle of "ultimate allegiance to God" as the boundary of their accommodation. Steadfastness in the exclusive worship of God was also the primary concern of Diaspora existence and the root of constant pagan hostility towards the people of God. Since their current alienation primarily stemmed from the ostracism of their pagan neighbours in their daily social life, the Diaspora Jews maintained as far as possible a harmonious relationship with the emperors and Roman officials, so as to concentrate on resisting the pressure to abandon God's commandments at provincial level. This is precisely the framework 1 Peter appropriates to the Christian Diaspora as part of the differentiated resistance in their social engagement. Hence, Christians are exhorted to submit to every human institution and honour the emperors, while enduring suffering for the sake of righteousness and without accomplishing the will of the Gentiles in their daily interactions with their pagan neighbours.

Furthermore, the dual elements of "resistance" and "accommodation" within the Diaspora social engagement owe their configuration to the dual dimensions of Diaspora consciousness. The eschatological dimension of a "longing" for an inheritance (homeland) elsewhere requires the Diaspora people of God to hold onto the grace/salvation of God, which necessarily requires their resistance to the pagan idolatrous culture. The existential dimension of a "belonging" to the existing place of residence, on the other hand, induces the exiles of Diaspora to express a degree of normality in their daily life. As I discussed in this chapter, this form of social engagement is especially fitting for the Petrine readers who are Gentile Christians having been born and brought up in a pagan world. Whereas it is of primary importance that they hold fast to their faith while waiting for the final revelation of their salvation, to allow room also for their continual settlement and contribution to the well-being of their native place actually serves to minimize unnecessary dislocation occasioned by their conversion.

Here lies the value of the Petrine appropriation of the Jewish experience and consciousness to Christians. Besides providing a mode of social engagement which best suits the need and circumstances of the early Gentile Christians, the primacy of religious conviction, which marks the Jewish social strategies, is also fundamentally important for Christians in the face of neighbours' hostility. For the Diaspora people of God, religious conviction always comes before any pragmatic consideration of survival or subsistence.

At the same time, it must be stressed that this appropriation of Jewish experience to Christians is implemented within the Petrine author's larger theological framework as I investigated in chapters 2 and 3. Besides being perceived as the appropriate identity expression of "Christian elect exiles of Diaspora," the Petrine "good works" are also connected to the reality unveiled by the historical appearance of the Messiah-Christ. Christians doing good and enduring suffering is merely their following the steps of Jesus Christ who himself suffered human rejection (1 Pet 2:4, 7) essentially as a resident-alien on the cross. "Differentiated resistance" also represents the form of Christ's engagement in the face of the cross. His acceptance of human suffering without retaliation is also the example (ὑπογραμμόν, 2:21) and, *at the same time*, regarded as fulfilling the Jewish ideal of seeking peace. It is precisely against this perception of the example of Jesus Christ as fulfilling the ideal mode of social engagement of the Diaspora people of God that the Jewish strategies are harmoniously incorporated into the Petrine ethics, and securely anchored to the letter's larger theological vision.

CHAPTER 5

Comparison Text I: Revelation

In the previous chapters, I concentrated on the shaping of Christian social behavioural instructions by theology in 1 Peter. I demonstrated that through the extensive use of OT language and images, the Petrine theological framework is constructed in terms of the Jewish eschatological visions. Jesus Christ is perceived as the Jewish expected Messiah who however suffered human rejection essentially as a resident-alien on the cross. Christians are also understood as the "elect exiles of Diaspora" inheriting the self-definition and eschatological hope of the Jewish Diaspora. For the Petrine author, Christians' identity on earth does not depend on being different from the wider world, but derives its origin from their exclusive relationship with God as his elect people brought about by the resurrection of Christ from the dead. Since their identity is determined by Christ, Christians also find themselves bound up with Christ just like individual elect stones of a spiritual temple grounding their existence and experience on that of the Messiah-Christ as its elect Cornerstone.

I then explored the Petrine social behavioural instructions from an insider perspective of the author's own religious convictions. I demonstrated that the theological framework mentioned in the last paragraph becomes the ideological basis on which the Petrine author devises the mode of Christian "good works" of "differentiated resistance" as a response to pagan pressure to accommodate. Ultimate allegiance to God remains his primary concern. This mode of Christian "good works" is underscored as the congruent identity expression of Christians as the "elect exiles of Diaspora" on earth, as well as a token of Christians following the steps of Christ as exemplified by the cross. Besides locating their vindication hope on God's ultimate visitation in terms of Jewish eschatological vision, Christians' present suffering for "doing good" and future glory is further perceived as participating in Christ's suffering and partaking in his glory. This Christ-Christians union is also a manifestation of the seamless unity of the Christian spiritual temple with Christ the Cornerstone.

In the previous chapter, I argued that by understanding Christians' existence as "elect exiles of Diaspora," the Petrine author further draws upon the experience and social strategies of the Jewish Diaspora especially in Asia Minor and Rome, whose social engagement also manifested the mode of "differentiated resistance." The Diaspora Jewish strategy of "maintaining harmonious relationship with the Roman emperor and officials, while concentrating on resisting pressure to accommodate at provincial level" is what 1 Peter is seen to have adopted. At the same time, the Jewish strategy of "seeking peace" and "maintaining a degree of normality" in the daily social life is also appropriated in 1 Peter to reflect Christians' existential "belonging" to their existing place of residence, although their "longing" for an eschatological inheritance (homeland) also requires the Diaspora people of God to stand firm in the salvation and hold onto their ultimate allegiance to God, which necessarily render them different from the pagan idolatrous environment.

In this and the next chapters, I will proceed to highlight these features of the shaping of the Petrine social ethics by comparing the letter with two other early Christian texts: Revelation and the *Epistle to Diognetus*. I will demonstrate how the early Christians' different theological perceptions of God/Christ and their relationship with the world gave rise to their different formulations of Christians' response to surrounding pagan hostility. In this chapter, I will first compare 1 Peter with Revelation.

Revelation can serve as an interesting comparison text because it bears a lot of similarities to 1 Peter but is, at the same time, very different. Just as 1 Peter is addressed to the churches in Asia Minor (Pontus, Galatia, Cappadocia, Asia, and Bithynia, 1 Pet 1:1), the intended readers of Revelation were also located in Asia Minor (Ephesus, Smyrna, Pergamum, Thyatira, Sardis, Philadelphia and Laodicea, Rev 1:11). In addition, most scholars nowadays accept that Revelation was written in the latter years of the reign of Domitian who ruled between 81–96 CE.[1] Among the evidence offered so far, particularly notable is the account of Irenaeus who testified that the Apocalypse was seen (ἑωράθη) by the end of Domitian's reign.[2] Although Irenaeus' record is flawed by his having attributed Revelation to the apostle John,[3] his testimony still carries much weight because he himself came from Asia Minor and lived in the second century CE, which was not too long after the time of Domitian.[4] Indeed, Irenaeus' record is corroborated by the fact that Babylon as a coded name for Rome[5] appears in Jewish literature only after 70 CE.[6] Furthermore, the names of the twelve apostles are seen inscribed on the foundations of the wall of the New Jerusalem in Revelation 21:14. As Yabro Collins convincingly argues, this remark reflects "a situation in which the time of the apostles is past."[7] Therefore, the argument for dating Revelation to the latter years of Domitian's reign (i.e. early 90s CE) is well supported by both external and internal evidence. All these observations on the geographical destination

---

1. E.g. J. P. M. Sweet, *Revelation*, SCM Pelican Commentaries (London: SCM, 1979), 21–27; Collins, *Crisis*, 54–77; Thompson, *Revelation*, 13–15; G. K. Beale, *The Book of Revelation: A Commentary on the Greek Text*, NIGTC (Grand Rapids, MI: Eerdmans, 1999), 4–27; Philip L. Mayo, *"Those Who Call Themselves Jews": The Church and Judaism in the Apocalypse of John*, Princeton Theological Monograph Series 60 (Eugene, OR: Pickwick, 2006), 4–17.

2. *Ad. Haer.* 5.30.3 = Eusebius, *Hist. eccl.* 3.18.3.

3. *Ad. Haer.* 2.22.5; 3.3.4; 5.30.1. If Irenaeus' record were accurate, it would mean that John would have well been over 90 when Revelation was written which, though not impossible, is unlikely. See also Sweet, *Revelation*, 36–37.

4. Irenaeus actually reported to have known Polycarp (*Haer.* 3.3.4) who was martyred only around 155–160 CE (Thompson, *Revelation*, 15). See also Michael W. Holmes, *The Apostolic Fathers: Greek Texts and English Translations*, 3rd ed. (Grand Rapids, MI: Baker Academic, 2007), 301.

5. It is commonly recognized that "the harlot" of Babylon (Rev 17:5) sitting on the seven hills (Rev 17:9) refers to the city of Rome (e.g. G. B. Caird, *A Commentary on the Revelation of St. John the Divine*, 2nd ed., BNTC (London: A & C Black, 1984), 216–217; Collins, *Crisis*, 57; Thompson, *Revelation*, 15; Ian Boxall, "The Many Faces of Babylon the Great: Wirkungsgeschichte and the Interpretation of Revelation 17," in *Studies in the Book of Revelation*, ed. Steve Moyise (Edinburgh: T&T Clark, 2001), 53–54.

6. Collins, *Crisis*, 58 asserts that it is "highly unlikely that the name would have been used before the destruction of the temple by Titus." Beale, *Revelation*, 18 also considers this to be "the strongest internal evidence for a post-70 date" for Revelation.

7. Collins, *Crisis*, 27.

and the date of Revelation therefore bring its readers under a similar sociopolitical context to that of 1 Peter, which I date also in the 90s CE.[8]

Another factor which renders Revelation a pertinent comparison text to 1 Peter is that while the Petrine author extensively appropriates OT language to construct his theological thought world, OT allusions and images also constitute the primary ingredients in the composition of John's symbolic universe in Revelation. Christ is also highlighted as the Jewish Messiah, and the Passover Messianic Lamb (ἀρνίον, e.g. 5:6, 8, 12–13; 7:10, 14, 17; 12:11; 13:8; 14:1; 17:14; cf. ἀμνοῦ in 1 Pet 1:19) in particular,[9] while Christians are also perceived as the people of God in extention to the nation of Israel.

However, despite all its similarities, Revelation actually calls for much more "undifferentiated" resistance and a more definite dissociation from the pagan culture in contrast to the Petrine preservation of an element of accommodation within its social strategies. An investigation into the relationship between theology and ethics in Revelation can, therefore, highlight the features of the Petrine author's grounding his comparatively pacifist social ethics on his particular theological framework. It also provides an answer to those scholars who argue that 1 Peter advocates one-sided resistance to assimilation such as Elliott[10], Achtemeier[11] and Green.[12] If 1 Peter were rejecting accommodation *per se*, we should expect 1 Peter to have presented a much more dualistic and polemical vision of the relationship between God/Christ and culture as exemplified in Revelation.

In fact, the close relationship between 1 Peter and Revelation is from time to time noted by scholars.[13] However, few attempts have been made to set the two texts side by side to understand the difference in their social

---

8. See my discussions on page 13 above.

9. Elisabeth Schüssler Fiorenza, *The Book of Revelation–Justice and Judgment* (Philadelphia, PA: Fortress Press, 1985), 73; Richard Bauckham, *The Climax of Prophecy: Studies on the Book of Revelation* (Edinburgh: T&T Clark, 1993), 184.

10. Elliott, *Home*.

11. Achtemeier, "Newborn Babes," 218–222.

12. Green, "Identity," 85–92.

13. E.g. Moule, "Nature," 9–10; F. Gerald Downing, "Pliny's Prosecutions of Christians: Revelation and 1 Peter," *JSNT* 34 (1988): 105–123; Thomas B. Slater, *Christ and Community: A Socio-Historical Study of the Christology of Revelation*, JSNTSup 178 (Sheffield: Sheffield Academic Press, 1999), 19–22.

strategies with reference to their respectively distinctive theological visions, which renders my study in this chapter particularly worthwhile.

In the following discussion, I will first investigate John's social behavioural instructions and his comprehension of the existing socio-economic and political system of the Roman Empire. I will demonstrate how the difference in the formulations of social ethics in 1 Peter and Revelation is due to the authors' different assessments of the Roman system and, thus, their different perceptions of what constitute proper Christian strategies for living within this system. In the second section of this chapter, I will then explore the theological thought world of John on which his approach of more undifferentiated resistance is grounded. I will argue that although both the Petrine author and John start their reflections with Jesus Christ's death on the cross, John's emphasis is more in line with the typical Jewish perception of the Messiah as a warrior-king. Christians are thus presented in Revelation as the twelve tribes of the Israelite army participating in Christ's Messianic War against Satan and his allies. It is against this vision of a warfare that Christians are called to take sides with Christ and abstain from any collaboration with the pagan culture. In the course of this analysis and by way of comparison, I will then highlight the Petrine author's choice of images to portray Christ and Christian existence on earth, which in turn gives rise to the configuration of his Christian social ethics.[14]

5.1 Social Behavioural Instructions in Revelation

In the last two chapters, I showed that the Petrine behavioural instructions are directed primarily against the harassments suffered by Christians from their neighbours at local, provincial level in Asia Minor, which informal accusations could also lead to official persecutions in sporadic cases. This observation actually finds support from Revelation.

Nowadays, many scholars recognize that there is no concrete evidence of widespread state-initiated persecution of Christians during Domitian's reign.[15] However, it by no means follows that Thompson's assessment is

---

14. I therefore do not intend my study of Revelation to be exhaustive. I will only focus on those aspects of Revelation which serve to highlight the characteristics of 1 Peter.

15. Please refer to the references in n. 65 on page 14 above.

accurate when he remarks, "For the most part, however, Christians lived peacefully with their neighbours in the Roman political order."[16] Indeed, 1 Peter actually presupposes real happenings of alienations and slanders against Christians by their neighbours (1 Pet 2:15; 4:4, 12) and for the name of Christ (4:14, 16). These local accusations could occasionally result in official persecutions and even death (Pliny, *Ep*. 10.96–97; Rev 2:13). Just as in 1 Peter, the behavioural instructions in Revelation are also formulated as a response to pagan pressure to compromise their faith and to accommodate to the wider culture, especially in the light of John's "imminent expectation of intensifying persecution on a widening and programmatic scale."[17]

In this section, I will firstly explore the background and purpose of John's behavioural instructions. Based on his overriding concern for Christians' clear-cut resistance and separation from the wider socio-economic and political system, I will then analyse his exhortations both in his seven letters (2:1–3:22) and apocalyptic visions (4:1–22:5).

5.1.1 Purpose of the Revelation Social Behavioural Instructions

While the readers of Revelation share a similar socio-political context with that of 1 Peter, Revelation further unveils three particular threats to Christians' existence in Asia Minor which 1 Peter has not expressly specified: (1) imperial cult (Rev 13:4–8, 12–15); (2) economic deprivation resulting from refusal to participate in emperor worship and the civic religion (13:17); and (3) harassment by the Diaspora Jews (2:9; 3:9).

Besides forming part of the wider polytheistic culture,[18] worship of emperors was regarded as a token of solidarity with the Roman Empire and within the cities. On the one hand, emperor cult provided the opportunity for the cities to show their loyalty to the empire and for the provincial officials and local elites to flatter the emperor by endowing him with elaborate

---

16. Thompson, *Revelation*, 172.

17. Beale, *Revelation*, 12; See also David A. deSilva, *Seeing Things John's Way: The Rhetoric of the Book of Revelation* (Louisville, KY: Westminster John Knox Press, 2009), 50–55.

18. Steven J. Friesen, *Imperial Cults and the Apocalypse of John: Reading Revelation in the Ruins* (New York: Oxford University Press, 2001), 75; deSilva, *Seeing Things*, 43.

honour.[19] On the other hand, it was a matter of honour and pride for the cities to obtain the status of *neokoros* (i.e. the temple warden), and to build temples with provincial status for the emperors.[20] Imperial festivals were also such important occasions of provincial life that the whole city was expected to support and join in the sacrifices, processions, celebrations and even games.[21]

Cities in Asia Minor were especially well known for their enthusiasm for the imperial cult. As succinctly described by Thompson, among the seven cities addressed in Revelation 2:1–3:22, "Five of the seven cities had imperial altars (all but Philadelphia and Laodicea), six had imperial temples (all but Thyatira), and five had imperial priests (all but Philadelphia and Laodicea)."[22]

In addition, Pergamum was the official centre of the imperial cult.[23] Ephesus even built a temple at the heart of the city to honour the living emperor, Domitian.[24] It is, therefore, imaginable how Christians' refusal to worship the emperors could attract criticisms for being disloyal to the empire and antisocial in city life.

Besides political and social advantages, Revelation further reveals that participation in the imperial cult and the civic religion also brought with them economic implications. In Revelation 13:17, John remarks that only those who have worshipped the first beast (the Roman Empire) are able to buy and sell, which is related to the wealth of Rome (17:4; 18:16) and the economic benefits that will ensue to those who enthusiastically embrace the Roman economic system (18:3, 15, 18–19). Since it is probable that many of the early Christians were artisans and traders,[25] the continual member-

---

19. Collins, *Crisis*, 77; Beale, *Revelation*, 10–11, 15.

20. Price, *Rituals*, 64–67. See also Thompson, *Revelation*, 158–161.

21. Price, *Rituals*, 108–113, 121; Beale, *Revelation*, 14–15; Steven J. Friesen, "The Beast from the Land: Revelation 13:11–18 and Social Setting," in *Reading the Book of Revelation: A Resource for Students*, ed. David L. Barr (Atlanta, GA: SBL, 2003), 59.

22. Thompson, *Revelation*, 159.

23. Elisabeth Schüssler Fiorenza, "The Followers of the Lamb: Visionary Rhetoric and Social-Political Situation," *Semeia*, 36 (1986): 136.

24. deSilva, *Seeing Things*, 42.

25. E.g. Paul, Aquila and Priscilla were tentmakers (Acts 18:2–3). Lydia the Thyatiran is also mentioned in Acts 16:14 as a seller of purple cloth. Wayne A. Meeks, *The First Urban Christians: The Social World of the Apostle Paul* (New Haven, CT: Yale University Press,

ship in the trade guilds was essential for their survival. However, dinners and ceremonies of these trade guilds usually involved cultic sacrifices and paying honour to the patron deities (and the emperor). In an inscription found in Pergamon and probably dated about 110 CE,[26] a singers' guild was said to have a priest and rites to the emperor. Newly elected members of the guild were also required to pay a contribution to the gods and for sacrifices to Rome and the emperor as an entrance fee. Christians' failure to pay this kind of fee or to participate in the sacrifices and common meals would necessarily mean loss of business and economic boycotts.[27]

The third threat to Christian existence as disclosed in Revelation was the harassments from the local Jewish communities: "Those who say they are Jews and are not" (Rev 2:9; 3:9). In the last chapter, I mentioned that the Jewish Diaspora were granted imperial privileges to observe their ancestral customs, and were thus officially exempted from participating in the imperial cult and other pagan religions. They also participated in existing socio-economic system by being parties to business transactions[28] and indeed, flourished in Asia Minor. The Jewish harassments against Christians in Asia Minor probably took the form of verbal slanders (τὴν βλασφημίαν, 2:9; ψεύδονται, 3:9). What started as verbal assault could, however, result in Christians being brought before the Roman authorities (cf. Acts 17:6–7; 18:12–17)[29] and put into prison or even death (Rev 2:10).[30]

1983), 64–65 further observes that passages such as 1 Thess 4:11–12 and Eph 4:28 were addressed to free handworkers or craftsmen.

26. Naphtali Lewis, *The Roman Principate: 27 B.C.–285 A.D.*, Greek Historical Documents (Toronto: Hakkert, 1974), 125–127.

27. See also deSilva, "Social Setting," 290–291; Paul R. Trebilco, *The Early Christians in Ephesus from Paul to Ignatius,* WUNT 166 (Tübingen: Mohr Siebeck, 2004), 319–320; Kirsi Siitonen, "Merchants and Commerce in the Book of Revelation," in *Imagery in the Book of Revelation*, eds. Michael Labahn and Outi Lehtipuu (Leuven: Peeters, 2011), 159.

28. Josephus, *Ant.* 16.27–28.

29. Claudia J. Setzer, *Jewish Responses to Early Christians: History and Polemics, 30–150 C.E.* (Minneapolis, MN: Fortress Press, 1994), 100–101.

30. This observation actually renders it unlikely for "synagogue of Satan" in Rev 2:9 and 3:9 to refer to Judaizing Gentile Christians. A Gentile adopting Jewish customs would be in a too vulnerable position to bring charge against another Christian group before the Roman authorities. See Setzer, *Jewish Responses*, 208 n.7; Adela Yarbro Collins, "Vilification and Self-Definition in the Book of Revelation," *HTR* 79 (1986): 313. The understanding of the "synagogue of Satan" as the ethnic Jews is further in line with John 8:44 in which Jesus rebukes the Jews as being "from (your) father, the devil."

By designating the Jews as a "synagogue of Satan," John is connecting the Jewish communities with the evil force supporting the Roman Empire (Rev 13:2, 4). Therefore, although the content of their slanders is not explicitly stated in the text, it is probable that these accusations involved calling into question the loyalty of Christians to the empire so that the attention of the authorities could be invoked. A possible example of these accusations can be found in Acts 17:6–7 in which Christians were charged for saying that "there is another king, Jesus." This may also explain why the church in Philadelphia is said to be enduring a situation where they were required to deny the name of Christ (Rev 3:8), which actually recalls the test imposed by Pliny on people to curse Christ and worship the emperor (Pliny, *Ep.* 10.96).[31] All these only rendered Christians all the more under pressure to compromise their faith, and to adopt the pagan idolatrous way of life to ease tension with the hostile environment.

In the face of these political, social and economic pressures to accommodate to the wider culture, John's seven letters to the seven churches in Revelation 2:1–3:22 reveal three possible modes of social response on the part of the Christians in Asia Minor as he sees it.[32] The first one represented a liberal approach as adopted by the Nicolaitans in Ephesus (2:6) and Pergamum (2:15), Balaam in Pergamum (2:14), and Jezebel in Thyatira (2:20),[33] who had no problem with Christians eating the food sacrificed to idols.[34] This approach represented a comparatively unreserved accommodationist tendency to the existing Roman system as it enabled Christians to

---

31. Setzer, *Jewish Responses*, 101–102. Beale, *Revelation*, 240 also proposes that the specific accusations of the Jews could also include that Christians were upsetting the peace of the *status quo* and were not a Jewish sect.

32. It is commonly recognized that these seven letters set out the context and John's purpose with reference to which the whole Revelation should be read (e.g. Thompson, *Revelation*, 180; Jonathan Knight, "The Enthroned Christ of Revelation 5:6 and the Development of Christian Theology," in *Studies in the Book of Revelation*, ed. Steve Moyise [London: T&T Clark, 2002], 44).

33. For the OT background of Balaam and Jezebel leading the Israelite people to idolatry, see Num 25:1–9; 31:16; cf. Josephus, *Ant.* 4.126–130 (Balaam); 1 Kgs 21:25–26; 2 Kgs 9:22 (Jezebel).

34. Many scholars believe that Nicholaitans, Balaam and Jezebel belonged to the same movement of accommodationist approach to pagan culture (e.g. Collins, *Crisis*, 43; Schüssler Fiorenza, *Revelation*, 116; David E. Aune, "The Social Matrix of the Apocalypse of John," *BR* 26 [1981]: 28; Trebilco, *Ephesus*, 311). In the light of the similarity in the teachings of the three groups, this view is well founded.

get fully involved in the social and economic life of the cities by participating in cultic meals, whether during festivals or in the trade guilds,[35] and in contexts that John sees as idolatrous (πορνεύω, 2:14, 20; πορνείας, 2:21).[36]

The second mode of possible Christian response represented what Aune calls a "centrist" approach to pagan pressure to accommodate, which Aune sees as adopted by those in Ephesus who had not followed the teachings of Nicolaitans but whom John regards as having failed to do the works (ἔργα) they did at first (2:5), in Sardis whose works (ἔργα) John does not find complete (πεπληρωμένα) before God (3:2), and in Laodicea whose works (ἔργα), for John, only characterize them as neither cold nor hot (3:15).[37] This centrist approach is characterized by a general abstention from participating in actual pagan worships and cultic meals. Besides the fact that Christians in Ephesus were found to have hated the works of the Nicolaitans (2:6) and, thus, refused to eat food offered to idols (cf. 2:15), John also does not reproach Christians in Sardis or in Laodicea for having followed this practice. In the light of his bitter disgust at Christians getting involved in idolatry (cf. κἀγὼ μισῶ, 2:6, πορνεύω, 2:14, 2:20, πορνείας, 2:21), we would expect him to have mentioned it if eating food offered to idols were an issue in these two churches. However, John obviously does not regard "refusal to eat idol food alone" to be enough for Christians' faithful witness in a predominantly pagan culture.

The churches of Sardis and Laodicea probably represent a more unrestrained accommodationist lifestyle within the centrist approach. As Thompson observes, "Among the seven letters in the Book of Revelation, only those addressed to Sardis and Laodicea do not mention specific adversaries, either Jewish (Smyrna and Philadelphia) or Christian (Ephesus, Pergamum, and Thyatira)."[38]

---

35. This approach would have made life much easier for Christians especially in Ephesus, Thyatira and Pergamum. As Schüssler Fiorenza, *Revelation*, 117 states, "Ephesus was a great trading city, Thyatira had an unusually great number of trade guilds, and Pergamum was the center of various pagan cults and one of the main places of the emperor cult."

36. Trebilco, *Ephesus*, 308; Friesen, *Imperial Cults*, 193.

37. Aune, "Social Matrix," 29.

38. Thompson, *Revelation*, 124.

This is so notwithstanding the presence of well-settled Jewish communities in both Sardis and Laodicea.[39] Neither is there any reference to any ostracisms or persecutions suffered by these churches from their neighbours. It therefore appears that although Christians in Sardis and Laodicea were cautious not to eat food offered to idols at cultic meals, they also sought ways to have peaceful coexistence with the other elements of society. They may have fitted into the wider socio-political and economic systems, by making a high profile presence at festivals and pagan rituals and cooperating with the trade guilds, although they would not participate in their cultic meals. This mode of active participation in city life actually earned Christians in Sardis the reputation of being "alive" (ὄνομα ἔχεις ὅτι ζῇς, 3:1).[40] Those in Laodicea even took advantage of the economic opportunities available in the city and became wealthy (πλούσιός εἰμι καὶ πεπλούτηκα καὶ οὐδὲν χρείαν ἔχω, 3:17).

As for Christians in Ephesus, they are reproached by the risen Christ for having left their first love (τὴν ἀγάπην . . . τὴν πρώτην, 2:4) and are called upon to do their first works (τὰ πρῶτα ἔργα, 2:5). Many scholars have understood this first love that has been abandoned as love "for each other,"[41] "for both God/Christ and humans"[42] or "a general quality of love as opposed to hatred."[43] On the other hand, there is a growing trend in scholarship to depart from this debate by proposing that the leaving of the first love in 2:4 refers to Christians leaving their love for God/Christ by

---

39. Josephus, *Ant.* 14.235, 259–261; 16.171 (Sardis); 14.241–243 (Loadicea).

40. Sweet, *Revelation*, 98. I agree with Ian Boxall, *The Revelation of Saint John*, BNTC 18 (Peabody, MA: Hendrickson, 2006), 68 that this reputation of being "alive" may be not just among other Christian communities but also "among their pagan and Jewish fellow-citizens." Since "white garments" are reserved for those who bear faithful witness "to the world" (3:5; cf. 6:11; 7:9, 13–14; 19:14), the reference to Christians in Sardis having "soiled their garments" (3:4) indicates that the issue in question is still Christians' witness "to the world" and not just among Christians.

41. E.g. G. R. Beasley-Murray, *The Book of Revelation*, NCB (London: Oliphants, 1974), 75; George Eldon Ladd, *A Commentary on the Revelation of John*, (Grand Rapids, MI: Eerdmans, 1972), 39; Boxall, *Revelation*, 50.

42. E.g. Colin J. Hemer, *The Letters to the Seven Churches of Asia in Their Local Setting*, The Biblical Resource Series (Grand Rapids, MI:Eerdmans, 2001), 41; Robert H. Mounce, *The Book of Revelation* (London: Marshall, Morgan and Scott, 1977), 88; Grant R. Osborne, *Revelation*, BECNT (Grand Rapids, MI: Baker Academic, 2002), 115–116.

43. E.g. Caird, *Commentary*, 31–32; Wilfrid J. Harrington, *Revelation*, SP 16 (Collegeville, MN: Liturgical Press, 1993), 57.

"witnessing to him in the world."⁴⁴ For example, Trebilco argues that the clue to understand the content of the "first works" in 2:5 is to read them together with the "works" (ἔργα) of the Nicolaitans in the following 2:6, which relates to eating food offered to idols (2:14–15). Since the "works" (ἔργα) of Nicolaitans represented an accommodationist tendency towards pagan culture, the works (ἔργα) which the Ephesians are called to go back point to an opposite direction (i.e. what John regards as necessary to retain a clear boundary with the world).⁴⁵ Therefore, John saw the Christians in Ephesus as having been "too lax"⁴⁶ and (as Knight observes) having reduced their "high social boundaries."⁴⁷ As Thompson asserts, John exhorts the Ephesians "to keep to the exclusivism that they had at first,"⁴⁸ while Aune also suggests that John probably views the Ephesian Christians as having "developed a comfortable accommodation with the pagan world."⁴⁹ Although the text has offered too little information to render any proposal conclusive, it appears that this line of interpretation fits the context better, especially in view of the fact that the previous verse 2:3 speaks of the patient endurance of the Ephesian Christians, while the following verse 2:6 mentions the hating of the works of the Nicolaitans (i.e. both of these statements concern the witness of the Ephesian Christians to the world).

It is interesting to note that if this latter line of interpretation is accepted, the Ephesian Christians can be seen as probably having also adopted a mode of "differentiated resistance" towards the wider culture. On the one hand, they preserved what they perceived as necessary to express their ultimate allegiance to God by resisting the teachings of the false apostles (2:2)⁵⁰ and of the Nicolaitans (2:6). On the other hand, they may have allowed for

---

44. Beale, *Revelation*, 230–231.

45. Trebilco, *Ephesus*, 305–306.

46. Ibid., 305.

47. Jonathan Knight, *Revelation,* Readings: A New Biblical Commentary (Sheffield: Sheffield Academic Press, 1999), 43.

48. Leonard L. Thompson, "Ordinary Lives: John and His First Readers," in *Reading the Book of Revelation: A Resource for Students,* ed. David L. Barr (Atlanta, GA: SBL, 2003), 43.

49. David E. Aune, *Revelation 1–5,* WBC 52A (Dallas: Word Books, 1997), 155.

50. For the view that the teachings of these false apostles may be similar to those of the Nicholaitans, see Aune, "Social Matrix," 27; Knight, *Revelation*, 42–43. The text however offers too little information to render any suggestion conclusive.

a degree of accommodation by participating in those aspects of the wider social and economic life which they did not consider as inconsistent with their religious conviction to God, for example, honouring the emperor in a non-cultic sense, but which John still saw as "too lax" and reducing their "high social boundaries." At the same time, the Ephesian accommodationist stance must have been restrained and so, fell short of their neighbours' expectations, as is apparent from their "bearing up (ἐβάστασας) on account of Christ's name" and "patient endurance" (ὑπομονήν) (2:3), both of which bear the connotation of persecution.[51]

I hold that the Petrine social strategies of "differentiated resistance" actually bear traits of this centrist approach to pagan alienation. As I discussed in the last two chapters, although 1 Peter posits "ultimate allegiance to God" as the boundary of Christians' social accommodation, which renders any involvement in idolatry or any cultic meals out of question, Christians are at the same time instructed to seek peace (1 Pet 3:11) and to stay inside the current system by responsibly discharging their societal roles whether as subjects (2:13–14) of the empire, or as slaves (2:18), wives (3:1) and husbands (3:7) within the households. This Petrine centrist stance further serves to account for the fact that despite current Jewish hostility in Asia Minor as unveiled in Revelation (2:9, 10; 3:9), the Petrine author does not express any reproof or disgust to the Jews, but instead, even draws upon the Diaspora Jewish social strategies as his own model of social engagement for Christians whom he perceives as the continuing "elect exiles of Diaspora."

What must be emphasized is that 1 Peter should not be taken as at the higher end of accommodation within this centrist approach of Christian social engagement in Asia Minor. While the strategy of peaceful coexistence in Sardis and Laodicea exonerated them from external harassments, the Petrine author actually perceives sufferings and alienations as part of Christian existence on earth (1 Pet 1:1, 6, 17; 2:11, 19–21, 3:14–17; 4:1, 4, 12–19; 5:9–10). His social strategy seems to be closer and, indeed, bears striking similarities to that of Christians in Ephesus, especially in the light of his admonishing Christians to endure suffering patiently (ὑπομενεῖτε, 1

---

51. Collins, *Crisis*, 113.

Pet 2:20; cf. ὑπομονὴν ἔχεις, Rev 2:3) and to accept insults for the name of Christ (ἐν ὀνόματι Χριστοῦ, 4:14; cf. διὰ τὸ ὄνομά μου, Rev 2:3).

However, no matter how controlled 1 Peter's allowance for Christians' social accommodation is, it seems that the Petrine author is allowing more room for Christians' accommodation to the existing system than John, whose teachings in Revelation represent the third mode of Christians' response to pagan pressure to compromise: "undifferentiated resistance" to the pagan systems. He expresses unreserved hatred (cf. Rev 2:6) of the teachings of the Nicolaitans, Balaam and Jezebel which, according to John, represent an unreserved embrace of the pagan culture. For John, they are no more than practising idolatry and, thus, fornication (πορνεύω, 2:14; 2:20; πορνείας, 2:21) with idols and apostasy.[52] Christians who follow their teachings are likewise committing adultery (μοιχεύοντας, 2:22) and apostasy.

At the same time, to those who adopt a centrist approach of social engagement, John's attitude is similarly reproaching. The church of Sardis is regarded by John as spiritually "dead" (νεκρὸς εἶ, 3:1; ἔμελλον ἀποθανεῖν, 3:2). The wealthy church of Laodicea is also viewed as spiritually "wretched and pitiable and poor and blind and naked" (3:17) and on the verge of being spewed out by Christ (3:16), that is, losing its place as a believing church of Christ.[53] If the Ephesians leaving their first love (2:4) is interpreted as their having become too lax in witnessing to Christ/God, the traits of their accommodation, though restrained, are also regarded by John as costing them the status of being a church (κινήσω τὴν λυχνίαν σου, 2:5).[54]

Indeed, John does not permit anything less than a clear-cut separation from the wider socio-economic and political systems on the part of Christians. As Mayo remarks, "For John, Rome is the incarnation of evil in the world."[55] Christians can hardly get involved in the Roman system without participating in evil and soiling their garments (3:4). Even the ethnic Jewish communities are pronounced by him as those who say that they

---

52. Trebilco, *Ephesus*, 312.

53. Boxall, *Revelation*, 77; Beale, *Revelation*, 305.

54. For this understanding of Christ's removing their lampstand from its place, see Beale, *Revelation*, 232.

55. Mayo, *Those Who Call*, 20.

are Jews when "they are not" (καὶ οὐκ εἰσίν) and in fact are a "synagogue of Satan" (2:9, 3:9). As Setzer convincingly argues, John may simply mean that "they are Jews who do not live up to the name 'Jews.'"[56] As I mentioned above, by designating the Jewish communities in Smyrna and Philadelphia as a "synagogue of Satan," John is connecting them with Satan, the evil force supporting the Roman Empire (Rev 13:2, 4). Therefore, for John, the Jews' slandering and making use of the wider evil system to persecute the Christian people of God had rendered them "tools of Satan,"[57] and disqualified from being the people of God.[58] Likewise, any attempt of Christians to cooperate with the Roman systems is also inconsistent with their identity as the continuing people of God.

For John, the only option available to Christians is therefore a total resistance to the wider Roman systems. Whereas those enjoying peaceful coexistence and prosperity in Sardis and Laodicea received unequivocal reproach, those who became poor (σου . . . τὴν πτωχείαν, 2:9) in Smyrna, and powerless (μικρὰν ἔχεις δύναμιν, 3:8) in Philadelphia received solely commendations from the risen Christ for suffering deprivation and harassment from the wider world.

The behavioural instructions in Revelation are therefore directed to facilitate Christians' definite resistance to the surrounding pagan systems although it may mean deprivation and oppression. In Revelation, any allowance for accommodating to the wider systems necessarily implies compromise in faith and attracts Christ's rebukes. This stance is notably different from 1 Peter. Although the purpose of 1 Peter is also to reinforce Christians' faith in the face of pagan hostility, the Petrine author does not consider it irreconcilable for Christians to follow the current societal order to some degree, while at the same time, keeping intact their identity and ultimate allegiance to God. His formulation of Christians' "good works," allowing for an element of accommodation, is actually what he regards as the congruent identity expression of Christians' status as God's elect people of the Diaspora.

---

56. Setzer, *Jewish Responses*, 100. See also Collins, "Vilification," 310.

57. Osborne, *Revelation*, 131.

58. See also Beale, *Revelation*, 240–241.

Indeed, many of the Christians under John's rebukes probably did not regard their participating in normal social and economic life of the wider society as committing idolatry or compromising faith.[59] They may have considered such participation necessary for Christians' witness and gaining room to maintain their faith in God. Many, like 1 Peter, may hope to silence the slanders of their neighbours (cf. 1 Pet 2:15) and even lead to their conversion (cf. 1 Pet 3:1–2). But for John, he himself was suffering persecution (ἐν τῇ θλίψει . . . ὑπομονῇ, 1:9), Antipas had been executed (2:13), some churches were already undergoing tribulations and persecutions (2:3, 9, 13; 3:8), and it was likely that their situations would become worse (2:9–10). Furthermore, he was probably witnessing the local authorities putting pressure on the city populace to show support for the imperial religion.[60] The Roman officials and the local aristocracy were probably addressing Domitian as "lord and god" (cf. Suetonius, *Dom.* 13) as their way of flattering the emperor to gain his favour.[61] This course of events seems to be heading towards a situation where Christians would have no choice, and no room to negotiate between resistance and accommodation. As Beale observes, Revelation points to John's "imminent expectation of intensifying persecution on a widening and programmatic scale."[62]

As apparent from Revelation, John's particular stance is due to what Yarbro Collins observes as "the conflict between the Christian faith itself, as John understood it, and the social situation as he perceived it."[63] Although the prosperity and security offered by the empire may look appealing, all these are viewed by John as no more than deception by the satanic forces (πλανάω, 2:20; 12:9; 13:14; 18:23; 19:20; 20:3; ψευδής, 2:2; 21:8; ψεύδονται, 3:9).[64] It is his "particular religious view of reality . . . which is the framework within which John interpreted his environment."[65]

---

59. Some scholars believe that John actually represents a minority view in Asia Minor. E.g. Aune, "Social Matrix," 28–29; Thompson, *Revelation*, 191–194; Trebilco, *Ephesus*, 339–340.

60. E.g. Price, *Ritual*, 99–100, 102–103, 111–114, 120–121.

61. Collins, *Crisis*, 72; Beale, *Revelation*, 10–12.

62. Beale, *Revelation*, 12.

63. Collins, *Crisis*, 106.

64. See also Friesen, *Imperial Cults*, 188–189.

65. Collins, *Crisis*, 106–107.

Therefore, like 1 Peter, theology once again plays a key role in shaping John's attitude towards the Roman systems and, thus, what he considers as the appropriate social expression of Christians' identity on earth. It is also the difference in theological perceptions between John and the Petrine author that leads to the different formulations of Christian behavioural instructions in Revelation and 1 Peter.

5.1.2 Social Behavioural Instructions of Revelation

As I mentioned in chapter 3, there are included in the Petrine behavioural instructions the exhortations to "be subject to" (ὑποτάσσω, 2:13, 18; 3:1, 5) the existing socio-political institutions, to "honour" (τιμάω, 2:17) the emperor and other members of society, to "bless" (εὐλογέω, 3:9), and to "seek peace" (ζητέω εἰρήνην, 3:11). It is noticeable that these notions of "being subject to," "honouring," "blessing" and "seeking peace" are all absent from John's Christian social ethics in Revelation.

Instead, "patient endurance" (ὑπομονή, 2:2, 3, 19; 3:10), "faithfulness" (πίστις, 2:13; 19; πιστός, 2:13), "holding fast" Christ's name (ἐβάστασας διὰ τὸ ὄνομά μου, 2:3; κρατεῖς τὸ ὄνομά μου, 2:13; οὐκ ἠρνήσω τὸ ὄνομά μου, 3:8) and "keeping" (τηρέω) Christ's word (3:8) and the word about his patient endurance (τὸν λόγον τῆς ὑπομονῆς μου, 3:10),[66] are grounds for commendations for Christians' "perseverance" against pressure to accommodate. "Perseverance" expressed in terms of being "faithful" (πιστός, 2:10), "holding fast" (κρατέω, 2:25; 3:11) and "keeping" Christ's works/Christian truths[67] (τηρέω, 2:26; 3:3) remains the theme of John's exhortations to the seven churches.[68] Particularly remarkable is the fact that in each of the seven letters, John emphatically calls the one who endures to the end "the one who conquers" (ὁ νικῶν, 2:7, 11, 17, 26; 3:5, 12, 21). For John, the church is in irreconcilable conflict and, indeed, warfare with the satanic force which is behind the Roman socio-economic and political system. The current systems are not something "to be subject to" or "to be honoured" as 1 Peter allows to a degree. For John, any temptation

---

66. Beale, *Revelation*, 289.
67. Osborne, *Revelation*, 176.
68. Ibid., 42–46.

or pressure to accommodate to the current systems must be "conquered" through persevered resistance at the cost of suffering, deprivation and, even death (2:10).

This notion of conquering, not by taking up arms, but by enduring resistance is what John considers the pertinent mode of Christians' witness on earth. This mode is modelled on that of Jesus Christ who himself is the first faithful witness (ὁ μάρτυς ὁ πιστός, 1:5; 3:14) through patient endurance (cf. τῆς ὑπομονῆς μου, 3:10) unto death.[69] It is also on account of this witness of Jesus Christ (τὴν μαρτυρίαν Ἰησοῦ Χριστοῦ, 1:2; τὴν μαρτυρίαν Ἰησοῦ, 1:9),[70] that John himself bears witness (ἐμαρτύρησεν, 1:2) and patiently endures (cf. ὑπομονῇ, 1:9) tribulation. Likewise, Antipas, who is the only one specifically named as having been killed under pagan persecution, is also designated by Christ as "my witness, my faithful one" (ὁ μάρτυς μου ὁ πιστός μου) in 2:13.

Hence, for John, Christians' patient endurance of persecutions to the point of death is precisely what Jesus Christ's sacrificial death on the cross exemplified. Just as Jesus Christ has already conquered evil on the cross (ὡς κἀγὼ ἐνίκησα, 3:21; cf. 5:5),[71] Christians are called upon to join John and other examples of faithful witness, like Antipas, to conquer the pressure to accommodate through the same faithful witness, even at the cost of their lives. As Reddish comments, "those who conquer are the ones who remain faithful, who hold the testimony of Jesus, even when confronted with death."[72]

This motif of "conquest through faithful witness, and perseverance unto death" is what links John's seven letters in 2:1–3:11 to his visions in 4:1–22:5. As Schüssler Fiorenza remarks, "Eschatological vision and

---

69. Beale, *Revelation*, 190.

70. I agree with scholars such as Knight, *Revelation*, 31 and Beale, *Revelation*, 183–184 that Ἰησοῦ (Χριστοῦ) of the phrase τὴν μαρτυρίαν Ἰησοῦ (Χριστοῦ) (1:2, 9; 12:17; 19:10; 20:4) can afford both nuances of a subjective and an objective genitive (i.e. Jesus Christ is both the agent and the content of the testimony. John is retaining the ambiguity to underscore Christians' identifying with Christ when witnessing him.

71. Allison A. Trites, *The New Testament Concept of Witness*, SNTSMS 31 (Cambridge: Cambridge University Press, 1977), 159.

72. Mitchell G. Reddish, "Martyr Christology in the Apocalypse," *JSNT* 33 (1988): 88.

parenesis have the same function in Revelation,"[73] while Pattemore also observes, "If the messages of the first vision (1:12–3:22) have urged the hearers to 'conquer,' the images of the second vision (4:1–22:9) have not only painted in terms of a military conflict but have ironically redefined conquering as following Jesus in the nature of his witness and death."[74] The function of the apocalyptic section Revelation 4:1–22:5 is therefore to bring John's behavioural instructions, already laid down in his seven letters, to the fullest expression.

Just as the motif of "conquest" is prominently reiterated in John's seven letters in 2:1–3:22, the whole cosmic universe is further portrayed as polemically belonging to two opposing military camps in his visions in 4:1–22:5. One camp includes God, Christ (the Lamb, e.g. 5:6, 12; 6:16; 7:9, 14, 17; 12:11; 13:8; 14:1, 4, 10; 17:14), God's angels (e.g. 12:7; 14:10, 15–19), worshippers of God/Christ who have the seal of God and whose names are in the book of life (e.g. 7:2–8; 14:1–5; 21:27; 22:3–4; cf. 3:12), and the Lamb's bride (the New Jerusalem, e.g. 19:7–8; 21:2, 9–10). The opposing camp includes Satan (the dragon, e.g. 12:3–17; 13:2; 16:13–14; 20:2), the beast from the sea (probably the Roman Empire,[75] e.g. 11:7; 13:1–8; 19:19–20) and the beast from the land (probably the whole network of socioreligious institutions involved in the imperial cult,[76] e.g. 13:11–17), Satan's angels (12:7, 9), worshippers of the dragon/beast who bear the mark of the beast (earth-dwellers, e.g. 11:10; 13:3–4, 8; 17:8), and the harlot Babylon (the city of Rome, e.g. 17:1–7; 18:2–24).[77] God/Christ and the pagan world are therefore in irreconcilable opposition and the two camps are consistently at war (πόλεμος, 11:7; 12:7; 12:17; 13:7; 16:13–14; 19:19; 20:8; πολεμέω,12:7; 17:14; 19:11; cf. 2:16). The only option

---

73. Schüssler Fiorenza, *Revelation*, 4.

74. Stephen Pattemore, *The People of God in the Apocalypse: Discourse, Structure, and Exegesis*, SNTSMS 128 (Cambridge: Cambridge University Press, 2004), 218.

75. Sweet, *Revelation*, 206–208; David E. Aune, *Revelation 6–16*, WBC 52b (Nashville, TN: Thomas Nelson, 1998), 779; Mayo, *Those Who Call*, 61. As scholars commonly recognize, the portrayal of the beast in Rev 13:1–2 is based on a combination of the features of the four beasts described in Dan 7:1–8. Since these four beasts represent four successive empires, it is likely that the beast in Rev 13:1–2 also represents an empire which was the Roman Empire at the time of John.

76. Friesen, "Beast," 62–63 followed by Siitonen, "Merchants," 147.

77. See also Collins, *Crisis*, 141–142.

available for Christians is to participate in the war as members of the camp of God/Christ.⁷⁸ There is no room for them to take a centrist stance or to preserve their allegiance to God without definitely setting themselves apart from the systems of the Roman Empire.

This dualistic view of the relationship between Christ and the wider socio-economic and political systems actually stems from John's perception that, although the Roman Empire has brought prosperity and trading opportunities to the whole empire (cf. 13:17), the source of its authority and power only comes from "Satan" (13:2, 4), who has been thrown down to earth (12:9). This understanding of the larger socio-political context is once again in marked difference from 1 Peter. Although the devil (διάβολος; cf. Διάβολος καὶ ὁ Σατανᾶς, Rev 12:9; 20:2) is also mentioned in 1 Peter as the ultimate adversary who seeks to procure Christians to give up their exclusive allegiance to God through persecutions (1 Pet 5:8–9), the Petrine author noticeably does not expressly identify him as the evil force behind the empire or its socio-economic system. In addition, although the Petrine author also recognizes Rome as an oppressor of the Christian people of God (Βαβυλῶνι, 5:13), he nevertheless still understands every human institution as merely part of God's creation (κτίσει, 1 Pet 2:13),⁷⁹ and the governors sent by the emperor as having the capacity "to punish those who do evil and to praise those who do good"(2:14). Therefore, in so far as Christians' exclusive and ultimate allegiance to God is not jeopardized, the Petrine author does not consider Christians "honouring the emperor" (1 Pet 2:17) and "subjecting themselves to every human institution (creature)" (1 Pet 2:13–14) as collaborating with the evil force and, thus, problematic *per se*. However, such honouring and subjection would have been impossible for John because, for him, such bestowing of honour and obedience on the imperial institutions necessarily amounts to accepting and expressing loyalty to the satanic force behind them.⁸⁰

---

78. Bauckham, *Climax*, 213, 233–234.
79. Michaels, *1 Peter*, 124.
80. See also Philip A. Harland, "Honouring the Emperor or Assailing the Beast: Participation in Civic Life among Associations (Jewish, Christian and Other) in Asia Minor and the Apocalypse of John," *JSNT* 77 (2000): 117.

Furthermore, since the economic system is bound up with pagan religions, the city of Rome, with all its wealth and economic influence (17:4; 18:16), is viewed by John as merely a harlot, deceiving the whole of humanity into idolatry (fornication) (οἶνος ... τῆς πορνείας αὐτῆς, 14:8; 17:2; 18:3).[81] His critique is further intensified by linking Rome's wealth with its self-glorification: "I sit as a queen and I am no widow, and I will never see mourning" (18:7). Although accommodating to Roman economic structures may bring people wealth for the time being (πλουτέω, 18:3, 15, 19), they are, for John, no more than committing idolatry (fornication) (πορνεύω, 17:2; 18:3, 9)[82] and joining in similar arrogance (18:9–10, 16, 19; cf. 3:17).

John's challenge to Christians is, therefore, the same call for a total disassociation from the pagan socio-economic system: "Come out of her, my people, lest you participate in her sins, and lest you receive her plagues" (18:4). This disassociation involves not so much a total physical withdrawal from city life as refusal to collaborate with the pagan idolatrous way of political and economic undertakings.[83] Although the society at large is supporting the Roman Empire (13:3–4, 8) and Christians' failure to cooperate with the larger socio-economic structure may put their livelihood (13:16–17), and even their lives (16:6; 17:6; 18:24; 19:2) at risk, John's exhortation is still Christians' steadfast faithfulness (πίστις, 13:10; 14:12) and patient endurance (ὑπομονή, 13:10; 14:12). Furthermore, keeping (τηρέω, 12:17; 14:12; cf. 16:15, 22:7, 9) and holding (ἔχω, 6:9; 12:17; cf. 19:10) "the word of God and the witness" of Jesus Christ (6:9; cf. 1:2, 9; 20:4), and its alternative formulations (i.e. the commandments of God and the witness of Jesus, 12:17; the commandments of God and the faith of Jesus, 14:12), are repeatedly emphasized as the characteristics of Christians who persevere in faithful witness of Christ, and even to the point of death (6:9; 20:4; cf. 12:11).

Although captivity and death (ἀποκτείνω, 6:11; 11:7; 13:10, 15 cf. 2:13; σφάζω, 6:9; 18:24) appear to be signs of Christians having been conquered (νικάω, 11:7; 13:7) by the evil empire (the beast), the true reality

---

81. Collins, *Crisis*, 121; Friesen, *Imperial Cults*, 205.
82. Siitonen, "Merchants," 159.
83. See Beale, *Revelation*, 898.

is that Christians in fact conquer (νικάω,12:11; 15:2; 21:7) Satan and the beast through sacrifices of their lives, just as Jesus Christ has already decisively conquered (ἐνίκησεν, 5:5; cf. ἐνίκησα, 3:21) evil through his sacrificial death (cf. σφάζω, 5:6, 9, 12; 13:8) on the cross.[84] Christians are therefore called upon to continue the conquest of Christ, whose ultimate victory over the beast and his allies (νικήσει, 17:14; cf. 14:14; 19:15) has already been brought into view.

Against this totally combatant attitude towards the pagan culture advocated in Revelation, the Petrine exhortations to Christians to seek peace (1 Pet 3:11), to bless (3:9) their neighbours, and to defend their faith with "gentleness" (3:15–16) become remarkable. Although the Petrine strategy of "differentiated resistance" also calls for Christians' resistance (ἀντίστητε, 1 Pet 5:9) to the devil, steadfastness in faith (πίστις, 1 Pet 1:5, 7, 9, 21; 5:9) and patient endurance of sufferings (ὑποφέρει, 1 Pet 2:19; ὑπομενεῖτε, 1 Pet 2:20; πάσχω, 1 Pet 2:19–20; 3:14, 17; 4:1, 19; 5:10), an element of accommodation is also retained to silence the slanders of unbelievers (2:15) and to gain room to uphold Christians' exclusive allegiance to God. For the Petrine author, the wider socio-political system is not to be dissociated from but is one within which Christians have to stay as responsible subjects (2:13–14), slaves (2:18), husbands (3:7) and wives (3:1–2), and fellow citizens (4:15) during the period of their sojourn (1:17) on earth. It is precisely through this contrast with Revelation that the arguments of those scholars, who maintain 1 Peter to be concerned solely with resisting assimilation, appear untenable. If 1 Peter were advocating total resistance, we should expect the author to be much more definite in calling upon Christians to adopt a clear-cut disassociation with the wider socio-economic and political systems as exemplified in Revelation.

Section Summary: Features of Petrine Social Behavioural Instructions

In this section, I highlighted the characteristics of John's social strategy in Revelation and contrasted them with those in 1 Peter. I showed that notably different vocabularies are employed in the two texts, which serve

---

84. See also Pattemore, *People*, 175; M. Eugene Boring, "Narrative Christology in the Apocalypse," *CBQ* 54 (1992): 715–716.

to highlight the different emphases of the authors' respective social strategies. Whereas 1 Peter, besides its admonitions on resistance, also teaches Christians to "subject themselves," to "honour," to "bless," and to "seek peace," these terms are not found in Revelation. The terms repeatedly appearing in John's text are rather those relating to "patient endurance," "keeping," and "holding fast" which become his mode of Christian "faithful witness" to "conquer" the temptation to conform to the larger socio-economic and political system.

These notions of "subjecting," "honouring," "blessing" and "seeking peace" actually underscore the elements of accommodation allowed by the Petrine strategy to ease tension with the wider world for the higher purpose of enabling the Christian readers to gain room to hold fast to their ultimate allegiance to God. A comparison of 1 Peter with a much more resistant writing like Revelation, therefore, renders it unlikely that the Petrine author is solely concerned with resisting assimilation.

Indeed, the stance chosen in 1 Peter is aligned with the "centrist" approach adopted by some Christians in Asia Minor, as reflected in John's seven letters in Revelation 2:1–3:22. While the Petrine author will not agree to Christians eating idol food in any cultic settings (1 Pet 4:3),[85] he at the same time gives room for Christians to look for a more peaceful existence in the city by submitting to the current societal order and responsibly discharging their civic and social duties. This centrist stance may account for the reason why 1 Peter does not evince any polemic against the Diaspora Jews, although Revelation actually unveils existing harassment by the Jewish communities against Christians in Asia Minor. Besides the fact that the Petrine author perceives the Jewish mode of social engagement in the Diaspora to be relevant for the formulation of his social instructions for the Christian elect exiles of Diaspora, this absence of reproach against the Jews is also consistent with his overall strategy to steer Christians away

---

85. In view of the commonly recognized affinities between 1 Peter and Paul's letters, it is likely that the Petrine author would agree with Paul's position on eating food sacrificed to idols as set out in 1 Cor 8:1–13 and 10:1–11:1. For a succinct overview of Paul's position, see Gordon D. Fee, *The First Epistle to the Corinthians,* NICNT (Grand Rapids, MI: Eerdmans, 1987), 357–363.

from unnecessary tension with their neighbours in so far as their salvation in God is not at stake.[86]

At the same time, the approach of 1 Peter is different from that of the Christians in Sardis and Laodicea as represented by John's letter in that the Petrine author is not prepared to push Christians' social accommodation to such an extent as to avoid any hostility, nor does he place "peaceful coexistence" as the sole objective of his Christian social engagement. The Petrine author actually stresses that Christians must stand firm when their exclusive commitment to God is in issue, for example, they must refuse idolatry (1 Pet 4:3) and accept suffering for the name of Christ (1 Pet 4:14; cf. 4:16). If it is accepted that "first love" in Revelation 2:4 refers to Christians' witness to the world, the Petrine approach seems to be more akin to that of the Ephesian church, which allowed for some accommodationist leeway in their social engagement, but still needed to endure suffering for the name of Christ.

In any case, if the Petrine text were placed before John, it is probable that he would have regarded the Petrine strategy to be incompatible with Christians' allegiance to God. This is borne out of his assessment of the current systems as an instrument of Satan to place the world under his authority (Rev 13:4), which is significantly different from that of the Petrine author who understands human institutions as merely part of God's creation (1 Pet 2:13). It is here that lies the value of comparing 1 Peter with Revelation as an *entrance imaginatively* to understand the Petrine author's own point of view. Besides, placing the Petrine social ethics in the larger religious landscape of Asia Minor, it also serves to highlight the

---

86. Although Betsy Bauman-Martin, "Speaking Jewish: Postcolonial Aliens and Strangers in First Peter," in *Reading First Peter with New Eyes: Methodological Reassessment of the Letter of First Peter*, eds. Robert L. Webb and Betsy Bauman-Martin (London: T&T Clark, 2007), 144–177, argues that the Petrine appropriation of Jewish identity to Christians constitutes a "replacement of the old elect group" (169) which replacement is "so complete that the original group no longer exists" (175), this observation appears to be inconsistent with the general tenor of the whole letter which stresses submission, honour and gentleness. Indeed, the appropriation of Jewish self-definitions to Christians does not necessarily imply leaving nothing for the ethnic Jewish people of God. The view expressed by Michaels, *1 Peter*, xlix that "there is no hint of exclusivity or possessiveness in Peter's identitifcation of his Gentile Christian readers as Jews . . . The actual Jewish community is simply ignored," seems to me to be judicious and more balanced and, thus, likely represents the Petrine author's position.

Petrine author's comparatively more positive view about the pagan world, which in turn accounts for his allowance for a degree of Christian social accommodation.

In fact, the Petrine perception of the larger world is closely related to the author's understanding of Jesus Christ's suffering on the cross and of what denotes Christians' faithful following of the Messiah-Christ as the people of God, which can be further highlighted by comparing with Revelation.

5.2 Shaping of Social Behavioural Instructions by Theology in Revelation

In chapter 2, I argued that the extensive use of OT language in 1 Peter enables the author to construct his theological framework with reference to Jewish eschatological visions. Jesus Christ is understood as the expected Messiah while the Christian community, which came into existence through his death and resurrection, is also perceived as the elect exiles of the Diaspora inheriting and fulfilling the self-identifications as well as the eschatological hope of Jewish people of God. A similar function is also served by the rich OT allusions in Revelation.

However, the Christ-Messiah underlined in Revelation is again notably different from that in 1 Peter. Whereas 1 Peter focuses on the rejection of Jesus Christ by human beings and identifies him as a resident-alien on earth in essence, the Messiah-Christ in Revelation is essentially a warrior-king. Likewise, while Christians are perceived in 1 Peter as an exilic people of Diaspora, suffering alienation on earth, the Christian people of God are underscored in Revelation as the army of the Messiah engaging in the Messianic War with Christ against Satan and his allies.

It is this understanding of Christians' tension with the pagan world as part of the larger war between Christ and Satan that further gives shape to John's perception of what Christians following Christ connotes, and what constitutes the correct behavioural expression of Christians' identity as Christ's Messianic army on earth.

5.2.1 Messiah-Christ in Revelation

When I explored the Petrine Christology in chapter 2, I pointed out that the reflection on Jesus Christ's earthly life in 1 Peter concentrates very much on his suffering on the cross which characterizes him as a resident-alien on earth: He was rejected by human beings (1 Pet 2:4) just like a stone rejected by the builders (2:7) and was sacrificed as a meek Passover Lamb (1:18–19). The passion story of Jesus Christ further underscores him as the Suffering Servant (2:22–25), submitting to sufferings in accordance with the current societal order: He accepted human afflictions without retaliation and without reviling or threatening in return (2:22–23). Hence, for the Petrine author, following Christ's steps (2:21) includes seeking peace and submitting to human afflictions without "returning evil for evil, or reviling for reviling" (3:9).

It is therefore remarkable that although addressing readers of similar geographical and social situations to those of 1 Peter, John actually puts emphasis on "resistance unto death," rather than "submitting to suffering in accordance with existing societal order," as the example Jesus Christ has left for Christians on the cross.

For John, the existing pagan hostility is merely part of the Messianic War expected within the Jewish eschatological vision, in which the Messiah as the Davidic king will war against the enemies of Israel and ultimately establish the kingdom of God over the whole mankind.[87] The cross is then the place where Christ the messianic warrior-king has won his decisive victory over evil and brought about the redemption of Christians (Rev 1:5). Although Satan and the beast (the Roman Empire) attempt to claim sovereignty and worship from the world, it is actually Jesus Christ whose death and resurrection proves him to be the true king of kings and, to whom worship from mankind should be due. Therefore, instead of perceiving Christ as the meek rejected Messiah submitting to human order on earth as in 1 Peter, John actually focuses on Christ's exaltation as the warrior-king, which becomes the theme of his Christology as best exemplified in four passages of the book (i.e. 1:4–8, 1:12–20; 5:1–14; 19:11–16).

---

87. Richard Bauckham, *The Theology of the Book of Revelation*, New Testament Theology (Cambridge: Cambridge University Press, 1993), 67–68. See also Schürer, *History*, 2:525–538.

i. 1:4–8

As early as in his salutation, John has already made explicit his idea of Jesus Christ as "the faithful witness (ὁ μάρτυς, ὁ πιστός), the firstborn of the dead (ὁ πρωτότοκος τῶν νεκρῶν) and the ruler of the kings on earth (ὁ ἄρχων τῶν βασιλέων τῆς γῆς)" (1:5). This threefold designation of Christ probably derives from a combination of LXX Psalm 88: 28, 38 (MT 89:28, 38) and Isaiah 55:4.[88] In LXX Psalm 88:28, David is named as the firstborn (πρωτότοκον) and higher than the kings of the earth (τοῖς βασιλεῦσιν τῆς γῆς), and in LXX Psalm 88:38, the eternity of the Davidic throne is comparable to the faithful witness (ὁ μάρτυς ... πιστός) of the moon. In LXX Isaiah 55:4, it is also David who is said to be a testimony (μαρτύριον) and a ruler (ἄρχοντα) at the same time. Christ is therefore perceived by John as the Messianic Davidic king in fulfilment of the Jewish eschatological expectation.[89]

It is noticeable that John also starts his reflection on Christ's messiahship with the cross, which underscores him as the "first" faithful witness to God to the point of death (cf. 3:14), and as the paradigm of Christians' faithful witness through unyielding resistance throughout the book (μάρτυς, 2:13; 11:3–7; 17:6; cf. μαρτυρία, 1:2, 9; 6:9; 11:7; 12:11, 17; 19:10; 20:4).

It is by first going through death, and as a consequence of his resurrection, that Christ is now exalted as the "firstborn," entitled to kingship and becomes the ruler of the "kings of the earth."[90] Although "these kings of the earth" (τῶν βασιλέων τῆς γῆς) are antagonistic to the rule of God/Christ at the moment (6:15; 17:2, 18; 18:3, 9; 19:19; cf. τοὺς βασιλεῖς τῆς οἰκουμένης ὅλης, 16:14), they ultimately will be subject to the rule of Christ after his final conquest of Satan and his allies (19:19–21; 21:24) as the divine warrior.

This connection of Christ's exaltation as the warrior-king with his martyr death is further seen in Revelation 1:7, when John once again combines

---

88. Sweet, *Revelation*, 65–66; Beale, *Revelation*, 190–192.

89. Also, Rebecca Skaggs and Thomas Doyle, "Revelation 7: Three Critical Questions," in *Imagery in the Book of Revelation*, eds. Michael Labahn and Outi Lehtipuu (Leuven: Peeters, 2011), 181.

90. Beale, *Revelation*, 191.

Christ's future coming "with the clouds" with his having been "pierced" by human beings. In Daniel 7:13–14, the messianic "one like a son of man" is said to come with the "clouds of heaven" and was given "dominion . . . and a kingdom."[91] In addition, "riding on clouds" further relates to the image of God as the divine warrior in the OT (e.g. Ps 104:3; Isa 19:1). Although Jesus Christ seems to have been conquered by human beings in his death, John expects that Christ will soon come back as the messianic warrior-king for judgment, when those who have pierced him will mourn on account of him.[92]

ii. 1:12–20

In this passage, Christ is once again portrayed as a majestic warrior-judge, now in the midst of seven lampstands (1:12–13) and holding seven stars in his right hand (1:16). As 1:20 unveils, these lampstands are the seven churches and the seven stars are likely the seven angels who are the counterparts and corporate representatives of these churches.[93] Christ's being amidst the lampstands and holding the seven stars in his hand, therefore, signify his sovereignty and oversight not only over unbelievers, but also over his own churches. Those who are lax in Christian witness will receive his rebuke, while those who keep their faithful witness will receive his commendations as is highlighted in his seven messages in 2:1–3:22.

Here, Christ is expressly described as "one like a son of man" (ὅμοιον υἱὸν ἀνθρώπου, 1:13), which immediately relates him to the "one like a son of man" in LXX Daniel 7:13 (ὡς υἱὸς ἀνθρώπου) and, thus, the messianic warrior-king within the Jewish eschatological visions.[94] His portrayal in Revelation 1:13–16 is probably based on a cluster of OT traditions which underscore his function as the righteous eschatological judge. Long robes

---

91. See also the Messianic warrior figure flying with the clouds of heaven in *4 Ezra* 13.3.

92. Knight, *Revelation*, 36–37. This vision of Christ's second coming for judgment is further elaborated in Rev 14:14–20 in which the "one like a son of man" is seen sitting on the cloud with a sharp sickle (δρέπανον) in his hand (14:14) which also symbolizes Christ's future coming as the judge of mankind (cf. δρέπανον, Mark 4:29; δρέπανα, LXX Joel 4:13).

93. Beasley-Murray, *Revelation*, 69; Sweet, *Revelation*, 73; Beale, *Revelation*, 217–219.

94. For the understanding of the Danielic "one like a son of man" as the messianic warrior-king within Jewish literature, see e.g. *1 En.* 46, 48, 62, 63, 69, 70 and 71; *4 Ezra* 13.

(ποδήρη, 1:13) were generally worn by dignitaries and rulers.[95] Particularly noticeable is that the figure in long robe (ποδήρη) in LXX Ezekiel 9:2 was one who is about to put God's judgment in action. Christ's eyes like a flame of fire (1:14) further recalls the eyes like torches of fire of the heavenly figure in Daniel 10:6, who is also wearing a golden belt (Dan 10:5; cf. ζώνην χρυσᾶν, Rev 1:13), and whose appearance is also related to the unveiling of God's judgment.[96] Indeed, this image of Christ's eyes like a flame of fire further marks his perceptive power to judge righteously, as underlined in Revelation 2:18 (cf. 2:23) and 19:11–12.[97]

Furthermore, the sharp two-edged sword from Christ's mouth (Rev 1:16) recalls the Messianic Davidic eschatological judge in Isaiah 11:3–4 and the messianic Servant in Isaiah 49:2. It also foreshadows the judicial role of Christ to the churches (2:16) and the pagan world (19:15). The description of Christ's feet like burnished bronze (1:15) probably also alludes to those of the heavenly figure in Daniel 10:6.[98]

Especially noticeable is that John's description of Christ's head and hair "like white wool" (1:14) likely derives from that of the Ancient of Days (God) in Daniel 7:9, while his voice "like the sound of many waters" (1:15) also recalls that of God as underscored in Ezekiel 1:24 and 43:2. In addition, although the image of Christ's face like the shining sun (1:16) probably alludes to the heavenly figure in Daniel 10 whose face is like "the appearance of lightning" (Dan 10:6), this image is also comparable to the glorious God who is actually said to be like "the sun" in MT Psalm 84:12. Therefore, John is exalting Christ to the utmost measure by underscoring him as sharing divine attributes with God.

This deliberate identification of Christ with God is even more obviously seen in Christ's self-designation as "the first and the last" (1:17; cf. 2:8; 22:13), which is the same title by which God designates himself in the OT (Isa 41:4; 44:6; 48:12). Moreover, this designation of "the first and the last" is comparable to the phrase "Alpha and Omega" which God

---

95. Osborne, *Revelation*, 89.
96. Beale, *Revelation*, 209.
97. See also Slater, *Christ*, 100.
98. A further possible reference is Ezek 1:7 in which the feet of the cherubim were gleaming like burnished bronze.

designates himself in Revelation 1:8 and 21:6. Christ's combining both "Alpha and Omega" and "the first and the last" to address himself in 22:13 is, therefore, further indication of John's vision of Christ's divine status as comparable to God.

Once again, this universal sovereignty of Christ as "the first and the last" is the product of John's reflection on the cross. It is only through his death that Jesus Christ is now seen as the resurrected and the ever living one (ὁ ζῶν, 1:18). Besides controlling life, the fact that Christ has entered death and won his victory manifests his sovereignty and control over (τὰς κλεῖς) even death and its realm (1:18).[99] It is with this control over life and death that Christ the righteous divine judge, and not the Roman emperor, keeps the book of life (13:8; 21:27; cf. 2:10).

This discrepancy between what things "seem to be" and those "truly are" is precisely how John understands the present reality. Instead of a sorrowful defeated one on the cross, Christ is actually the most exalted, truly divine warrior-king, which renders any worship of the emperor unthinkable. Likewise, suffering/death is not something that Christians need to avoid by conforming to pagan expectations. The true destiny of life/honour and death/punishment is in fact in the hands of Christ.

iii. 5:1–14

In this passage, Christ is introduced as an answer to the question of who is worthy to unveil God's plan for the last phase of the history of the present heaven and earth by opening the scroll.

In 5:5, Christ is designated as "the lion of the tribe of Judah" and "the root of David" (cf. Rev 22:16). These titles probably allude respectively to Genesis 49:8–12 and Isaiah 11:1–10, both of which receive a messianic interpretation in Jewish literature.[100] Particularly noticeable is that in *4 Ezra* 11–2, the Messiah who arises from "the posterity of David" is seen as "a lion" (12.31-2) and he declares the doom of the eagle (11.38–46), which symbolizes Rome as the fourth empire (11.40; 12.11).[101] Therefore, Christ

---

99. Osborne, *Revelation*, 95–96.

100. Gen 49:8–12: e.g. *Tg. Onq.* Gen 49:8–12; Isa 11:1–10: e.g. *Pss. Sol* 17.24, 35–37; *1 En.* 49.3; 62.2.

101. Michael E. Stone, *Fourth Ezra: A Commentary on the Book of Fourth Ezra*, Hermeneia (Minneapolis, MN: Fortress Press, 1990), 348, 353.

is once again portrayed as the messianic warrior-king who is combatant towards the Roman Empire.

In this passage, John starts his portrayal of Christ as the Messianic Davidic king once again from the cross. The "lion of Judah" and "root of David" who has conquered (ἐνίκησεν, 5:5) is none other than the Lamb "as if slain" (ὡς ἐσφαγμένον, 5:6), that is, he appears to have been conquered.[102] Since the blood of this Lamb is seen as a ransom payment (ἠγόρασας, 5:9; cf. λύσαντι, 1:5) for people and as making them a kingdom and priests (5:9–10; cf. 1:6) which recalls the Exodus account (cf. Exod 19:6), Christ is likely seen in this passage as the Passover Lamb.[103] However, for John, the sacrificial death of this Passover Lamb is paradoxically the means through which Christ the Messiah is seen to have conquered the satanic force as the divine warrior-king (cf. 5:9). As Beasley-Murray observes, "The warrior-Lamb then has conquered through accepting the role of the passover Lamb."[104]

Therefore, instead of the meek messianic Passover Lamb exemplifying peace and submission in 1 Peter (1 Pet 1:18–19; cf. 2:23), John's messianic Lamb is one with seven horns and seven eyes (Rev 5:6) denoting complete royal power[105] and complete omniscience.[106] Within John's vision, sacrificial death is in fact indicative of Christ's victory and, thus, his exalted status as the warrior-king and the righteous judge (cf. 1:14). It is also this example of Christ that Christians are called upon to follow by taking part in Christ's Messianic War, and continuing his victory through unyielding resistance to the wider systems to the point of sacrificial death.

Indeed, for John, it is sacrificial death that deserves the most elaborate praise and honour. Christ's sacrificial death entitles him (5:9, 12) to receive heavenly adoration and worship (5:8–12), and even share worship with God (5:13–14) which, as Hurtado remarks, is the most "direct and

---

102. Slater, *Christ*, 169.
103. Beasley-Murray, *Revelation*, 125; Bauckham, *Climax*, 184, 215.
104. Beasley-Murray, *Revelation*, 125.
105. Horns: e.g. Num 23:22; Deut 33:17; Dan 7:7.
106. Eyes: e.g. Zech 4:10.

forceful way to express Jesus' divine status."[107] Prostration in worship (5:8, 14; cf. 19:10; 22:8–9), prayers (5:8) and angelic hymn (5:12) are gestures of reverence and allegiance that are commonly offered to God in the OT.[108] Although Christ probably is not seen as sharing the same throne with God in this scene,[109] he is unambiguously presented as sharing the same throne with God in 3:21 and 22:1.

It is precisely this high view of Christology that serves as the basis of John's demand for Christians' uncompromising resistance to the pagan culture. On the one hand, since "the highest, truest"[110] worship can be due to Christ/God only, any worship to any other object, whether in the pagan religions or the imperial cult, is no more than a farce and any participation, an absurdity. On the other hand, since Christ's sacrificial death is paradoxically the means to his entitlement to divine kingship (5:6) and sharing the throne of God, sacrificial death on the part of Christians is also what entitles them to share the throne of Christ (3:21; cf. 5:10; 20:4, 6). It is on account of this extreme honour and exhilarating eschatological hope that Christians are motivated to pay any price for the realization of such expectation.

iv. 19:11–16

In this passage, Christ's image as the divine warrior-king is most blatantly presented. He is portrayed as a glorious rider on a white horse, who comes to judge and to make war (πολεμεῖ, 19:11; cf. 2:16) on Satan and his allies.

Here, the depiction of Christ recalls his various images already presented in the book and, thus, brings John's Christology to a coherent unity. His eyes like "a flame of fire" (φλὸξ πυρός, 19:12; cf. φλὸξ πυρός, 1:14; 2:18), the "sharp sword" (ῥομφαία ὀξεῖα, 19:15; cf. ῥομφαία ... ὀξεῖα, 1:16, 2:12; ῥομφαίᾳ, 2:16) from his mouth and his ruling with a rod of

---

107. Larry W. Hurtado, *Lord Jesus Christ: Devotion to Jesus in Earliest Christianity*, paperback ed. (Grand Rapids, MI: Eerdmans, 2005), 592–593.

108. See Osborne, *Revelation*, 258; Cf. Bauckham, *Climax*, 139; Slater, *Christ*, 170–173.

109. The fact that the Lamb needs to come (ἦλθεν) to the throne to take the scroll (5:7), and the conscious distinction between the One sitting on the throne and the Lamb (5:13) make it unlikely that the Lamb is envisioned as on the same throne as God (Caird, *Commentary*, 75–76. See also Bauckham, *Climax*, 139).

110. Cf. Hurtado, *Lord*, 591.

iron (ποιμανεῖ ... ἐν ῥάβδῳ σιδηρᾷ, 19:15; cf., ποιμαίνειν ... ἐν ῥάβδῳ σιδηρᾷ, 12:5) are all found in his previous appearances, and once again endow him with a messianic overtone (cf. LXX Ps 2:9; *Pss. Sol.* 17.21–25). In addition, his name "Faithful and True" (19:11) also echoes his designation as the "faithful and true witness" in 3:14. "Word of God" (19:13) similarly recalls his faithful witness to the word of God (1:2, 9; cf. 6:9; 20:4), but is now accentuated as his coming to deliver God's true and righteous judgment (ἐν δικαιοσύνῃ κρίνει, 19:11; cf. δίκαιος, 15:3, 16:5, 7; 19:2) and to vindicate his own witness on the cross.[111]

Furthermore, Christ the warrior-king is distinctively pictured as having "many" diadems (19:12) on his head, which obviously downplay the "seven" diadems on the heads of the dragon (12:3) and the "ten" diadems on the horns of the beast (13:1) – it is Christ who is the true "king of kings and lord of lords" (19:16; cf. 17:14) rather than the false sovereignty of the Roman Empire. John is once again exalting Christ to extreme honour and glory in somewhat hyperbolic terms that demands Christians to respond accordingly by adopting a polemical stance against the pagan systems.

Similar extremity within John's vision is further betrayed by his dramatizing Christians' ultimate vindication in terms of Christ's robe frightfully "dipped in blood" of his enemies (19:13).[112] This severity of Christ's judgment is further heightened by the image of the blood of enemies flowing like grape juice from a "wine press" (19:15), which recalls 14:20 where the blood flows from the wine press "up to horses' bridles" and "for 1600 stadia."

This portrayal of Christ as the glorious warrior serves double purposes of both assurance of vindication and warning of judgment. Just as extreme honour in an alternative reality serves as the incentive for Christians' clearcult disassociation from the pagan social structure and paying whatever

---

111. Cf. Beale, *Revelation*, 957–958.

112. I agree with the view of scholars such as Mounce, *Revelation*, 345; Beasley-Murray, *Revelation*, 280; Osborne, *Revelation*, 682–683; Slater, *Community*, 224–225 that the blood on Christ's robe refers to the blood of the enemies rather than the blood of Christ himself. This interpretation is in line with the image of the conqueror in Isa 63:3, who has trodden on the wine press and has the blood of his enemies sprinkled on his garments. This combination of "treading the wine press" with "garments sprinkled with blood" convincingly renders Isa 63:3 a probable OT background of Rev 19:13 and 19:15.

price for such honour, extreme suffering and punishment in the future, on the other hand, becomes a warning to Christians not to compromise for the sake of better comfort in the present life. Within John's perception, there is no middle way.

Subsection Summary

Although John also starts his christological reflection with the cross and also emphasizes the messiahship of Jesus Christ just like 1 Peter, his choice of images to portray Christ is notably different from 1 Peter. While 1 Peter focuses more on Jesus Christ as the rejected stone, the submissive sacrificial Lamb, Suffering Servant and the shepherd, much more emphasis is put by John on the divine status of Christ as a glorious messianic king, divine warrior and an eschatological judge.

It is in the light of such exaltation of Christ to extreme honour that for John, there are only two possible forms of response to pagan pressure to compromise. On the one hand, just as the extreme suffering of Christ on the cross proves him entitled to the divine status of extreme honour and glory even comparable to God, Christians should have no reluctance in unambiguously dissociating themselves from the current socio-economic and political structures even if death (i.e. the extreme form of suffering), may be the consequence.

On the other hand, Christ the warrior-king and supreme judge requires absolute allegiance from Christians who can only choose to be either on his side or on the side of his enemies in the Messianic War. While choosing Christ leads to extreme honour, choosing the pagan systems can only lead to extreme punishment from Christ.

All these further account for John's perception of Christians as the army of the Messiah. For John, "following Christ by taking part in the Messianic War to the point of death" is the only choice available to Christians as the proper expression of their identity in the present world.

5.2.2 Christian Messianic Army in Revelation

In the previous chapters, I demonstrated that 1 Peter perceives Christians' existence in the present world as "elect exiles of Diaspora." This perception entails Christians seeking peace and maintaining a degree of normality in their city life, provided that their ultimate allegiance to God is kept intact.

Besides understanding this mode of "differentiated resistance" as a congruent identity expression of the Christian Diaspora, "seeking peace" and "submission in accordance with current societal order" are also perceived in 1 Peter as one aspect of the social response Christ himself adopted when facing human rejection as a resident-alien, and which Christians can follow in his steps (1 Pet 2:21).

John's perception of Christian existence on earth is again notably different from 1 Peter. Although OT language and images are also employed to apply the titles and attributes of the people of God of Israel to Christians, John's focus is not so much on the existence of the *exilic people of God living as resident-aliens* in society as on their participation in the Messianic War as *the army of the Messiah-Christ*. For John, the people of God are those who faithfully follow Christ in the conquest of Satan by unambiguously resisting the wider culture, and drawing a clear-cut frontier with the Roman socio-economic system to the point of sacrificial death. This vision of Christian existence in Revelation is what I am going to explore in the following discussion with reference to John's apocalyptic visions.

As symbolized by the leaving out of the outer court[113] of the temple from measurement,[114] which is given to the Gentiles to be trampled for forty-two months in 11:2,[115] it is within John's vision that Christians are living in a designated period of physical persecutions on earth. His expectation of Christians undergoing persecutions for "forty-two months" (three and a half years) actually recalls "a time, times and half a time" (Dan 7:25; 12:7), "half a week" (Dan 9:27), and "1,290 days" (Dan 12:11), which denotes the time in which evil prevails and the saints have to undergo persecutions before the arrival of the eschaton. Besides "forty-two months," John also designates this period as "1,260 days" (counting 30 days a month, Rev 11:3; 12:6) and "time, times and half a time" (Rev 12:14).[116]

---

113. For the view that the outer court of the temple refers to the outward life of the church, see Sweet, *Revelation*, 184; Mounce, *Revelation*, 220.

114. For the notion that "measuring" refers to God's preservation and protection, see Ezek 40–43:12; Zech 2:5–9; *1 En.* 61.3–5.

115. For John's identification of the Holy City (11:2) with the faithful church, see Rev 21:2. See also Sweet, *Revelation*, 183–184; Osborne, *Revelation*, 413.

116. See also Osborne, *Revelation*, 414.

Indeed, John actually takes the present tension between Christians and the pagan world to the cosmic plane as part of the warfare between God and Satan in heaven, and understands the present persecutions of Christians as the war waged by Satan (πόλεμον, 12:17, cf. 12:13) following his defeat, which has already taken place. For John, Christians' existence on earth is not just a period of sojourn (cf. 1 Pet 1:17), negotiating their existence between a longing for an alternative homeland and a belonging to the present world, but rather, a time of continuous warfare with the satanic force. Since Satan has already met his decisive defeat both by the Messiah-Christ (12:4–5) and by God's angels (12:7–9), the persecutions inflicted on Christians are no more than Satan's last desperate attempt to conquer the people of God which he knows has no chance to triumph (εἰδὼς ὅτι ὀλίγον καιρὸν ἔχει, 12:12). Christians, as the army of the Messiah-Christ, therefore, have to face the war and continue the conquest of Satan (ἐνίκησαν, 12:11) already achieved on the cross (διὰ τὸ αἷμα τοῦ ἀρνίου, 12:11) through perseverance in faithful witness for Christ to the point of death (12:11). For John, there is no room for Christians to ease tension with the larger world.

It is remarkable that in John's vision of the heavenly woman in 12:1–17, those on whom Satan makes war are the offspring of the heavenly woman (12:17), who is portrayed with reference to the people of Israel. Her linkage to the sun, moon and twelve stars (12:1) is often recognized by scholars as owing its background to Genesis 37:9[117] in which the sun and moon refer to Jacob and Leah while the eleven stars, to their sons. Moreover, the fact that she was carried by two wings of a great eagle into the wilderness (12:14; cf. Exod 19:4; Deut 32:10–11) and saved by God from the flood (12:15–16; cf. Exod 15:12) further relates her to Israel in the Exodus account. At the same time, her offspring are designated as those who "keep the commandments of God and hold to the testimony of Jesus" (12:17). This heavenly woman therefore represents corporately the people of God of all times including the church in extension to the nation of Israel. For John, facing the war of Satan by "keeping the commandments of God and

---

117. E.g. Osborne, *Revelation*, 456; Mayo, *Those Who Call*, 149; Boxall, *Revelation*, 178; Edmondo F. Lupieri, *A Commentary on the Apocalypse of John*, trans. Maria Poggi Johnson and Adam Kamesar (Grand Rapids, MI: Eerdmans, 2006), 189.

bearing the witness of Jesus" (12:17; cf. 1:2, 9; 6:9; 14:12; 20:4) is actually the gist of Christians' existence as the continuing faithful people of God.

This conviction of John is also highlighted in his vision of the two witnesses in 11:3–13. They are called μάρτυσίν (11:3) which immediately relates them to Jesus Christ (μάρτυς, 1:5; 3:14) and the faithful martyr Antipas (μάρτυς, 2:13). They are further designated as "two lampstands" (λυχνίαι) and "two olive trees" (11:4), which further relate them to the whole church (cf. λυχνίαι, 1:20) assuming the role of Israel as priests and kingdom (cf. Zech. 4:3, 14; Rev 1:6; 5:10; 20:6).[118]

It is this faithful church that is empowered to prophesy during the period of 1,260 days (11:3) of Satan's apparent victory. Far from seeking peace or releasing tension with the neighbours, proper Christian witness is supposed to be a torment (ἐβασάνισαν, 11:10) to the world around them. Therefore, John does not shun from admitting the hatred and seemingly disheartening situation that Christians may plunge into by drawing a clear boundary with the wider culture. The two witnesses ended up facing the persecutions (war, πόλεμον) of the beast (the empire) and appeared to be conquered (νικήσει, 11:7; cf. 13:7). The hatred and opposition they aroused were so great that the world around them (11:9–10) rejoiced over their death and refused to let their dead bodies be placed in a tomb.[119]

While pagan hatred and hostility are parts of Christian existence on earth, sacrificial death is also considered by John as a token of Christians' identification with Christ in the conquest of Satan. Thus, the two witnesses died in the great city "where their Lord was crucified" (11:8). They were resurrected after "three and a half days" (11:11) and "went up to heaven in a cloud" (11:12). Just as the cross is where Christ the Lamb has decisively conquered Satan, Christians' sacrificial death is also their continuing Christ's conquest over Satan and his allies.

This perception of "sacrificial death" as an identification with Christ is also reflected in John's vision of the souls of the martyred saints under the

---

118. Zech 4:14 clarifies these two olive trees as the two anointed ones whom are commonly recognized as Joshua and Zerubbabel and respectively the high priest and the Davidic governor of Judah at the time of their return from exile. See e.g. Beasley-Murray, *Revelation*, 183–184; Beale, *Revelation*, 577; Boxall, *Revelation*, 163–164.

119. For the notion of exposing the dead body without a burial as a gesture of total lack of mercy, see e.g. Philo, *Ios.* 25.

altar in 6:9–11. The deaths of these saints are explained as due to their having kept "the word of God and the witness" of Jesus (6:9; cf. 20:4), which is further clarified as refusing to worship the beast or its image and to receive the mark of the beast (20:4; cf. 13:16) (i.e. they had failed to conform to the expectation of the larger world).[120] They are notably underscored as having been slain (ἐσφαγμένων, 6:9) which immediately relates them to Christ the Lamb in the conquest of the satanic force (ἐνίκησεν, 5:5) through being slain (ἐσφαγμένος, 5:6, 12; ἐσφάγης, 5:9).

It is through this vision of the martyred saints that John perceives death as not to be avoided but embraced. The fact of each martyr saint being given a white robe (στολὴ λευκή, 6:11; cf. 7:9, 13–14)[121] denotes their purity and righteous deeds (19:8),[122] and therefore, signifies their victory over pressure to conform.[123] Furthermore, white garments are also the eschatological gift promised in 3:4–5 (ἱματίοις λευκοῖς) to the one who conquers (ὁ νικῶν). Therefore, the overriding context of Christian existence is still that of a continuing warfare. There is simply no room for neutrality or avoidance of tension with the larger pagan milieu.

Indeed, John's comprehension of Christians' existence as Christ's army on earth is most blatantly manifested in 7:4–8, where the number of Christians receiving the seal of God is said to be 144,000, 12,000 of which belong to each tribe of Israel.[124] This numbering of each tribe is reminiscent of a census of the tribes in the wilderness (e.g. Num 1:20–46; 26:5–51) for the preparation of upcoming wars (e.g. Num 1:2–3; 26:2) in the OT.[125] The heading of Judah in the tribal lists further recalls Christ the Lamb as the "lion of the tribe of Judah" (5:5). Therefore, this vision of the

---

120. Beale, *Revelation*, 715; Osborne, *Revelation*, 517–518.

121. See also white garments (ἱμάτια λευκά) in 3:5, 18; 4:4; white linen (βύσσινον λευκόν) in 19:14 (cf. βύσσινον, 19:8); and the image of Christians washing their robes (στολὰς αὐτῶν) in the Lamb's blood in 7:14 and 22:14.

122. Beale, *Revelation*, 394.

123. Bauckham, *Climax*, 225. For the Roman background of a conquering general leading a victory procession in a white toga, see Osborne, *Revelation*, 319.

124. It is commonly recognized that John's list of the twelve tribes does not follow any list in the OT. The list in Rev 7:5–8 is likely to be the product of John's own reworking. See the detailed discussion in Mayo, *Those Who Call*, 79–87.

125. Bauckham, *Climax*, 217–218; Osborne, *Revelation*, 313; Pattemore, *People*, 138–139.

144,000 actually highlights John's understanding of Christians as the messianic army following the lead of Christ as their warrior-king.[126]

This idea of Christians following Christ in the Messianic War is even more prominently conveyed in 14:1–5, where the victory of Christ is seen in the Lamb standing on Mount Zion with the company of the Christian 144,000. Mount Zion is the place where the Messiah is expected in the Jewish literature to appear, defeat the ungodly, and gather the people of God under his protection (*4 Ezra.* 13.35–50; *2 Bar.* 40.1–3). In accompanying the Lamb on Mount Zion, Christians are the army of the people of God following the Messiah wherever he goes (14:4). While following Christ's steps in 1 Peter refers to Christians following the examples of Christ the resident-alien in doing good and enduring suffering (1 Pet 2:20–21), Christians following Christ, for John, entails following the Messiah as his army in his war (cf. Rev 17:14; 19:14).

In order to fight their war as the army of Christ, Christians are to uphold the true witness of Christ by maintaining their purity through clearly disassociating themselves from the larger Roman systems. Therefore, they must preserve their chastity (παρθένοι, 14:4) by not aligning themselves with the idolatrous pagan culture (cf. 19:7–8).[127] While the whole of mankind is now deceived (πλανάω, 2:20; 12:9; 13:14; 18:23; 19:20; 20:3) by Satan and his allies, who are underscored as no more than liars (ψευδής, 2:2; 21:8; ψεύδονται, 3:9), the Christian army of Christ are to maintain a clear distinction by having "no lie" (οὐχ εὑρέθη ψεῦδος, 14:5) in their mouth, even if it may result in persecutions and death.

Once again, Christians' participation in the Messianic War is not by bearing arms, but rather, by way of sacrifice to God. As Pattemore remarks, "The battle in which the messianic army is engaged consists of the life of the saints."[128] Therefore, the Christian army are the sacrifices of "first fruits" (ἀπαρχή, 14:4; cf. Exod 23:19; Lev 23:10; Deut 18:4; Neh 12:44) offered to God, and they are "without blemish" (ἄμωμοί, 14:5), that is, without being profaned by the larger evil culture.

---

126. Bauckham, *Climax*, 216.
127. So Beale, *Revelation*, 739; Schüssler Fiorenza, "The Followers," 133.
128. Pattemore, *People*, 195.

Indeed, based on this vision of Christians as Christ's Messianic army, John further portrays the celebration of Christians' victory in heaven as the restoration of the people of God in accordance with the Jewish eschatological vision. In the vision of the innumerable multitude in 7:9–17, the promise of no more hunger, thirst or burning heat (7:16) likely alludes to Isaiah 49:10, and God's wiping away the tears of his people (7:17) also recalls Isaiah 25:8. In addition, the notion of the Lamb shepherding the Christian people (7:17) once again relates Jesus Christ to the Davidic Messiah promised in the OT to come and shepherd the flock of the people of God (Ezek 34:23–24; 37:24–25). The celebration of the victory of Christians is thus also the celebration of the victory of the Messiah in his Messianic War, which brings about the establishment of his kingdom.

Likewise, in the vision of millennium reign in 20:4–6, Christians sharing the throne of Christ is also portrayed in terms of the messianic kingdom having conquered the evil force in the Messianic War within Jewish expectations. As commonly recognized, this scene alludes to Daniel 7:9–27,[129] in which the kingdom of all peoples is given to the one like a son of man (7:14). Indeed, the notion of an interim period of messianic kingdom before the consummation of history is also found in Jewish literature (e.g. *2 Bar.* 29.1–30.5; *4 Ezra* 7.28–29). This placing of the millennium kingdom within the Jewish vision is even more obvious when John connects the reign of Christians with their service as priests (Rev 20:6), which recalls their having been made both a kingdom and priests in 1:6 and 5:10. Christians are thus placed in the context of the New Exodus (cf. Exod 19:6) in which Israel will experience their eschatological restoration.[130]

The perception of Christians inheriting the restoration hope of Israel is further brought to a climax in the vision of the New Heaven and New Earth in Revelation 21:1–22:5. Here, the eschatological reward for faithful Christians is portrayed as their gaining a new existence as/in the New Jerusalem (21:2, 9–10), with the gates named after the twelve tribes of Israel (21:12–13) and the foundations of the wall, after the twelve apostles

---

129. E.g. Beasley-Murray, *Revelation*, 292–293; Sweet, *Revelation*, 288; Osborne, *Revelation*, 705–706.

130. For the Jewish vision of the future restoration as a New Exodus, see page 24 in chapter 2 above.

(21:14). At the same time, this New Jerusalem is God's eternal dwelling with Christians and the fulfilment of his promise to accept Israel as his people (21:3; cf. 7:15; Lev 26:11–12). Since the same promises of God's dwelling and of acceptance to be his people are also given to Israel in Ezekiel 37:27, Christians are again underscored as the extension of the old covenant people of God. Their reconstitution as the New Jerusalem is also the fulfilment of the Jewish hope for a return to the New Jerusalem from the exile after the Messianic War has been won.[131]

What is noticeable is that all those fabulous eschatological blessings found in the New Jerusalem are underscored as inheritance for "the one who conquers" (ὁ νικῶν, 21:7) the pressure to accommodate to the pagan culture. Indeed, the eschatological promises to those who conquer in the seven letters (ὁ νικῶν, 2:7, 11, 17, 26; 3:5, 12, 21) are now seen realized in the New Heaven and Earth and the New Jerusalem.[132] The blessedness enjoyed is therefore envisioned as the award to the Christian army for their having won their victory in the Messianic War through faithfully following the Messiah-Christ (cf. 14:4; 17:14; 19:14).

In direct contrast (δέ), those who are cowards (δειλοῖς) and faithless (ἀπίστοις) are the first two on the lists of sinners in 21:8, who will end up meeting their eternal second death in the lake of fire. These fearful cowards and faithless are obviously those who succumb to the threat of persecutions by conforming to the pagan systems and in direct antithesis to John's exhortations to Christians to be fearless (μηδὲν φοβοῦ) and faithful unto death (γίνου πιστὸς ἄχρι θανάτου, 2:10).[133] The dualism within John's thought is therefore blatantly clear – Christians can only choose either to participate in Christ's war and inherit the eschatological award for their victory, or to avoid confrontations by accommodating to the demands of the pagan world and meet their terrible fate of eternal death. John does not allow for any middle way in-between.

---

131. E.g. Jer 31:1–6 (LXX 38:1–6); Zech 8:3–8. For the view that John's vision owes its background to Ezek 40–48 and Isa 40–66, see Boxall, *Revelation*, 293.

132. 2:7=22:2; 2:11=21:7–8; 2:17=21:2; cf. 19:7–9 (Beale, *Revelation*, 251–253); 2:26–28=22:5; cf. 20:4; 3:5=21:2 cf. 19:8+21:27; 3:12=21:22–23+22:4; 3:21=22:5; cf. 20:4. See also Beale, *Revelation*, 1058 followed by Osborne, *Revelation*, 739.

133. Beale, *Revelation*, 1059.

Section Summary: Features of the Shaping of Social Behavioural Instructions by Theology in 1 Peter

In this section, I sought an empathic understanding of the different formulations of Christian social strategies in 1 Peter and Revelation from the perspective of the authors' own emphasis in their perceptions of Jesus Christ and Christian existence on earth.[134] Although both the Petrine author and John begin their reflections with the cross, John understands the death of Jesus Christ as part of the cosmic warfare between God/Christ and Satan. The cross is ironically where Christ has decisively conquered Satan and testifying to his exalted status as the divine Messianic warrior-king. Likewise, the tension and persecutions experienced by Christians are only a continuation of the warfare waged by the satanic force, so that Christians are understood as the army of Christ taking part in the Messianic War on earth. Hence, Christians following Christ entails accompanying him in his war and continuing his conquest through perseverance in faithful witness and facing sacrificial death if necessary. There is no room for Christians to seek peace or cooperate with the wider socio-economic and political systems.

It is precisely through contrasting with Revelation that the distinctive features of the Petrine choice of images for Christ and Christian existence is blatantly thrown into light. For the Petrine author, the cross denotes not only *the death* but also *the manner* of Jesus Christ in submitting to current societal order and accepting pagan inflicted suffering essentially as a resident-alien and stranger on earth. Although Christ is also exalted as the messianic king in 1 Peter (1 Pet 3:22), more attention is devoted on Christ as the "meek sacrificial Passover Lamb" (1 Pet 1:18–19; cf. 1 Pet 2:23), the "rejected stone" (2:4, 7) and the "Suffering Servant" (2:22–25). The Petrine Messiah-Christ is not so much underscored as a combatant warrior as a patient sufferer submitting to human course for the higher purpose of accomplishing the divine purpose of God. Besides "patient resistance," to "seek peace without retaliation" is also what the Petrine author perceives Christ's cross to denote.

---

134. Since my focus is on the empathic understanding of the shaping of different social strategies by different theological emphasis in the two texts, I do not intend to offer further (sociological/psychological) analysis into the factors contributing to these different theological understandings of reality on the part of the two authors. In any event, 1 Peter is offering too little information about its author to make such investigation feasible.

It is based on this understanding of the Messiah-Christ as a meek and peaceful figure that the Petrine author grounds his understanding of Christian existence on earth. Besides the exhortations to arm (ὁπλίσασθε, 4:1) with the same thought of Christ and resist the devil as their adversary (1 Pet 5:8–9), emphasis is also placed on Christians' identity as resident-aliens and exiles of Diaspora (1 Pet 1:1; 2:11) suffering human alienation as Christ did on earth. They are to seek peace without retaliation (3:9–12) and to defend their faith "with gentleness" (3:15–16). Since the cross of Jesus Christ denotes his accepting suffering without violating the existing societal order, Christians following Christ's steps (2:21) also entails similar submission and responsibly discharging their societal roles, which are notably absent in John's visions.

5.3 Chapter Conclusion

In this chapter, I tried to place 1 Peter in the larger religious landscape of Christians in Asia Minor by comparing it with Revelation as an entrance to seek an empathic understanding of the shaping of the Petrine social ethics by the author's own theological vision. I argued that among the different modes of Christian response to pagan hostility as presented by John in his seven letters, the Petrine social strategy of "differentiated resistance" represents a centrist approach adopted by Christians in Asia Minor. The comparatively pacifist approach in 1 Peter becomes noticeable when seen in the light of the "undifferentiated resistance" adopted in Revelation. I also demonstrated in this chapter that this difference in social strategies adopted in the two texts is attributed to the two authors' different theological emphasis especially on the relationship between Christ and the world and, thus, Christians' existence on earth.

All these observations serve to demonstrate that even when dealing with similar problem of pagan hostility in similar social and geographical contexts, the early Christians were open to devise different modes of social response, with different acceptable degrees of social accommodation, in accordance with what they perceived as sufficient to express Christians' allegiance to God. In the process, different authors would put emphasis on different images of Christ and Christians to construct their own visions of the relationship between Christ and the wider world, and of what following Christ in the unbelieving world entails. For John, Christ is the warrior-king and Christians are his army. Following Christ means participating in Christ's Messianic War to conquer any pressure to conform to the wider culture. For the Petrine author, Christ is at the same time the meek sacrificial Lamb, rejected stone and the Suffering Servant suffering human rejection essentially as a resident-alien, while Christians are likewise resident-aliens negotiating their sojourn in this world as the exilic people of God. Besides holding fast to their ultimate allegiance to God, following Christ in 1 Peter also includes seeking peace without disrupting existing societal order as Christ himself has exemplified.

Therefore, when investigating the social behavioural instructions in 1 Peter, one has to look into the letter's theology in its own right, rather than incorporating into the Petrine text one's impression of the other texts in the Bible. Those proposals, which argue that the Petrine social strategy represents one-sided resistance to assimilation, seem to be presenting a conclusion which can be reached only with reference to Revelation, rather than what can be derived from 1 Peter itself.

CHAPTER 6

Comparison Text II: The *Epistle to Diognetus*

In the last chapter, I highlighted the more accommodationist element within the Petrine social strategy of "differentiated resistance" by comparing 1 Peter with Revelation. I demonstrated that although these two texts are addressed to readers of similar temporal, geographical and, thus, sociopolitical contexts, the teachings in 1 Peter reflects a centrist approach of both resistance and pacifism to pagan alienations, whereas the resistance advocated in Revelation appears much more "undifferentiated." I further argued that these different emphases on the part of the two authors stem from their different theological views of the relationship between Christ and the wider culture as underscored by the cross, which in turn affect their understanding of what Christians following Christ connotes. For the Petrine author, Christ's suffering on the cross denotes his being rejected by human beings essentially as a resident-alien on earth. His "differentiated resistance" to human hostility, as reflected by his holding fast to his ultimate loyalty to God *while* seeking peace and submitting to sufferings in accordance with current societal order, is what Christians following Christ as "exiles of Diaspora" on earth entails.

In this chapter, I will further elucidate the shaping of this Petrine social strategy of differentiated resistance by comparing 1 Peter with another early Christian writing: The *Epistle to Diognetus*. This anonymous writing, probably dated in the second half of the second century,[1] is fitting to serve

---

1. Also e.g. Paul Foster, "The Epistle to Diognetus" in *The Writings of the Apostolic Fathers*, ed. Paul Foster (London: T&T Clark, 2007), 149–150; Benjamin H Dunning, *Aliens and Sojourners: Self as Other in Early Christianity,* Divinations: Rereading Late

as a comparison text for our purpose because, as in 1 Peter, Christians are also perceived as resident-aliens, strangers and foreigners (πάροικοι, 5.5; ξένοι, 5.5; ἀλλόφυλοι, 5.17; cf. παρεπιδήμοις, 1 Pet 1:1; παροίκους καὶ παρεπιδήμους, 1 Pet 2:11) sojourning (παροικοῦσιν, 6.8; cf, τῆς παροικίας ὑμῶν, 1 Pet 1:17) on earth amidst pagan hostility. They are "hated" (μισεῖ, 6.5 cf. 5.17) by the world even though they have not done any wrong. They are "persecuted" (διώκω, 5.11, 17), "condemned" (κατακρίνονται, 5.12), "put to death" (θανατοῦνται) (5.12), "dishonoured" (ἀτιμοῦνται), "slandered" (βλασφημοῦνται) (5.14), "reviled" (λοιδοροῦνται), "insulted" (ὑβρίζονται) (5.15), "punished" (κολάζω, 5.16; 6.9; 7.8; 10.7) and "warred upon" (πολεμοῦνται) (5.17). At the same time, the coexistence of both resistance and accommodation within Christians' social engagement in the face of pagan alienation is even more elaborately and eloquently explicated in *Diognetus*: Christians are distinguished from the rest of humanity neither by country, language nor customs[2] (5.1) *but at the same time* demonstrate the remarkable and admittedly paradoxical (παράδοξον) order[3] of their own citizenship (5.4).

Although *Diognetus* is in essence an apologetic-protreptic treatise in an epistolary form,[4] seeking to accentuate the attractiveness and superiority of

---

Ancient Religion (Philadelphia, PA: University of Pennsylvania Press, 2009), 64. As Markus, N. A. Bockmuehl, *Jewish Law in Gentile Churches: Halakhah and the Beginning of Christian Public Ethics* (Edinburgh: T&T Clark, 2000), 215 observes, "the relative absence of a personal christology, liturgy, ecclesiology and a canon of Scripture, along with the stereotypical but still relatively naïve development of standard apologetic *topoi*, render a date in the later second century plausible to many" although Bockmuehl himself prefers to date the document earlier to the middle of the second century (*Jewish Law*, 216), which is also the date ascribed by Henry G. Meecham, *The Epistle to Diognetus: The Greek Text, with Introduction, Translation and Notes* (Manchester: Manchester University Press, 1949), 19. Whether *Diognetus* should be dated more specifically to the middle or to the later part of the second century does not affect my present investigation.

2. I agree with most scholars that ἔσθεσι (meaning "clothing"), which appears on the manuscript in Codex Argentoratensis Graecus ix, should probably be read as ἔθεσι (meaning "customs"). As Meecham, *Epistle*, 108 argues, having "customs" to follow "country" and "language" in 5.1 completes the "threefold correspondence" to "cities, speech, life" in 5.2. Meecham's observation is followed in Dunning, *Aliens*, 146 n. 9. Holmes, *Apostolic*, 700 also adopts this reading but without mentioning the emendation of the manuscript.

3. See Meecham, *Epistle*, 79 for the rendering of "order" for κατάστασιν.

4. See also Rudolf Brändle, *Die Ethik der Schrift an Diognet: Eine Wiederaufnahme paulinischer und johanneischer Theologie am Ausgang des zweiten Jahrhunderts* (Zürich: Theologischer Verlag, 1975), 15; Dunning, *Aliens*, 64–65; Meecham, *Epistle*, 8–9; Henry G. Meecham, "The Theology of the Epistle to Diognetus," *ExpTim* 54 (1943): 97.

the Christian religion to those outside their community,[5] this writing still provides valuable information about how early Christians perceived their own existence[6] and, thus, what constitutes appropriate lifestyle in the contemporary world. As Townsley observes, "Central to the author is the exaltation of the life and function of Christians in the world,"[7] while Meecham also comments that the author's main object is to "show the reasonableness of the Christian faith and its appeal as a way of life."[8] A comparison of 1 Peter with *Diognetus*, therefore, serves to demonstrate how the correlation of both resistance and accommodation within the Petrine strategy of "differentiated resistance," which was probably still in its earliest form in 1 Peter, was further developed into a coherent mode of social expression of Christians' self-understanding as resident-aliens on earth in the second half of the second century. What remains implicit or appears ambiguous in the Petrine social strategies becomes more clearly and explicitly formulated in *Diognetus*. A study of this later document, therefore, once again provides an entrance to give depth to the appreciation of the shaping of the Petrine social behavioural instructions, which probably cannot be achieved by looking at 1 Peter alone.

In the following chapter, I will firstly investigate the mode of Christian social engagement as portrayed in *Diognetus*. I wish to demonstrate that for the early Christians, the two limbs of resistance (identity maintenance) and accommodation are not mutually exclusive, nor necessarily in tension with each other. It is precisely through being the best citizens and complying with the norms of society most diligently, in so far as the boundary of their ultimate allegiance to God is not overstepped, that Christians mark themselves out as a distinct, morally superior group in society. Though comparatively more implicit, traits of this vision of Christians' moral superiority in society are also present in 1 Peter.

In the second section of this chapter, I will proceed to explain how the mode of Christian social engagement portrayed in *Diognetus* is also derived

---

5. See also Foster, "Diognetus," 150, 156.

6. Dunning, *Aliens*, 65.

7. Ashton L. Townsley, "Notes for an Interpretation of the Epistle to Diognetus," *RSC* 24 (1976): 6.

8. Meecham, *Epistle*, 4.

from the author's perception of the relationship between God/Christ and the world, as manifested by the salvation event fulfilled on the cross. Although neither the cross nor the death of Jesus Christ is mentioned in the writing,[9] the sacrifice of the Son is still the starting point of the author's reflection that gives rise to his perception of Christian existence and, thus, his formulation of corresponding Christian social ethics on earth. This once again shows that one cannot properly appreciate the dynamics within the social ethics in a given early Christian document, such as 1 Peter, without at the same time giving due consideration to the theological vision of the author, which renders my present study particularly worthwhile.

As most scholars agree, *Diogn.* 1–10 and *Diogn.* 11–12 probably come from two different sources.[10] Particularly convincing is the argument that the two sections notably differ in style, subject matter and purpose. Whereas chapters 1–10 are clearly apologetic-protreptic in tone and purpose with an outsider of the church in view, chapters 11–12 appear to be a homily with believers within the church the target readers.[11] Therefore, I will confine my present investigation to *Diogn.* 1–10, so as to avoid the possibility of exploring the relationship between the theology and the social ethics of respectively two different early Christian documents.

6.1 Christian Social Engagement Portrayed in the *Epistle to Diognetus*

In chapter 3, I argued that the real concern of the Petrine social behavioural instructions is Christians standing firm in the grace/salvation of God despite constant pressure to accommodate to the pagan idolatrous culture. Subject to the overriding boundary of "ultimate allegiance to God," (i.e. such as avoidance of idolatry and any social activities that have religious implications), the Petrine author actually exhorts Christians to adopt the

---

9. Indeed, the terms "Jesus" and "Christ" are not used in *Diognetus*. The title most frequently employed to refer to Jesus Christ include the "Child" (παῖς, 8.9, 11; 9.1) and the "Son" (υἱός, 9.2, 4; 10.2; cf. 7.4).

10. E.g. E. H. Blakeney, *The Epistle to Diognetus* (London: SPCK, 1943), 13; Meecham, *Epistle*, 64–68; Brändle, *Ethik*, 13–14; Foster, "Diognetus," 149; Bockmuel, *Jewish Law*, 215; Michael Heintz, "Μιμητὴς Θεοῦ in the Epistle to Diognetus," *JECS* 12 (2004): 111.

11. See Meecham, *Epistle*, 64–65; Foster, "Diognetus," 151–154.

highest moral ideals and to be the best citizens in accordance with standards of the wider society. This becomes obvious when one compares, for example, the vice list in 1 Peter 4:3b with contemporary Greco-Roman moral teachings.[12] I also argued that in order to inspire their slanderers to glorify God at the end (1 Pet 2:12) and to "silence the ignorance of the foolish men" (2:15), Christians' "good works" must considerably overlap with what the larger society recognizes as such.[13] It is noticeable that all these elements of Petrine social behavioural instructions are present and, in fact, more directly and explicitly elucidated in the portrayal of Christians' social engagement in the *Epistle to Diognetus*.

As a matter of fact, right at the beginning of his answers to the inquiries of Diognetus in chapter 2, the author first of all underscores the distinctiveness of the Christians by drawing a clear polemic against pagan idolatry. His critique centres on the pagans' irrationality to offer worship to images, which are no more than creatures made by human hands (2.3–4). These lifeless and perishable objects of stone, bronze, wood, silver, iron and pottery (2.2) are in essence no different from other utensils moulded by the craftsmen for everyday use (2.2–4). The idols' lack of perception (ἀναισθητέω, 2.8, 9; cf. ἀναίσθητος, 2.4; 3.3) is betrayed by the pagans' own offerings of blood and steaming fat, which are no more than a punishment to these idols if they really had perception.

It is by way of ridicule and contempt for the pagan gods that a clear boundary is drawn by the author between Christians and the pagans. In view of the nullity of the pagan gods, Christians can hardly be enslaved (δεδουλῶσθαι, 2.10) by them, and this becomes the root of pagan hatred and alienation: "This is why you hate Christians, because they do not consider these to be gods" (2.6). While Christians are often accused by their pagan neighbours of being atheists,[14] facts speak for themselves that it is the pagans themselves that are truly atheistic.[15] They despise (καταφρονεῖτε), mock (χλευάζετε) and insult (ὑβρίζετε) those they regard as gods by locking up and guarding some at night for fear of theft, but leaving out

---

12. See pages 107–109 above.
13. See pages 78, 81 above.
14. See page 110 above.
15. Brändle, *Ethik*, 34.

the rest as not worth looking after (2.7; cf. 2.2). Their offerings of blood and steaming fat to the idols were no more than a punishment (κολάζετε, 2.8; κολάσεως, 2.9) to them. By calling these objects gods, serving them and worshipping them, the pagans become just like them (2.5): deaf and blind (2.4) and, thus, incapacitated from having access to the truth of the Christian faith (cf. ἀκούω, 1.2; ἀκροατής, ἴδε, 2.1).[16] Therefore, for the author of *Diognetus*, the fundamental difference between Christians and pagans is not so much their lifestyle or any of their peculiar social practices, as it is their religious orientation (i.e. their exclusive loyalty to God). "Ultimate allegiance to God," as the overriding boundary of Christian accommodation, is what *Diognetus* and 1 Peter both share.

What distinguishes *Diognetus* from 1 Peter is that, whereas 1 Peter does not expressly evince polemics against the Jews, a clear distance (ἀπέχονται, 4.6) between Christians and Jews is blatantly underscored in *Diognetus*. Although the Jews' monotheistic faith of God is acknowledged (3.2), their method of worship (ch. 3) and ritual observances (ch. 4) reveal that they have failed to put God in the right perspective (i.e. the line drawn between Christians and Jews is also religious). By offering sacrifices to God as if he were in need of these things, the Jews are not offering God the worship which is seemly to his honour as the Creator and Provider of the universe (3.2–4). They are in fact sharing the same folly (ἀφροσύνης, μωρίαν, 3.3) as the Greeks by worshipping God in the same manner as the pagans offering lavish honour (φιλοτιμίαν)[17] to their dumb and deaf idols (3.5; cf. 3.2).

The impiety and folly of the Jews is then further amplified in chapter 4 with reference to their ritual observances. Their scruples about food virtually amount to a rejection of part of God's creation as useless and superfluous (4.2). Their false allegation of God about his forbidding (κωλύοντος) men's good deeds on Sabbath is also impiety (πῶς οὐκ ἀσεβές) (4.3). In addition, Jews are laughable for taking pride in the mutilation of the flesh (μείωσιν τῆς σαρκός), that is, circumcision, as a sign of God's election and special love (4.4). Their observance of the lunar calendar and arbitrary designation of times of festivals and mourning also constitutes a

---

16. Horacio E. Lona, *An Diognet,* Kommentar zu Frühchristlichen Apologeten 8 (Freiburg: Herder, 2001), 100.

17. Meecham, *Epistle*, 103.

violation of God's created order and an example of their foolishness just like the Greeks (ἀφροσύνης ... δεῖγμα, 4.5; cf. ἀφροσύνης δεῖγμα, 3.3). Therefore, the distinction between Christians and Jews is concerned with proper worship and the correct ritual expression of their faith in God and is, therefore, also primarily religious. This observation is confirmed by the fact that in 4.6, and after asserting Christians keeping away from the silliness and deceit of the Greeks, as well as the meddlesomeness and pride of the Jews (4.6),[18] the author immediately turns to the mystery (μυστήριον) of the Christians' religion/service to God (θεοσεβείας) as a contrast to that of the pagans and the Jews.

It is worth notice that by upholding the religious superiority of Christians, the author of *Diognetus* does not endow Christians only with an "internal" sense of identity, but at the same time posits them as a distinctive "externally recognizable" group in society. Lieu comments that the external identity of Christians as portrayed in *Diognetus* is marked by "a lack of visible differentiation,"[19] and Feldmeier also argues, "Externally, Christians are in no respect different (according to Dg. 5:1ff) from other people: they do not live in different cities, and do not lead remarkable lives. They are, however, marked by a special inner attitude to all these things."[20]

But these impressions of *Diognetus* have actually underrated the implications of Christians' abstention from the religious cults of both pagans and Jews, which actually makes them distinctively and externally observable by their neighbours.

As I have mentioned in the previous chapters, religion is bound up with every fabric of city life, whether political, household or social, in the ancient Greco-Roman world. As exemplified by Tertullian's *Idolatry*, besides refusing to oberve holy-days connected with idolatry (ch. 13) or participate in priestly function and sacrifices in private and social solemnities (ch. 16), Christians' abstention from pagan idolatry further includes forms of oath, attestation and legal formalities (chs. 20–23). It also includes choices of

---

18. I agree with Meecham, *Epistle*, 106 that "τῆς ... κοινῆς εἰκαιότητος καὶ ἀπάτης" and "τῆς Ἰουδαίων πολυπραγμοσύνης καὶ ἀλαζονείας" refer to the faults of Greeks and Jews respectively. The two occurrences of τῆς indicate that the author is referring to two separate groups of people. Also Lona, *Diognet*, 139. Contra Brändle, *Ethik*, 58.

19. Lieu, *Jew nor Greek*, 179–189.

20. Feldmeier, "Nation," 265.

profession and trade (chs. 8–12). Even being a school master is regarded as idolatrous because he has to preach the pagan gods and to observe their solemnities and festivals (ch.10). Furthermore, according to Tertullian, there were among the Romans gods of entrances, so that Christians had to avoid using lamps and laurels to decorate their entrances (ch. 15).

Indeed, Pliny's letter also reveals that the emergence of Christianity had observable social effects: temples were almost deserted, sacred festivals were interrupted, sales of sacrificial animals were also affected (*Ep.* 10.96). Even in *Diognetus* itself, the author makes it clear that the pagans hate Christians because Christians do not join them in considering their idols as gods (2.6), and remain different by not denying the Lord/God (7.7; 10.7). Jews are also seen standing on the same front as the Greeks in alienating Christians as foreigners, probably on the ground of religious difference and, therefore, cannot state the reason for their hostility (5.17).

Therefore, in Greco-Roman antiquity, Christians' exclusive worship and ultimate allegiance to God was not just a matter of internal piety. It was embodied in the various aspects of Christians' external way of life, and required to be translated into observable social behaviour in their day-to-day engagement with the wider idolatrous world. It is precisely against this overriding boundary imposed by Christians' religious orientation of exclusive allegiance to God that their relatively positive social engagement as mentioned in *Diogn.* 5–6 and 10 should be understood.

At the same time, while *Diognetus* shares with 1 Peter the same overriding principle of "ultimate allegiance to God" as the boundary of Christian social accommodation, it ventures further by asserting more blatantly and boldly that Christians are distinguished from the rest of humanity neither by country, language nor customs (5.1), nor do they practice any peculiar mode of life (5.2). They take part in all things as ordinary citizens (5.5), and have no problem following the customs and mode of life of the other inhabitants of the cities in which Christians find themselves (5.4). In effect, the author is claiming that Christians' understanding of their own distinctiveness is not primarily sociological, but religious/theological. In so far as they are not required to get involved in any customs and practices that may be inconsistent with their ultimate allegiance to God, Christians do not mind adopting the social norms and practices of the larger society. This mode of Christian social engagement is reflective and indeed, represents a second-century amplification of the configuration of Petrine Christian "good works" of "differentiated resistance" as I explained in chapter 3 above.

Even more noticeable is the fact that while the Petrine author perceives "differentiated resistance," comprising an element of accommodation, as the congruent behavioural expression of Christians' identity as "elect exiles of Diaspora," *Diognetus* also understands Christians following the commonly accepted customs and practices of the wider society as part of the visible demonstration (ἐνδείκνυνται) of the order of their own citizenship (κατάστασιν τῆς ἑαυτῶν πολιτείας, 5.4) in heaven (5.9). As Meecham observes, "for *Diognetus* the Christian lives here and now in the heavenly city."[21] The positive features of the Christian ethos are just those which "attest its divine origin and nature"[22] (cf. 5.3). Therefore, Christians are now in the flesh but in fact do not live according to the flesh (οὐ κατὰ σάρκα ζῶσιν) (5.8).

It is based on this perception of Christians' true citizenship in heaven that the author further claims that Christians are in fact the best citizens complying faultlessly with current societal norms and practices. Save those customs and practices that have religious implications and, thus, inconsistent with their ultimate allegiance to God, the author of *Diognetus* does not consider the Christian way of life as necessarily incompatible with the moral philosophies of the wider world. Besides their exclusive allegiance to God, what really distinguishes Christians from the wider world is that they actually excel their pagan neighbours in living out the highest moral ideal recognized by the larger society. As Dunning remarks, Christians "outstrip the Romans in their ability to fulfil Roman norms."[23] This superior quality of Christians' moral life, recognizable with reference to the standard of the wider society, is interpreted by the author as the visible expression on earth of the invisible reality of Christians' higher citizenship in heaven, which is apparent from his portrayal of Christians' (1) civil life; (2) household life; and (3) daily social life.

---

21. Meecham, *Epistle*, 108.
22. Ibid., 107.
23. Dunning, *Aliens*, 66.

6.1.1 Christian Engagement in Civil Life

Similar to 1 Peter in which Christians are exhorted to stay within the wider socio-political system by honouring the emperor (1 Pet 2:17) and subjecting themselves to every human creature (institution) including the governors, who have the capacity to decide who does evil and who does good (2:13–14), *Diognetus* also underscores Christians' perfect compliance with the city norms by taking up their civic responsibilities (μετέχουσι πάντων ὡς πολῖται, *Diogn.* 5.5),[24] obeying the prescribed laws of the state (5.10) and indeed, doing no wrong (ἀδικούμενος, 6.5) to the world.

Where *Diognetus* goes further is that, besides merely positing Christians as exemplary citizens adopting the norms and practices of the wider society, *Diognetus* indeed underscores Christians as "conquering" (νικῶσι) the laws in their own mode of life (ἰδίοις βίοις, 5.10). By aligning their own life with the order of their citizenship in heaven (ἐν οὐρανῷ πολιτεύονται, 5.9), Christians outrun the legal requirements demanded by human institutions and, thus, render the normative function of societal laws superfluous.[25] For the author of *Diognetus*, Christians' citizenship in heaven and the laws laid down by the secular authorities are not inherently incompatible. When they comply with the established laws of the world, they are no more than living out the higher order of their invisible religion/service of God (cf. ἀόρατος . . . θεοσέβεια, 6.4) as citizens of heaven.

On the other hand, since Christians are already living in the order of their citizenship in heaven, human laws are no longer the standard against which their conduct is measured. Just as 1 Peter, which emphasizes that while the emperor is to be honoured (τιμᾶτε) just like others (πάντας τιμήσατε), it is God who is to be feared (φοβεῖσθε) (1 Pet 2:17), the author of *Diognetus* also has no hesitation in emphasizing Christians' readiness to resist the demands of the larger society when their ultimate allegiance to God is at stake. Whereas Christians conquer (νικῶσι, *Diogn.* 5.10) the human laws in their own mode of life, they themselves are not conquered (νικωμένους, 7.7) when they are thrown to wild beasts to make them deny (ἀρνήσωνται, 7.7; cf. ἀρνήσασθαι, 10.7) the Lord. Although Christians

---

24. Blakeney, *Epistle*, 50; Brändle, *Ethik*, 183.
25. Lona, *Diognet*, 168.

indeed outrun their pagan neighbours in obeying the prescribed laws, their obedience is not without boundary. When they are required to cross the boundary, such as to participate in the state religions, to offer worship to the emperors or to curse Christ,[26] the laws of their own citizenship in heaven always are to prevail.

Therefore, "differentiated resistance" is also seen as Christians' social strategy in *Diognetus*. When the author claims that Christians comply with the laws of the secular society, he does not mean to forego Christians' religious distinctiveness or focus only on Christians' social accommodation for the sake of apology. Within the boundary of their "ultimate allegiance to God," they are still seen as a distinctive group in society, maintaining a high moral standard better than the pagans.

6.1.2 Christian Engagement in Household Life

In *Diogn.* 5.6–7, the author highlights the normality of Christian family life by emphasizing that Christians get married and have children in accordance with wider societal expectations. In a similar vein to 1 Peter, in which slaves are exhorted to subject themselves (ὑποτασσόμενοι, 1 Pet 2:18) to their masters, and wives, to their husbands (ὑποτασσόμεναι, 3:1), *Diognetus* also perceives Christians as a people who uphold the current family system of society. Remarkably, *Diognetus* once again goes further in stating even more explicitly that Christians conduct their family life just like the others (ὡς πάντες, *Diogn.* 5.6). For the author of *Diognetus*, Christians living as resident-aliens on earth does not necessarily imply detachment or lack of commitment to society, devoting their hope and efforts only in the alternative reality of their home in heaven. Instead, they are ready to settle in this earthly world by raising families, and indeed participating in human procreation.

At the same time, *Diognetus* obviously does not perceive Christians leading normal family life as endangering their distinctive identity. What marks Christians out from the rest of society is again their excelling the pagans in preserving proper familial order, and living out the best of their family life on earth. When doing so, Christians are measured, again, not

---

26. E.g. Pliny, *Ep.*10.96; *Mart. Pol.* 9.3.

according to human expectations but by the standard of their citizenship in heaven: they are in the flesh, but do not live according to the flesh (5.8).

Therefore, although Christians have children as others, they do not expose (ῥίπτουσι) their children (5.6). Abandonment of unwanted children, if born deformed or as products of rape and incest, was frequent in antiquity. Poverty and family limitation could also be the causes for exposure of children.[27] Once exposed, the unwanted children could likely be killed or taken to be raised for a brothel. In a letter found in Oxyrhynchus, a man remarkably wrote in Alexandria to his wife that if she bore a child, "if it is a male let it be, if a female expose (ἔκβαλε) it."[28]

In fact, ancient moral philosophers did from time to time express their reservations about child exposure. For example, Epictetus reproaches Epicurus's admonition "Let us not bring up children" with disgust,

> But a sheep does not abandon its own offspring, nor a wolf; and yet does a man abandon his? . . . Why, in my opinion, your mother and your father, even if they had divined that you were going to say such things, would not have exposed you![29]

However, as Boswell observes, "Most ancient moral writers evince indifference toward or acceptance of abandonment."[30] Although child abandonment might be viewed as far from morally ideal, this practice was endured and accepted by the Roman society at large.[31]

Therefore, when *Diognetus* claims that Christians do not expose their children, the author is underlining Christians' distinctiveness in fulfilling the pagans' moral philosophical ideals better than the pagan society itself.[32]

---

27. J. R. Sallares, "Infanticide," *OCD*: 757.

28. Bernard P. Grenfell and Arthur S. Hunt, *The Oxyrhynchus Papyri*, vol. iv (London: Egypt Exploration Fund, 1904), no. 744.

29. Epictetus, *Diatr.* 1.23.7–10 (Oldfather, LCL). See also Tactitus, *Germ.* 19. For the view that Tacitus is revealing a certain public opinion in the Greek world against infanticide, see A. Cameron, "The Exposure of Children and Greek Ethics," *The Classical Review* 46 (1932): 113.

30. John Boswell, *The Kindness of Strangers: The Abandonment of Children in Western Europe from Late Antiquity to the Renaissance* (New York: Pantheon, 1988), 88. I derive this reference from Dunning, *Aliens*, 70.

31. See e.g. the records in Minucius Felix, *Oct.* 30.2; Tertullian, *Apol.* 8–9; Philo, *Spec.* 3.113–115.

32. Also Dunning, *Aliens*, 70.

This moral superiority of Christians in maintaining the family order is then further highlighted in *Diogn.* 5.7, where the author asserts that Christians offer free board (τράπεζαν κοινήν)[33] but not their marriage bed (κοίτην).[34] This claim of *Diognetus* is probably directed against frequent pagan charges of Christians for promiscuous and incestuous intercourses.[35] It is noticeable that although pagans often accused Christians of sexual promiscuity, sexual purity and sanctity of marriage were not something always respected by the pagans themselves. For example, Minucius Felix, when defending Christians against charges of incestuous practices, writes:

> Among the Persians it is lawful for sons to have intercourse with their mothers, and in Egypt and Athens the marriage of brother and sister is legal. Your tales and tragedies display cases of incest in boastful language, and you read and listen to them with pleasure. In like manner you worship gods joined in incestuous wedlock with a mother, a daughter, or a sister. It is not to be wondered at, then, if among you cases of incest are often discovered and constantly being perpetrated." (*Oct.* 31.3–4)[36]

Likewise, Tertullian also remarks that the pagans,

> not only usurp the marriage rights of their friends, but they even hand over their own rights to their friends with the greatest equanimity. This results, I suppose, from the teaching they have learned from those who were older and wiser, the Greek Socrates and the Roman Cato, who shared with their friends the wives whom they had married, so that they could bear children in other families, too. (*Apol.* 39.12)[37]

---

33. Translation rendered in Meecham, *Epistle*, 81.

34. As with most scholars, the reading κοίτην seems to make more sense than κοινήν as appears in Codex Argentoratensis Graecus ix (e.g. Blakeney, *Epistle*, 51; Meecham, *Epistle*, 41; Bockmuehl, *Jewish Law*, 221). Indeed, rebutting pagan accusation of promiscuity is a theme frequently found in Christian apologetic writings. See note 35 below.

35. See e.g. Justin, *1 Apol.* 26; *Dial.* 10; Athenagoras, *Leg.* 31; Theophilus, *Autol.* 3.4; Tertullian, *Apol.* 7.

36. Translation rendered in Tertullian and Felix, *Apologetical Works*, 387.

37. Ibid., 100.

Hence, by emphasizing Christians' abstention from child exposure and maintaining purity in marriage, *Diognetus* is once again underscoring Christians' moral superiority in complying with the moral norms of the wider society, which marks them out from the rest of the world. This preservation of the existing familial order of the wider society on the part of Christians is translated by the author as the visible behavioural expression of their invisible citizenship in heaven, so that Christians are no longer living in accordance with the standard of the world but of their heavenly citizenship (5.8).

6.1.3 Christian Engagement in Daily Social Life

Closely related to Christians "living not in accordance with the flesh" (οὐ κατὰ σάρκα ζῶσιν, 5.8) is the notion that they are hated by the world, just as the soul (τὴν ψυχήν) is hated by the flesh (ἡ σάρξ) (6.5). In *Diognetus*, two reasons are given to account for pagan hatred towards Christians: (1) Christians do not consider that pagan idols are gods (2.6), and (2) Christians hinder the world from indulging in fleshly pleasures (ἡδοναῖς, 6.5). Indeed, even within Platonic philosophy, the pleasures (ἡδοναί) of the body are also to be restrained and avoided by the soul of the philosopher in order to seek virtue, wisdom and truth.[38] Therefore, subject to their maintaining the boundary of ultimate allegiance to God, Christians are once again seen as outdoing their pagan neighbours in fulfilling the moral philosophical ideals of the larger world. Christians are hated not because they have done any wrong (6.5), but only because they are different.

This perception of Christians' existing social situation is in line with what the Petrine author observes as the source of Christians' alienation: Their neighbours "are surprised that you no long go with (them) in the same excess of dissipation, they slander (you)" (1 Pet 4:4). It is noticeable that while the Petrine author exhorts Christians not to return reviling for reviling (λοιδορίαν ἀντὶ λοιδορίας) but, to bless (εὐλογοῦντες) (1 Pet 3:9), *Diognetus* also asserts that Christians are reviled, and they bless (λοιδοροῦνται καὶ εὐλογοῦσιν); they are insulted, and they honour (τιμῶσιν; cf. πάντας τιμήσατε, 1 Pet 2:17) (*Diogn.* 5.15). Like 1 Peter, "non-retaliation"

---

38. E.g. *Phaed.* 65A–C; 68E–69D; 83B; 114C–E.

is also the mode of Christian response to pagan hostility as claimed in *Diognetus*.

Where the author of *Diognetus* goes further is that, besides passively enduring persecutions and hatred without retaliation, it also underscores Christians' positive commitment to the world in their love for all people (ἀγαπῶσι πάντας, 5.11),[39] including those who hate them (τοὺς μισοῦντας ἀγαπῶσιν, 6.6). In Diognetus' original inquiry about the religion of Christians (τὴν θεοσέβειαν τῶν Χριστιανῶν, 1.1), he was only referring to the love Christians have "for one another" (φιλοστοργίαν . . . πρὸς ἀλλήλους, 1.1). This question is then extended and answered by the author with reference to Christians' φιλανθρωπία, concretized in their taking up the burden of their neighbours, wishing to benefit those who are worse off than themselves and supplying for those in need (10.6).[40] Although it can also be derived from the instructions of 1 Peter that Christians are to promote the welfare of cities, so as to do what is good in the eyes of those in authority (1 Pet 2:14) and to silence the ignorance of the slanderers (1 Pet 2:15),[41] Christians' love and concern for the benefits of the wider society are now unambiguously and eloquently expounded in *Diognetus*. Despite all the alienations and ostracism suffered from the host society, Christians actually do not consider themselves a marginalized sect separating from the rest of society.

On the contrary, it is through taking up their social responsibility as the best citizens that Christians manifest their superiority and identity in society. Through providing for the needs of their neighbours, Christians become gods to those who receive their benefits (θεὸς γίνεται τῶν λαμβανόντων, 10.6). When they imitate God (μιμητής ἐστι θεοῦ, 10.6) in the acts of sharing what they have received from God (παρὰ τοῦ θεοῦ λαβών, 10.6), Christians are sharing in God's nature and his role to human beings. This claim that Christians share in God's divine nature when imitating him in endowing benefits to their neighbours is in line with the exhortation of Gregory of Nazianzus, "Become more eminent than your neighbor by showing yourself more generous; become a god to the unfortunate, by

---

39. Brändle, *Ethik*, 183.
40. Meecham, *Epistle*, 111; See also Heintz, "Μιμητὴς Θεοῦ," 115.
41. See pages 81, 84 above.

imitating the mercy of God" (*Or. Bas.* 14.26).[42] Likewise, Ignatius, when expressing his gratitude for the provision of the Trallian Church, also states that "I received therefore your godly benevolence through him, and gave God glory that I found you, as I had learnt, imitators of God."[43]

Although *Diognetus* does not mention Christians following in the steps of Christ as in 1 Peter (cf. 1 Pet 2:21), Christians' social strategies, for the author of *Diognetus*, is still closely related to their theology (i.e. the nature and attribute of the God they believe in). It is due to God the Creator's love for the whole of mankind (φιλάνθρωπος, 8.7; φιλανθρωπίας, 9.2; τοὺς ἀνθρώπους ἠγάπησε, 10.2) and his goodness (χρηστότης, 9.1, 2, 6; 10.4) that Christians receive what they need for life (4.2; 8.7; 9.6). Christians' love for God and their imitation of his goodness find concrete expression in their transmitting similar love and goodness not only to their fellow believers, but to the rest of mankind (10.4–6).[44]

Indeed, this imitation of God in terms of love to neighbours is none other than part of Christians' way of proclaiming (λαλεῖν) the mysteries of God (μυστήρια θεοῦ, 10.7), which recalls the mystery of their own religion/service of God (τὸ ... τῆς ἰδίας αὐτῶν θεοσεβείας μυστήριον) in 4.6. Instead of loss of distinctiveness, Christians taking up their social responsibility and performing their function as model citizens in loving and serving the rest of humanity is, therefore, understood as putting their otherwise invisible religion/service of God (ἀόρατος ... αὐτῶν ἡ θεοσέβεια μένει, 6.4) into concrete visible expression.

Section Summary: Petrine Resonances in the *Epistle to Diognetus*

In this section, I demonstrated that sometime in the second half of the second century, the author of the *Epistle to Diognetus* understood Christians' social engagement as resident-aliens (ὡς πάροικοι, 5.5; cf. παροικοῦσιν, 6.8) on earth in a similar vein to 1 Peter. Religious orientation and proper worship to the only one true God are what *Diognetus* considers to be what

---

42. Translation rendered by Brian Daley, *Gregory of Nazianzus*, The Early Church Fathers (London / Routledge, 2006), 90. I derive this reference from Meecham, *Epistle*, 144.
43. Ignatius, *Ad Trall.* 1.2 (Lake, LCL).
44. Brändle, *Ethik*, 74, 126, 144–145.

really distinguish Christians from the rest of society. Within the overriding boundary of their ultimate allegiance to God, Christians remain the best citizens in society, adopting and complying with the same societal and household norms as their pagan neighbours.

Where *Diognetus* goes further is that, it states more boldy and explicitly that Christians are distinguished from the rest of humankind not by customs (ἔθεσι, 5.1) or mode of life (βίον, 5.2). Indeed, Christians go beyond meeting the basic requirements of following societal norms, and fulfil the moral ideals of society better than the pagans themselves. As citizens of heaven, they outdo (νικῶσι) the laws in their own mode of life (5.10), excel their pagan neighbours in maintaining the family order (5.6–7), and take up their social responsibility by benefitting their neighbours (10.6).

Here lies another point of contact between 1 Peter and *Diognetus* in allowing room for Christians to adopt the current social norms and practices without losing their sense of identity. Similar to 1 Peter, in which Christians' strategy of "differentiated resistance" is understood as the congruent expression of Christians' identity of "elect exiles of Diaspora," and a token of their following in the steps of Christ (1 Pet 2:21), *Diognetus* also understands Christians living out the highest moral ideals of society as merely reflecting their true identity as citizens of heaven and their imitation of God on earth.

These observations again demonstrate that for the early Christians, at least for the authors of 1 Peter and *Diognetus*, Christians' distinctive identity does not depend on separating or being different from the wider culture *per se*. Nor did early Christians seek to uphold their difference just for the sake of being different. Their theology, especially the vision of the relationship between Christ/God and culture, and their understanding of their own existence on earth always play a part in the formulation of their social engagement.

6.2 Shaping of Social Behavioural Instructions by Theology in the *Epistle to Diognetus*

In the previous chapters, I argued that the Petrine Christian social strategy is devised largely with reference to the author's understanding of Jesus

Christ's suffering on the cross and what following Christ's steps entails. For the Petrine author, the cross denotes Christ's suffering human rejection essentially as a resident-alien on earth, whose response to human afflictions notably reflects the form of "differentiated resistance." His example on the cross is remarkably consistent with the Jewish social strategies to seek peace (cf. 1 Pet 3:10–12) and to follow the current societal order in so far as their ultimate allegiance to God is kept intact. Hence, Christians' "good work" of "differentiated resistance" is perceived as *both* a token of following Christ's steps (2:21) *and* a congruent behavioural expression of Christians' identity as "elect exiles of Diaspora" on earth.

Although the author of *Diognetus* does not mention Christians following Christ's steps, but rather their imitation of God (μιμητής, *Diogn.* 10.4, 6; μιμήσασθαι, 10.5), his understanding of Christians' social strategies is still based very much on his perception of God and what imitation of his goodness (10.4) entails. In this section, I will firstly investigate *Diognetus'* perception of God and his relationship with the world as decisively manifested by the salvation event fulfilled through Christ, his son/child. As in 1 Peter and Revelation, the sacrifice of the Son of God as a ransom for humanity (9.2) is the starting point of the author's reflection and from which Christians derive their existence as eschatological citizens of the heavenly kingdom, which I will explore in the second subsection. Although Christians consistently find themselves alienated by the surrounding world, this status of "resident-aliens" is notably viewed by *Diognetus* not with self-pity or sullenness, but self-esteem. Moral superiority and positive social contributions by the Christian resident-aliens in society are merely the visible expressions of their privileged citizenship of heaven.

6.2.1 All-loving God/Christ in the *Epistle to Diognetus*

As Meecham asserts, "The theological content of the Epistle lies mainly in chs. vii–ix"[45] which "set forth the divine plan of salvation."[46] For the author of *Diognetus*, this redemption plan of God is where God's love and goodness to humankind are most evidently revealed (9.2) through his sending

---

45. Meecham, *Epistle*, 19.
46. Ibid., 22.

of his Son "not to condemn the world but to save it."⁴⁷ Although no reference is made to any event of Jesus Christ's life on earth, the coming of the Son to the world is succinctly underlined as, "He himself gave up His own Son as a ransom for us" (9.2). The cross of Jesus Christ is still the starting point to appreciate God's love and goodness for humanity.

For the author, Christians' knowledge of God is not derived from earthly invention or human mysteries (7.1). It is God who made himself known especially through his Son (7.2–4; cf. 8.5). From this perspective, "to imitate God" is to a certain extent "to imitate Christ." As Heintz comments, "it is the Incarnate Son who gives definition and shape to this imitation."⁴⁸ It is therefore important to note that although the Son is the "Designer and Artisan of the universe himself" (7.2) and was sent as a king and, indeed, as God (ὡς θεόν) (7.4), he came not to rule by tyranny, fear, and consternation (7.3), but was sent in gentleness and meekness (7.4). What the cross represents is God's salvation not by overpowering (βια-ζόμενος, 7.4; cf. βιάζεσθαι, 10.5), but by persuasion. Furthermore, when God sent his Son, he did so as one calling and loving, rather than one persecuting or judging (7.5). God's dealing with humanity through the Son is therefore marked by kindness, goodness, truth and without anger (8.8), because violence (βία) is not an attribute belonging to God (οὐ πρόσεστι τῷ θεῷ, 7.4).

In addition, just as 1 Peter understands Christ's suffering as the example for Christians seeking peace and submitting to suffering without retaliation, *Diognetus* also understands the gentleness and meekness (ἐπιεικείᾳ καὶ πραΰτητι, *Diog.* 7.4; cf. πραΰτητος, 1 Pet 3.16) demonstrated by the Son as the mode of Christians' imitation of God not to retaliate to pagan hatred with violence. They are, rather, to respond with blessings (5.15) and good works (ἀγαθοποιοῦντες, 5.16; cf. χρηστότητος, 10.4; ἀγαθός, 8.8), and without lording over or overpowering (βιάζεσθαι) their neighbours, which is outside God's majesty (10.5).

Furthermore, God's salvation plan for humanity is also revealed (8.11) and accomplished by the Son on the cross (9.2) and, thus, manifesting his

---

47. Blakeney, *Epistle*, 13.
48. Heintz, "Μιμητὴς Θεοῦ," 118.

patience and love for all people (φιλάνθρωπος, 8.7; φιλανθρωπίας, 9.2). This salvation plan has already been prepared by God from the very beginning and is meant to enable all to participate in his benefits (εὐεργεσιῶν, 8.11; cf. 9.5). Within the thought world of *Diognetus*, what the cross of the Son reflects is God's openness and goodwill to humanity and, therefore, is notably different from the notion of God/Christ engaging in warfare with the evil forces of the world as emphasized in Revelation. Hence, for *Diognetus*, Christians' imitation of God involves their taking up their social responsibility to love and to benefit the world around them (5.15–16; 6.6; 10.6).

At the same time, God does not take pleasure in our sins (9.1). After God had shown humanity's moral inability to attain life and to enter the kingdom of God (9.1, 6), and when our unrighteousness (ἀδικία; cf. τῶν ἀδίκων) had been fulfilled (πεπλήρωτο) so that punishment and death can only be expected (9.2), God took upon himself our sin (τὰς ἡμετέρας ἁμαρτίας ἀνεδέξατο) and gave up his own Son as a ransom for us (9.2). The sacrifice of the one righteous (δικαίῳ ἑνί, 9.5; cf. τὸν δίκαιον, 9.2; ἐκείνου δικαιοσύνη, 9.3; δικαιοσύνη ... ἑνός, 9.5) Son brings about the justification/making righteous (δικαιόω, 5.14; 9.4, 5) of us, the many lawless (πολλοὺς ἀνόμους, 9.5; τοὺς ἀνόμους, 9.4; ἀνόμων, 9.2; cf. ἀνομία ... πολλῶν, 9.5) and sinners (cf. τὰς ἡμετέρας ἁμαρτίας, 9.2; τὰς ἁμαρτίας ἡμῶν, 9.3). As Brändle succinctly observes, "He (God) takes men out of the power sphere of the time of unrighteousness and relocates them in that of righteousness."[49]

Therefore, the atonement by the Son is viewed in *Diognetus* mainly from the perspective of moral transformation within people.[50] In the former time (πρόσθεν χρόνου, 9.1), the lives of Christians were marked by undisciplined impulses (ἀτάκτοις φοραῖς),[51] pleasures and cravings (9.1), and they were incapable (ἀδύνατος, 9.1, 6; cf. τὰ ἀδύνατα, 9.6) of moral living and of entering the kingdom of God. After God inaugurated the time (ἦλθε ... ὁ καιρός, 9.2; cf. καιρῷ ... τῆς δικαιοσύνης δημιουργῶν, 9.1) in

---

49. "Er entnimmt die Menschen der Machtsphäre des Kairos der Ungerechtigkeit und versetzt sie in die der Gerechtigkeit" (Brändle, *Ethik*, 65).

50. Meecham, *Epistle*, 24.

51. Translations rendered in Holmes, *Fathers*, 709.

which Christians were justified/made righteous through the sacrifice of the Son, they are enabled (δυνατοί, 9.1; δύναται, 10.4) by the power of God (δυνάμει, 9.1; δύναμιν, 9.2; cf. ἠδυνήθη, 9.3; δυνατόν, 9.6) to enter the kingdom of God, to become citizens of heaven and even to imitate God.[52] It is through this empowerment to moral living, and as a token of their imitation of God that Christians discharge their commitment and social responsibility to the world. Just as God's works in his Son put an end to the time of Christians "being led astray by pleasures and cravings" (ἡδοναῖς καὶ ἐπιθυμίαις, 9.1), Christians also hinder the world from indulging in pleasures (ἡδοναῖς, 6.5). Likewise, just as God settled all things according to their order (κατὰ τάξιν διακρίνας, 8.7), and has created (δημιουργῶν) the present time of righteousness (9.1) to enable Christians to resume the proper moral order of life, Christians also serve to hold the world together (συνέχουσι, 6.7), preserving intact its moral, social and political order, and saving it from plunging into chaos.

Indeed, according to *Diognetus*, redemption and creation stand close to each other. The Son sent by God is none other than the "Designer and Artisan of the universe himself" (αὐτὸν τὸν τεχνίτην καὶ δημιουργὸν τῶν ὅλων, 7.2), just as God is the Creator (παντοκτίστης, 7.2) and the one God of the universe (θεὸν ἕνα τῶν πάντων) and the Master (δεσπότην) (3.2), who provides us all with what we need (3.4). Hence, having revealed his goodness (χρηστότης, 9.1, 2) and love for humanity (φιλανθρωπίας, 9.2), and having demonstrated the saving power of the Saviour in contrast to human powerlessness to attain life, God expects people to have faith in his goodness (χρηστότητι; cf. χρηστός, 8.8), and regard him as nurse (i.e. the one who provides sustenance [τροφέα]), so that they no longer need to be anxious about clothing and food (τροφῆς) (9.6).

Therefore, the relationship between God and humanity is marked by God's love for people from the very beginning: For "God loved humanity," he made the world for their sake (δι᾽ οὕς), subjected all to them and gave them reason and mind (10.2). Furthermore, God formed humans after his own image, sent to them his only-begotten Son, and promised them the

---

52. Also Heintz, " Μιμητὴς Θεοῦ," 117.

kingdom in heaven (10.2). It is God who always takes the initiatives.[53] It is he who loved humanity first (προαγαπήσαντά, 10.3), showed himself when no one had yet seen or known him (8.5), conceived the design for the salvation of people (8.9) and created the time of righteousness for them (9.1). What is manifested by God's dealings with humans is his generosity and constant commitment for their good. Even imitation of God is not possible for Christians if God does not will it (10.4).

When Christians translate God's dealings with humanity into their mode of social engagement, as a token of imitating him (10.4) and in response to his love (10.3–4), they can only mark their dealings with their fellowmen with similar loving kindness and benevolence. Just as God did not hate us, nor reject us nor remember our misdeeds (9.2), Christians also love those who hate them (6.6). Likewise, while God took upon himself (ἀνεδέξατο) the sins of humanity (9.2), allows them to participate in his benefits (εὐεργεσιῶν) (8.11), and provides them with what they need (χορηγῶν ὧν προσδεόμεθα) (3.4), Christians also take upon themselves (ἀναδέχεται) the burden of their neighbours, benefit (εὐεργετεῖν) those who are worse off than themselves, and provide those in need (τοῖς ἐπιδεομένοις χορηγῶν) what they have received from God (10.6).

At the same time, Christians' insistence on preserving their exclusive loyalty to God is also derived from their faith (πίστιν, 10.1) and knowledge of God's love. Through faith, they are able to see (cf. διὰ πίστεως ᾗ μόνῃ θεὸν ἰδεῖν συγκεχώρηται, 8.6) that God rules in heaven, just as their true life is in heaven (10.7). Their life is no longer governed by the earthly standard, but the heavenly one. Hence, Christians prefer to be punished (κολαζομένους, 10.7; cf. κολάζω, 5.16; 6.9; 7.8) rather than to deny God (ἀρνήσασθαι θεόν, 10.7; cf. ἀρνήσωνται τὸν κύριον, 7.7). Although refusal to deny God may lead to death (cf. 5.12), including being thrown to beasts (7.7), Christians regard this death as only apparent (δοκοῦντος . . . θανάτου, 10.7) and it can do no true harm to them.[54] The true reality is that they are brought to life (5.12). As those justified/made righteous (δικαιόω, 5.14; 9.4, 5) through the redemption accomplished by the Son, Christians

---

53. Meecham, *Epistle*, 23.
54. Brändle, *Ethik*, 189.

are prepared to endure the transitory fire (τὸ πῦρ τὸ πρόσκαιρον)⁵⁵ for the sake of their righteousness (ὑπὲρ δικαιοσύνης) (10.8), knowing full well that it is the punishment (κολάσει, cf. κόλασις καὶ θάνατος, 9.2) of real death (τὸν ὄντως θάνατον) and eternal fire (τὸ πῦρ τὸ αἰώνιον) (10.7) that Christians should really fear.

To sum up this subsection, the mode of Christian social engagement, as portrayed in *Diognetus*, hangs on the author's perception of God/Christ and his relationship to the human world just as in 1 Peter and Revelation. The sacrifice of Jesus Christ on the cross is still the pivotal event from which the author starts his reflection. Although *Diognetus* applies the notion of "imitation of God," rather than "following Christ's steps" employed in 1 Peter, as the conceptual basis for Christians' social engagement, God's love and commitment to do good for humans also constitutes the basis, on which Christians understand themselves as committed to the common good of society and to do their best to preserve a positive relationship with their neighbours.

Although this positive participation in the wider social life necessarily entails upholding the existing societal order and adopting current social norms to some degree, Christians' identity is not thereby lost. Just as 1 Peter understands "good works" as a token of Christians' solidarity with Christ, the degree of social accommodation allowed in *Diognetus* is merely Christians' way of imitating their God. It is precisely on the basis of this perception of imitating God that any participation in any customs and practices that may contradict their allegiance to God becomes out of question. Religious conviction, rather than simply a concern for external distinction or separation, is once again the prime consideration of Christians when negotiating their existence in the non-believing world.

At the same time, the form of social engagement adopted by the early Christians also depends on their own understanding of Christian existence on earth. As revealed in *Diognetus*, this self-portrayal of Christians is another source of their sense of identity and, indeed, superiority amidst pagan alienation in the current world.

---

55. As followed by many scholars, the reading πρόσκαιρον forms part of the phrase τὸ πῦρ τὸ πρόσκαιρον and thus, serves as a neat contrast to τὸ πῦρ τὸ αἰώνιον in 10.7. So Meecham, *Epistle*, 135.

6.2.2 Christian Resident-Aliens in the *Epistle to Diognetus*

Just as 1 Peter perceives Christians' "good works" of "differentiated resistance" as the congruent expression of their identity as "elect exiles of Diaspora," *Diognetus* also regards "differentiated resistance" as the necessary outcome of Christians' earthly existence as "resident-aliens" (ὡς πάροικοι, 5.5, παροικοῦσιν, 6.8). While 1 Peter makes use of OT language and images to construct the identity of the Christian "elect exiles of Diaspora" so that they become "an elect race," "a royal priesthood," "a holy nation" and "God's own people" (1 Pet 2:9), inheriting the special privileges of the ethnic Jews before God, *Diognetus* also interprets Christians' identity as "resident-aliens" as an indicator of their special sense of distinctiveness on earth. It is due to their self-understanding as a universal people determined by their exclusive worship and ultimate allegiance to God,[56] which results in their being excluded by the wider culture as outsiders, that Christians also view themselves as a "new race" (καινὸν . . . γένος, 1.1), that is, a distinct people,[57] being neither Greeks (cf. 3.3; 5.4, 17), nor Jews (cf. 3.1; 5.17), nor barbarians (cf. 5.4).

Just as 1 Peter understands the Christian "elect exiles of Diaspora" as an *elect race* (γένος ἐκλεκτόν, 1 Pet 2:9) without the necessary ethnic link with the Jews, but steming from their religious identity as the elect people of God, *Diognetus* also does not regard the Christian *race* as determined by ethnicity or by country, language or customs (5.1), but from their theological existence brought about by the redemption accomplished by the Son. Having been justified/made righteous in the Son (cf. 9.4), Christians are now enabled to enter into their new life (τὸ ἀληθῶς ἐν οὐρανῷ ζῆν, 10.7) as citizens of God's Kingdom in heaven (5.4, 9; 10.2). As Brändle asserts, "Their life stands in the eschatological horizon."[58] Although Christians

---

56. See also Denise Kimber Buell, *Why This New Race: Ethnic Reasoning in Early Christianity* (New York: Columbia University Press, 2008), 90.

57. Cf. Bockmuehl, *Jewish Law*, 217–218. Although Henri Irénée Marrou, *À Diognète: introduction, édition critique, traduction et commentaire* (Paris: Cerf, 1951), 132 argues that "new race" is a remark that the author aims to reject, his view overlooks the fact that this identity marker of "new race" serves to accentuate Christians' sense of distinctiveness as resident-aliens amidst the pagan world. See Buell, *Race*, 32; See also Dunning, *Aliens*, 146 n.11 for other criticisms of Marrou's observation.

58. "Ihr Leben steht im eschatologischen Horizont" (Brändle, *Ethik*, 79).

remain living in the earthly realm, their new eschatological existence has already been inaugurated.

Hence, the term "resident-aliens" actually denotes Christians moving between the two dimensions of *both* "already" *and* "not yet" of their eschatological existence.[59] On the one hand, Christians' life is now determined by the paradoxical order (παράδοξον ... κατάστασιν) of their new citizenship in heaven (5.4, 9). While sojourning (παροικοῦσιν) among mortals (φθαρτοῖς), they are in fact waiting (longing) (προσδεχόμενοι) for the immortality (ἀφθαρσίαν) in heaven (6.8; cf. 10.7). On the other hand, Christians still have their residence (κατοικοῦντες, 5.4; κατοικεῖ, 6.8; οἰκοῦσιν, 5.5) and timespan (διατρίβουσιν, 5.9) on earth while awaiting the final consummation of their ultimate immortality. Although this earthly habitation is marked by their being constantly subject to hatred (2.6; 5.15; 6.5, 6) and enduring alienation as strangers (ὡς πάροικοι; ὡς ξένοι), so that every fatherland (πατρίς) is a foreign land (ξένη) to them, Christians still have a sense of belonging to the world and view every foreign land as their fatherland (πατρίς) (5.5).[60] These dual senses of a "longing" for an alternative reality to the present alienation *and* a "belonging" to the existing place of residence within Christians' existence as resident-aliens are once again in line with the Petrine perception of Christians' Diaspora consciousness as I explained in chapter 4, and indeed even more profoundly highlighted in *Diognetus*.

At the same time, it is on the basis of this understanding of Christians as a distinct people of resident-aliens having their abode on earth, but living according to the order of their citizenship in heaven, that their social engagement necessarily reflects the mode of "differentiated resistance." As citizens of heaven living on earth, there is inevitably some distance which Christians must maintain from the surrounding world. They are no longer living according to the standard of the flesh (5.8) or the norms of the world

---

59. Brändle, *Ethik*, 82.

60. Although Paul Hanly Furfey, "Christian Social Thought in the First and Second Centuries," *The American Catholic Sociological Review* 1 (1940): 15 asserts that Christians renounce this world not by literally withdrawing from it, but "by living in it physically while being mentally separated," he has overlooked the fact that by regarding every land as their fatherland, Christians necessarily have certain attachment and commitment to this world rather than mentally separating from it.

(6.3). Any pagan customs or practices inconsistent with their ultimate allegiance to God, such as denial of the Lord (7.7)/God (10.7) or participation in idolatry or improper worship of God (2.6; 3.1; 4.6), are what Christians must resist at all cost.

Therefore, the uniqueness of the Christian existence as resident-aliens is actually marked by the ongoing hatred and persecutions around them. Just as 1 Peter exhorts Christians not to be surprised by the fiery ordeal that comes for testing them (1 Pet 4:12), *Diognetus* also understands ostracism and alienation as parts and parcels of Christians sojourning experience on earth. They are punished as evildoers even when they are doing good (ἀγαθοποιοῦντες, 5.16; cf. ἀγαθοποιοῦντας . . . πάσχειν, 1 Pet 3:17). While they are hated by the world, the world actually does not know them (5.12), suffers no wrong (6.5), and cannot state the reason for its hostility (5.17) (i.e. Christians are persecuted for simply being Christians [cf. 1 Pet 4:16]). Thus, persecutions and sufferings are none other than the identity marker of Christians, and the opportunity for them to demonstrate their ultimate allegiance to God (7.7; 10.7) and his presence (παρουσίας)[61] with them (7.9).

Although the primary purpose of *Diognetus* is apologetic-protreptic, it can still reflect the author's own conviction that alienations and ostracism do not thereby turn Christians sullen or misanthropic, nor does their experience as resident-aliens make them a pathetic people standing detached from the larger society, and enclosing themselves to their own community. The vitality of this people of resident-aliens is evidenced by the fact that when they are deprived of their daily supply, they get better still (6.9), and the more they are punished every day, the more they multiply exceedingly well (πλεονάζουσι μᾶλλον, 6.9; πλεονάζοντας, 7.8). Christians are not a people that can be conquered (μὴ νικωμένους, 7.7) by threats against their life. Hence, sufferings are now given a positive interpretation. It is amidst hostility and alienation that Christians are seen to be endowed with true life (ζωοποιοῦνται, 5.12; ζωοποιούμενοι, 5.16), glorified (δοξάζονται, 5.14), deemed righteous (δικαιοῦνται, 5.14), blessed (μακαρίσεις, 10.8) and to rejoice (χαίρουσιν, 5.16; cf. χαίρω, 1 Pet 4:13).

---

61. For the understanding of παρουσίας in *Diogn*. 7.9 as denoting God's presence rather than his return, see Meecham, *Epistle*, 123; Brändle, *Ethik*, 96–97.

Besides passively enduring alienation with an inner positive attitude, Christians' invisible citizenship in heaven (6.4) is also made visible in their external daily life. Similar to 1 Peter, in which Christians' good works are interpreted as their offering spiritual sacrifices to God as his royal priesthood (1 Pet 2:5, 9), *Diognetus* also regards Christians expressing their moral superiority and discharging their social responsibility, within the boundary of exclusive allegiance to God, as a means to express their religion/life service to God (τὸ . . . τῆς ἰδίας αὐτῶν θεοσεβείας μυστήριον, 4.6; μυστήρια θεοῦ, 10.7). Although the world (κόσμος) is in some sense the sphere of the anti-divine power[62] marked by deceit and error (10.7) and where Christians are hated (6.5), it is also the creation of God for the sake of humanity (10.2) and the present living space of Christians as citizens of heaven (6.1–4, 7–8; cf. ἐπὶ γῆς διατρίβουσιν, 5.9). In it, Christians are appointed to an important position (εἰς τοσαύτην . . . τάξιν ἔθετο, 6.10) by God,[63] having a task and a responsibility to discharge.

This sense of responsibility and commitment of Christians to the wider world is especially underscored by their function to hinder the world from indulging in its pleasures (6.5) and, thus, to maintain the moral, social and political order of the larger world like the soul to the body (6.1). Once again, Christians' existence as resident-aliens is not equated in *Diognetus* with withdrawal and self-enclosure within their own church community. Although the Christian heavenly citizens are now detained (φρουρεῖται, 6.4; ἐγκέκλεισται, κατέχονται, 6.7) among mortals while awaiting their ultimate immortality (6.8), it is precisely through their dispersion (ἔσπαρται, 6.2) as resident-aliens that Christians maintain their presence in the world, and indeed hold it together (συνέχω, 6.7) like the human soul permeating throughout the body (6.2).

The preservation function of Christians can be traced back to the traditions of Jesus in which Christians are designated as "salt" and "light" of the world (Matt 5:13–15). This perception of Christians as salt is interpreted by Origen as referring to the function of Christians that, "they preserve the order of the world; and society is held together (συνέστηκε) as long as the

---

62. Brändle, *Ethik*, 169.
63. Ibid., 86.

salt is uncorrupted" (*Cels.* 8.70).[64] Clement of Alexandria, when referring to Christians as "light of the world" and "salt of the earth," also comments that Christians are "the seed" (σπέρμα; cf. ἔσπαρται, *Diogn.* 6.2) sent here "on a kind of foreign service" and "all are held together (συνέχεται) so long as the seed remains on earth."[65] At the same time, a further connotation of Christians "holding the world together" is put forth by Meecham, who preferred to understand συνέχω as to "keep under control" or "keep within bounds," such as appears in Luke 19:43; 2 Corinthians 5:14 and *1 Clem.* 20.5, and thus, denoting Christians' "mastery" over the world.[66] It is probably based on a combination of these connotations that Christians' role of holding the world together should be understood: By restraining the world from going astray in its lusts and pleasure (6.5), Christians *at the same time* preserve intact the moral, social and political order of the world, and prevent it from falling into disarray.

As recognized by scholars,[67] this notion of Christians permeating the world, as the soul throughout the body, probably owes its background to current philosophies. On the one hand, Plato also perceives the immortal (ἀθάνατος, *Phaed.* 100B, 105E, 106E–107A, 107C, 114D;[68] cf. ἀθάνατος, *Diogn.* 6.8) and invisible (ἀειδές, ἀόρατον, *Phaed.* 79A–B; cf. ἀόρατος, *Diogn.* 6.4) soul as imprisoned (ἔν τινι φρουρᾷ, *Phaed.* 62B;[69] cf. φρουρεῖται, *Diogn.* 6.4; ἐν φρουρᾷ, *Diogn.* 6.7) in the visible (ὁρατός, *Phaed.* 79A–B, 80C; cf. ὁρατῷ, *Diogn.* 6.4) body. The soul of the philosopher also seeks to restrain and reject the pleasures of the body (e.g. *Phaed.* 65A–C; 69A–D; 83B; 114C–E; cf. *Diogn.* 6.5), and to depart from the body into the immortal realm (ἐκεῖσε οἴχεται εἰς . . . ἀθάνατον, *Phd.* 79D;[70] cf. τὴν ἐν οὐρανοῖς ἀφθαρσίαν προσδεχόμενοι, *Diogn.* 6.8). At the same time, while Plato regards the soul as *despising* the body and seeking to *flee* from

---

64. Translation rendered in Origen, *The Writings of Origen*, vol. 2, 2 vols., trans. Frederick Crombie (Edinburgh: T&T Clark, 1872), 553.
65. Clement of Alexandria, *Quis div.* 36 (Butterworth, LCL).
66. Meecham, *Epistle*, 115.
67. E.g. Meecham, *Epistle*, 44; Dunning, *Aliens*, 150 n. 52.
68. See also *Phaedr.* 245C–246A.
69. See also εἰργμοῦ, δεδεμένος, δεδέσθαι, *Phaed.* 82E; δεσμωτηρίων, *Phaed.* 114B.
70. See also *Phaed.* 81A.

it (*Phaed.* 65D),[71] *Diognetus* actually likens Christians to the soul, which *loves* the flesh (the world) and is committed to *sustain and contribute* to the welfare of the world (*Diogn.* 6.6–7).

On the other hand, it is within Stoic thoughts, as portrayed by Marcus Aurelius, that the world (κόσμος) is a unified living whole (cf. συνεχῶς, *Meditations* 4.40; συνεχείας, *Meditations* 5.8.5; cf. συνέχει, *Diogn.* 6.7) to which "all is absorbed into the one consciousness," and all things are compassed "with a single purpose" (*Meditations.* 4.40).[72] The indwelling world soul (ψυχή; cf. ψυχή, *Diogn.* 6.4–9) is the informing reason (*Meditations* 5.32) and principle of life,[73] which governs (οἰκονομοῦντα, 5.32; διοικέω, 4.46; 5.13; 6.1, 4) the whole world. Furthermore, Epicurus also conceives the soul of the human body as diffused (παρεσπαρμένον, *Hdt.* 63; cf. ἔσπαρται, *Diogn.* 6.2) throughout the physical structure, and animating the whole body by communicating "sensations and feelings" (*Hdt.* 63)[74] to it. At the same time, *Diognetus* obviously does not perceive Christians' existence on earth as providential and eternal (cf. διὰ παντὸς τοῦ αἰῶνος, *Meditations* 5.32), unlike the world soul within the Stoic thought. Moreover, whereas Epicurus asserts that the soul of the human body needs to be protected by the enclosure of the human structure (*Hdt.* 64),[75] so that if the whole human structure is dissolved, the soul is also dispersed (*Hdt.* 65), Christians as citizens of heaven do not base their existence on the earthly world. Although they reside in the world, they in fact are not of the world (*Diogn.* 6.3).

Therefore, it is most probable that the author of *Diognetus* makes use of the language of current philosophies to drive home his own perception of *both* transcendence *and* immanence[76] within Christians' existence as resident-aliens on earth. While language of Platonic thoughts underscores

---

71. See also *Phaed.* 65B, 66D, 67E.
72. Translation provided in Marcus Aurelius, *The Meditations of the Emperor Marcus Antoninus*, vol. 1, 2 vols., trans. Arthur Spenser Loat Farquharson (Oxford: Clarendon, 1944), 67, 69.
73. Commentary by Farquharson in Marcus Aurelius, *Meditations*, vol. 1, 322.
74. Translation by Cyril Bailey, *Epicurus: The Extant Remains* (Oxford: Clarendon, 1926), 39.
75. Bailey, *Epicurus*, 226.
76. Using the terminology of Marrou, *Diognète*, 136.

the otherworldliness of Christians' true citizenship in heaven, the idea of the soul diffusing throughout the body highlights Christians' embodiment in the world for love and positive service to the whole of humanity.[77] As Townsley remarks, Christians living in this world are at once "a part of it and apart from it."[78]

Indeed, by comparing Christians as the soul and the world as the body, the author once again pinpoints the prominence and superiority of Christians to the rest of society. As Plato remarks, "the soul is most like the divine and immortal and intellectual and uniform and indissoluble and ever unchanging, and the body, on the contrary, most like the human and mortal and multiform and unintellectual and dissoluble and ever changing."[79]

In addition, while the Stoic world soul as the governing principle of life is obviously superior to the rest of the cosmic whole, even Epicurus, who rejects the incorporeality of the human soul, also recognizes the eminence of the soul when he asserts that, in so far as the soul remains in the body, the soul will not lose sensation, even though a portion of the body is lost. However, the reverse does not hold true because the body cannot retain its sensation if any sum of the atoms constituting the soul, however small it may be, are lost (*Hdt.* 65).[80]

To sum up this subsection, although the term "resident-aliens" accurately highlights the objective reality of Christians being constantly estranged and ostracized in society, it does not follow that Christians subjectively regard themselves as merely a group of pitiful outsiders standing aloof from the rest of humanity. Indeed, just as 1 Peter highlights Christians living in this world with *both* senses of "longing" *and* "belonging" by calling them "exiles of Diaspora" on earth, *Diognetus* also perceives Christians as *both* "longing" for their immortality in heaven (6.8), *and* having a sense of "belonging" to this world in regarding every foreign land as their fatherland (5.5). Christians' visible existence as "resident-aliens" on earth is actually

---

77. See also Adrian Hasting, "Christianity and Nationhood: Congruity or Antipathy," *JRH* 25 (2001): 249.

78. Townsley, "Notes," 14.

79. Plato, *Phaed.* 80B (Fowler, LCL).

80. Bailey, *Epicurus*, 230.

viewed with a sense of self-esteem, because it merely reflects the invisible reality of their simultaneous eschatological citizenship in heaven. They are a "new race" dispersed (6.2) throughout the world, as the soul throughout the body, enduring the hatred of the world with a positive attitude, and expressing their religion/service to God in their everyday life with moral superiority and commitment for the good of their fellowmen.

Section Summary: Features of the Shaping of Social Behavioural Instructions by Theology in 1 Peter

In this section, I argue that *Diognetus* shares a similar approach to 1 Peter in understanding Christians' social engagement of "differentiated resistance" as a token of solidarity with Christ/God, and the congruent expression of their self-understanding on earth. Both the Petrine author, and the author of *Diognetus*, start their theological reflection from the sacrifice of Jesus Christ on the cross, and both understand the cross as inaugurating the eschatological existence of Christians as the elect people of God/citizens of heaven sojourning as resident-aliens on earth.

It is noticeable that whereas 1 Peter understands Jesus Christ's suffering on the cross as *both* his enduring suffering for the sake of righteousness (1 Pet 2:24; 3:18) *and* seeking peace by submitting to suffering, *Diognetus* states more positively that the Son's sacrifice testifies to the love of God for people from the very beginning and his goodness to benefit them with his abundance. Just as the Petrine author perceives the suffering of Christ as the basis for Christians to follow his steps by *both* enduring suffering *and* seeking peace in the city, *Diognetus* also understands the love and goodness of God as the model for Christians' imitation in loving without the use of violence, and sharing what they receive from God with their fellowmen.

Furthermore, while both 1 Peter and *Diognetus* regard sufferings and persecutions as part and parcel of Christians' existence on earth, both authors view Christians' identity as resident-aliens with a sense of superiority and self-esteem. While the Petrine author designates the Christian "elect exiles" as "an elect race," "a royal priesthood," "a holy nation" and "God's own people," *Diognetus* also views the Christian "resident-aliens" as a "new race" and "the soul of the world." Therefore, at least for both the authors of 1 Peter and *Diognetus*, Christians' self-understanding as "resident-aliens" on earth does not thereby turn them sullen. Their dual citizenship of both heaven and earth actually requires them to express their eschatological existence through taking up their social responsibility and relating constructively with the wider world, within the overriding boundary of their ultimate allegiance to God.

6.3 Chapter Conclusion

In this chapter, I demonstrated that the *Epistle to Diognetus* falls into the trajectory of 1 Peter in the formulation of Christians' social strategies as resident-aliens on earth, and in basing these strategies on the author's perception of God/Christ and of Christians' existence on earth. While 1 Peter represents a centrist approach to pagans' pressure to accommodate, allowing room for Christians to adopt pagan values and practices to a certain degree, by the end of the first century,[81] *Diognetus* shows that sometimes in the second half of the second century, there remained in the Christians' circle an understanding of Christians' existence as resident-aliens much in line with that in 1 Peter. Although we do not know whether the author of *Diognetus* had access to 1 Peter, *Diognetus* certainly reflects a consistent line of development of the social ethics of Christian resident-aliens represented by 1 Peter.

It is therefore remarkable that *Diognetus* actually serves to verify my findings concerning the Petrine social strategy in the previous chapters, and indeed states even more explicitly and eloquently what 1 Peter could have further developed on the interaction between the two elements of resistance and accommodation within Christians' "good works" of "differentiated resistance." While both 1 Peter and *Diognetus* make it clear that for Christians to participate in idolatry (1 Pet 4:3; *Diogn.* 2.6; 4.6) and to deny the Lord (1 Pet 3:15; 4:14, 16; *Diogn.* 7.7; 10.7) is out of the question, *Diognetus* gives a clearer and bolder account of the overlap between the Christian and pagan way of life by stating expressly that, Christians are distinguished from the rest of humanity neither by country, language nor mode of life (*Diogn.* 5.1–2), and indeed participate in all things as citizens (i.e. as members of the cities [5.5]). Whereas the Petrine author confines his ethics on Christians' interactions with the pagans mainly in terms of

---

81. See my analysis in chapter 5.

"submission" (1 Pet 2:13, 18; 3:1, 5) to the current civic and household orders, "seeking peace" (3:9–12) and gentleness (3:16), *Diognetus* goes further to underscore the positive contributions of Christians to society as the soul of the world and the benefactors of their neighbours. Likewise, while Christians' sense of belonging to the earthly native cities can be derived from 1 Peter with reference to its identification of Christians as "exiles of Diaspora,"[82] *Diognetus* once again makes blatantly clear Christians' attachment and social responsibility to the earthly cities by asserting that they regard every foreign land as their fatherland (*Diogn.* 5.5). A study of the *Epistle to Diognetus* therefore serves to manifest what remains latent in 1 Peter and what can be further elaborated from its Christian social ethics.

In any event, *Diognetus* sets a clear example as how Christians do not regard their distinctive identity as depending on maintaining difference or separation from the wider culture, nor do they regard accommodation to the values and practices of the wider world as *by itself* a threat to their new identity obtained through Christ. The superiority of Christians in complying with the moral ideals of the pagan world is just part of the visible expression of their true invisible identity in heaven, and a token of imitating God in his dealings with the human world. This approach actually bears resemblance to the Petrine author who understands Christians' good works as a token of their solidarity with Christ, and the congruent expression of their identity as "elect exiles of Diaspora."

Therefore, although Elliott argues that the Petrine author accentuates Christians' conflict and struggle with the outside world, in order to motivate their clear distance from Gentile influence and maintenance of internal communal cohesion,[83] my investigation of *Diognetus* actually demonstrates that alienation and ostracism do not necessarily push Christians towards sectarianism, nor cause them to keep an irreconcilable distance from the rest of society. For the author of *Diognetus*, as well as the author of 1 Peter, the congruent expression of Christians' existence as resident-aliens is to comply with the moral ideals of the society to their best, and demonstrate their commitment to the whole of humanity through discharging

---

82. See section 4.2.2 in chapter 4 above.
83. Elliott, *Home*, 101–150.

their civil responsibilities and benefitting their pagan neighbours, as an expression of their invisible identity as citizens of heaven/members of the people of God.

On the other hand, although Balch asserts that the apologetic purpose of the Petrine household code involves Christians' acculturating to the Hellenistic social values "even in tension with the early Jesus movement, changes that raise questions about continuity and identity in early Christianity,"[84] *Diognetus* actually shows that when early Christians engaged in apology, they did not mean to blur Christians' distinctiveness just for sake of apology. The author of *Diognetus* has no hesitation in pointing out Christians' ultimate allegiance to God as their fundamental difference with the wider culture, which had significant implications for their external way of life, and indeed results in their being constantly subject to pagan hatred. Even when the convergence of Christian and pagan lifestyles is mentioned, *Diognetus* actually goes further to underscore Christians' unique moral superiority in following societal norms better than the rest of society. The fundamental nature of Christianity as a religious movement is not changed, nor is Christians' identity being given up by the apologetic purpose of the writing. I hold that this is also how the Petrine household code should be understood.

Therefore, my comparison of 1 Peter with *Diognetus* in this chapter provides a further basis to understand the Petrine social behavioural instructions from the author's own religious point of view. Theology again plays a crucial role in the shaping of early Christians' social ethics. Any investigation of the Petrine social behavioural instructions without seriously taking into account of the author's theological perspective as his *ultimate concern* is clearly inadequate.

---

84. Balch, "Hellenization/Acculturation," 81.

CHAPTER 7

Conclusion

In the above study, I sought an empathic understanding of the shaping of the Petrine social behavioural instructions from the author's own theological vision as his ultimate concern.

I argued that the primary concern of the Petrine author is Christians' steadfastness in standing firm in the grace/salvation of God in the face of constant pagan hostility and pressure to abandon their allegiance to God and is, therefore, religious. This religious concern is by no means merely a matter of internal piety, but is required to be translated into concrete behavioural expression, especially in the context of the Greco-Roman world, in which people's social life was virtually inseparable from their religious expressions. This is precisely how the Petrine "good works" of "differentiated resistance" should be understood. The gist of Christians' resistance lies in their abstention from any pagan activies involving religious or cultic implications. Subject to Christians keeping their exclusive allegiance to God intact, the author actually does not regard Christians complying with current societal order as ideal citizens, and adopting commonly accepted social norms and practices as, *by itself*, incompatible with their identity before God. Especially for those Christians who are in vulnerable situations, such as slaves and wives in unbelieving households, to silence slanders surrounding them was particularly crucial for them to gain room to preserve their exclusive worship of God in their already precarious circumstances.

Therefore, for the Petrine author, the major question is not whether Christians should separate from or accommodate to the wider pagan culture, but whether their behaviour is consistent with their religious commitment to God. His formulation of Christians' "good works" is actually the *outcome* of his theological perception of what Jesus Christ exemplified on the cross *and* what Christians' identity on earth entails. Jesus Christ is understood as the Messiah expected within the Jewish eschatological vision but paradoxically experienced rejection by human beings as a resident-alien, which alienation is what Christians are experiencing and should expect on earth. The author's perception of Christians' existence on earth is then underscored also in Jewish terms as "elect exiles of Diaspora," inheriting the self-definitions and eschatological promises of the Jewish elect exiles of the Diaspora, which becomes the controlling metaphor of Christian identity in 1 Peter. Since Jesus Christ's response to human alienation on the cross reflects the form of "differentiated resistance" and, remarkably, fulfilled the Jewish ideal of seeking peace without returning abuses, Christian "good works" of "differentiated resistance" is perceived as expressive of Christians' solidarity with Christ, and a congruent behavioural expression of their existence as "elect exiles of Diaspora."

Therefore, for the Petrine author, Christians' identity does not depend on whether they are socially distinctive enough or whether they are too accommodating to the wider culture *per se*, but is derived from their unique conviction of Christians' particularly privileged status before God brought about by their new faith in Christ. As manifested by my comparison of 1 Peter with the *Epistle to Diognetus*, this particular nature of Christians' self-understanding is what generates Christians' continual vitality and commitment to the larger society, based on their understanding of the nature of God/Christ, and regardless of constant pagan hostility and alienation, which is actually beyond human reason and, therefore, resists sociological generalization.

I therefore wish that my above study can contribute to current Petrine scholarship by arousing scholars' interest in taking the author's own theological conviction seriously *in its own right* to understand his social behavioural instructions. As I have demonstrated in the above discussion, an approach focusing on the author's theological orientation is still competent in answering the questions posed by scholars who are interested in the paraenetic concern of 1 Peter. An approach giving full credit to the author's theological conviction actually serves to avoid imposing on the text questions that are in fact not relevant to the author's own concern, and allows the voice of the text to be properly heard.

Indeed, the Petrine social strategy of "differentiated resistance," with its primary concern of Christians' salvation and, thus, their abstention from idolatry and other pagan cultic practices, actually retains its instructional value even today for Christians living in those societies, where Christianity remains a minority religion amidst a polytheistic wider culture. Nowadays, many Christians living in Asia are still living in societies where ancestral worship and domestic cults are common in individual households, and where participation in various folk religions is just part of the social norms. Christians failing to participate in these ancestral rites and common cultic practices can similarly result in social rebukes for being stubbon, exclusivist and even impious towards the ancestors. My exploration of the Petrine behavioural instructions in this study is actually instructive to Christians in these societies to devise their social strategies by focusing on matters that are relevant to their faith, and striving for room to uphold their ultimate allegiance to God by being good citizens and family members recognizable as such by the larger society.

Even for places where Christians are increasingly marginalized, and where "secularization" becomes the trend of the day, my study also challenges Christians to focus on the essential nature of the Christian faith, and not to insist on being different just for the sake of being different. For the early Christians, at least for the authors of 1 Peter and *the Epistle of Diognetus*, overlap between Christians' way of life and that of the wider world is not something to be avoided *by itself.* Religious orientation and loyalty to the one true God, are always the primary basis of Christians' discernment of what constitutes congruent behavioural expressions of their exclusive faith and allegiance to God. At the same time, Christians' religious difference from the wider world is not a matter of internal piety, but is required to be translated into concrete behaviour which necessarily renders Christians externally and visibly different from the rest of society.

Even where Christians have different emphases of what constitutes proper expression of their ultimate allegiance to God, such as between the Petrine author and John in Revelation, theological reflections of what the cross of Jesus Christ denotes, and what Christians following the example of Christ entails, are still the starting point for both authors to formulate their respective Christian social ethics. The fact that the early church chose to place both 1 Peter and Revelation, with their notably different Christian social strategies, as canonical books of the Bible, actually challenges Christians to continue their reflection on the essence of their Christian faith, and to devise their forms of social engagement in accordance with their convictions of what Christian existence, and what upholding Christians' allegiance to God, entail in their particular situations.

In situations where pressure to accommodate remains primarily at a social level, and where governmental actions are not imminent, Christians can formulate their social strategies with reference to 1 Peter in order to gain some room to keep their faith to God intact. But for Christians who are facing actual governmental arrests and even executions for their faith, and where they simply do not have choice or room to negotiate, John's call in Revelation may be particularly relevant in their circumstances.

Finally, although my approach to posit the author's theological conviction as the starting point of investigation involves going *inside* the text, and adhering to its (apparently) obvious meaning as far as possible, I also tried to integrate my study of the text with a historical investigation of the socio-political background *behind* the text, and utilize this socio-historical information *as an entrance* to understand imaginatively the vision of the Petrine author, and the implications of his Christian social instructions. My study of the actual Jewish social engagement in the Diaspora serves to throw light on the author's understanding of the nature of Christians' existence on earth when addressing them as "elect exiles of Diaspora" and, thus, further concretizes the working of the Petrine strategy of "differentiated resistance" in reality. Likewise, a comparison of 1 Peter and Revelation serves to place the text in its own religious landscape of Asia Minor, and highlights the Petrine social ethics within the dynamics of the diverse forms of social engagement current in Asia Minor. A comparison of 1 Peter with the *Epistle to Diognetus* also reveals how the Petrine idea of Christians' existence as resident-aliens on earth could be further developed in the second half of the second century CE.

Therefore, I further wish to demonstrate through my study that a theological approach and a socio-historical approach to study the biblical text are not inherently incompatible, in so far as we properly prioritize one over the other, and are conscious of our basic task in trying to understand a biblical text such as 1 Peter. Since 1 Peter is *by its nature* an internal correspondence between Christians, theological/religious convictions of the parties should be taken as the starting point of investigation, so as to enable the voice of the author to be properly heard. On the other hand, if one's interest is in understanding Christianity as a religioius movement in the Greco-Roman world (e.g. its growth and development, its social structure and effect, etc.), more weight can be placed on sociological viewpoints, and relevant social theories can be introduced to serve as frames of reference. However, even then, theological/religious conviction, as the *genuine concern* of early believers, must be taken into consideration. After all, religion was what in fact generated Christianity into existence.

Bibliography

Primary Sources

Apuleius. *Metamorphoses*. Translated by John Arthur Hanson. 2 vols. Loeb Classical Library. Cambridge, MA: Harvard University Press, 1989.

Augustine. *The City of God against the Pagans*. Translated by R. W. Dyson. Cambridge: Cambridge University Press, 1998.

Bailey, Cyril. *Epicurus: The Extant Remains*. Oxford: Clarendon, 1926.

Daley, Brian. *Gregory of Nazianzus*. The Early Church Fathers. London: Routledge, 2006.

Chilton, Bruce. *The Isaiah Targum: Introduction, Translation Apparatus and Notes*. The Aramaic Bible 11. Edinburgh: T&T Clark, 1987.

Cicero. *De Natura Deorum Academica*. Translated by H. Rackham. Loeb Classical Library. London: William Heinemann, 1933.

Clement of Alexandria, *Clement of Alexandria*. Translated by G. W. Butterworth. Loeb Classical Library. London: William Heinemann, 1919.

Collins, J. J. trans. "Sibylline Oracles." Pages 317–472 in *The Old Testament Pseudepigrapha*, edited by James H. Charlesworth. 2 vols. Peabody, MA: Hendrickson, 2009 (1st published, 1983).

Columella, Lucius Junius Moderatus. *On Agriculture*. Vol 1. Translated by Harrison Boyd. The Loeb Classical Library. London: William Heinemann, 1941.

Epictetus. *The Discourses as Reported by Arrian, the Manual, and Fragments*. Translated by W. A. Oldfather. 2 vols. The Loeb Classical Library. London: William Heinemann, 1926–1928.

———. *Moral Discourses: Enchiridion and Fragments*. Translated by Elizabeth Carter. London: Dent & Sons, 1910.

Frey, Jean Baptiste. *Corpus Inscriptionum Iudaicarum: recueil des inscriptions juives qui vont du IIIe siècle avant Jésus-Christ au VIIe siècle de notre ère*. 2 vols. Sussidi allo studio delle antichità cristiane 1, 3. Vatican: Pontificio Istituto di archeologia cristiana, 1936–1952.

Grenfell, Bernard P., and Arthur S. Hunt. *The Oxyrhynchus Papyri*. Vol. 4. London: Egypt Exploration Fund, 1904.
Holmes, Michael W. *The Apostolic Fathers: Greek Texts and English Translations*. 3rd ed. Grand Rapids, MI: Baker, 2007.
Isaac, E., trans. "1 (Ethiopic Apocalypse of) Enoch." Pages 5–89 in vol. 1 of *The Old Testament Pseudepigrapha*. Edited by James H. Charlesworth. 2 vols. Peabody, MA: Hendrickson, 2009 (1st published, 1983).
Josephus. *Jewish Antiquities*. Translated by Ralph Marcus. 9 vols. The Loeb Classical Library. London: William Heinemann, 1933–1963.
———. *Josephus*. Translated by J. Thackeray. 10 vols. The Loeb Classical Library. London: William Heinemann, 1926–1981.
———. *The New Complete Works of Josephus*. Translated by William Whiston, rev. ed. Grand Rapids, MI: Kregel, 1999.
Kee, Howard Clark, trans. "Testaments of the Twelve Patriarchs." Pages 775–828 in vol. 1 of *The Old Testament Pseudepigrapha*. Edited by James H. Charlesworth. 2 vols. Peabody, MA: Hendrickson, 2009 (1st published, 1983).
Lake, Kirsopp. *The Apostolic Fathers*. 2 vols. Loeb Classical Library. London: William Heinemann, 1912–1913.
Lewis, Naphtali. *The Roman Principate: 27 B.C.–285 A.D. Greek Historical Documents*. Toronto, ON: Hakkert, 1974.
Livy. *Livy*. Translated by B. O. Foster. 14 vols. Loeb Classical Library. London: William Heinemann, 1919–1959.
Noy, David. *Jewish Inscriptions of Western Europe*. 2 vols. Cambridge: Cambridge University Press, 1993–1995.
Marcus Aurelius. *The Meditations of the Emperor Marcus Antoninus*. Translated by Arthur Spenser Loat Farquharson. 2 vols. Oxford: Clarendon 1944.
Musurillo, Herbert. *The Acts of the Christian Martyrs, Introduction, Texts and Translations*. Oxford: Clarendon Press, 1972.
Origen. *The Writings of Origen*. Translated by Frederick Crombie. 2 vols. Edinburgh: T&T Clark, 1872.
Philo. *The Works of Philo: Complete and Unabridged*. Translated by C. D. Yonge. New updated ed. Peabody, MA: Hendrickson, 1993.
Plato. *Laws*. Translated by R. G. Bury. 2 vols. Loeb Classical Library. London: William Heinemann, 1926.
———. *Plato, with an English Translation. Apology; Crito; Phaedo; Phaedrus*. Translated by Harold North Fowler. Reprint ed. The Loeb Classical Library. London: Heinemann, 1913.
Pliny, the Younger. *Letters*. Translated by William Melmoth. Revised by W. M. L. Hutchinson. 2 vols. Loeb Classical Library. London: William Heinemann, 1915.

Plutarch. *Moralia*. Translated by Frank Cole Babbitt. 14 vols. Loeb Classical Library. London: William Heinemann, 1957.
Saint Justin Martyr. *Dialogue with Trypho*. Translated by Thomas P. Halton. Selections from the Fathers of the Church 3. Washington, DC: Catholic University of America Press, 2003.
Seneca. *Moral Essays*. Translated by John W. Basore. 3 vols. Loeb Classical Library. London: William Heinemann, 1928–1935.
———. *Seneca's Letters to Lucilius*. Translated by Edward Phillips Barker. 2 vols. Oxford: Clarendon, 1932.
Stec, David M. *The Targum of Psalms: Translated with a Critical Introduction, Apparatus, and Notes*. The Aramaic Bible 16. London: T&T Clark, 2004.
Strack, Hermann L., and Paul Billerbeck. *Kommentar zum Neuen Testament aus Talmud und Midrasch*. 6 vols. Munich: C. H. Beck, 1922–1961.
Suetonius. *The Lives of the Caesars*. Translated by J. C. Rolfe. 2 vols. The Loeb Classical Library. London: William Heinemann, 1913–1914.
Tacitus. *The Histories and The Annals*. Translated by Clifford H. Moore and John Jackson. 4 vols. The Loeb Classical Library. London: William Heinemann, 1925–1937.
Tatian. *Oratio Ad Graecos and Fragments*. Translated by Molly Whittaker. Oxford: Clarendon Press, 1982.
Tertullian, and Marcus Minucius Felix. *Tertullian: Apologetical Works and Minucius Felix Octavius*. Translated by Rudolph Arbesmann, Emily Joseph Daly and Edwin A. Quain. The Fathers of the Church 10. Washington, DC: Catholic University of America Press, 1950.
Tcherikover, Victor, Alexander Fuks, Menahem Stern, and David M. Lewis, eds. *Corpus Papyrorum Judaicarum*. 3 vols. Cambridge, MA: Harvard University Press, 1957–1964.
Wiedemann, Thomas. *Greek and Roman Slavery*. London: Croom Helm, 1981.
Wright, R. B., trans. "Psalms of Solomon." Pages 639–670 in vol. 2 of *The Old Testament Pseudepigrapha*. Edited by James H. Charlesworth. 2 vols. Peabody, MA: Hendrickson, 2009 (1st published, 1983).
Xenophon. *Memorabilia and Oeconomicus*. Translated by E. C. Marchant. The Loeb Classical Library. London: William Heinemann, 1923.

Dictionaries, Lexicons and Grammars

Bauckham, Richard. "Spirits in Prison." Pages 177–178 in vol. 6 of *The Anchor Bible Dictionary*. Edited by D. N. Freedman. 6 vols. New York: Doubleday, 1992.

Ferguson, E. "Religion, Greco-Roman." Pages 1006–1011 in *Dictionary of the Later New Testament & Its Developments*. Edited by Ralph P. Martin and Peter H. Davids. Downers Grove, IL: InterVarsity, 1997.

Garrett, Susan R. "Sociology of Early Christianity." Pages 89–89 in vol. 6 of *The Anchor Bible Dictionary*. Edited by D. N. Freedman. 6 vols. New York: Doubleday, 1992.

Kittel, G., and G. Friedrich, eds. *Theological Dictionary of the New Testament*. Translated by G. W. Bromiley. 10 vols. Grand Rapids, MI: Eerdmans, 1964–1976.

Miles, John R. "Lamb." Pages 132–134 in vol. 4 of *The Anchor Bible Dictionary*. Edited by D. N. Freedman. 6 vols. New York: Doubleday, 1992.

Sallares, J. R. "Infanticide." Page 757 in *The Oxford Classical Dictionary*. Edited by Simon Hornblower and Antony Spawforth. Oxford: Oxford University Press, 2003.

Wallace, Daniel B. *Greek Grammar Beyond the Basics: An Exegetical Syntax of the New Testament*. Grand Rapids, MI: Zondervan, 1996.

Secondary Literature

Achtemeier, Paul J. *1 Peter: A Commentary on First Peter*. Hermeneia. Minneapolis, MN: Fortress Press, 1996.

———. "Newborn Babes and Living Stones: Literal and Figurative in 1 Peter." In *To Touch the Text: Biblical and Related Studies in Honor of Joseph A. Fitzmyer, S. J.*, edited by Maurya P. Horgan and Paul J. Kobelski, 207–236. New York: Crossroad, 1989.

———. "Suffering Servant and Suffering Christ in 1 Peter." In *The Future of Christology: Essays in Honor of Leander E. Keck*, edited by Abraham J. Malherbe and Wayne A. Meeks, 176–188. Minneapolis, MN: Fortress Press, 1993.

Aageson, James W. "1 Peter 2:11–3:7: Slaves, Wives and the Complexities of Interpretation." In *A Feminist Companion to the Catholic Epistles and Hebrews*, edited by Amy-Jill Levine and Maria Mayo Robins, 34–49. London: T&T Clark, 2004.

Andriessen, Dom P. "The Authorship of the Epistula Ad Diognetum." *Vigiliae Christianae* 1 (1947): 129–136.

Applebaum, S. "The Legal Status of the Jewish Communities in the Diaspora." In *The Jewish People in the First Century: Historical Geography, Political History, Social, Cultural and Religious Life and Institutions*, edited by S. Safrai and M. Stern, vol. 1, 2 vols., 420–463. Assen: Van Gorcum, 1974.

Attridge, Harold W. *The Epistle to the Hebrews: A Commentary on the Epistle to the Hebrews*. Hermeneia. Philadelphia, PA: Fortress Press, 1989.

Aune, David E. *Revelation 1–5*. Word Biblical Commentary 52A. Dallas, TX: Word Books, 1997.

———. *Revelation 6–16*. Word Biblical Commentary 52B. Nashville, TN: Thomas Nelson, 1998.

———. "The Social Matrix of the Apocalypse of John." *Biblical Research* 26 (1981): 16–32.

Bakhos, Carol. "Introduction." In *Ancient Judaism in Its Hellenistic Context*, edited by Carol Bakhos, 1–7. Leiden: Brill, 2005.

Balch, David. "Hellenization/Acculturation in 1 Peter." In *Perspectives on First Peter*, edited by Charles H. Talbert, 79–101. Macon, GA: Mercer University Press, 1986.

———. *Let Wives Be Submissive: The Domestic Code in 1 Peter*. Society of Biblical Literature Monograph Series 26. Atlanta, GA: Scholars Press, 1981.

Bammel, E. "The Commands in 1 Peter II. 17." *New Testament Studies* 11 (1964/65): 279–281.

Barclay, John M. G. "Introduction: Diaspora Negotiations." In *Negotiating Diaspora: Jewish Strategies in the Roman Empire*, edited by John M. G. Barclay, 1–6. New York: T&T Clark, 2004.

———. *Jews in the Mediterranean Diaspora: From Alexander to Trajan (323 BCE–117 CE)*. Edinburgh: T&T Clark, 1996.

———. "Snarling Sweetly: Josephus on Images and Idolatry." In *Idolatry: False Worship in the Bible, Early Judaism, and Christianity*, edited by Stephen C. Barton, 73–87. London: T&T Clark, 2007.

Barnard, L. W. "The Epistle Ad Diognetum: Two Units from One Author?" *Zeitschrift für die neutestamentliche Wissenschaft* 56 (1965): 130–137.

Barr, David L. "Doing Violence: Moral Issues in Reading John's Apocalypse." In *Reading the Book of Revelation: A Resource for Students*, edited by David L. Barr, 97–108. Atlanta, GA: Society of Biblical Literature, 2003.

Barton, Stephen C. "Historical Criticism and Social-Scientific Perspectives in New Testament Study." In *Hearing the New Testament: Strategies for Interpretation*, edited by Joel B. Green, 61–89. Grand Rapids, MI: Eerdmans, 1995.

Bauckham, Richard. *The Climax of Prophecy: Studies on the Book of Revelation*. Edinburgh: T&T Clark, 1993.

———. *The Theology of the Book of Revelation*. New Testament Theology. Cambridge: Cambridge University Press, 1993.

Bauman-Martin, Betsy. "Speaking Jewish: Postcolonial Aliens and Strangers in First Peter." In *Reading First Peter with New Eyes: Methodological Reassessment of the Letter of First Peter*, edited by Robert L. Webb and Betsy Bauman-Martin, 144–177. London: T&T Clark, 2007.

Beale, G. K. *The Book of Revelation: A Commentary on the Greek Text*. The New International Greek Testament Commentary. Grand Rapids, MI: Eerdmans, 1999.

Beare, Francis Wright. *The First Epistle of Peter: The Greek Text with Introduction and Notes*. 3rd (rev. and enlarged) ed. Oxford: Blackwell, 1970 (1st published, 1958).

Beasley-Murray, George Raymond. *The Book of Revelation*. New Century Bible. London: Oliphants, 1974.

Bechtler, Steven Richard. *Following in His Steps: Suffering, Community, and Christology in 1 Peter*. Society of Biblical Literature Dissertation Series 162. Atlanta, GA: Scholars Press, 1998.

Bennett, H. "The Exposure of Infants in Ancient Rome." *The Classical Journal* 18, no. 6 (1923): 341–351.

Best, Ernest. *1 Peter*. New Century Bible. London: Oliphants, 1971.

———. "1 Peter II, 4-10 – A Reconsideration." Novum Testamentum 11 (1969): 270–293.

Bhabha, Homi K. *The Location of Culture*. London: Routledge, 1994.

Bickerman, Elias J. "The Name of Christians." *Harvard Theological Review* 42 (1949): 109–124.

Binder, Donald D. *Into the Temple Courts: The Place of the Synagogues in the Second Temple Period*. Society of Biblical Literature Dissertation Series 169. Atlanta, GA: Society of Biblical Literature, 1999.

Bird, Jennifer G. *Abuse, Power and Fearful Obedience: Reconsidering 1 Peter's Commands to Wives*. Library of New Testament Studies 442. London: T&T Clark International, 2011.

Blakeney, E. H. *The Epistle to Diognetus*. London: Society for Promoting Christian Knowledge, 1943.

Blendinger, Christian. "Kirche als Fremdlingschaft." *Communio viatorum* 2–3 (1967): 123–134.

Bockmuehl, Markus N. A. *Jewish Law in Gentile Churches: Halakhah and the Beginning of Christian Public Ethics*. Edinburgh: T&T Clark, 2000.

Boismard, M. -É. Quatre hymnes baptismales dans la première épître de Pierre. Lectio divina 30. Paris: Cerf, 1961.

Bonnington, Mark. "Fleeing Idolatry: Social Embodiment of Anti-Idolatry in the First Century." In *Idolatry: False Worship in the Bible, Early Judaism, and Christianity*, edited by Stephen C. Barton, 107–119. London: T&T Clark, 2007.

Borgen, Peder. "'Yes,' 'No,' 'How Far?': The Participation of Jews and Christians in Pagan Cults." In *Paul in His Hellenistic Context*, edited by Troels Engberg-Pedersen, 30–59. Minneapolis, MN: Fortress, 1995.

Boring, M. Eugene. "Narrative Christology in the Apocalypse." *Catholic Biblical Quarterly* 54 (1992): 702–723.

———. "Narrative Dynamics in First Peter: The Function of Narrative World." In *Reading First Peter with New Eyes: Methodological Reassessments of the Letter of First Peter*, edited by Robert L. Webb and Betsy Bauman-Martin, 7–40. London: T&T Clark, 2007.

Boswell, John. *The Kindness of Strangers: The Abandonment of Children in Western Europe from Late Antiquity to the Renaissance*. New York: Pantheon, 1988.

Boxall, Ian. "The Many Faces of Babylon the Great: Wirkungsgeschichte and the Interpretation of Revelation 17." In *Studies in the Book of Revelation*, edited by Steve Moyise, 51–68. Edinburgh: T&T Clark, 2001.

———. *The Revelation of Saint John*. Black's New Testament Commentaries 18. Peabody, MA: Hendrickson, 2006.

Bradley, K. R. *Slaves and Masters in the Roman Empire: A Study in Social Control*. Collection Latomus 185. Bruxelles: Latomus, 1984.

Brändle, Rudolf. *Die Ethik der Schrift an Diognet: Eine Wiederaufnahme paulinischer und johanneischer Theologie am Ausgang des zweiten Jahrhunderts*. Zürich: Theologischer Verlag, 1975.

Brown, Jeannine K. "Just a Busybody? A Look at the Greco-Roman Topos of Meddling for Defining ἀλλοτριεπίσκοπος in 1 Peter 4:15." *Journal of Biblical Literature* 3 (2006): 549–568.

Brubaker, Rogers. "The Return of Assimilation? Changing Perspectives on Immigration and Its Sequels in France, Germany, and the United States." *Ethnic and Racial Studies* 24 (2001): 531–548.

Buell, Denise Kimber. *Why This New Race: Ethnic Reasoning in Early Christianity*. New York: Columbia University Press, 2008.

Caird, G. B. *A Commentary on the Revelation of St. John the Divine*. 2nd ed. Black's New Testament Commentaries. London: A&C Black, 1984.

Callahan, Allen D. "Apocalypse as Critique of Political Economy: Some Notes on Revelation 18." *Horizons in Biblical Theology* 21 (1999): 46–65.

Cameron, A. "The Exposure of Children and Greek Ethics." *The Classical Review* 46 (1932): 105–114.

Campbell, Barth L. *Honor, Shame, and the Rhetoric of 1 Peter*. Society of Biblical Literature Dissertation Series 160. Atlanta, GA: Scholars Press, 1998.

Carter, Warren. "Going All the Way? Honoring the Emperor and Sacrificing Wives and Slaves in 1 Peter." In *A Feminist Companion to the Catholic Epistles and Hebrews*, edited by Amy-Jill Levine and Maria Mayo Robbins, 14–33. London: T&T Clark, 2004.

Chesnutt, Randall D. "Jewish Women in the Greco-Roman Era." In *Essays on Women in Earliest Christianity*, edited by Carroll D. Osburn, vol. 1. 2 vols. 93–130. Joplin, MS: College Press 1993.

Chester, Andrew, and Ralph P. Martin. *The Theology of the Letters of James, Peter, and Jude*. Reprinted edition. Cambridge: Cambridge University Press, 1996.

Chin, Moses. "A Heavenly Home for the Homeless: Aliens and Stranger in 1 Peter." *Tyndale Bulletin* 42 (1991): 96–112.

Cohen, Shaye J. D. "Crossing the Boundary and Becoming a Jew." *Harvard Theological Review* 82 (1989): 13–33.

———. *From the Maccabees to the Mishnah*. Library of Early Christianity 7. Philadelphia, PA: Westminster Press, 1987.

———. "Was Judaism in Antiquity a Missionary Religion?" In *Jewish Assimilation, Acculturation and Accommodation: Past Traditions, Current Issues and Future Prospects*, edited by Menahem Mor, 14–23. Lanham, MD: University Press of America, 1992.

Cohick, Lynn H. *Women in the World of the Earliest Christians: Illuminating Ancient Ways of Life*. Grand Rapids, MI: Baker, 2009.

Collins, Adela Yarbro. *Crisis and Catharsis: The Power of the Apocalypse*. Philadelphia, PA: Westminster Press, 1984.

———. "Eschatology in the Book of Revelation." *Ex auditu* 6 (1990): 63–72.

———. "Political Perspective of the Revelation to John." *Journal of Biblical Literature* 96 (1977): 241–256.

———. "Vilification and Self-Definition in the Book of Revelation." *Harvard Theological Review* 79 (1986): 308–320.

Collins, John Joseph. *Between Athens and Jerusalem: Jewish Identity in the Hellenistic Diaspora*. New York: Crossroad, 1983.

Connolly, R. H. "Notes and Studies: The Date and Authorship of the Epistle to Diognetus." *The Journal of Theological Studies* 36 (1935): 347–353.

Corley, Kathleen E. "1 Peter." In *Searching the Scriptures*, edited by Elisabeth Schüssler Fiorenza, vol 2, 2 vols., 349–359. London: SCM, 1994.

Cranfield, C. E. B. *The First Epistle of Peter*. London: SCM Press, 1950.

Cross, F. L. *I. Peter: A Paschal Liturgy*. London: A. R. Mowbray, 1954.

Crowe, Brandon D. "Oh Sweet Exchange! The Soteriological Significance of the Incarnation in the Epistle to Diognetus." *Zeitschrift für die neutestamentliche Wissenschaft* 102 (2011): 96–109.

Danker, Frederick W. Review of John Elliott, *A Home for the Homeless: A Sociological Exegesis of 1 Peter, Its Situation and Strategy*. *Interpretation* 37 (1983): 84–88.

Daube, David. "κερδαίνω as a Missionary Term." *The Harvard Theological Review* 40 (1947): 109–120.

Davids, Peter H. *The First Epistle of Peter*. New International Commentary on the New Testament. Grand Rapids, MI: Eerdmans, 1990.

Davies, W. D. *The Setting of the Sermon on the Mount*. Brown Judaic Studies 186. Atlanta, GA: Scholars Press, 1989.

Dalton, William J. *Christ's Proclamation to the Spirits: A Study of 1 Peter 3:18–4:6*. Analecta Biblica 23. Rome: Pontifical Biblical Institute, 1965.

deSilva, David A. *Seeing Things John's Way: The Rhetoric of the Book of Revelation*. Louisville, KY: Westminster John Knox Press, 2009.

———. "The Social Setting of the Revelation to John: Conflicts within, Fears Without." *Westminister Theological Journal* 54 (1992): 273–302.

de Ste. Croix, G. E. M. "Why Were the Early Christians Persecuted?" *Past & Present* 26 (1963): 6–38.

Deterding, Paul E. "Exodus Motifs in First Peter." *Concordia Journal* 7 (1981): 58–65.

Dowden, Ken. *Religion and the Romans*. Classical World Series. London: Bristol Classical, 1992.

Downing, F. Gerald. "Pliny's Prosecutions of Christians: Revelation and 1 Peter." *Journal for the Study of the New Testament* 34 (1988): 105–123.

Dryden, J. de Waal. *Theology and Ethics in 1 Peter: Paraenetic Strategies for Christian Character Formation*. Wissenschaftliche Untersuchungen zum Neuen Testament 2/209. Tübingen: Mohr Siebeck, 2006.

Dubis, Mark. *1 Peter: A Handbook on the Greek Text*. Waco, TX: Baylor University Press, 2010.

———. *Messianic Woes in First Peter: Suffering and Eschatology in 1 Peter 4:12–19*. Studies in Biblical Literature 33. New York: Peter Lang, 2002.

———. "Research on 1 Peter: A Survey of Scholarly Literature since 1985." *Currents in Biblical Research* 4 (2006): 199–239.

Duff, Paul B. "Literary Opposition and Social Tension in the Revelation of John." In *Reading the Book of Revelation: A Resource for Students*, edited by David L. Barr, 65–79. Atlanta, GA: Society of Biblical Literature, 2003.

Dunning, Benjamin H. *Aliens and Sojourners: Self as Other in Early Christianity*. Divinations: Rereading Late Ancient Religion. Philadelphia, PA: University of Pennsylvania Press, 2009.

Elliott, John H. "Backward and Forward "in His Steps": Following Jesus from Rome to Raymond and Beyond. The Tradition, Redaction, and Reception of 1 Peter 2:18–25." In *Discipleship in the New Testament*, edited by Fernando F. Segovia, 184–209. Philadelphia, PA: Fortress Press, 1985.

———. "Disgraced yet Graced. The Gospel according to 1 Peter in the Key of Honor and Shame." *Biblical Theology Bulletin* 25 (1995): 166–177.

———. *The Elect and the Holy: An Exegetical Examination of 1 Peter 2:4–10 and the Phrase Basileion Ierateuma*. Supplements to Novum Testamentum 12. Leiden: Brill, 1966.

———. *1 Peter*. AB 37B. New Haven, CT: Yale University Press, 2000.

———. "1 Peter, Its Situation and Strategy: A Discussion with David Balch." In *Perspectives on First Peter*, edited by Charles H. Talbert, 61–78. Macon, GA: Mercer University Press, 1986.

———. *A Home for the Homeless: A Social-Scientific Criticism of 1 Peter, Its Situation and Strategy*. Eugene, OR: Wipf & Stock, 2005. This is the paperback edition of *A Home for the Homeless: A Sociological Exegesis of 1 Peter, Its Situation and Strategy*. Philadelphia, PA: Fortress, 1981 with a new preface, introduction and subtitle.

———. Review of Steven Richard Bechtler, *Following in His Steps: Suffering, Community, and Christology in First Peter*. *Theology Today* 57 (2000): 288.

———. "Social-Scientific Criticism of a Biblical Text: 1 Peter as an Example." In *Social-Scientific Approaches to New Testament Interpretation*, edited by David G. Horrell, 339–358. Edinburgh: T&T Clark, 1999.

Fee, Gordon D. *The First Epistle to the Corinthians*. The New International Commentary on the New Testament. Grand Rapids, MI: Eerdmans, 1987.

Feldman, Louis H. "The Concept of Exile in Josephus." In *Exile: Old Testament, Jewish, and Christian Conception*, edited by James M. Scott, 145–172. Leiden: Brill, 1997.

———. *Jew and Gentile in the Ancient World: Attitudes and Interactions from Alexander to Justinian*. Princeton, NJ: Princeton University Press, 1993.

Feldmeier, Reinhard. *Die Christen als Fremde: die Metapher der Fremde in der antiken Welt, im Urchristentum und im 1. Petrusbrief*. Wissenschaftliche Untersuchungen Zum Neuen Testament 70. Tübingen: Mohr, 1992.

———. *The First Letter of Peter: A Commentary on the Greek Text*. Translated by Peter H. Davids. Waco, TX: Baylor University Press, 2008.

———. "The 'Nation' of Strangers: Social Contempt and Its Theological Interpretation in Ancient Judaism and Early Christianity." In *Ethnicity and the Bible*, edited by Mark G. Brett, 241–270. Leiden: Brill, 1996.

Filson, Floyd Vivian. "Partakers with Christ: Suffering in First Peter." *Interpretation* 9 (1955): 400–412.

Fitzpatrick-McKinley, Anne. "Synagogue Communities in the Graeco-Roman Cities." In *Jews in the Hellenistic and Roman Cities*, edited by John R. Bartlett, 55–87. London: Routledge, 2002.

Foster, Paul. "The Epistle to Diognetus." In *The Writings of the Apostolic Fathers*, edited by Paul Foster, 147–156. London: T&T Clark, 2007.

Frankfurter, David "Jews or Not? Reconstructing the 'Other' in Rev 2:9 and 3:9." *Harvard Theological Review* 94 (2001): 403–425.

Friesen, Steven J. "The Beast from the Land: Revelation 13:11–18 and Social Setting." In *Reading the Book of Revelation: A Resource for Students*, edited by David L. Barr, 49–64. Atlanta, GA: Society of Biblical Literature, 2003.

———. *Imperial Cults and the Apocalypse of John: Reading Revelation in the Ruins*. New York: Oxford University Press, 2001.

———. "Satan's Throne, Imperial Cults and the Social Settings of Revelation." *Journal for the Study of the New Testament* 27 (2005): 351–373.

Furfey, Paul Hanly. "Christian Social Thought in the First and Second Centuries." *The American Catholic Sociological Review* 1 (1940): 13–20.

Furnish, Victor Paul. "Elect Sojourners in Christ: An Approach to the Theology of 1 Peter." *The Perkins School of Theology Journal* 28 (1975): 1–11.

Gafni, Isaiah. *Land, Center and Diaspora: Jewish Constructs in Late Antiquity*. Journal for the Study of the Pseudepigrapha Supplement Series 21. Sheffield: Sheffield Academic Press, 1997.

Gärtner, Bertil. *The Temple and the Community in Qumran and the New Testament: A Comparative Study in the Temple Symbolism of the Qumran Texts and the New Testament*. Society for New Testament Studies Monograph Series 1. Cambridge: University Press, 1965.

Goppelt, Leonhard. *A Commentary on I Peter*. Translated by John E. Alsup. Edited by Ferdinand Hahn. Grand Rapids, MI: Eerdmans, 1993.

Gordon, Milton Myron. *Assimilation in American Life: The Role of Race, Religion, and National Origins*. New York: Oxford University Press, 1964.

Grant, Michael. *The Jews in the Roman World*. London: Phoenix Giant, 1999 (1st published, 1973).

Green, G. L. *Theology and Ethics in 1 Peter*. PhD diss. University of Aberdeen, 1979.

———. "The Use of the Old Testament for Christian Ethics in 1 Peter." *Tyndale Bulletin* 41 (1990): 276–289.

Green, Joel B. "Identity and Engagement in a Diverse World: Pluralism and Holiness in 1 Peter." *Asbury Theology Journal* 55 (2000): 85–92.

———. *1 Peter*. The Two Horizons New Testament Commentary. Grand Rapids, MI: Eerdmans, 2007.

———. "Living as Exiles: The Church in the Diaspora in 1 Peter." In *Holiness and Ecclesiology in the New Testament*, edited by K. E. Brower and Andy Johnson, 311–325. Grand Rapids, MI: Eerdmans, 2007.

———. "Modernity, History and the Theological Interpretation of the Bible." *Scottish Journal of Theology* 54 (2001): 308–329.

Greer, Rowan. "Alien Citizens: A Marvelous Paradox." In *Civitas: Religious Interpretations of the City*, edited by Peter S. Hawkins, 39–56. Atlanta, GA: Scholars Press, 1986.

Grudem, Wayne A. "Wives Like Sarah, and the Husbands Who Honor Them: 1 Peter 3:17." In *Recovering Biblical Manhood and Womanhood: A Response to Evangelical Feminism*, edited by John Piper and Wayne A. Grudem, 194–208. Wheaton, IL: Crossway, 1991.

Gruen, Erich S. *Diaspora: Jews amidst Greeks and Romans*. Cambridge, MA: Harvard University Press, 2002.

Gundry, Robert H. "Further Verba on Verba Christi in First Peter." *Biblica* 55 (1974): 211–236.

———. "'Verba Christi' in 1 Peter: Their Implications Concerning the Authorship of 1 Peter and the Authenticity of the Gospel Tradition." *New Testament Studies* 13 (1967): 336–350.

Hall, Randy. "For to This You Have Been Called: The Cross and Suffering in 1 Peter." *Restoration Quarterly* 19 (1976): 137–147.

Hanson, Anthony. "Salvation Proclaimed, 1 Peter 3:18–22." *The Expository Times* 93 (1981/82): 100–105.

Harland, Philip A. *Associations, Synagogues, and Congregations: Claiming a Place in Ancient Mediterranean Society*. Minneapolis, MN: Fortress, 2003.

———. "Honouring the Emperor or Assailing the Beast: Participation in Civic Life among Associations (Jewish, Christian and Other) in Asia Minor and the Apocalypse of John." *Journal for the Study of the New Testament* 77 (2000): 99–121.

Harrington, Wilfrid J. *Revelation*. Sacra Pagina 16; Collegeville, MN: Liturgical Press, 1993.

Hasting, Adrian. "Christianity and Nationhood: Congruity or Antipathy." *The Journal of Religious History* 25 (2001): 247–260.

Heintz, Michael. "'Μιμητής Θεοῦ' in the Epistle to Diognetus." *Journal of Early Christian Studies* 12 (2004): 107–119.

Hemer, Colin J. *The Letters to the Seven Churches of Asia in Their Local Setting*. Biblical Resource Series. Grand Rapids, MI: Eerdmans, 2001.

Hill, David. "'To Offer Spiritual Sacrifices' (1 Peter 2:5): Liturgical Formulations and Christian Paraenesis in 1 Peter." *Journal for the Study of the New Testament* (1982): 45–63.

Hillyer, Norman. "'Rock-Stone' Imagery in 1 Peter." *Tyndale Bulletin* 22 (1971): 58–81.

Holloway, Paul A. *Coping with Prejudice: 1 Peter in Social-Psychological Perspective*. Wissenschaftliche Untersuchungen Zum Neuen Testament 244. Tübingen: Mohr Siebeck, 2009.

Homcy, Stephen L. "'To Him Who Overcomes': A Fresh Look at What 'Victory' Means for the Believer according to the Book of Revelation." *Journal of the Evangelical Theological Society* 38 (1995): 193–201.

Homans, George Caspar. *The Human Group*. International Library of Sociology and Social Reconstruction. London: Routledge & Kegan Paul, 1975.

Holmes, Michael W. "*Polycarp*, Epistle to the Philippians." In *The Writings of the Apostolic Fathers*, edited by Paul Foster, 108–125. London: T&T Clark, 2007.

Horrell, David G. "Between Conformity and Resistance: Beyond the Balch-Elliott Debate towards a Postcolonial Reading of First Peter." In *Reading First Peter with New Eyes: Methodological Reassessments of the Letter of First Peter*, edited by Robert L. Webb and Betsy Bauman-Martin, 110–143. London: T&T Clark, 2007.

———. *The Epistles of Peter and Jude*. Epworth Commentaries. Peterborough: Epworth Press, 1998.

———. *1 Peter*. New Testament Guides. London: T&T Clark, 2008.

———. "The Label Χριστιανός: 1 Peter 4:16 and the Formation of Christian Identity." *Journal of Biblical Literature* 126 (2007): 361–381.

———. "'Race,' 'Nation,' 'People': Ethnic Identity-Construction in 1 Peter 2:9." *New Testament Studies* 58 (2012): 123–143.

Hubbard, Moyer V. *Christianity in the Greco-Roman World: A Narrative Introduction*. Peabody, MA: Hendrickson, 2010.

Humphrey Edith M. "A Tale of Two Cities and (at Least) Three Women: Transformation, Continuity, and Contrast in the Apocalypse." In *Reading the Book of Revelation: A Resource for Students*, edited by David L. Barr, 81–96. Atlanta, GA: Society of Biblical Literature, 2003.

Hurtado, Larry W. *Lord Jesus Christ: Devotion to Jesus in Earliest Christianity*. Paperback ed. Grand Rapids, MI: Eerdmans, 2005.

Hyde, Walter Woodburn. *Paganism to Christianity in the Roman Empire*. New York: Octagon Books, 1970.

Jefford, Clayton N. *The Apostolic Fathers and the New Testament*. Peabody, MA: Hendrickson, 2006.

Jeremias, Joachim. "Eckstein – Schlußstein." *Zeitschrift für die neutestamentliche Wissenschaft* 36 (1937): 154–157.

———. *The Eucharistic Words of Jesus*. Translated by Normal Perrin. New Testament Library. London: SCM Press, 1966.

———. "Κεφαλὴ γωνίας – Ἀκρογωνιαῖος." *Zeitschrift für die neutestamentliche Wissenschaft* 28 (1929): 264–280.

Jobes, Karen H. *1 Peter*. Baker Exegetical Commentary on the New Testament. Grand Rapids, MI: Baker, 2005.

Johnson, Sherman E. "Early Christianity in Asia Minor." *Journal of Biblical Literature* 77 (1958): 1–17.

Joshel, Sandra R. *Slavery in the Roman World*. Cambridge Introduction to Roman Civilization. New York: Cambridge University Press, 2010.

Kee, Howard Clark. *Who Are the People of God?: Early Christian Models of Community*. New Haven, CT: Yale University Press, 1995.

Kelly, J. N. D. *A Commentary on the Epistles of Peter and of Jude*. Black's New Testament Commentaries. London: Adam & Charles Black, 1969.

Kaminsky, Joel S. "Israel's Election and the Other in Biblical, Second Temple, and Rabbinic Thought." In *The "Other" in Second Temple Judaism: Essays in Honor of John J. Collins*, edited by Daniel C. Harlow, Karina Martin Hogan, Matthew Goff and Joel S. Kaminsky, 17–30. Grand Rapids, MI: Eerdmans 2011.

Knight, Jonathan. "The Enthroned Christ of Revelation 5:6 and the Development of Christian Theology." In *Studies in the Book of Revelation*. Edited by Steve Moyise, 43–50. London: T&T Clark, 2002.

———. *Revelation*. Readings: A New Biblical Commentary. Sheffield: Sheffield Academic Press, 1999.

Kraabel, A. Thomas, and Robert S. MacLennan. "The Disappearance of the 'God-Fearers.'" *Numen* 28 (1981): 113–126.

———. "The God-Fearers – a Literary and Theological Invention." In *Diaspora Jews and Judaism: Essays in Honor of, and in Dialogue with A. Thomas Kraabel*, edited by J. Andrew Overman and Robert S. MacLennan, 131–143. Atlanta, GA: Scholars Press, 1992.

———. "The Roman Diaspora: Six Questionable Assumptions." *Journal of Jewish Studies* 33 (1982): 445–464.

Krentz, Edgar. "Order in the 'House' of God: The Haustafel in 1 Peter 2:11–3:12." In *Common Life in the Early Church: Essays Honoring Graydon F. Snyder*, edited by Graydon F. Snyder, Julian Victor Hills and Richard B. Gardner, 279–285. Harrisburg, PA: Trinity Press International, 1998.

Ladd, George Eldon. *A Commentary on the Revelation of John*. Grand Rapids, MI: Eerdmans, 1972.

LaFargue, Michael. "Sociohistorical Research and the Contextualization of Biblical Theology." In *The Social World of Formative Christianity and Judaism: Essays in Tribute to Howard Clark Kee*, edited by Jacob Neusner et al., 3–16. Philadelphia, PA: Fortress Press, 1988.

Lawson, John. *A Theological and Historical Introduction to the Apostolic Fathers*. New York: Macmillan, 1961.

Leaney, A. R. C. "1 Peter and the Passover: An Interpretation." *New Testament Studies* 10 (1963/1964): 238–251.

Leon, Harry J. *The Jews of Ancient Rome*. The Morris Loeb Series. Philadelphia, PA: Jewish Publication Society of America, 1960.

Levine, Étan. "The Jews in Time and Space." In *Diaspora: Exile and the Jewish Condition*, edited by Étan Levine, 1–11. New York: J. Aronson, 1983.

Lienhard, Joseph T. "The Christology of the Epistle to Diognetus." *Vigiliae Christianae* 24 (1970): 280–289.

Lieu, Judith. *Neither Jew nor Greek?: Constructing Early Christianity*. London: T&T Clark, 2002.

Little, Vivian Agincourt Spence. *The Christology of the Apologists, Doctrinal*. Studies in Theology. London: Duckworth, 1934.

Lindars, Barnabas. "Enoch and Christology." *Expository Times* 92 (1981): 295–299.

Lona, Horacio E. *An Diognet*. Kommentar zu Frühchristlichen Apologeten 8. Freiburg: Herder, 2001.

Longenecker, Richard N. *The Christology of Early Jewish Christianity*. Studies in Biblical Theology, 2nd Series, 17. London: SCM Press, 1970.

Lupieri, Edmondo F. *A Commentary on the Apocalypse of John*. Translated by Maria Poggi Johnson and Adam Kamesar. Grand Rapids, MI: Eerdmans, 2006.

Magie, David. *Roman Rule in Asia Minor: To the End of the Third Century after Christ*. 2 vols. Princeton, NJ: Princeton University Press, 1950.

Marrou, Henri Irénée. À Diognète: introduction, édition critique, traduction et commentaire. Paris: Cerf, 1951.

Martin, Troy W. *Metaphor and Composition in 1 Peter*. Society of Biblical Literature Dissertation Series 131. Atlanta, GA: Scholars Press, 1992.

———. "The Rehabilitation of a Rhetorical Step-Child: First Peter and Classical Rhetorical Criticism." In *Reading First Peter with New Eyes: Methodological Reassessments of the Letter of First Peter*, edited by Robert L. Webb and Betsy Bauman-Martin, 41–71. London: T&T Clark, 2007.

Matera, Frank J. *New Testament Christology*. Louisville, KY: Westminster John Knox Press, 1999.

Mattingly, Harold B. "The Origin of the Name Christiani." *The Journal of Theological Studies* 9 (1958): 26–37.

Mayo, Philip L. *"Those Who Call Themselves Jews": The Church and Judaism in the Apocalypse of John*. Princeton Theological Monograph Series 60. Eugene, OR: Pickwick, 2006.

Mbuvi, Andrew Mūtūa. *Temple, Exile, and Identity in 1 Peter*. Library of New Testament Studies 345. London: T&T Clark, 2007.

McCartney, Dan G. " λογικός." *Zeitschrift für die neutestamentliche Wissenschaft* 82 (1991): 128–132.

McKelvey, R. J. *The New Temple: The Church in the New Testament*. Oxford Theological Monographs. London: Oxford University Press, 1969.

Meecham, Henry G. *The Epistle to Diognetus: The Greek Text, with Introduction, Translation and Notes*. Manchester: Manchester University Press, 1949.

———. "The Theology of the Epistle to Diognetus." *The Expository Times* 54 (1943): 97–101.

Meeks, Wayne A. *The First Urban Christians: The Social World of the Apostle Paul.* New Haven, CT: Yale University Press, 1983.

———. *The Origins of Christian Morality: The First Two Centuries.* New Haven, CT: Yale University Press, 1993.

Metzger, Bruce M. *A Textual Commentary on the Greek New Testament.* 2nd edition. London: United Bible Societies, 1994 (1st published, 1971).

Michaels, J. Ramsey. *1 Peter.* WBC 49. Waco, TX: Word Books, 1988.

———. *1 Peter.* Word Biblical Themes. Dallas, TX: Word Publishing, 1989.

———. "Review of Troy W. Martin, *Metaphor and Composition in 1 Peter.*" *Journal of Biblical Literature* 112 (1993): 358–360.

Minear, Paul Sevier. "The House of Living Stones: A Study of 1 Peter 2:4–12." *Ecumenical Review* 34 (1982): 238–248.

Mitchell, Stephen. *Anatolia: Land, Men, and Gods in Asia Minor.* Vol. 1, 2 vols. Oxford: Clarendon, 1993.

Moehring, Horst R. "The Persecution of the Jews and the Adherents of the Isis Cult at Rome A.D. 19." *Novum Testamentum* 3 (1959): 293–304.

Moule, C. F. D. "The Nature and Purpose of 1 Peter." *New Testament Studies* 3 (1956/1957): 1–11.

Mounce, Robert H. *The Book of Revelation.* London: Marshall, Morgan and Scott, 1977.

Moyise, Steve. "Isaiah in 1 Peter." In *Isaiah in the New Testament*, edited by Steve Moyise and Maarten J. J. Menken, 175–188. London: T&T Clark, 2005.

Munro, Winsome. *Authority in Paul and Peter: The Identification of a Pastoral Stratum in the Pauline Corpus and 1 Peter.* Society for New Testament Studies Monograph Series 45. Cambridge: Cambridge University Press, 1983.

Neusner, Jacob. "Exile and Return as the History of Judaism" In *Exile: Old Testament, Jewish and Christian Conceptions*, edited by James M. Scott, 221–237. Leiden: Brill, 1997.

Nilsson, Martin P. *Opuscula Selecta.* Vol. 3, 3 vols. Lund: CWK Gleerup, 1960.

North, J. Lionel. Review of Campbell, Barth L., *Honor, Shame, and Rhetoric of 1 Peter* and Bechtler, Steven Richard, *Following in His Steps: Suffering, Community, and Christology in First Peter. Journal for the Study of the Old Testament* 84 (1999): 161–162.

Noy, David. *Foreigners at Rome: Citizens and Strangers.* London: Duckworth, 2000.

Olsson, Birger. "A Social-Scientific Criticism of 1 Peter." In *Texts and Contexts: Biblical Texts in Their Textual and Situational Contexts: Essays in Honor of Lars*

Hartman, edited by Tord Fornberg and David Hellholm, 827–846. Oslo: Scandinavian University Press, 1995.

O'Neill, J. G. "The Epistle to Diognetus." *The Irish Ecclesiastical Record* 85 (1956): 92–106.

Osborne, Grant R. *Revelation*. Baker Exegetical Commentary on the New Testament. Grand Rapids, MI: Baker, 2002.

Osborne, Thomas P. "Guide Lines for Christian Suffering: A Source-Critical and Theological Study of 1 Peter 2, 21–25." *Biblica* 64 (1983): 381–408.

Osiek, Carolyn, and David L. Balch. *Families in the New Testament World: Households and House Churches*. Louisville, KY: Westminster John Knox Press, 1997.

Overman, J. Andrew. "The God-Fearers: Some Neglected Features." In *Diaspora Jews and Judaism: Essays in Honor of, and in Dialogue with, A. Thomas Kraabel*, edited by J. Andrew Overman and Robert S. MacLennan, 145–152. Atlanta, GA: Scholars Press, 1992.

Pattemore, Stephen. *The People of God in the Apocalypse: Discourse, Structure, and Exegesis*. Society for New Testament Studies Monograph Series 128. Cambridge: Cambridge University Press, 2004.

Pearce, Sarah. "Belonging and Not Belonging: Local Perspectives in Philo of Alxandria." In *Jewish Local Patriotism and Self-Identification in the Graeco-Roman Period*, edited by Siân Jones and Sarah Pearce, 79–147. Sheffield: Sheffield Academic Press, 1998.

Perdelwitz, R. *Die Mysterienreligion und das Problem des 1 Petrusbriefes: ein literarsicher und religionspeschichtlicher Versuch*. Giessen: Topelmann, 1911.

Piper, John. "Hope as the Motivation of Love: 1 Peter 3:9–12." *New Testament Studies* 26 (1979/80): 212–231.

Price, S. R. F. *Rituals and Power: The Roman Imperial Cult in Asia Minor*. Cambridge: Cambridge University Press, 1984.

Pryor, John W. "First Peter and the New Covenant." *Reformed Theological Review* 45 (1986): 1–4, 44–51.

Radin, Max. "The Exposure of Infants in Roman Law and Practice." *The Classical Journal* 20 (1925): 337–343.

Rajak, Tessa. "Benefactors in the Greco-Jewish Diaspora." In *Geschichte–Tradition–Reflexion: Festschrift für Martin Hengel zum 70. Geburtstag*, edited by Peter Schäfer, vol. 1, 3 vols., 305–319. Tübingen: J. C. B. Mohr (Paul Siebeck), 1996.

———. "The Jewish Community and Its Boundaries." In *The Jews among Pagans and Christians in the Roman Empire*, edited by John A. North, Tessa Rajak and Judith Lieu, 9–28. London: Routledge, 1992.

———. "The Synagogue within the Greco-Roman City." In *Jews, Christians, and Polytheists in the Ancient Synagogue: Cultural Interaction During the Greco-Roman Period*, edited by Steven Fine, 161–173. London: Routledge, 1999.

———. *Translation and Survival: The Greek Bible of the Ancient Jewish Diaspora*. Oxford: Oxford University Press, 2009.

———. "Was There a Roman Charter for the Jews?" *The Journal of Roman Studies* 74 (1984): 107–123.

Reddish, Mitchell G. "Martyr Christology in the Apocalypse." *Journal for the Study of the New Testament* 33 (1988): 85–95.

Regev, Eyal. "Were the Early Christians Sectarians?" *Journal of Biblical Literature* 130 (2011): 771–793.

Richardson, Peter. "Augustan-Era Synagogues in Rome." In *Judaism and Christianity in First-Century Rome*, edited by Karl P. Donfried and Peter Richardson, 17–29. Grand Rapids, MI: Eerdmans, 1998.

———. *Israel in the Apostolic Church*. Society for New Testament Studies Society for New Testament Studies Monograph Series 10. London: Cambridge University Press, 1969.

Robinson, P. J. "Some Missiological Perspectives from 1 Peter 2:4–10." *Missionalia* (1989): 176–187.

Rosenberg, Roy A. "Exile, Mysticism, and Reality." In *Diaspora: Exile and the Jewish Condition*, edited by Étan Levine, 43–48. New York: Jason Aronson, 1983.

Rowland, Christopher. *Revelation*. Epworth Commentaries. London: Epworth, 1993.

Royalty, Robert M. *The Streets of Heaven: The Ideology of Wealth in the Apocalypse of John*. Macon, GA: Mercer University Press, 1998.

Russell, Ronald. "Eschatology and Ethics of 1 Peter." *The Evangelical Quarterly* 47 (1975): 78–84.

Rutgers, Leonard Victor. *The Hidden Heritage of Diaspora Judaism*. Contributions to Biblical Exegesis and Theology 20. Leuven: Peeters, 1998.

———. "Roman Policy toward the Jews: Expulsions from the City of Rome during the First Century C.E." In *Judaism and Christianity in First-Century Rome*, edited by Karl P. Donfried and Peter Richardson, 93–116. Grand Rapids, MI: Eerdmans, 1998.

Sanders, Jack T. *Ethics in the New Testament: Change and Development*. London: SCM Press, 1975.

Schertz, Mary H. "Nonretaliation and the Haustafeln in 1 Peter." In *The Love of Enemy and Nonretaliation in the New Testament*, edited by Willard M. Swartley, 258–285. Louisville, KY: Westminster, 1992.

Schürer, Emil. *The History of the Jewish People in the Age of Jesus Christ (175 BC–AD 135)*. 3 vols. Revised English ed. Edited by Fergus Millar, Geza Vermes, Matthew Black. Edinburgh: T&T Clark, 1973–1986.

Schüssler Fiorenza, Elisabeth. "Babylon the Great: A Rheorical-Political Reading of Revelation 17–18." In *The Reality of Apocalypse: Rhetoric and Politics in the Book of Revelation*, edited by David L. Barr, 243–269. Atlanta, GA: Society of Biblical Literature, 2006.

———. *The Book of Revelation–Justice and Judgment*. Philadelphia, PA: Fortress Press, 1985.

———. "The Followers of the Lamb: Visionary Rhetoric and Social-Political Situation." *Semeia* 36 (1986): 123–146.

Schutter, William L. *Hermeneutic and Composition in 1 Peter*. Wissenschaftliche Untersuchungen zum Neuen Testament 30/2. Tübingen: J. C. B. Mohr, 1989.

Schweizer, E. "Traditional Ethical Patterns in the Pauline and Post-Pauline Letters and Their Development (Lists of Vices and House-Tables)." In *Text and Interpretation: Studies in the New Testament Presented to Matthew Black*, edited by Ernest Best and Robert McLachlan Wilson, 195–209. Cambridge: Cambridge University Press, 1979.

Scott, James C. *Domination and the Arts of Resistance: Hidden Transcripts*. New Haven, CT: Yale University Press, 1990.

Scott, James M. "Exile and the Self-Understanding of Diaspora Jews in the Greco-Roman Period." In *Exile: Old Testament, Jewish, and Christian Conceptions*, edited by James M. Scott, 173–218. Leiden: Brill, 1997.

Scroggs, R. "The Sociological Interpretation of the New Testament: The Present State of Research." *New Testament Studies* 26 (1980): 164–179.

Seland, Torrey. *Strangers in the Light: Philonic Perspectives on Christian Identity in 1 Peter*. Biblical Interpretation Series 76. Leiden: Brill, 2005.

Selwyn, Edward Gordon. "Eschatology in 1 Peter." In *The Background of the New Testament and Its Eschatology*, edited by W. D. Davies and David Daube, 394–401. Cambridge: University Press, 1956.

———. *The First Epistle of St. Peter: The Greek Text with Introduction*. 2nd (repr.) ed. London: Macmillan, 1952 (1st published, 1946).

Senior, Donald. "1 Peter." In *1 Peter, Jude and 2 Peter*, edited by Daniel J. Harrington, 3–158. Collegeville, MN: Liturgical Press, 2003.

Setzer, Claudia J. *Jewish Responses to Early Christians: History and Polemics, 30–150 C.E.* Minneapolis, MN: Fortress Press, 1994.

Sevenster, Jan Nicolaas. *The Roots of Pagan Anti-Semitism in the Ancient World*. Supplements to Novum Testamentum 41. Leiden: Brill, 1975.

Siitonen, Kirsi. "Merchants and Commerce in the Book of Revelation." In *Imagery in the Book of Revelation*, edited by Michael Labahn and Outi Lehtipuu, 145–160. Leuven: Peeters, 2011.

Skaggs, Rebecca, and Thomas Doyle. "Revelation 7: Three Critical Questions." In *Imagery in the Book of Revelation*, edited by Michael Labahn and Outi Lehtipuu, 161–181. Leuven: Peeters, 2011.

Slater, Thomas B. *Christ and Community: A Socio-Historical Study of the Christology of Revelation*. Journal for the Study of the New Testament Supplement Series 178. Sheffield: Sheffield Academic Press, 1999.

Sleeper, C. Freeman. "Political Responsibility according to 1 Peter." *Novum Testamentum* 10 (1968): 270–286.

Smallwood, E. Mary. *The Jews under Roman Rule: From Pompey to Diocletian*. Studies in Judaism in Late Antiquity 20. Leiden: Brill, 1976.

Snodgrass, K. "I Peter II. 1-10: Its Formation and Literary Affinities." *New Testament Studies* 24 (1977/78): 97–106.

Spencer, Aída Besançon. "Peter's Pedagogical Method in 1 Peter 3:6." *Bulletin for Biblical Research* 10 (2000): 107–119.

Stenschke, Christoph. "Reading First Peter in the Context of Early Christian Mission." *Tyndale Bulletin* 60 (2009): 107–126.

Stern, M. "The Jewish Diaspora." In *The Jewish People in the First Century: Historical Geography, Political History, Social, Cultural and Religious Life and Institutions*, edited by S. Safrai and M. Stern, vol. 1, 2 vols., 117–183. Assen: Van Gorcum, 1974.

Steuernagel, Valdir R. "An Exiled Community as a Missionary Community: A Study Based on 1 Peter 2:9, 10." *Evangelical Review of Theology* 10 (1986): 8–18.

Stone, Michael E. *Fourth Ezra: A Commentary on the Book of Fourth Ezra*. Hermeneia. Minneapolis, MN: Fortress Press, 1990.

Stowers, S. K. "The Social Sciences and the Study of Early Christianity." In *Approaches to Ancient Judaism Vol. 5, Studies in Judaism and Its Greco-Roman Context*, edited by W. S. Green, 149–181. Atlanta, GA: Scholars Press, 1985.

Sweet, J. P. M. "Maintaining the Testimony of Jesus: The Suffering of Christians in the Revelation of John." In *Suffering and Martyrdom in the New Testament: Studies Presented to G. M. Styler by the Cambridge New Testament Seminar*, edited by William Horbury and Brian McNeil, 101–117. Cambridge: Cambridge University Press, 1981.

———. *Revelation*. SCM Pelican Commentaries. London: SCM, 1979.

Talbert, Charles H. "Once Again: The Plan of First Peter." In *Perspectives on First Peter*, edited by Charles H. Talbert, 141–151. Macon, GA: Mercer University Press, 1986.

Tcherikover, Victor. *Hellenistic Civilization and the Jews.* Translated by Shimon Applebaum. New York: Atheneum, 1970.

Theissen, Gerd. *Social Reality and the Early Christians: Theology, Ethics and the World of the New Testament.* Translated by Margaret Kohl. Edinburgh: T&T Clark, 1993.

Thompson, James W. "The Submission of Wives in 1 Peter." In *Essays on Women in Earliest Christianity*, edited by Carroll D. Osburn, vol. 1, 2 vols., 377–392. Joplin, MO: College Press, 1993.

Thompson, Leonard L. *The Book of Revelation: Apocalypse and Empire.* New York: Oxford University Press, 1990.

———. "Ordinary Lives: John and His First Readers." In *Reading the Book of Revelation: A Resource for Students*, edited by David L. Barr, 25–47. Atlanta, GA: Society of Biblical Literature, 2003.

———. "A Sociological Analysis of Tribulation in the Apocalypse of John." *Semeia* 36 (1986): 147–174.

Thurén, Lauri. *Argument and Theology in 1 Peter: The Origins of Christian Paraenesis.* Journal for the Study of the New Testament: Supplement Series 114. Sheffield: Sheffield Academic Press, 1995.

———. *The Rhetorical Strategy of 1 Peter: With Special Regard to Ambiguous Expressions.* Åbo: Åbo Akademis forlag, 1990.

Tidball, Derek. *An Introduction to the Sociology of the New Testament.* Exeter: Paternoster, 1983.

Tite, Philip L. *Compositional Transitions in 1 Peter: An Analysis of the Letter-Opening.* San Francisco, CA: International Scholars Publications, 1997.

Townsley, Ashton L. "Notes for an Interpretation of the Epistle to Diognetus." *Rivista di studi classici* 24 (1976): 5–20.

Trebilco, Paul R. *The Early Christians in Ephesus from Paul to Ignatius.* Wissenschaftliche Untersuchungen Zum Neuen Testament 166. Tübingen: Mohr Siebeck, 2004.

———. *Jewish Communities in Asia Minor.* Society for New Testament Studies Monograph Series 69. Cambridge: Cambridge University Press, 1991.

Trites, Allison A. *The New Testament Concept of Witness.* Society for New Testament Studies Monograph Series 31. Cambridge: Cambridge University Press, 1977.

Tuñi, José Oriol. "Jesus of Nazareth in the Christology of 1 Peter." *The Heythrop Journal* 28 (1987): 292–304.

van Unnik, W. C. "Christianity according to 1 Peter." *The Expository Times* 68 (1956/1957): 79–83.

———. "The Critique of Paganism in 1 Peter 1:18." In *Neotestamentica et semitica: Studies in Honour of Matthew Black*, edited by E. Earle Ellis and Max Wilcox, 129–142. Edinburgh: T&T Clark, 1969.

———. *Sparsa Collecta*. Part 2, 3 vols. Leiden: E. J. Brill, 1980.
———. "The Teaching of Good Works in 1 Peter." *New Testament Studies* 1 (1954/1955): 92–110.
Volf, Miroslav. "Soft Difference: Theological Reflections on the Relation between Church and Culture in 1 Peter." *Ex Auditu* 10 (1994): 15–30.
Warden, Duane. "Imperial Persecution and the Dating of 1 Peter and Revelation." *Journal of the Evangelical Theological Society* 34 (1991): 203–212.
Wardy, Bilhah "Jewish Religion in Pagan Literature during the Late Republic and Early Empire." In *Aufstieg Und Niedergang der römischen Welt: Geschichte und Kultur Roms im Spiegel der neueren Forschung*, 19.1:592–644. Part 2, *Principat*, 19.1. Edited by Wolfgang Haase. Berlin: Walter de Gruyter, 1979.
Wells, Jo Bailey. *God's Holy People: A Theme in Biblical Theology*. Journal for the Study of the Old Testament Supplement Series 305. Sheffield: Sheffield Academic Press, 2000.
Wilcox, Max. "The 'God-Fearers' in Acts – a Reconsideration." *Journal for the Study of the New Testament* 13 (1981): 102–122.
Wilken, Robert L. *The Christians as the Romans Saw Them*. New Haven, CT: Yale University Press, 1984.
———. "Toward a Social Interpretation of Early Christian Apologetics." *Church History* 39 (1970): 437–458.
Williams, Margaret. "Jews and Jewish Communities in the Roman Empire." In *Experiencing Rome: Culture, Identity and Power in the Roman Empire*, edited by Janet Huskinson, 305–333. London: Routledge in association with the Open University, 2000.
Wilson, Bryan R. "An Analysis of Sect Development." *American Sociological Review* 24 (1959): 3–15.
———. *Magic and the Millennium: A Sociological Study of Religious Movements of Protest among Tribal and Third-World Peoples*. London: Heinemann, 1973.
———. *Sects and Society: A Sociological Study of Three Religious Groups in Britain*. London: Heinemann, 1961.
Windisch, H. *Die katholischen Briefe*. 3rd rev. and augmented ed. with appendix by H. Preisker. HNT 15. Tübingen: Mohr (Siebeck), 1951 (1st published, 1911).
Winter, Bruce W. "The Public Honouring of Christian Benefactors." *Journal for the Study of the New Testament* 34 (1988): 87–103.
———. *Seek the Welfare of the City: Christians as Benefactors and Citizens*. Grand Rapids, MI: Eerdmans, 1994.
Wire, Antoinette. Review of John H. Elliott, *A Home for the Homeless: A Sociological Exegesis of 1 Peter, Its Situation and Strategy* and David L. Balch,

Let Wives Be Submissive: The Domestic Code in 1 Peter. Religious Studies Review 10 (1984): 209–216.

Wolff, Christian. "Christ und Welt im 1. Petrusbrief." *Theologische Literaturzeitung* 100 (1975): 333–342.

Wright, N. T. *The New Testament and the People of God.* Christian Origins and the Question of God 1. London: SPCK, 1992.

Zerbe, Gordon M. *Non-Retaliation in Early Jewish and New Testament Texts: Ethical Themes in Social Contexts.* Journal for the Study of the Pseudepigrapha Supplement Series 13. Sheffield: JSOT Press, 1993.

Zimmerli, W., and J. Jeremias. *The Servant of God.* Rev. ed. Studies in Biblical Theology 20. London: SCM Press, 1965 (1st published, 1952).

Langham Literature and its imprints are a ministry of Langham Partnership.

Langham Partnership is a global fellowship working in pursuit of the vision God entrusted to its founder John Stott –

> *to facilitate the growth of the church in maturity and Christ-likeness through raising the standards of biblical preaching and teaching.*

Our vision is to see churches in the majority world equipped for mission and growing to maturity in Christ through the ministry of pastors and leaders who believe, teach and live by the Word of God.

Our mission is to strengthen the ministry of the Word of God through:
- nurturing national movements for biblical preaching
- fostering the creation and distribution of evangelical literature
- enhancing evangelical theological education

especially in countries where churches are under-resourced.

Our ministry

Langham Preaching partners with national leaders to nurture indigenous biblical preaching movements for pastors and lay preachers all around the world. With the support of a team of trainers from many countries, a multi-level programme of seminars provides practical training, and is followed by a programme for training local facilitators. Local preachers' groups and national and regional networks ensure continuity and ongoing development, seeking to build vigorous movements committed to Bible exposition.

Langham Literature provides majority world preachers, scholars and seminary libraries with evangelical books and electronic resources through publishing and distribution, grants and discounts. The programme also fosters the creation of indigenous evangelical books in many languages, through writer's grants, strengthening local evangelical publishing houses, and investment in major regional literature projects, such as one volume Bible commentaries like *The Africa Bible Commentary* and *The South Asia Bible Commentary*.

Langham Scholars provides financial support for evangelical doctoral students from the majority world so that, when they return home, they may train pastors and other Christian leaders with sound, biblical and theological teaching. This programme equips those who equip others. Langham Scholars also works in partnership with majority world seminaries in strengthening evangelical theological education. A growing number of Langham Scholars study in high quality doctoral programmes in the majority world itself. As well as teaching the next generation of pastors, graduated Langham Scholars exercise significant influence through their writing and leadership.

To learn more about Langham Partnership and the work we do visit **langham.org**